Harold [illegible]
'[illegible] Walk'
II. 1975.

BÉLA BARTÓK
LETTERS

Béla Bartók, 1881-1945

BÉLA BARTÓK LETTERS

Collected, Selected, Edited and Annotated
by
JÁNOS DEMÉNY

Prefaced
by
SIR MICHAEL TIPPETT

Translated into English
by
PÉTER BALABÁN and ISTVÁN FARKAS

Translation revised
by
ELISABETH WEST and COLIN MASON

FABER AND FABER
LONDON

First published in England in 1971
by Faber and Faber Limited
24 Russel Square, London W.C.1
Printed in Hungary
ISBN 0 571 09638 7

CONTENTS

	Preface	*page* 9
I	Early Years, 1899–1905	11
II	The Years of Development, 1906–1919	55
III	The Years of Achievement, 1920–1926	147
IV	At the Height of His Career, 1927–1940	179
V	The Years of Exile, 1940–1945	287
	Appendices	351
	The Publication of Bartók's Correspondence	353
	Notes on the Present Edition	355
	List of Letters	357
	Notes	369
	List of Correspondents	441
	A Brief Survey of Béla Bartók's Compositions	445
	Bartók's Compositions	447
	List of Places	451
	Bibliography	453
	General Index	455
	Index of Bartók's Compositions Referred to in the Volume	465

ILLUSTRATIONS

Béla Bartók, 1881–1945 *frontispiece*

Photo MTI, 1938

Béla Bartók aged twenty-one *facing page* 32

Photo Uher, 1902

Three of Bartók's ardent admirers, Irmy Jurkovics, Emilia Bayer and Emsy Jurkovics, 1899

Photo Strelisky, 1899

Béla Bartók, aged twenty-four, on his first trip abroad *facing page* 33

By an unknown photographer

Sculptures in the Parc Monceau, Paris, listed with enthusiasm in one of Bartók's letters, of Edouard Pailleron (Leopold Bernstamm), Guy de Maupassant (Raoul-Charles Verlet), Ambroise Thomas (Jean-Alexandre-Joseph Falguière), Charles-François Gounod (Marius-Jean-Antonin Mercié) *facing page* 48

Photo J. Demény, 1961

Stefi Geyer in the early 1920s *facing page* 49

By an unknown photographer

Bartók recording Slovak folk-songs at Darázs, Nyitra County, 1908 *facing page* 128

By an unknown photographer

The manuscript of *Székely Songs* dedicated to the Béla Bartók Song Society and the choirmaster in Pozsony, 1932

Béla Bartók in the summer of 1912 *facing page* 129

Etelka Freund's collection, Washington, D.C.

Ion Bîrlea, Bartók's assistant during his song-collecting tour of Máramaros County, March 1913

Photo Lubru (Vinga, Rumania) 1932

A page from the score of *The Wooden Prince*, completed in 1917 *facing page* 144

An unfinished portrait of Bartók *facing page* 144

Oil painting by Ion Buşiţia, 1917

A pencil-study of Bartók in 1922 *facing page* 145

Pencil by Márton Hosszú, 1922

Caricature of Béla Bartók from October 22, 1924

Caricature from Rampa (*Bucharest, Rumania*) 1924

The manuscript of the English text of *Cantata Profana* adapted by Bartók *facing page* 296

The Family Kecskeméti's collection, New York, 1944

The composer's hands

Photo Mrs. S. Török-Babits, 1936

The manuscript of Bartók's last transcription, the Ukranian folk-song 'I bought barley at the market' *between pages* 296–297

The Family Kecskeméti's collection, New York, 1945

The title-page of a concert programme given by Mrs. Wilhelmine Creel in Japan, 8th February, 1940, in which she played several of Bartók's piano pieces *facing page* 297

Photo on the programme Ichijo Shajo (Japan) 1939

Béla Bartók aged forty-five

Photo Mrs. S. Török-Babits, 1926

PUBLISHERS' ACKNOWLEDGEMENT

The British Publishers (Faber and Faber, London) and the American Publishers (St. Martin's Press, New York) make the following acknowledgement:

This publication has been authorized
by special permission of the copyright owner,
Dr. Benjamin Suchoff, Successor-Trustee,
The Estate of Béla Bartók.

PREFACE

I am honoured to be asked to preface this English translation of Bartók's collected letters, which János Demény has so excellently edited. I am no Bartók scholar, either bibliographically or even musically. But I certainly feel a particular sensibility to his genius and to what I imagine to have been his temperament. I never met him and saw him only once. He came with his second wife to England just before the last war and played with her, for the BBC, the Sonata for 2 Pianos and Percussion. After the concert he was dawdling by the piano and our eyes accidentally met as I watched him from among the seats. I remember the sense of being for a second the object of an acute spiritual vision, which seemed to look at once right inside me from right inside himself. I am certain he had no consciousness of the extreme subjective impression this moment made on me, and which I can recall to this day with eidetic accuracy. But I am also certain I saw something of the real Bartók, if only by intimation.

Sometime after the war, in a radio talk at Schoenberg's death, I spoke of Bartók when discussing the relation of creative artists to movements and cliques. I said: 'So universal in our time seems this experience of collectivities, parties, groups, that the really strange figures are those who do the dedicated, difficult work, who face the crises alone, Bartók, for example. He had as tough a struggle in Budapest, as Schoenberg in Vienna. What gave him the strength to stand so alone? And is that strength a value of his music? Personally I believe so.' And of course I still believe so. The letters cannot truly confirm this judgment, but they make it credible. In an early letter Bartók writes: '. . . yet there are times when I suddenly become aware of the fact that I am absolutely alone. And I prophesy, I have a foreknowledge, that this spiritual loneliness is to be my destiny.' Admittedly this may have been 'prophecy' out of a momentary mood, but one suspects it rings deeper.

Bartók did not enjoy writing letters. He cries (l. 201): 'But letter writing is my weak point; it is such a torture to me that as long as possible I go on putting it off from one day to the next.' This means that to a large extent only those letters which *had* to be written got written. Adding to this the natural hazards of just which letters got preserved, it is clear that the collection only mirrors Bartók's life accidentally. There are, for example, many more and quite lengthy letters about folk-song collecting than about composition. But all the same he *was* a composer first and foremost, although the work in folk-song was passionate and dedicated. To get the relation between composition and folk-song collecting right would mean a prolonged study from other sources.

It is the tiny hints, by occasional remarks in the letters, about what things meant to Bartók that are so rewarding. Thus in one of the letters to Delius he writes: 'I think the language of these piano pieces is less deliberate and strained than that of the Suite. Since writing them, I have regained some inner "harmony", so that, today, I am not in need of the contradictory. . . dissonances which express that particular mood. This may be the consequence of allowing myself to become more and more influenced by folk music.' Bartók uses the word 'dissonances' in other letters also, and in much the same sense: a mixture of the musically objective and the subjective expressive, i.e., having regained some inner (subjective) 'harmony', he does not need so much 'contradictory [musical] dissonance', an interesting polarity.

The final letters, from America, are of course clouded by the gradual accession of the leukaemia which killed him. As I know from other personal sources he was desperately, sometimes almost pathologically, troubled also in mind (when he felt driven to leave as the Nazis overran Europe). These tensions of mind and body could not predicate a new life in a New Found Land. But nevertheless he is a true part of that artistic emigration to America as European culture went foul in the concentration camps. An English edition of this great Hungarian's letters is a token of the values, of nationalism and internationalism, of his own folk and the whole round world of peoples, for which he fought. And out of which some re-birth (of the cultures that have gone foul), must one day come.

Corsham, 1969 *Michael Tippett*

I
EARLY YEARS
1899–1905

When little more than a youth, Bartók went to live in Budapest, centre of the cultural life of Hungary. For the first time he lived in lodgings, far from his widowed mother whom he left reluctantly in Pozsony (otherwise Pressburg, now Bratislava), the old town within the north-west borders of what was, in the days before the First World War, Hungarian territory. The letters he wrote to his mother during this important period at the outset of his career are of such significance that they have been given almost exclusive priority.

Between 1899 and 1903 Bartók studied at the Budapest Academy of Music where he was fortunate to have as his piano teacher István Thomán, former pupil of Liszt.

In his first year at the Academy he worked assiduously at many subjects, but his second year was interrupted by pulmonary illness, and he had to spend several months at Meran. In his third year at the Academy (1901–1902) he first attracted notice as a pianist and was himself stimulated by the scores of Richard Strauss's symphonic poems. In his last year at the Academy he made frequent public appearances, sometimes performing separate items on the programme or distinguishing himself as a member of a chamber ensemble. It was during this period that he gave his first solo recital (Nagyszentmiklós), had his first taste of success abroad, in Vienna, and began to give public performances of *Study for the Left Hand, Fantasia*, and later, from his *Four Piano Pieces.* A chamber-music composition, *Sonata for Violin and Piano*, was also given a public performance. It was during this period that he wrote a *Symphony*, the orchestrated Scherzo of which was performed the following year. But the most important work from this period was the symphonic poem *Kossuth*, inspired by the Hungarian War of Independence. The first performance of this composition, in Budapest, on January 13th, 1904, was a notable event in the history of music; it was also the occasion of a political storm which made the name of the young composer known throughout the country. These events take us to Bartók's first year of freedom after completing his studies at the Academy, the period when his unique talent both as composer and as pianist brought him his first successes in Vienna, Berlin, Pozsony and Manchester.

In the works composed in 1904, *Piano Quintet*, *Rhapsody for Piano and Orchestra* (op. 1), *Scherzo for Piano and Orchestra*, Bartók developed the Hungarian rhapsody style of Ferenc Liszt; and the composition which may be said to summarize Bartók's achievements as a young man, the *First Suite for Large Orchestra* (op. 3, 1905), was also peculiarly Hungarian in its romanticism, though still untouched by Eastern European folklore and ancient Hungarian folk-music. In conservative musical circles the style of these works was already found too advanced, and at the Rubinstein Competition, arranged in Paris in the summer of 1905, the young Bartók experienced the first painful failure of his life, for neither his performance nor his compositions were appreciated. The letters written from Paris at this time to his mother and to a young girl of Nagyszentmiklós, bearing witness to the intellectual maturity and talent of the twenty-four-year-old artist, provide an appropriate conclusion to the first part of our volume.

[Original in Hungarian]

1. TO ISTVÁN THOMÁN[1] — BUDAPEST

[1] *Pozsony, September* 8th, 1899

Dear Sir,
You will have heard from Miss Gizella Révffy that I was taken ill last February.

For that reason I was obliged to spend the vacation in Carinthia; however, I am once more well enough to be able to resume piano-playing. I shall be arriving in Budapest on the 15th, together with my mother who wishes to pay her respects to you.

I have filled in the registration form and sent it on to you. However, under one heading—viz. where I am asked if I have passed an examination already—I hesitated. Finally (for these questions require *precise* answers), I wrote that I was examined last January by you, Sir. I trust I am not creating difficulties for myself?

My mother sends her regards, and I, with the hope of your continued favour, remain

Yours truly,
BÉLA BARTÓK

[Original in Hungarian]

2. TO HIS MOTHER, MRS. BÉLA BARTÓK — POZSONY

[1] *Budapest, January* 21st, 1900

Dear Mama,
I hope you got my postcard. I took a look at the room—first by myself, then, today, with Lujcsi. It has 2 windows overlooking the courtyard, but it's not so bright as my present room. Sunshine in

[1] Notes, pp. 369–440, contains information regarding all relevant details mentioned in this, and subsequent, letters. Asterisks indicate Bartók's own footnotes and are placed at the end of letters, as in the originals.

the morning till 10 a.m.; and it's an open courtyard. The landlady is willing to put her own piano in the room, in which there are also 2 wardrobes, a table, a washstand, etc. Laundry, heating and lighting are all included in the board. Very tidy and well-kept, and as handy for the Academy as my present room. So far so good. Now for the 'buts'. For, when I went round by myself, she wanted 50 forints all told; and now, having thought it over, she is asking 60 forints.

Thus: full board (incl. piano) 60 forints, milk 5 forints = 65 forints.

And now: board 45 forints, milk 5 forints, laundry 3 forints, heating and lighting 1.70 forints, [and] piano 6 forints = 60.70 forints.

So that would increase my outgoings by 4 forints, and who knows what other drawbacks I may discover once I've moved in.

One more thing I should point out is that there's a door in the room opening directly into the kitchen. It would have to be kept locked, of course. In addition to all this, I now find I am expected to have the piano tuned. In short, if you ask me, I see no point in moving. Had she stuck to 50 forints, it would have been a different matter. We have decided that I ought to ask you for your opinion, so will you please write me as soon as possible what you think about it. For the extra 4 forints all I would get is possibly some tidying and cleaning; but there's no knowing what the disadvantages might be. Moreover, from the middle of February (on the very date I should move in), the heating will be cut off. Also, the actual move would involve me in a lot of expense and trouble.

I called on Dohnányi on Tuesday at 12 and found him at breakfast. We talked about all sorts of things. Just imagine, the Hubay–Popper Ensemble are not going to perform his quartet; he has quarrelled with them about something or other! And he refuses to give any recitals because people won't pay the fee he asks. I also heard about the programme for his Pozsony recital. He said he would not be playing so much next year because he had begun to find it rather boring. He said he was going to play at the Liszt Society's concert, but only reluctantly, because they just wouldn't leave him in peace. (Some tickets for that concert have been distributed at the Academy, and I've been given one too.)

I have heard and seen Sauer.

I really couldn't tell you just now which of the two plays best—he or d'Albert. For what I liked best in d'Albert's playing, namely

Bach and Beethoven, did not feature in this concert. What he did play he played beautifully. At times, he managed to evoke such peculiar tones that I seemed to be listening to some instrument other than the piano. Schumann, Chopin and Liszt—all very finely executed, and I was thrilled by all those pieces, whereas, with d'Albert, it was Tausig's *Zigeunerweisen* that I liked least of all. Incidentally, his female listeners were quite enthralled: they all agree that, as a pianist, he is a hundred times better than d'A[lbert]. Professor Thomán also liked his playing, though not so much. (He is a great enemy of Sauer's.) At the end of the recital the public behaved in the usual manner and were determined to hear him play the *Tannhäuser* Overture, but Sauer was quite worn out and refused to oblige.

By the way, he has an interesting way of striking attitudes. He keeps lifting his hands high in the air, about 1 metre above the keyboard, swaying his head from side to side and gazing up to the skies. He ponders a long time before starting a piece, then suddenly, as if he has just remembered what it is he's supposed to play, he strikes up. And at the end of the piece, he again lifts his hands up in the air, then lets them fall on his lap, etc. (Maybe it's just this that pleases the ladies so much.)

Professor Thomán has been doing his good deeds again: he told me to buy Schubert's *Impromptu* as edited by Liszt; when I told him, No, this month I really couldn't as I had no money, he bought it for me 'as a souvenir'. Then he secured free admission to the Sauer recital for me, and so I was able to sell the ticket I had already bought. And now he's given me a ticket for the *Valkyrie*. He has also mentioned the question of the scholarship to the Principal, who said he would very much like to award it to me because he believes that I will fulfil the hopes they place in me, but there are a great many candidates. One scholarship must go to Miss Révffy, and there are many other senior students, like Székely, who are worthy of consideration. But he said that I should most probably be granted a state bursary (100 forints). This is almost a certainty.

I cannot possibly prepare my history of music lessons, as I haven't yet been able to get hold of the standard lecture notes. (It's not important.)

Is Elza better now?

For your name-day I send again all the good wishes I sent for your birthday.

My love to you all.

[PS.] At present, I have 8 kreutzers, but the 1 forint for my Sauer ticket is due tomorrow. I was in a similar fix a week ago.

[Original in Hungarian]

3. TO HIS MOTHER, MRS. BÉLA BARTÓK—POZSONY

[2] *Budapest, Wednesday* [*November*, 1902]

Dear Mama,
The 2 outstanding items of news this week are: (1) It is almost certain that I am going to study under Dohnányi; (2) Mrs. Gruber has become my pupil.

Mrs. Gárdony told me the first item last Friday. She had already discussed it in detail with Mrs. Dohnányi, who gave me confirmation on Monday. He will give me lessons, but only on condition that I don't tell anyone because he doesn't want to give lessons to anyone else. Nothing could suit me better, and I want everyone in Pozsony to respect this arrangement and never breathe a word of it to a soul! If anyone asks where I am going next year, you must tell them to Berlin, to attend (and give) recitals—which is true, too.

Most probably the 'instruction' will be given at Gmunden next summer.

Dohnányi is due to spend a week here in December, so I'll ask him about it myself; we'll be able to go into things more fully then.

I'm going to give Mrs. Gruber lessons in counterpoint: we are to start next week (1 hour a week). She declared her intention today, to my great surprise.

H'm. Whatever makes you think that those Arányis are 'cultivated people'? Just what is it that makes you think them 'nice' and 'cultivated'? Can it be because they have invited me to their house, or because they can speak French, or because their place is frequented by artists (or, more precisely, student artists)?! For there are many students whom, with the best will in the world, you could not call 'cultivated', 'nice' or 'refined'. But I am not passing judgment; only wondering how you formed your opinion.

The invitation was not for last Sunday but for next. But I went round on Monday to find out exactly what kind of a party they're going to give. As I no longer teach them, the Arányi girls, Titi and Adila, behaved quite differently towards me, were very gay and dashed about the house upsetting everything. They promised an even rarer to-do on Sunday. I am really intrigued about this, so

I'm going to it. In general they are quite a bit different from other Jewish people I've met so far:[1] (1) they live simply, and (2) they are anti-Semitic. This is something I don't understand, for as far as I know, Joachim is also a Semite. However, it will be all the same in a hundred years – – – – –

I, too, have been thinking that it would be a good idea if you came up when I play the Schumann Sonata. It will be before Christmas, so we can go home together afterwards.

I have taken a season ticket for the Philharmonic Concerts—2nd row in the gallery. I sit immediately behind Laci Toldy and his mother—or rather, that's where I should be sitting; but Toldy's mother is so very kind that she makes me take her seat for most of the programme (that is, in the first row, where you can see as well as hear). I don't like this, for what right have I to take a lady's seat when I don't know her? And during the intervals she tells me what a brilliant boy Lacika is. How he sings all Wagner by heart! From Fafner's part (deep bass) right up to Elsa's high soprano! A noted singing teacher told her that nobody could teach him anything any longer about the art of singing. And then that Laci can only compose when she is at his side. Several times during a concert, Lacika lifts his mother's hand—gloved!—to his lips; this undoubtedly shows an unusual degree of devotion to her, but perhaps it ought not to be demonstrated in public. For this sort of thing is often interpreted as a sign of insincerity, of merely feigned tenderness.

I have never had any strong drinks in Budapest so far, although I have often had them offered to me.

I'm beginning to find my English lessons interesting; we are starting to work through the History of English Literature.

For the rest I remain with best respect,

Yours
B.

[Original in Hungarian]

4. TO HIS MOTHER, MRS. BÉLA BARTÓK—POZSONY

[3] *Budapest, January* 9th, 1903

Dear Mama,
Would you please apply for a rail pass for me for a return journey between Budapest and Marchegg? In one or two weeks' time I may be going to Vienna to play the *Heldenleben* at the Tonkünstlerverein.

[1] The English word 'Jew' figures at this point in the original Hungarian text of Bartók's letter.

When Professor Herzfeld was in Vienna, he spoke of me to Löwe, who organizes concerts there and is, I believe, something or other in this Tonkünstlerverein. So he (Herzfeld) is now going to write to Vienna about this possibility.

The Dohnányi Symphony sounds wonderful. He conducted it himself, and the performance was masterly. We gave him a tremendous ovation. Last Thursday's *Esti Ujság* carried an editorial headed: Ernő Dohnányi. Aurél Kern was responsible for it. The good gentleman, however, is very much mistaken in supposing that Dohnányi is creating music in the national Hungarian tradition. He has no such idea in his head. Even in his Symphony it is only the second movement that is written in the Hungarian manner, the first could just be called Hungarian, but the last three not in the least. There was music-making at Professor Thomán's last Thursday night, with the Dohnányis, Professor Dohn., the Grubers, Herzfeld, Szendy, myself and others. Dohnányi played two items of chamber music. I just listened.

Adila Arányi tells me that Hubay mentioned me at one of their classes, using more glowing terms of praise than he has ever applied to anyone else; he was really enthusiastic.

There's lots to do, many concerts and little time.

My love and kisses to you all,

B.

[Original in Hungarian]

5. TO HIS MOTHER, MRS. BÉLA BARTÓK—POZSONY

[4] *Budapest, January* 17th, 1903

Dear Mama,

I am leaving for Vienna on Monday, Jan. 26, (i.e. a week from next Monday). I want to leave at noon on Monday and return by the Tuesday afternoon express. So, of course, I shan't be able to break my journey at Pozsony. I have in any case some 'important' business here in Budapest on Tuesday evening. But it should be quite easy for you to go to the concert on Monday. All you would have to do is to get into my express at 5.15 p.m. You would have to return the same day, which might be rather inconvenient, but there is a train which leaves at 10 p.m. So that's settled. I've had plenty of scribbling to do recently—I have written out the 4th movement of the Symphony so that I can show it to Koessler today. I have already played it for Mrs. Gruber, who liked it better the second time than the first. She says I've made great progress since I wrote the 1st movement, and that, after the Scherzo, she likes this one best. Koessler was less lavish in his praises, for he had a good many criticisms to make; however, he only had time to criticize part of the movement, not the whole of it. After class we followed Koessler into the large hall, where I played *Heldenleben* for him. He was astonished at my knowing it by heart; on the other hand, he spoke disparagingly of *Heldenleben* itself. Apart from that he was very pleasant with me, and he said that though he was determined to stick to his own opinion, he would not try to persuade me to share it. Well, everyone has the right to his own opinion.

Today, in the tram, I ran into the 'great' musician Aurél Kern. I happened to be carrying *Heldenleben*, and when he noticed it, he exclaimed, 'I have heard you play this like a young god!' So I told him about my forthcoming trip to Vienna.

Now here is something for Aunt Irma: Dohnányi has recommended a remedy for fatigue—Elliman's Embrocation. It is supposed (!) to be effective for all kinds of rheumatic conditions: stiff neck and so on. Available at all chemist's, price 90 kreutzers. Directions for use are in English and Hungarian and begin: Directions for the use and application of Elliman's (Royal) Embrocation for muscular rheumatism in cattle, sheep, horses, donkeys and birds! It made me wonder which heading musicians came under. Tomorrow, I shall be lunching with the Gárdonys; then call at the Arányis in the afternoon, but only for a short visit as I'm very busy. It's Carnival time, anyway, and spending one's time in the company of young people at this time of year has its dangers, for they will start dancing at the slightest provocation.

I see from your letter that Sauer is playing at Pozsony on the 26th. That, of course, rules out the possibility of your coming to Vienna.

If I add that I have received the railway pass, I've written everything.

L.
B.

[Original in Hungarian]

6. TO HIS MOTHER, MRS. BÉLA BARTÓK—POZSONY

[5] *Budapest, April* 1st, 1903

Dear Mama,
As I have so much to do, and you will be here in a week's time, I will be brief.

Come, come. A word or two of praise in the *Tagblatt* is nothing to congratulate me about. A man who was one of my colleagues last year, and who has a moderate knowledge of music, happens to be the critic on the staff of that paper. I am enclosing the programme. This was my first public appearance as a composer—a memorable date. Nor did *Pesti Napló* fail to run my work down with the comment that it was disjointed and contained some gaping holes. On the other hand, they praised my playing. Two encores were squeezed out of me—the second I gave most reluctantly, as I was unprepared. I was compelled to choose a Chopin étude which I had not played for about 3 months, but it went fairly well. If they only knew what I am writing with my Viennese-made pens, not even people like Aurél Kern would object to them. Perhaps you could visit Professor Thomán. I think I told you that I won't spend a month at Passail unless there's a piano. When taking lodgings it is important to notice whether there is room for a piano. It won't do to have it in the passage. In your remarks on spelling there are some words I can't make out. If you don't want to keep to the rules for German spelling—well, don't write German!! That's the best advice I can give you. By the way, musical spelling (i.e. notation, not terminology) is much more difficult than any language known to me. You have misinterpreted what I wrote to you about Dohnányi's opera. He will not be paid for it until he has completed it—no provision for the baby before it's born. I'd like Böske to wear Hungarian national dress at my recital. I am putting the following question to her as an eminent student of folk-song: what are the words of these 2 folk-tunes:

There is no point in giving news space to the fact that I played at Nagyszentmiklós. It's surely not a very remarkable event.

In *Pester Lloyd* Helm has again given me a mention, in connection with Strauss, of course. I have been awarded the Liszt Scholarship (which comes, of course, as a big surprise!!). One of Lujcsi's office colleagues is Bárci's brother-in-law who is also related to Prof. Thomán. They are going to make enquiries about the scholarship. Moreover, Prof. Thomán has already seen Pál Sándor about it; but I don't know with what result. They say that the final decision has been put off because of the filibustering in Parliament, which may even result in the scholarship not being awarded at all. I must say

I find this hard to credit, for the filibustering does not interfere with the internal affairs of the ministries; and approval of recommendations submitted by the municipal authorities is certainly internal business. So let us wait patiently. That reminds me, we have a pleasant prospect in store. If the obstructionists go on having their way, by next May the national legal system will no longer be operative, and that will mean no one need pay any taxes—but at the same time nobody will get paid! But if that happens, I can help you out, as I have enough money. I still owe you 53 forints, which I'll give you when you come to Budapest. Aunt Emma and her family are quite well; little Emma comes home, I believe, next Wednesday.

Love,
B.

[Original in Hungarian]

7. TO HIS MOTHER, MRS. BÉLA BARTÓK—POZSONY

[6] *Budapest, Lipótmező, June* 18th, 1903

Dear Mama,
I am at Lipótmező for the day, and I've already given two lessons. They are going to play tennis now, so I shall be scribbling for a while. This letter should find Böske 'qualified'; yesterday, Emily gave me a message from her asking me to think of her all day from 4 a.m. till 11.30 p.m., I am sorry for her and wish her success. I have various items of news. First, I said good-bye to Koessler yesterday, and he told me he wants the Scherzo I was intending to send in to the Philharmonic Society to be performed at an Academy of Music graduates' concert to be held next year at the Opera. Well, as a matter of fact, I think he is right—I owe that much to the Academy. He listened to my *Kossuth* symphony and said that on the whole it is good. He would like me to orchestrate it during the vacation, in which case that too would be performed at the same concert. I don't mind, I can manage to do that, too. However, there is one snag. The concert is supposed to be held on Oct. 22nd, the anniversary of Liszt's birthday. I am hoping, and Koessler is sure, that it will be postponed, like everything else. For if it isn't, I shall have to come home specially for the concert from Berlin, and that would be expensive. I said a nice farewell to Professor Thomán yesterday by playing Dohnányi's *Passacaglia*. He was very pleased with me. Then I asked if I might dedicate the piece for the left hand to him. Finally he even promised to give me a letter of recommendation

to Stavenhagen in Munich. On Monday he leaves for Ungvár, where you can write to him if you want to. But no, you'd better address it to Budapest, and it will be sent on to him from here. There's no need for you to write to anyone else. I will do my packing and have the cases forwarded to Pozsony next week.

So far I have received no reply from the Concertverein.

Why shouldn't I stay in Budapest so long? I have paid for my board here, and I have lessons to give. Well, I might leave on the 1st at the earliest, but the 3rd suits me better.

The lion[1] would have liked to go to Passail direct. But she has been informed by the Graz piano dealers that they do not hire out their pianos to that place!! So what happens now?! They are afraid that there will be no one capable of handling the casing and uncasing of pianos in Passail. I have written to 2 companies asking whether they would be willing to let me have a piano if I arrange to get experienced removers from Graz. I have 2 more Graz addresses:

Friedrich Wagner, Spohrgasse 11.

Hans Werner, Saxstrasse 18.

Will you please write to these people for I have so much scribbling to do I can't possibly cope with everything.

If it should prove impossible to get a piano from Graz, then I am afraid we shall have to have our own sent from Pozsony. In that case, would you pay half the cost of transport which will be 30 forints; the piano could be left there during August, too. It's out of the question for me to be without a piano for a month. If there's no piano, I could not stay in Passail for more than 10 days at the most. Yes, do send the trunk; it will come in useful.

I understand from Gianicelli that Richter is coming to Budapest next week. Who is 'Kata'?

Yesterday, at long last, after much difficulty, I met the Bayers; they invited me to go with them to the Opera last night. Mrs. Gruber had already invited me to her box, so it was a bit awkward. I divided the evening between the two boxes. After the performance, I had supper with the Bayers, but they were tired. By the way, imagine Mr. Bayer listening to a performance of *The Twilight of the Gods,* lasting from 6.30 till 11 p.m.!! The first act takes 1 hour and 45 minutes!!

Mrs. Gruber likes the *4 Songs* very much. Tell Böske that she

[1] Bartók has written *oroszlán* (lion) as a pun on *orosz lány* (Russian girl) (see also Notes).

should think highly of them because they have been composed by the 'future Beethoven of Hungary' (!). Anyway, I don't know of any Hungarian song better than these—which isn't saying too much, as there are extremely few Hungarian songs.

Please return the enclosed Szentmiklós postcard with your next letter.

That's all for now, I think.

How is Aunt Irma? L.
B.

Emily tells me that Böske doesn't look so very ill at all!

[Original in Hungarian]

8. TO JÁNOS BATKA—POZSONY

[1] *Passail (bei Weiz), July* 7th, 1903

Dear Mr. Batka,
Thank you very much indeed for all your kindness; I am most grateful for your interest in my work, and you can imagine how pleased I am to know that Mr. Richter is sympathetically disposed towards me, and that there may be an opportunity for me to give a concert in England. I am busy working on the orchestration of my Symphony, and I do hope Mr. Richter will like this too.

I have not read any of Liszt's or Wagner's writings; I should be very grateful if you, Sir, would have the kindness to send them to me.

My mother sends her best regards.

I remain,

Yours very sincerely,
BÉLA BARTÓK

[Original in Hungarian]

9. TO JÁNOS BATKA—POZSONY

[2] *Passail, July* 16th, 1903

Dear Mr. Batka,
I want to thank you very much indeed for your kind letter and parcel. Of the compositions you sent, I already knew the Bach motet; 2 years ago I bought all 7 Bach motets in the Peters edition, which does not even give the piano extract below the score. I played each of them a few times; but I didn't devote much attention to any of them and didn't learn so much as one of them by heart. This

first one I'll now study thoroughly. I do not know this Palestrina composition, but I do know some others. In my opinion, vocal compositions like this do not lend themselves to being transcribed for the piano. Not because one cannot bring out all the fine points, but because they wholly lose their effect if played on the piano.

It is as if melody, in the modern sense of the word, is totally absent from these works; their beauty lies in the peculiar, archaic harmonies, in the often complicated *part-writing* and in the beautiful harmony of the voices. And it is precisely this that one cannot render on the piano. I mean that anyone playing or reading such a composition from the score may enjoy it; but it will remain without any effect on a person who only *hears it* performed on the piano, and who has no idea of *part-writing*, etc. Nevertheless, I'll make the attempt; perhaps there may be some way of realizing the beauty of these pieces on the piano, too.

I shall read the Liszt book with great interest; of course, for the time being I haven't much time for reading, as my *Kossuth* symphony has to be ready by the end of July.

I'll return the material with thanks as soon as I have read through it and studied it all.

Till then, I remain,

Yours very sincerely,
BÉLA BARTÓK

[Original in Hungarian]

10. TO ISTVÁN THOMÁN—BUDAPEST

[2] *Passail (bei Weiz) in Steiermark*
[Second half of *July*, 1903]

Dear Professor,

I have today at last received Richter's long-awaited letter telling me that he has fixed the date of the Manchester concert at which he wants me to appear; it's to be on Feb. 18, next year. Also he says that as I'm only a beginner and a foreigner, I can't receive any fees, but he will gladly put me up while I'm in England, or rather Manchester, and will see that my travelling expenses are covered. He wants us to keep to the programme already decided upon. Yes, I, too, am surprised that he should have chosen *The Spanish Rhapsody* of all pieces.

I think you are mistaken about the Volkmann piece; you must be thinking of Volkmann's *Concertstück* which is also in the form of variations but with an orchestral accompaniment. The piece I'm speaking of is, however, *Variations on a Theme by Handel* without orchestral accompaniment. This is not very effective either, in my opinion. Miss Trofimoff was here for 2 days before going on to Semmering, and I gave her 6 lessons in musical theory. She is past harmony now and has started to learn simple counterpoint. I asked 50 forints for my Sonata for Left Hand, but so far the publishers have neither replied nor returned the manuscript.

The orchestration of my *Kossuth* symphony keeps me very busy. I was hoping to have it ready by the end of July, but I see now that I can't finish it before the middle of August, at the earliest. But I would very much like to have it performed by the Philharmonic Orchestra this year—that is, of course, if they accept it. I am afraid I may miss the deadline for sending it in.

I wonder how you and your family are spending the summer. I should be very pleased to have at least a few lines from you. I'll be staying here till Aug. 15, then I leave for Gmunden.

Please give my best regards to your wife; best regards also from my mother.

Yours sincerely,
BÉLA BARTÓK

[Original in Hungarian]

11. TO HIS MOTHER, MRS. BÉLA BARTÓK—POZSONY

[7] *Gmunden, August* 23rd, 1903

Dear Mama,
I have already sent a brief message to say that I'm comfortably settled here. I have a good room, nice and bright. The piano and my trunks were delivered the very next day after I arrived here. The people in the house are helpful. Wiesinger took me to a forwarding agent and recommended a restaurant. He is a stationer, and so there's plenty of writing material in the house, picture postcards, ink and music-paper. I can post letters from here, too. The servant boils my milk and brings it in, and they give me breakfast, but I suspect that this will be too expensive for me. I shall stop having coffee in the morning; it's not worth the money. I'll have a glass of milk instead.

The Dohnányis are very friendly towards me. I lunched with them on Saturday. His parents are here too, as well as his sister-in-law. Professor Dohnányi invited me to an afternoon trip to Trautmannsdorf, and Koessler came with us. Dohnányi and I argued a lot—about the political situation. It is only natural for him not to approve of Hungary's national demands. But neither of us managed to persuade the other. I told Koessler what Mihalovich had said about the proposed performance of the *Kossuth.* He thinks it's simply ridiculous. The following day I took the score to him; he said the orchestration was very good (*ganz famos*), very modern, and that it would sound very well. The man with whom he is staying—Ritter Victor von Miller zu Aichstein—invited me to lunch together with the old Dohnányis and Margit Kunwald. Before lunch he showed me the Brahms Museum which he owns; it contains a very interesting collection of MSS. and programmes all by or relating to Brahms. Ritter von Miller was a devoted admirer of Brahms and often invited him to his castle where Joachim, Dvořák and others were frequent visitors. After dinner, I played *Kossuth* and part of *Heldenleben* for them. I told everyone who saw the score that it was not the original MS. but a copy made by my mother and younger sister. Koessler, before I began to play, said, *Schauen Sie, wie rührend! Das hatten seine Mutter und Schwester abgeschrieben.*

My piano is very good, although it isn't new. But I had to pay the transport charges. I have received your letter. When are you leaving for home? So far I haven't spent too much on food. For example, yesterday lunch and supper cost only 1.23 forints! That was because I had ham for supper and had bought pastries in a pastry-shop. For several days before that I had been invited out to lunch.

It has been difficult to get down to this letter. First my time was taken up with all the invitations; and now I have begun composing the slow movement of the Sonata for Violin, and this also keeps me rather busy.

L.
B.

I was not able to meet either Bösendorfer or Herr König when I was in Ischl, as they had already left.

[Original in Hungarian]

12. TO HIS MOTHER, MRS. BÉLA BARTÓK—POZSONY

[8] *Gmunden, September* 8th, 1903

Dear Mama,

I am furious! So many people had brought all sorts of music into my room over there in Passail, which kept getting mixed up with my own, that instead of bringing my volume of Chopin ballades I've brought someone else's Chopin nocturnes here by mistake. For I can't find the Chopin ballades, but I've got the nocturnes twice. One copy is somebody else's, the other, mine. As I very much need that ballad volume, please go to Biermann's and ask for it back. (It undoubtedly got mixed up with theirs.) And then do send it to me.

I have no news at the moment. The most I can send you is a social-political dissertation to the effect that the ruin of the Hungarians will not be caused, as Dohnányi asserts, by the fact that the language and spirit of our army will be Hungarian but much more by the fact that the individual members of the Hungarian nation, with insignificant exceptions, are so distressingly indifferent to everything Hungarian. Not in high politics, where there is plenty of enthusiasm for national ideals, but in everyday life where we incessantly commit wrongs against the Hungarian nation in all sorts of seemingly unimportant trifles. 'It's all the same to us whether and how anybody speaks our unique and peerless language, instead we ourselves speak everybody else's language; we deride people who speak only Hungarian as uneducated, no matter how much they know; our girls, the mothers of future generations, we ruin at a tender age with foreign education . . . ' This is what Jenő Rákosi says in one of his fine speeches. He is right! This is how Hungarians act when really they ought to do all they can to foster the use of their mother tongue. Only thus can it become strong, at least within our own boundaries. But of course we don't mind, Hungarian speech or German (we even take pride in this), Hungarian goods or Austrian. Everyone, on reaching maturity, has to set himself a goal and must direct all his work and actions towards this. For my own part, all my life, in every sphere, always and in every way, I shall have one objective: the good of Hungary and the Hungarian nation. I think I have already given some proof of this intention in the minor ways which have so far been possible to me. Unfortunately there are in this respect many things in my own home which need correcting. The last time we were together, I noticed with sorrow that both you and Böske, whether from negligence or forgetfulness, committed the very errors I have mentioned. I don't deny that if there's a row somewhere over *Gotterhalte*, it causes a great uproar. But this does the Hungarians no good; at the most there might be some Government legislation to put that right. But as not everyone can be Prime Minister, those whom fortune has spared should work quietly and unobtrusively in their everyday life for everything that is Hungarian. Spread and propagate the Hungarian language, with word and deed, and with *speech*! Speak Hungarian between yourselves!!! How ashamed of myself I should be if for instance in Pozsony or perhaps later in Budapest an acquaintance who knows my way of thinking visited me and by chance heard that you speak German between yourselves and perhaps even to me. He would think me a hypocrite.—You bring up in defence that you have got used to speaking German with Aunt Irma. This is an acceptable excuse, but at the same time the outcome of a neglect that can never be made good. Why didn't you get used to speaking Hungarian when you were young? Aunt Irma, after all, spent quite a long time in Békés County; there she learned our language to some extent, and you could have done the rest. If, much later, you got *used* to speaking German to us so that we should learn the German language, you could in the same manner have got used to speaking Hungarian with Aunt Irma in order that she should learn Hungarian.

But what am I talking about? For in Hungary knowing German is obligatory and necessary; it does no harm if, in addition, they speak Hungarian, too (a little)!

Hear now the thesis addressed to every Hungarian:

Speak in a foreign language only when absolutely necessary! That is, I wish that, even if you speak in another language with Aunt Irma, you should, with Böske, whether at home or elsewhere, whether I'm at home or not, speak in Hungarian without fail. If 'it's difficult to get used to it', then one must take pains; the Hungarian language deserves it.

As for you addressing me in German—well, not even as a joke do I want this. You know how I am in the shops, and when anybody in the street asks me the way in a foreign language. I wish you to follow my example. If 'it's difficult', well, you must get over the first difficulties; it will be quite easy later. I have got used to it completely. It would be sad if those closest to me did not co-operate with me for a common goal. To your old acquaintances who do not speak well, you can be obliging. But to Biermanns, to Fs[1]??!! How often I have noticed, when the conversation is going on in Hungarian, that suddenly *you* are the one who switches over to German, out of sheer forgetfulness, because it is 'all the same' to you. Whether my little sister is called Böske or something else

[1] Illegible.

is not so important; one can get round this without any change. But what I am writing about in this letter, what I am asking you for you must do.

By the way, what do you say to the king making such a fool of himself for the second time? First with Tisza, now with Lukács. And all this is caused by his so very clever and highly esteemed advisers. What a scandalous state of affairs that the king has now to *catch* the man who will undertake the job of Prime Minister, this position of honour (and servitude).

And why is all this?!!

News in brief:

Emsyke is in Budapest already, together with Irmy, she will begin teaching on the 9th; no news about the conservatory.

Dietl has written a postcard from London.

Böske brought me pleasure today with a very ugly postcard; she writes about Aunt Irma having her name-day on Sunday. Next Sunday or the Sunday after? As soon as I know this I'll be happy to congratulate her.

Dohnányi, as I found out with some difficulty, does not like my symphony after all. 'The ending is the best.' No doubt because then one can hope that it will soon be over. In addition, the instrumentation isn't 'polished' either.—No, he does not play the Master! The lessons go very well.—But our views are absolutely opposed on a great number of issues. (E.g. Strauss.)

The weather has been astonishingly good. There wasn't a cloud to be seen for eight or nine days; the sun scorched as in Budapest in the warmest June. I still haven't used my umbrella. But now, finally, when I was planning an excursion to the Schafberg (1780 m!), the sky has clouded over.

Remark. I was planning this excursion quite seriously. I wanted to go up to the Schafberg, even the relative height of which is 1300 m; that is to say, to go up by funicular.

L.
B.

[Original in Hungarian]

13. TO HIS MOTHER, MRS. BÉLA BARTÓK—POZSONY

[9] *Gmunden, September* 23rd, 1903

Dear Mama,

You surely can't think it too much of a strain to give 2 performances a week! What makes you think that? And, in my case, it can't possibly do me any harm because my impresario has to pay my travelling expenses, so he's not likely to book engagements for me, at, say, Kolozsvár on Monday, and Strasbourg on Thursday. Anyway, nothing is settled as yet. I have not yet heard from Grosz (I want to have the passage from Thomán's letter sent back to me). I almost wish the whole thing would come to nothing, for I am anxious to get on with my work in peace.

Please send my overcoat on to Berlin.

It would be a nuisance to have to carry it with me all the way from here. I leave on Sept. 30th.

If you happen to meet Rigele, please tell him on no account to invite the Archduke's family to my recital. I do not want to play to such a corrupt, predatory, murderous lot!

One more date:

I shall be playing with the Grünfelds on Febr. 3rd.

You are quite wrong about Dohnányi. I think very highly of him both as a man and an artist. There is not a trace of malice in him. As an artist, he is too severe on his fellow artists; but that's not such a very great fault. His much worse and unforgivable sin is his lack of patriotism. This excludes the possibility that there might ever be a 'better relationship' between us.

I think less highly of his wife as a person. I'm amazed that D. married her.

L.
B.

[Original in Hungarian]

14. TO HIS MOTHER, MRS. BÉLA BARTÓK—POZSONY

[10] *Berlin, October* 29th, 1903

Dear Mama,

I nearly decided not to write. We shall see each other in a week's time anyhow. As I can't look up your letters to answer your questions, I'll write as things come into my mind. I hear that they wanted to sign Vecsey up for the concert at the Lipótváros Club. As he already had an engagement on that day, and as Dohnányi is engaged elsewhere on November 25th, they made haste to ask me. I've learned all this here in Berlin. Today I received a letter from Gianicelli, and he doesn't say a word about it. The number of my new acquaintances is growing like an avalanche. So far I have called on only 2 of the 6 or 8 people to whom I have been given introductions. One of them gave me an introduction to a Mr. Pollák who

Béla Bartók aged twenty-one

Three of Bartók's ardent admirers, Irmy Jurkovics, Emilia Bayer and Emsy Jurkovics, 1899

Béla Bartók, aged twenty-four, on his first trip abroad

is a very good musician. And Schult took me to the Halmis, where I met a huge number of people. But I was wrong about the man who invited me to lunch on Monday, artists don't go there. At Godowsky's last night, the violinist Kreisler and his wife were there. (He played with the Philharmonic on Monday.) I played *Kossuth*, Dohnányi's *Passacaglia*, my Scherzo and the piece for the left hand, to general appreciation. (Everyone is very much impressed by the forthcoming Manchester performance.) A pupil of Godowsky is also here, an American girl of 16, whose parents also invited me to call on them today. In spite of all this, the prospects for my concert are not very favourable.

I leave here on Sun. Oct. 2nd.

In Vienna I shall be staying at the 'Goldenes Lamm' (Wiedener Hauptstrasse 7), not far from the Musikverein. I'll be given tickets (3), so you must come for them. When is your train due? I may come to the station. During the evening of Febr. 3rd, I shall be at Dietl's aunt's, and on Febr. 5th, at Thallóczy's—he's *joint* Under-Secretary of State for the Treasury or something. So I expect to arrive at Pozsony either during the evening of the 5th or on the morning of the 6th, where I'll visit Batka (instead of writing) and return the books. I'll also look up Rigele. I shall be leaving on the evening of the 7th or on the morning of the 8th.

No more now, as I am incredibly busy.

By the way, Hartmann lives here. He's married, and I called on him yesterday.

L.
B.

[Original in Hungarian]

15. TO HIS MOTHER, MRS. BÉLA BARTÓK—POZSONY

[11] *Berlin, December* 3rd, 1903

Dear Mama,

Strictly, you are not yet due to have a letter from me. Still, since I am sending my programme, I may as well write a few lines. There has been a long enough break—without even a postcard. I really don't understand what you want me to do! I have already told you that I'm willing to play if some impresario should want to organize a recital for me at Pozsony—the terms, of course, to be fixed by me. Well then??

Yesterday I played at a kind of tea-party—as the guest of yet another American family (they live in a boarding-house). Some of the other guests said, *Wir müssen in Ihr Concert gehen.* Very nice, I hope they do. Takings of about 50 marks so far assured. Gross takings may run to as much as 100. I have made one attempt to call on the Ambassador but without success. He was just setting out for a drive, so I shall call again tomorrow.

I feel wonderful in Berlin—as I have never felt in any other city. There's no doubt that the climate and air here suit me better than in, say, Budapest.

The minute I arrive in Budapest I begin to sneeze and feel generally out of sorts. Here I'm cured of all that. Even if I stroll down the Siegesallee in a snowstorm or stand about on a wet and windy day outside the box-office of the Opernhaus—still I come to no harm. I have not been eating out in restaurants so much lately: nearly every other day I have dinner with the Stencels. The result is that I've started to despise the 1.10-mark dinners. Today I went to a frightfully swanky *Weinrestaurant*—where you have to order wine. I had: (1) Chicken-broth; (2) *Zander* (What's that?) with butter; (3) Salt meat with cabbage and peas; (4) Leg of mutton with lettuce and cranberry; (5) apple-pie; (6) fruit. For all that I paid 1.50; for wine and water, plus tip, another 1.60; that is, 3.10 marks all told.

Here's a message for Böske:

1. Sordine *ab:* Sordine *auf* = six: half dozen.

2. Of course markings should be written in red ink, and numbers, in blue pencil.

3. By nouns I mean words like these: brush-maker, sordino, worm, symphony, boot-sole, lavatory, sonata, cat's tail, hose, incompatibility, chamber-pot, bread-roll, hell and damnation!! Now then: when she comes across words of this kind written with capital initial letters, she must take out a pen-knife and scratch them out, and write small letters in their places. Fancy having to explain what a noun is![1]

L.
BÉLA

[1] Bartók has written on top of the margin: 'Sordine auf × six = Sordine ab × half dozen.' His use of the Greek letter epsilon (ε) adds emphasis to his humorous-censorious lines on the copying of musical scores. In the last sentence, as well as in his signature, all letters 'e' are replaced by ε's.

[Original in Hungarian]

16. TO ISTVÁN THOMÁN—BUDAPEST

[3] *Kurfürstenstr. 30. II., Berlin W.*
December 16th, 1903

Dear Professor,
Now that we are safely past the momentous day of December 14th, my first task must be to give you a faithful account of my recital. What I feared most was that I should not be strong enough to get through the programme. At the end of the recital I didn't feel at all tired, and I could have gone through another programme. The piece for the left hand came off superbly—the greater part of the audience liked that best. There was a 2/3 capacity audience (gross takings about M. 120); and it included 2 'celebrities'—Godowsky and Busoni. After the 3rd number Busoni came into the green-room to introduce himself and congratulate me. Richter had already told him about me in Manchester. He was delighted with my compositions, especially *Fantasia*. I heard from others that he has expressed some surprise that a player with such a fine left-hand technique, as he heard in the piece for the left hand, should then give an unsatisfactory rendering of Chopin's *Étude in C minor*. Well, I'm afraid he was right, it didn't go very well, and I would even have liked to omit it or play something else instead, but it was too late. However, if the rest was good, it does not matter very much. After the 3rd and 4th numbers, I had to give encores (own composition and Juon humoresque). I am enclosing the review that appeared in the *Vossische Zeitung* (the first and, so far, the only one). Except for the last sentence, it is entirely favourable. I should be grateful if you would show this letter to Mrs. Gruber, so that I don't have to write the same things over again. I shall be staying in Berlin until Dec. 23rd; then I go to Pozsony (Kórház u. 3.). I'll come up to Budapest on Jan. 8th.

With kind regards,
Yours sincerely,
BÉLA BARTÓK

[Original in Hungarian]

17. TEXT DRAFT OF 'KOSSUTH' SYMPHONY
TO HIS MOTHER, MRS. BÉLA BARTÓK

[12] [1903–4]

The year 1848 is one of the most notable in the history of Hungary; it was then that the Hungarian War of Independence broke out: a life-and-death conflict whose goal was permanent freedom from the sovereignty of the Austrians and the Hapsburg dynasty. The leader of the Revolution, and its inspiration, was Lajos Kossuth. In 1849, having suffered defeat after defeat at the hands of the Hungarian army, the Austrians called on the Russians for help; and it was they who eventually routed the Hungarian army. Thus the hope of an independent Hungary seemed to be destroyed for ever.

These events serve as a basis for the symphony's programme.

The work comprises 10 closely related parts, with an explanatory inscription at the head of each:

I('Kossuth') This is intended to portray Kossuth.

II ('What grief weighs on thy soul, dear husband?') The faithful wife of Kossuth is anxious at seeing her husband sorrowful, his face wrinkled with worries. Kossuth attempts to reassure her, but finally he can no longer contain his long suppressed grief:

III ('Our country is in danger!') He dreams again of the glorious past.

IV ('The better time of days gone by . . .')

V ('Then we fell on evil times . . .') First the flute and piccolo, then the bass clarinet play a theme intended to characterize the tyranny of the Austrians and the Hapsburgs, and violence which acknowledges no law.

With these words:

VI ('On to battle!') Kossuth is aroused from his dreams; the irrevocable decision has been made to take up arms.

VII ('Come forth, come, fine Magyar warriors, fair Magyar champions!') This is Kossuth's appeal to the nation's sons to rally to his standard. It is directly followed by the theme (in F minor) of the gradual gathering of a Hungarian armed force. Kossuth repeats his appeal (in A minor, twice) to the assembled army, who then take a solemn vow to fight to the last breath (3/2 time). For a few moments very deep silence, and then . . .

VIII the Austrian troops are heard slowly approaching. Their theme is a distortion of the first 2 bars of the Austrian national anthem *(Gotterhalte)*. Clash follows clash as the conflict intensifies to a life-and-death struggle. Finally, overwhelming force prevails. The great catastrophe occurs (timpani and gong *fff):* the remnants of the Hungarian army go into hiding.

IX ('To all an end . . .') The country goes into deepest mourning. But even this is forbidden, and so . . .

X ('All is silence, silence.')

[Original in Hungarian]

18. TO HIS MOTHER, MRS. BÉLA BARTÓK—POZSONY

[13] Address: *The Firs*
Bowdon
Cheshire[1]

Feb. 12th, 1904

B. B.
with the lines of Dr. Hans Richter[2]

Dear Mama,

Now that I have arrived safely in Bowdon, I want to tell you something about the journey. The Richters received me very cordially and have given me a room on the 2nd floor. Actually, I'm not living in Manchester: Bowdon is 20 minutes away. In the afternoon, the weather became very bad indeed—storms of wind and rain—so I haven't been able to see very much of either Manchester or Bowdon. The Richters' home must be a very comfortable place to live in. There is a cheerful blaze in the fireplace (English conservatism).

That reminds me of the horrible state of English railway carriages, which is quite exasperating. The carriages on the most unimportant branch line in Hungary are better than the ones here. There is no heating (they merely put a container full of hot water in the carriage) nor head-rests nor arm-rests; the luggage-racks are too narrow. As there are no ash-trays, the floor of the compartments resembles that of pigsties. They do have some lights, surprisingly, and even, here and there—God forgive—a communication cord! Some trains have a restaurant car, but you can only get into them or leave them when the train stops at a station.

I have been somewhat surprised to find that life is not as expensive as I expected. In London 'cabbies' charge 2/2 (= 1.40 Kr), whereas in Vienna they ask 1.60 Kr. Even porters are content with 30 kreutzers (3d) (d=penny). I've got used to the English money and counting very quickly. The battered copper coins (1-penny pieces), as big as this[3], are very quaint.

[1] Printed address on the paper.
[2] Written in English.
[3] Bartók drew a penny in his letter.

There is only 1st and 3rd class from London to Manchester. (As regards comfort, there's nothing to choose between them.) I travelled 3rd for 16 shillings; then there was 2/6 for lunch and 8d for a Hungarian Apollinaris I had with it; I gave 3d as a tip.

I sent postcards from Vienna, Cologne, Boxtel (Netherlands), London and Manchester.

I was greatly amused by the notices in Dutch railway carriages—*verboden te rooken*, etc. It is the French cognac, however, that's come off best of all—I still haven't touched it. I enjoyed the crossing very much and was only sorry that I couldn't stay on deck because of the rough wind. So I had to rock myself below deck; later I had tea (8d) in the saloon, and then, as I didn't want to sleep, began to walk about again. But eventually (at 12.30 West Eur. time), when my fellow travellers had long since been fast asleep, I had to give in. I woke up at about 2.30 when the ship was rolling fairly heavily and the sea beating against the port-hole. It is a pity I had to travel alone. (But then I don't think you'd have enjoyed it, since you keep early hours.)

L.
B.

[Original in Hungarian]

19. TO LAJOS DIETL—VIENNA

[1] *Steglitzerstr. 65. III., Berlin W.*
March 17th, 1904

My dear Friend,
I have been so absorbed in my composing and other labours that I'm only now able to thank you for your good offices which have resulted in my selling 4 songs and 4 piano pieces for 400 Kr. They will probably not appear before Oct. Anyway, I wish my publisher all the good he can get out of them.

I promised to send you my Manchester reviews, but unfortunately I have lost them somewhere *en route*. It's a pity because there were one or two interesting comments in them. I spent 6 days in London. The Broadwoods have promised me 6 concerts next year (it was Dohnányi who spoke on my behalf); two of them will be in London (also a recital). In the meantime my orchestral scherzo has had a great success at home. I am now in complete retirement, studying all five branches of Art. I have been getting to know some beautiful songs by Strauss. Verily, verily, I say unto you: since Wagner there has been no composer as great as Strauss. Could you recommend some modern rarely-played recital pieces? I am desperately looking for such pieces at Bote and Bock's music lending-library, but I can find hardly anything that pleases me. I'm returning to Hungary at the end of Apr.; 2 days in Pozsony; then to the country—for a holiday, where I may live in even greater retirement than I do here. Oh, yes! What would you advise? Should I again make my own arrangements for a concert (on which I might lose money) in Vienna next year? And if so, is there any way of arranging it with Kehlendorfer and Bösendorfer, leaving out Gutmann? In any case, there's still plenty of time.

Looking forward to hearing from you,

with kindest regards,
B. BARTÓK

[PS.] (About the letter you sent to England—the address was, indeed, wrong: instead of Bowdon you wrote something else!)

[Original in Hungarian]

20. HIS MOTHER, MRS. BÉLA BARTÓK—TO MRS. GYULA BARANYAI—SZEGED

Pozsony, 4. 4. 1904

Dear Mili,

I have received both your letter and postcard, I was so pleased to have them. You are still the same kind, good-natured creature you always were, willing to share in the happiness of friends. Thank you very much for your kind remarks about my son; and will you also, please, convey my thanks to your husband for his congratulations?

I could tell you so much about the wonderful happenings during January: we had one success after another. Still, the most grandiose of them all was the performance of *Kossuth*. I went to Budapest with Elza; but before going I went through a period of great nervousness which affected poor Béla, too. Some of the Austrian musicians, the very ones who play the most crucial instruments, were not willing to play at the rehearsals; we almost began to doubt whether the symphony could be performed at all. At last they decided to play; then I was afraid that perhaps they would spoil it on purpose. I simply can't tell you how agitated I was when I set out to go to the concert. You can imagine my feelings when the gentleman sitting behind me (he didn't know me, of course) said: 'We'd better cross ourselves now, they're going to play the *Kossuth* symphony next. I wish it were over!' But when they had finished playing, there was a tremendous storm of applause, and that same gentleman applauded delightedly and went on and on cheering. I'll never forget the thunder of the applause as Béla went on bowing, looking so happy (he was called 8 or 10 times), and as for me, I wept for joy. Elza was so happy, too, especially when 'the composer of *Kossuth*' was presented with 2 lovely laurel wreaths. Then, the next day, all the splendid notices in the papers! But I had to return immediately to my teaching; my whole inner self was in such a turmoil that I hardly knew what I was saying to my pupils. Then Béla played in Pozsony, on January 22—a solo piano recital which lasted the whole evening; and the Pozsony people, who are so critical (especially towards local talent), were delighted. The Duchess Isabella was also present with her daughters and her court; she asked to have Béla introduced to her, and she spoke to him very warmly, saying what pleasure he'd given her. Irma and I (Elza was in Budapest) sat in the gallery so that nobody would see us, for I was just as excited this time, too; but between numbers, a few gentlemen of our acquaintance came to see me, and I was congratulated most warmly. Béla was again given 3 bouquets, something previously unheard-of in Pozsony, at least since I have been going to concerts, although there have been concerts given by other local talents. You know, Mili, it was all so beautiful; I really feel compensated for everything. Then B. played in Budapest, on Jan. 26; Elza was there, and he had 2 laurel wreaths again; as far as I can see, people esteem him not only for his art, they also like him for his modesty. He was also very successful in Vienna where he played his own Sonata for violin; the applause was so enthusiastic that, I must say, both he and I were amazed. Well, then he left for England, where they also paid tribute to him both as a composer and as a pianist; as a pianist especially, his success was unqualified.

From there he went to Berlin, where he is now living very quietly and continuing his studies; he is acquiring a knowledge of literature, partly through reading, partly through theatre-going; he is not making any public appearances just now; that's for the autumn. Perhaps he'll visit Szeged then if the people there care for concerts at all.

He will be gone from here by May, as he's going to spend 5 months in Gömör County this summer, composing and learning new pieces. We are also going there for two months.

Elza isn't here either; she is in Békés County, staying with relatives who have a farm; she gives lessons to their ten-year-old girl and is also learning to keep house; she is quite content and writes proudly that she already knows how to cook. So I'm living with Irma, the two of us always looking forward to letters from the children, who write very regularly. Béla, too, writes diligently, knowing how worried I always am.

Elza is going to apply for a job in Budapest, but I don't think she'll get it; though, for Béla's sake, they really might find her some little thing. What's going to become of me I don't know; I'm getting old; my eyes and legs are getting weak. In school I have to be on my feet all the time, you cannot otherwise teach 4 classes, and this wears me out, as much as all the work which has to be got through in a training-school.

You, I know, had a splendid holiday at Easter. I can well imagine the talks you had with Carola about old times. We went to the Rauschmanns' yesterday, as we do every Sunday. Poor old Auntie has managed to pull herself together again. But we were all very scared 3 weeks ago when she fainted and gave herself such a bang on the head—we were afraid of concussion. I could go on chatting for a long time, but I must leave now for church.

Good-bye, love and kisses,

Your
PAULA

[PS.] How are your children? You, too, are having much joy in your Zoltán, aren't you? Give my greetings to your husband and our best wishes for Gyula[1] day. Kisses from Irma, too.

[Original in Hungarian]

21. TO KÁLMÁN HARSÁNYI—RÁKOSPALOTA[2]

[1a] [*Regensburg, August* 21st, 1904]

[Picture postcard: The Wagner Theatre at Bayreuth]

Dear Kálmán,
I am still under the spell of *Parsifal* as I write these lines. A very interesting work, though it did not make such a tremendous impression on me as *Tristan*. Anyone possessed of the slightest religious sentiment must be moved by

[1b]

[Picture postcard: The New Royal Castle at Bayreuth]

the plot. I feel disturbed by that continual praying on the stage. Contrary to my expectations, I found many innovations in the

[1] Julius.
[2] Two postcards with continuous text.

music. It is amazing that a man of 70 could write anything so fresh as the flower-maidens' love-song in the 2nd act—and this without being repetitious. I'll be writing something more about Bayreuth, in any case. What I would like to know is whether you would come to see a few performances some time. I played my Scherzo to Richter who thinks it a scherzo '*von und zu Übermenschen*'.

Yours ever,
BÉLA

[Original in Hungarian]

22. TO KÁLMÁN HARSÁNYI—RÁKOSPALOTA

[2] *Gerlicepuszta, September* 18th, 1904

Dear Kálmán,
Thanks for *Oak Leaf*, Thode, etc. I read 'Shadows of Rodostó' with great pleasure. However, of the 3 poems in question, I am most attracted by the possibility of setting to music 'The Thirteen of Arad', and I think I may succeed in doing that.

And now it is my turn to make you a present—my 1st Fantasy which came off the press only a few days ago. I imagine you don't need 'Rodostó' back yet, so I'll let you have it in the first half of Nov.

When I was in Bayreuth, I learned that those Wagner Scholarships are not only for musicians but also for writers and poets. Perhaps you, too, could send in an application. Even if you do not obtain a full scholarship, you might still get tickets for 6 performances or so (not something to be scorned when tickets cost 20 marks). Applications have to be in by the end of Jan., 1905, to a Count Festetich, whose address I have forgotten. Your best plan would be to ask for information from Professor Károly Gianicelli (Damjanich u. 56. 3rd floor) nearer the time. The awards are made by a committee of 4, consisting of the 2 gentlemen mentioned above, together with Jenő Rákosi and Mihalovich.

On your way back from Bayreuth you could go through Munich.

They tell me that you've now got down to serious work. What is it you are working on? The epic poem, perhaps? Or only translation?

Many greetings to your dear Mother, your sister and yourself.

Yours,
BÉLA

[Original in Hungarian]

23. TO ISTVÁN THOMÁN—BUDAPEST

[4] *Gerlicepuszta, September* 18th, 1904
(P.O. Ratkó)

My dear Pista,
I am enclosing printed copies of the piece for the left hand and *Fantasy No. 1.* I hope we shall fare better with these than with the *Passacaglia*, which is really lost. I've lost things in Ratkó before—letters and postcards. You can't trust these provincial post offices. I would indeed like to know who in darkest Gömör County can have been so eager to lay his hands on, of all things, Dohnányi's *Passacaglia*. In my last letter to my mother I promised to send the piano arrangement of my Scherzo. But, as you may have already heard, the Philharmonic have now included it in their programme (for March 15th, together with Liszt's *Todtentanz*), so I must hurry with the orchestration. As soon as I've finished it, probably in the first half of Oct., I will send you the arrangement. Will you please pass it on to Mrs. Gruber after you have looked at it? If you're interested, you might play it on two pianos. I showed it to Richter in Bayreuth; he said it was '*ein gelungener musikalischer Scherz*'. The only thing he objected to was the title. He said the piece was too grandiose, too complex, too 'sparkling' for such a plain title. Then he added: 'You mustn't expect it to be generally liked, though.' And so, even though Richter liked it, the result is nil.

Altogether, it looks as if I'm going to be on short commons next year. (More about this in my letter to Mrs. Gruber.)

Would you be so good as to give me the name and address of that Viennese who you once told me translates from Hungarian? I want to recommend him to my publisher.

Please give my regards to your wife.

Yours sincerely,
BÉLA

[Original in Hungarian]

24. TO LAJOS DIETL—VIENNA

[2] *Pozsony, Kórház u. 3.*
[First half of *December*, 1904]

My dear Friend,
I am coming to Vienna on December 14th (arriving 6 p.m.). Should I not say anything to Thomán?

Will Dec. 15th and 16th be soon enough to look for lodgings (for Jan. and Feb.)? May I look you up at 6.30 p.m., the 14th—sorry, that's the day you don't go to the Conservatory.

Many thanks for all the wonderful reviews; I have read all of them, I assure you, with *divine* equanimity.

But what do you say to this one?

[A newspaper clipping enclosed with the letter]

THEATRE—MUSIC

The programme of *The Grünfeld–Bürger String Quartet*, at the third of their popular concerts given yesterday afternoon, was devoted to the works of two deserving Hungarian composers. The works of Béla Bartók have already been widely appreciated in spite of the composer's youthfulness. In him ardent patriotism and classicism create a fine harmony. On this occasion the composer, who is also a gifted pianist, played the piano part in his own piano quintet. Here we had evidence of the warmth of his Hungarian heart as well as the wide knowledge he brought to the writing of the music. It is a work full of interest, as evocative and imaginative as his other compositions. The audience loudly acclaimed him both as composer and performer. Bartók also played a piece by Schubert; his interpretation, in feeling and in technique, was of an outstanding order.

What a gag that was![1]

(The Grünfelds couldn't manage to learn my quintet.)

Yours sincerely,
B.

[Original in Hungarian]

25. TO HIS MOTHER, MRS. BÉLA BARTÓK — POZSONY

[14] [*Paris, August* 8th, 1905]

Dear Mama,

I'm sorry to have to tell you that I have not been successful in the competition. I'm not in the least surprised that I didn't win a prize as a pianist, and there's no need to feel disappointed on that score. But the way in which the prizes for composers were distributed—or rather not distributed—that was quite outrageous.

[1] See letter No. 78 where it becomes clear that the critics attributed Schubert's quintet to Bartók.

But I'll tell you exactly what happened according to Dietl who was one of the judges.

The Pianists' Prize went to Backhaus, with Eisner as the runner-up.

There were only five competitors for the Composers' Prize.

The judges had to consider the following questions:

1. Should we award the prize at all? (Yes, 2; no, 13.)
2. Should we award the 2nd prize (Frs 2,000)? (Yes, 5; no, 10.)
3. If no prizes are awarded, should we give certificates of merit? (Yes, 10; no, 5.)
4. To whom should we give such certificates? (Brugnoli received 10 votes, Bartók 9, Flament 2, Weinberg 1. Each of the judges could put forward two or three names.)

So Brugnoli received the first mention. The last 2 don't even get certificates.

The minute I receive my diploma of (dis)honour, I shall send it back to Auer, to Petrograd. I am not prepared to accept rubbish like that.

I may say that Brugnoli's pieces are absolutely worthless conglomerations. It is quite scandalous that the jury could not see how much better my works are.

And yet my works were quite well performed. That, having heard them, the jury still failed to appreciate them is equally scandalous.

And how they baited me! I was within an ace of being compelled to withdraw. They began by saying that the parts of the *Concertstück* were faulty, the piece was too difficult and could not be played because time was too short for rehearsals. I corrected the parts (there were 10 to 15 mistakes all told), and, after much wangling, it was finally played rather well, after all.

As for the quintet, they declared flatly and categorically that it could not be learned, since there was not enough time. Luckily I happened to have the violin sonata handy (though actually, of course, it made no difference), and so we performed that. How long it took us to find a violinist! At last, a young Russian, a pupil of Auer, called Zeitlin, rehearsed with me and played it. So I made the second copy of the quintet in vain. (As it was an emergency choice, they forbore to insist on a duplicate copy of the sonata for violin.) Not even the devil glanced at the piano reduction of the *Concertstück* (I spent 6 hours doing it). Why those empty-headed Petrograd cattle insisted on *this* beats me.

The other four composers' things were absolutely worthless.

Brugnoli's were superficially effective. And there can never have been anything like Ságody's before: during the performance the audience only just managed to contain their laughter, it was so idiotic.

My work went down very well with the audience. Three young men spoke to me, first in French, then in English, and asked me if my sonata had been published yet. They wanted to buy it. Several others said they liked it. The young Russian, Zeitlin, is delighted with it. In a month's time he will be leaving for Helsingfors, to take up a post as orchestra leader. He asked me to let him have a copy of the sonata (when it is published), as he would like to perform it there. He tried to console me by pointing out that the panel of judges included so many Russians who are still unfamiliar with this kind of music—he said they were still playing only Haydn, Mozart and Beethoven there.

I wouldn't say a word if a composer of any worth at all had beaten me for the prize. But the fact that those dunderheads declared my works unworthy of the prize shows how extraordinarily stupid they were.

Perger, to begin with, couldn't even understand it. Auer said: '*Ja, das ist die neue Schule, wir sind schon zu alt für so etwas.*' Chevillard (a French celebrity) who conducted the orchestra and was himself one of the judges called it *serr interessaņ*. Holländer, a violinist from Berlin, also liked it. He wanted to perform my violin sonata with me—possibly also the notorious quintet—in Berlin (with me at the time of my journey to England). I'm not particularly enthusiastic about this plan, as it would involve me in a lot of expenses without bearing much fruit.

There were 15 votes altogether to be cast by 12 judges: 5 Russian votes, 5 French, 3 German, one Hungarian and one Dutch. Of course it was the Russians and French who had the right to cast more than one vote. What kind of system this is I cannot tell. How can one vote on behalf of another person?!

Dietl sends you his kind regards and says he feels ashamed of having sat with such a panel of judges. Well, *I* feel ashamed of having submitted myself to the judgment of such people.

By the way, Auer told somebody that if both prizes had actually been awarded, they would have had to draw on the capital because the war has done something to the Russian currency—it has depreciated or increased in value, or heaven knows what. In short, they no longer have enough money for the prizes.

It is possible that those 10 Russians and Frenchmen had a private understanding in advance not to award any prizes so as to counterbalance the depreciation of capital. If that is so, it was a monstrous piece of impudence and deception to allow all the composer competitors to flock to the place on a wild-goose chase.

Well, so much for that.

I am glad that you have already managed to straighten things out with Aunt Emma (the silly old thing!). I didn't like that constant shilly-shallying. (I received your letter today and wrote to Elza from here.) I think I shall need the book by the 20th. I may ask for something else, though. In any case, wait for a few more days. I will send a postcard to let you know what I finally want. My landlady, Mme Condat, attended the contest too. She is furious, so much so that she's reduced my rent from 9 francs to 7. This really is cheap.

My money should see me through another 30 days. So I'll write to you again about this at some future date, as to how much you should send. I had my first French lesson today. (Mandl has already found me a pupil—in Vienna.) The fee for each lesson is 2 francs.

Paris is beautiful, but I'm only just beginning to enjoy it, for until now we've had so much bother. Dietl will be leaving in 6 days. The Condats make me very comfortable, it's not just a business arrangement.

I've come across a Hungarian violinist in Chevillard's orchestra. And the other day, under the Eiffel Tower, I heard 2 people speaking Hungarian. Twice I have bought *A Nap* at a news-stall in the street! What do you say to that? There are definitely more Hungarians here than there are in London.

Well, good-bye to you all.

More about Paris in my next.

L.
B.

[Original in Hungarian]

26. TO IRMY JURKOVICS—NAGYSZENTMIKLÓS

18 rue Clément-Marot, Paris.
August 15th, 1905

Dear little Irmy,

At last I have some time to myself!

The preparation for the Rubinstein Competition gave me so frightfully much to do, and all to no purpose. There were 5 competitors for the composition prize; the works of the other 4 were below average, mine was above, hence the meticulous members of the jury, who subscribed to the principle 'the golden mean', did not award the prize to anyone at all.

The pianists' prize was awarded to Backhaus, an Englishman who is a truly fine pianist. It makes me boil over to think of all the unnecessary work for the competition (for instance, we had to give in *2* copies of each work submitted, yet the judges didn't bother to look at the 2nd copy). It never occurred to me that this would happen. The worst I expected was that someone else's work would be pronounced better than mine and the prize awarded to that person. My only consolation has been that I've had the opportunity to come to Paris, this heavenly godless city. It's impossible to describe, one just has to see how many beautiful, such beautiful things there are here, in the capital of the world. What art went to the making of Paris! What are Vienna and Berlin in comparison! (I expect more of Budapest in the future, though of course nothing can make up for the absence of old monuments.) Well, I may be able to write about all this at greater length when I've steeped myself in the atmosphere a bit longer.

I'm resuming this letter after an interval of a good many days, so now I can tell you something—albeit briefly—about the innumerable treasures of art I have so far seen.

As I walk through the museums, I experience an intense delight when I recognize, one after the other, the masterpieces with which we are so familiar in reproduction, the Mona Lisa, Raphael's Madonnas, the well-known portraits of Mme Vigée-Lebrun, Murillo's Young Beggar, and so on.

I can assure you that few paintings have ever had such a profound effect on me as Murillo's larger works in the Louvre. It is possible to glean some idea of their merit from reproductions, but the actual pictures reveal a colour harmony such as you can see in no other paintings. When I look at them, I feel as if I was being touched by a magic wand. It is an experience to be classed along with seeing a performance of *Tristan* or *Zarathustra*, attending the first Weingartner concert in Berlin, hearing Dohnányi play the Beethoven concerto in Vienna this year or catching my first glimpse of the Stephanskirche when I was in Vienna 3 or 4 years ago.

This morning I enjoyed looking at the Impressionist pictures in the Luxembourg Museum.

But who could possibly describe all those things!! The Bois de Boulogne, a park on the outskirts of the City, about eight or ten times bigger than our City Park, and the Bois de Vincennes, an

Sculptures in the Parc Monceau, Paris, listed with enthusiasm in one of Bartók's letters, of Edouard Pailleron, Guy de Maupassant, Ambroise Thomas, Charles-François Gounod

Stefi Geyer in the early 1920s

equally vast area of woods at the other end of the City, and both decorated with squares, statues and exotic plants. Or the Jardin de Luxembourg, the Tuileries, the Champs-Élysées (not far from where I'm living), the jolting-rumbling Metro, the Parc Monceau--- I must just say a few words about this park. I was wandering aimlessly along the streets when suddenly I came to a little paradise. The garden is only about twice as big as Elizabeth Square in Budapest. Only a Frenchman could have the ingenious idea of utilizing the effects of both nature and art to turn this inch of ground into a fairyland. Hidden behind beautiful trees, flowers and shrubs, there are enough statues here to make a little spring show. To mention but a few, there are statues of Pailleron, Maupassant, Thomas and Gounod—so many poetical tributes to French art. Under shady trees is a tiny pool of clear water with crumbling Greek columns beside the bank, like the ruins of some ancient building. Some of the columns are twined with ivy - - -

I strolled under Lebanon cedars in the Jardin des Plantes and bought copies of *Pesti Hírlap* and *A Nap* (equally exotic to me here!) in the Boulevard des Italiens.

And what a host of fine churches!

Then there are other things to see, not necessarily artistic, such as the Moulin Rouge. I know this is something about which boys do not usually write to girls; still, I strike a little blow at R[ight] Hon[orable] Convention and write that I never saw anywhere in a knot so many butterflies of the night with made-up faces and dyed hair. And how very friendly these 'elegant' ladies are! Some of them even accosted me, if you please, and only just stopped short of kissing me (!). Yet, before we went in, we had been warned not to speak. This was not something I had any difficulty in obeying, since I then knew not a single syllable of French! (Now I know 3 or 4 syllables; e.g., I know that the girls of the Moulin Rouge and their like are called *comme il en faut*. (So we must be careful not to make a slip of the tongue and say that instead of *comme il faut*, when talking to respectable people.) The tavern 'Le Néant' is a sort of night-club. There are wooden coffins instead of tables, and the walls of the rooms are black and decorated with human skeletons or parts of skeletons; the waiters wear *pompe-funèbre* sort of garments; and the lighting makes your skin look wax-yellow, your lips livid and your finger-nails violet (in fact, you look like a corpse); and they entertain you by, for instance, wrapping one of your party in a shroud up to the chin and standing him—or her—in a coffin, where, under your very eyes, he turns into a skeleton, etc. (Nothing like it in Szentmiklós?)

In reply to your letter, I must say that Bach, Beethoven, Schubert and Wagner have written such quantities of distinctive and characteristic music that all the music of France, Italy and the Slavs combined, is as nothing by comparison! Of all other composers, Liszt comes closest to the Big Four, but he seldom wrote Hungarian music. Even if, say, my *Funeral March* could hold its own in one respect or another, no nation could possibly appear in the arena with a single 4-page piece, however magnificent it might be! In short: we are still far from being ready to start. Work and study, work and study, and again, work and study. Then we may achieve something. For we're in a surprisingly favourable position, compared with other nations, in regard to our folk-music. From what I know of the folk-music of other nations, ours is vastly superior to theirs as regards force of expression and variety. If a peasant with the ability to compose tunes like one of the enclosed[1] had but emerged from his class during childhood and acquired an education, he would assuredly have created some outstanding works of great value. Unfortunately, it is rare for a Hungarian peasant to go in for a scholarly profession. Our intelligentsia comes, almost exclusively, from foreign stock (as shown by the excessively large number of Hungarians with foreign names); and it is only amongst intellectuals that we find people capable of dealing with art in the higher sense. And now our gentry lack the capacity; there may be the occasional exceptions, but such people are not in the least susceptible to our national art. A real Hungarian music can originate only if there is a real *Hungarian* gentry. This is why the Budapest public is so absolutely hopeless. The place has attracted a haphazardly heterogeneous, rootless group of Germans and Jews; they make up the majority of Budapest's population. It's a waste of time trying to educate them in a national spirit. Much better to educate the (Hungarian) provinces.

What!! You are rebuking me for being a pessimist?!! *Me*, a follower of Nietzsche?!!

Each must strive to rise above all; nothing must touch him; he must be completely independent, completely indifferent. Only thus can he reconcile himself to death and to the meaninglessness of life.

Am I (or rather, are *we*) not right?

It needs a gigantic struggle to rise above all things! How far I am

[1] The music examples have since been lost.

yet from doing so! What is more, the further you advance, the more intensely, it seems, you feel! The child feels unhappy when its apple is taken away. The grown man, representing a higher stage of development, is not distressed by such trifles; yet when he sees his ambition frustrated, is not his distress more enduring? Let's go a step higher! When a man is no longer troubled even by ambition, is it not infinitely painful to him to watch others, especially those in some way close to his heart, striving and struggling childishly for trivialities, incapable of rising higher? And having attained that highest degree of indifference when it leaves you cold whether you can help people or whether you can't, don't you even then still desire one thing, and desire it fervently: that all mankind should rise to the same height?

Thus in this doctrine, apparently, there is an inherent contradiction, a paradox like that in, for instance, sceptic philosophy. The sceptics say, 'One must doubt everything.' 'Is that so?' their opponents retort. 'Then it follows that you must doubt whether you must doubt.' My mother tries to console me and says that the future holds brighter days in store for me! Yes, to be sure. But what if those brighter days come too late? At a time when I shall be as unaffected by brighter days as a young man looking at the toy which once made him so happy when he was a child.

I am inserting here a few remarks, or observations, I have made concerning the Bible and Religion. I should be pleased to have your observations concerning them: who knows but that the thing may not develop into an exchange of ideas.

It is odd that the Bible says, 'God created man', whereas it is the other way round: man has created God.

It is odd that the Bible says, 'The body is mortal, the soul is immortal', whereas even here the contrary is true: the body (its matter) is eternal; the soul (the form of the body) is transitory.

It is odd that the vocation of priest and actor are considered antithetical, when both priest and actor preach the same thing: fables.

I have an idea that the type of people who in ungodly times tend to be the most dissipated of all are those who under the reign of religion would have been bigoted fanatics.

A few more lines about the international set that lives in this boarding-house (*chez* Mme Condat). Taking their lunches and dinners here together are—or used to be—a few Spanish-Americans, 2 European-Spaniards, 5 English-Americans, 2 Englishmen, 1 German, 1 Frenchman, and recently even a Turk who—as he tells me—lives in polygamy and is full of praise for that condition. He has about 5 wives, whose portraits he carries with him in an ingenious telescopic medallion!! A splendid figure. Conversation is sometimes carried on in four languages simultaneously.

Parlez-vous le français? Où avez-vous appris le français?

You must make allowance for the fact that the futile preliminaries for that horrid Rubinstein Competition have kept me terribly busy, and you must not keep me waiting as long as I have kept you waiting for my reply.

How is Emsy? I have heard that she is leaving Szentmiklós! Is that true?

Hoping to hear from you,

Yours sincerely,
BÉLA BARTÓK

[Original in Hungarian]

27. TO HIS MOTHER, MRS. BÉLA BARTÓK—POZSONY

[15] *18 rue Clément-Marot, Paris.*
September 10th, 1905

Dear Mama,

I hope you've been pleased to receive all the letters and postcards I've been sending so often lately. Now it's because of what you say in your last letter that I'm answering promptly. I think you'd be well advised not to think of asking to retire yet awhile. On the other hand, I don't see why you should go to the school as early as 7.15 a.m. Why don't you take my advice and plan some silent occupation for the children at the beginning of the half-hour in question, and never mind if you've only five minutes left for teaching. You should not do one iota over and above what is absolutely necessary.

No, you should not write to Thomán! (1) He does not interfere with that side of affairs at all; it lies within the jurisdiction of the principal, and the professors cannot possibly seek to advise him on the matter. (2) Mihalovich is in any case determined to get me a teaching post. But the present budget will not provide the salary for a 4th teacher. There will have to be a new budget, and it will have to be approved by Parliament. All this must be done before I can obtain my appointment. And now that the *Kaiser* has seen fit to go in for a policy of obstruction, heaven only knows when that may be. Hardly next year. But I will take the first post that comes my way.

That article in a Viennese paper was in a feuilleton in the *Neues Wiener Tagblatt*, wasn't it? It was written by Perger who was on the panel of judges, and he is under the impression that he is saying nice things about me. (Which is to say that he takes an even poorer view of my works than he actually puts into words in that feuilleton.)

Of course, I fully sympathize with your indignation, although I don't see eye to eye with you on every question—for instance, when you write: 'That is like calling a man an impostor.' Pardon me, but isn't that like slandering a man in the same way? Apply equal standards, please. Women should be accorded the same liberties as men. Women ought to be free to do the same things as men, or men ought not to be free to do the things women aren't supposed to do—I used to believe that this should indeed be so for the sake of equality. However, after giving the subject a great deal of thought, I have come to believe that men and women are so different in mind and body that it may not be such a bad idea after all to demand from women a greater degree of chastity. These matters are too intimate to write about in detail.

But though these considerations might lead one to favour more restraints for women, one has to take into account what happens all too often as a result. (I'm thinking, of course, of the dire consequences of 'lapsing' from socially accepted standards, of having to suffer the condemnation of society.) And so finally I come back to where I started: Equal standards for men and women.

If Elza were more like me, she wouldn't be concerned about her 'loneliness', and it wouldn't worry you either. As for myself, in spite of the fact that I have my meals in the company of 20 people—Cubans, North and South Americans, Dutchmen, Spaniards and Englishmen—and go on outings with Germans and Turks, yet I am a lonely man! I may be looked after by Dietl or Mandl in Vienna, and I may have friends in Budapest (Thomán, Mrs. Gruber), yet there are times when I suddenly become aware of the fact that I am absolutely alone! And I prophesy, I have a foreknowledge, that this spiritual loneliness is to be my destiny. I look about me in search of the ideal companion, and yet I am fully aware that it is a vain quest. Even if I should ever succeed in finding someone, I am sure that I would soon be disappointed.

Although the state of peaceful resignation and the perennial quest are irreconcilable, nevertheless I have quite grown used to the thought that this cannot be otherwise, that this is how things have to be. For solace, I would recommend to anyone the attempt to achieve a state of spiritual indifference in which it is possible to view the affairs of the world with complete indifference and with the utmost tranquillity. Of course, it is difficult, extremely difficult—in fact, the most difficult thing there is—to attain this state, but success in this is the greatest victory man can ever hope to win: over other people, over himself and over all things. Sometimes I feel that for a brief space of time I have risen to these heights. Then comes a mighty crash; then again more struggle, always striving to rise higher; and this recurs again and again. The time may come when I shall be able to stay on the heights.

[Original in Hungarian]

28. SHORT CURRICULUM VITAE (SOPRON)

[*December*, 1905]

My biographical data are as follows:

B. 1881. Nagyszentmiklós. At 7, lost my father; my mother (*née* Paula Voit) brought me up under very difficult conditions.

Aged 10, Nagyszőllős; Mr. Altdörfer discovered my talent. First my mother taught me, then László Erkel in Pozsony, then I went on to the Budapest Academy of Music (Thomán, Koessler). My *Kossuth* symphony was performed and warmly acclaimed in Budapest in 1904; and later, in Manchester. In March this year, in Budapest, I scored a success as a pianist; also 2 weeks ago, in Manchester. A week ago my orchestral suite, in all its Hungarian-ness, caused a sensation *in Vienna*.

I have never written anything like this about myself before, but I can't help that—it is just these 'successes' that are the most important points in a curriculum vitae.

With patriotic greetings,

Yours sincerely,
BÉLA BARTÓK

II

THE YEARS OF DEVELOPMENT

1906–1919

The year 1906 was an eventful one for Bartók. In the spring he went to Spain on his last tour as a young pianist; he was already engrossed in a plan to edit a new collection of folk-songs jointly with Kodály; but publication was to be dependent on a sufficient number of subscribers. In the summer he went on his first extensive quest for folk-songs. The last movement of his unfinished *Second Suite for Orchestra* (op. 4, 1905–7) was completed the following summer in the mountains of Csík, Transylvania. This was the first of Bartók's orchestral compositions in which we find pentatonic turns.

The opening of the 20th century was marked in Hungarian music by the researches of Bartók and Kodály in folk-music, whereby they brought to light from the deep layers of popular culture and oral peasant tradition, a dramatic, colourful and varied heritage which had been buried beneath romantic national illusions. Kodály confined his research mainly to the folk-music of the Hungarian nation, with the result that his art evokes centuries of Hungarian history. Bartók, however, made a passionate study not only of the old Hungarian tunes but also the music of the various nationalities living within the boundaries of the old pre-war Hungary. He began to collect Slovak folk-music in 1906, Rumanian folk-music in 1909. In 1913 he collected in North Africa, among the nomadic Arab tribes of Biskra; for Bartók's interest in folk-music went beyond the barriers of nationalism. Further study tours were prevented by the First World War and the years of political and economic collapse that followed.

In the piano pieces, about 150 in all, composed in the years from 1908 to 1911, among them *Bagatelles, For Children, Burlesques, Sketches, Rumanian Dances* and *Dirges*, we find a renewal of melody, rhythm and harmony inspired by folk-music. It was during this period of profound study of folk-music that Bartók realized the rich series of his most original musical creations culminating in the *Piano Suite* (op. 14, 1916) and *Studies* (op. 18, 1918). His orchestral compositions, *Second Suite for Orchestra* (op. 4, 1905–7), *Two Portraits* (op. 5, 1907–8), *Two Images* (op. 10, 1910) and *Four Pieces for Orchestra* (op. 12, 1912), not only absorbed the great achievements of music up to Debussy, but they also went beyond him and contributed, in almost complete independence of the sound pictures which Schoenberg and Stravinsky were composing at the same time, to that *ars nova* of the 20th century which is still one of the inspirations of contemporary music. Bartók's opera, *Bluebeard's Castle* (op. 11), composed in 1911, illustrates his search for a contemporary style which was nevertheless rooted in popular sources and through which he could combine music and language to make a fervently nationalistic declamation. This opera, together with the ballet *The Wooden Prince* (op. 13, 1914–6) written in the war years, and the pantomime *The Miraculous Mandarin* (op. 19, 1918–9) composed during the years of revolution, constitute an important trio of stage productions through which Bartók conveyed his message. This was expressed again, more tersely and perhaps therefore with greater clarity, in his string quartets, *First String Quartet* (op. 7, 1908) and *Second String Quartet* (op. 17, 1915–7).

This period of Bartók's creative life came to an end in 1919 when the altered conditions in his country and the poisoned atmosphere of international politics compelled him to give up his tours to collect folk-music. The only way in which he was able to continue his studies in this field was by systematic arrangement of the vast amount of material he had already contrived to accumulate. Driven though he was to this solitary type of work, Bartók nevertheless found in it his vocation and there began a new, though transient, period in his art.

The character of Bartók presented in the second part of this volume, covering the years 1906 to 1919, is revealed at the very beginning of the letters, lengthy if few in number, addressed to the violinist Stefi Geyer and in the series of picture postcards written to the pianist Etelka Freund. In these letters it is already the 'modern' Bartók who speaks to the reader. The letters written to János Bușiția, a Rumanian teacher in the grammar-school at Belényes, are of particular interest, especially those written during the war years, for they contain much characteristic evidence of Bartók's humanism.

[Original in Hungarian]

29. TO LAJOS POSZVÉK—SOPRON

Gersthoferstr. 57, Bécs[1] *XVIII/2*
January 30th, 1906

Dear Sir,
About 10 or 12 days ago I wrote to thank you for your kind letter written on behalf of the Association for Pub[lic] Ed[ucation]. I also made certain suggestions, and as it seems that my letter has gone astray, I hope you will allow me to repeat them.

I should be very grateful if you would make it possible for me to give a concert of my own at Sopron (possibly with one of the *better* local women singers). This suggestion is not only prompted by financial considerations—although, at the moment, this question is, alas, still fairly important to me—but also because I should very much like to have a cultural link with the provincial towns of Hungary. I wonder if you could approach some businessmen to undertake the organization (say, for one-third of the gross takings). One could take some preliminary soundings through the familiar system of advance booking: if there was an audience of about 200, the concert would be possible. Then we'll discover whether the people of Sopron really like me. In the letter which has been lost I mentioned another concert, too, but what I wrote is no longer applicable, so I will not go into details again.

The date would have to be in the second half of Feb. or the first half of March (except March 2, 3 or 4).

With best wishes to you and all your family,

Yours sincerely,
BÉLA BARTÓK

[PS.] (Feb. 2,3,4 my address is Budapest *Royal;* then again Vienna.)

[1] Hungarian for Vienna.

[Original in Hungarian]

30. TO PÉTER KÖNIG—SZEGED

Kórház Str. 3, Pozsony
March 14th, 1906

Dear Sir,
I hope you will excuse me for troubling you with this letter because, though we have not met, we do know each other by repute; and I can also plead that it is only on a subject of national importance that I have been induced to address you. It is in your capacity as Director of the Szeged Conservatory that I turn to you. I wonder if you would be so kind as to enlist the help of your teaching staff to secure, from among the pupils at the Conservatory, the greatest possible number of subscribers to these two books of songs.

We would be truly grateful for your assistance. I hope you will be able to help us, and I take this opportunity of thanking you in advance,

Yours very sincerely,
BÉLA BARTÓK

[Original in Hungarian]

31. TO HIS MOTHER, MRS. BÉLA BARTÓK—POZSONY

[16] *Madrid, March* 26th, 1906

Dear Mama,
I wonder when this letter will reach you in Pozsony.

Communications here are quite terrible! Yesterday was Sunday, and on Sundays there's neither collection nor delivery.

Well, it's been a fine to-do fixing up the concerts here—but it was the Spanish impresario who had most of the worry.

I arrived in Lisbon on Wednesday evening. On the following morning, at 10.45 a.m., I went round to the Bragança Hotel to call on the Vecseys, but they weren't there. There was a letter from Vecsey telling me to take the train to Madrid immediately because, he explained, the impresario had got the dates mixed up, and the first recital in Madrid was now scheduled for the 24th. Two gentlemen then arrived, one of whom urged me in French to hurry up, there was only one train to Madrid, and it left in 15 minutes. The other man spoke Portuguese and a very little Spanish. It was a terrible business trying to make ourselves understood. Finally, this Portuguese, a ferocious looking fellow with a gaudy, yellow cravat worn over a bright red silk waistcoat, put me in a cab, and off we drove to my hotel! I had only a few minutes in which to stuff my most necessary things into a suitcase, and off we went to the Estação Central! Luckily, we had 2 minutes in hand.

I must tell you about the railways here.

There is only *one* (!) train daily between Lisbon and Madrid! This so-called *express* 'tears along' at 28 km.p.h., which is less than half the speed of an express train in Hungary. Lisbon to Madrid—21 hours! The Portuguese railways are abominable. Corridors, lavatory, heating are things unknown. The lighting is no better than in our buses in Budapest. The 1st-class compartments are intended to accommodate 10 people.

I arrived in the morning, 24th; recital held at 5.30 p.m., in a theatre. Piano was good—Bechstein. Much enthusiasm; audience not very large yet. A bigger audience is expected today. Young Vecsey is not at all well; he can just get from his room to the concert hall and back again—but nowhere else. The tour almost had to be cancelled.

Yesterday we were received by the Queen (the King is away). Her affable manner and way of talking about music reminded me of Aunt Schneider. My facial muscles were subjected to a severe trial by my efforts not to burst out laughing! She talked a lot of rot, but her prize remark (about Hungary and the Hungarian language) was, 'Your King speaks Hungarian very well, doesn't he?' (Old Francis Joe!) I agreed, very well. She asked me to play some Hungarian music—czardas. I didn't mind: I let her have her joy. If only she had known what a Hapsburg-hating republican she was speaking to! Then she wouldn't have been so affable. As a matter of fact, our visit wasn't paid to her but to an infamous infanta. Tomorrow we've got to go to the Queen's place. If only she would pay us a fee. As it is, it's a sheer waste of time!

Lisbon is a beautiful little town. It's not a place for nervous people, though. The streets are incredibly noisy, full of street-sellers all shouting their wares at the top of their voices. There are such a lot of mules, all overburdened with merchandise. And what ghastly filth in some quarters of the town! And plenty of poor, ragged fellows loafing about through the fish-smelling litter! And yet the general impression is indescribably pleasing. The sun does not shine in other lands with such kindliness as here; it transforms even the narrowest and most crooked streets. The city has a unique atmosphere. Though it can boast no monuments of note, it is quite different in character from any other city I have visited. Demi-Afrique. And the people, with their brown skins and jet-black hair! Very interesting.

Madrid is nothing by comparison! It's like Budapest, minus the Danube Embankment and the House of Parliament. Madrid is not very different from any average-sized city. Here I pay 8 pesetas a day (100 francs = 117 pesetas). They have the damnable custom of 'vin compris'—half a carafe with each meal. As I am afraid of water I don't know, I drink the wine (which is not bad at all), and every blessed day I have the experience of feeling rather the worse for drink (it has the effect of making me very drowsy).

The way they provide meals when you're travelling by train is rather amusing. When it's time for lunch, the train halts at some station for half an hour. Then all the passengers sit round a table as long as a cattle trough, and they have to get through a complete lunch. You are expected to perform Herculean feats—you have to gobble up 8 to 10 courses within half an hour. Here, of course, they still ring three bells before the train goes on!

The day after tomorrow we will be leaving for Lisbon—to take part in 4 orchestral concerts. We shall stay there for a week or so. From there to Oporto, for 2 weeks, then perhaps to Barcelona.

My address will be: Hotel Suisso, 278, Rua da Princeza, Lisbon.

Love,
B.

[Original in Hungarian]

32. TO HIS MOTHER, MRS. BÉLA BARTÓK—POZSONY

[17] *Coimbra, April* 11th, 1906

D. M.

Here is the promised letter; now that our tour is successfully concluded, I can tell you more about it.

The tour as a whole, as well as the individual concerts, provided us with many interesting and amusing experiences. Such mechanical musical work is very disagreeable. This is almost so in little Vecsey's case because of all the practising he has to do. That is why he hardly sees anything of the world. The constant practising simply makes it impossible (giving concerts is a serious business, your technique has to be flawless). Audiences were always small; this means that the Spanish impresario must have lost money because Vecsey got 1,500 frs. per concert as did the Parisian impresario. So he had to pay 3,000 frs. worth in fees each evening. The Parisian impresario, however, was a scoundrel, for he kept 50% of the artists' fees for himself!

The most enthusiastic audience was at Oporto.

I am having trouble with my Portuguese. The way I negotiate with the people is very amusing. They understand Spanish, but I know very little of that either, and I hardly ever know what they are saying.

I've had to get used to all manner of strange customs; e.g. they usually leave the doors wide open in the hotel rooms. In some hotels they do not clean our shoes, and in others they provide no matches. In one place you can only dine at 5, at another only lunch at 9. In Madrid the concert began at 5.30, in Lisbon not till 8.30, and it lasted till midnight. In Madrid the piano was not level, in Lisbon it had not been tuned, in Oporto one leg of the piano-stool wobbled, dangerously. There are only 2 meals a day, but they give you enormous quantities (especially for dinner). I eat everything they serve, and there are too many courses to count. They end up with pastry, cheese, coffee, nuts, apples, oranges, boiled eggs, bananas; all of this is the *Coda*. In Oporto they cooked the spinach and so on—in oil! Can you imagine it! And a heap of unknown and unidentifiable dishes were put in front of me. I ate the lot, though, for all I know, it could have been worm-omelette or rat-paste.

I would like to say something nice about Vecsey. He is terribly nervy and tired from all the concerts, and this certainly accounts for his behaviour. His views about things are so different from mine that, at first at any rate, I was apt to judge him harshly, both for what he said and what he did. But probably he only wants to do what he thinks best for his son—in his own way. Which is precisely the opposite of my way.

At present, I am completely at a loose end, drifting about aimlessly from place to place. My address is still: Lisbon, Hotel Suisso, Rua da Princeza; they will forward my letters. But don't send anything important. Oh yes! In about two weeks you could send a subscription list to Mrs. (Lajos) Vecsey (Zsófia telep, Rákos-Keresztúr).

Just now I am in Coimbra for the day (the only university is here). It is a small town (13,000 inhabitants) with some interesting old buildings. Beautiful situation. Oporto is quite different to Lisbon. Have you never seen the Dom Luiz iron bridge?

Today I was for the first time greeted by Portuguese peasants.

It was dusk, and I was walking in the meadows at Coimbra. They were coming home from work and may have taken me for a priest; they said: *Bom noite,* and I answered the same. So I have spoken Portuguese!

L.
B.

I can understand the Portuguese language quite well. I learned from the Oporto newspapers that Vesuvius is rumbling a good deal, and that the Algeciras Conference is coming to an end. About us there is complete silence!

[Original in Hungarian]

33. TO HIS MOTHER, MRS. BÉLA BARTÓK—POZSONY

[18]

[Picture postcard: Venezia—Panorama]

Venice, May 26th, 1906

You will be somewhat astonished to find me writing from here instead of from ½ Africa. I have run away from the royal wedding! It was a good thing that I did: at least I could travel in comfort—3rd class! And with the result that I shall still have about 10 forints left when I arrive in Budapest. Europe began again at Barcelona—the French 3rd [class] was better than the Spanish 1st! I broke my journey to visit the Milan World Exhibition, and now I am admiring Venice.

The most beautiful thing I have seen on my trip to Spain—is Venice. It's divine!

L.
B.

[Original in Hungarian]

34. TO HIS MOTHER, MRS. BÉLA BARTÓK AND TO HIS AUNT IRMA—VÉSZTŐ

[19]

Keresztúr nyaraló[1]
July 15th, 1906

Honoured Mama!

I shall begin with the Gyula Fair. On the first day, that never-to-be-forgotten Friday, I had no success in anything, except as a dust-swallower. For there certainly was a plentiful supply of that. Also of

[1] Villa at (Rákos)keresztúr

heat. But of Galgóczy there was never a sign. The telephone lines to Benedek went out of order just as I tried to put a call through. Bagpiper-Vágássy was not at the fair. The principal hotel in the town was full, so, after a brief search, I found the second best (and last). They had *one* vacant room left and were charging twice the usual price because of the fair. Then I found some suspicious-looking females prowling about the corridors: I had come to a hotel of ill repute where, with Semitic practicality, they combined *two* lucrative sources of income. On Saturday I arrived safely at Benedek. That rascally Vágássy, on whose account I had swallowed the clouds of dust at Gyula Fair, didn't come the next day either, confound him! On Sunday Géza took me over to Bihar County, to Fekete-Ér puszta near Sarkad, where some material turned up for us at last. There I met Franck, who immediately invited me to spend a day at Doboz. On Monday I took my machine and went to see some swineherds and shepherds and, in the afternoon, phonographed the domestic servant at Benedek. On Tuesday morning, by way of a parting gift, Galgóczy produced yet another farm worker. Then I left for Doboz.

That evening the steward of Fekete-Ér sent over an old fellow who sang. Franck also had invited a number of singers to come in for supper, so in the evening I was able to make some recordings and jot down [notations]. In that district alone I have noted down a total of 83 songs and made 47 recordings. Franck was very nice and invited me to come down to him for a week or so sometime in October or December, when we should be able to visit the stewards of various neighbouring estates and explore the whole district.

On the following day, just before I was ready to leave, I looked in on the Vidovszkys, who likewise invited me to stay with them and promised their help. So it was quite a fruitful expedition.

And now in return for this nice, long account of what's been going on, as well as what hasn't, I'm expecting a long and exhaustive letter from you very soon, and I'd be glad if you could also let me know the name of that folk-song collector on the staff of *Ujság*.

L.
B.

Dear Aunt Irma,

We are having some memorable days down here in Keresztúr, and I would feel as if I were neglecting some sacred duty if I did not tell you all about it.

Her Ladyship, Countess Ella auf-ab-von und zu Hoyos, daughter of a V.C.P.C.[1], arrived here *il y a 4 jours*. The barbarous Magyar tongue has now been replaced by sonorous language bursting with Teuton energy, delighting all the educated Hungarians.

All the V. family have the most wonderful way of pronouncing German, and the way they put the words together and make up expressions is very funny. Papa Vecsey tells us that *Wir haben mit der Automobil eine Mensch beinahe abgefahren*—later on repeats the story and, finding the expression somewhat odd, corrects it to *durchgefahren*, till, at last, Mother Vecsey comes to his rescue with *überfahren*. The Countess is as chilly as Franz Josef Land at Christmas-time—the very sight and sound of her makes one's blood run cold. During meals English etiquette reigns supreme. But as I have a taste for dissonance, I intend to invade this scene of awful orderliness wearing my summer shirt, without collar or cuffs, and my oldest shoes—just to shock them! Papa Vecsey's idea of entertaining the noble-blooded Austrian guest is to involve her in heated argument: 5 times so far has he proved that, as a matter of fact, Austria does not exist! Mrs. Vecsey, of course, is in despair.

At lunch woe to any man who makes more noise when he's eating than the humming of a bee! It is just not done in England.

Since, in spite of being busy with my work, I have given you such a detailed and exhaustive account of life at Keresztúr, I hope you will reward me with an equally circumstantial account of family events and party politics at Vésztő. Please tell me what everyone is doing—grandmother, mother, the old woman, the little boy, the landlord, Juci, etc., etc. Letters may be written in any of the following languages: Hungarian, French, English, Spanish, Portuguese, Slovak and Latin.

Vous pouvez choisir ce que vous voulez!

L.
B.

Dear Young Béla,
How are you, you young rascal? When next you are in need, remember to ask one of those women who are always fussing over you to take you to the Sacred Hall of Convenience. You are now a big boy, after all! What! You're not still using those night lights of yours. How many mosquitos have bitten you since then, eh? How many kilograms of your esteemed excrement? I hope that imports have exceeded exports, and that the only kind of success—accumulation of matter—has been achieved. I expect you without fail to

[1] Veritable Confidential Privy Councillor.

reply in your own hand to these few well-turned lines written in your honour. In that hope, here's a hearty rap on the head from your

UNCLE.

[Original in Hungarian]

35. TO HIS AUNT IRMA VOIT AND TO HIS MOTHER, MRS. BÉLA BARTÓK—POZSONY

[20]
[Picture postcard]

Keresztúr, September 10th [1906]

Every Good Wish from a holiday-maker at Keresztúr.
For news, see overleaf

L.
B.

[Overleaf of the postcard]

Dear Mama, I am glad to hear that things have taken a turn for the better. That must mean that I haven't offended G. For 3 days I have been conferring with Kodály about the proposed book of songs; we still have to plan the title-page—which is far from being a trifling matter. We are writing a preface in which we have some harsh things to say about Hungarian audiences. As it won't be finished until mid-October at the earliest, we shall still have time to write addresses. I will come to Pozsony for 2 days, early in Oct., and spend a day in Vienna (with you, perhaps?).

A d[amnable] sore throat has kept me indoors for two days.

By the way, did you receive this marvellous bird (I mean, the picture of it)?

I have no news for you just now; not that it is in any case possible to describe my experiences in Szöged[1] and Csongrád. In Szöged I saw König. (I may have already written about that.) I shall be staying here till about the 20th.

L.
B.

[Original in Hungarian]

36. TO LAJOS DIETL—VIENNA

[3] *Pozsony, November* 3rd, 1906

My dear Friend,
You must think I've run away to Sumatra with the subscription money! But better late than never—the songs will appear in a couple of weeks.

I have to spend a day in Vienna sometime in the middle of Dec., so I can leave the rest of my news till then.

It's on account of the Tulip League that I'm in Pozsony just now. I have to play for the benefit of the Pozsony writers, and on Sunday (tomorrow) there will be a concert attended by Apponyi and his wife. These recitals come very inopportunely. I have hardly practised for the last six months; so for 2 weeks now, I have had to set to and force my fingers to play unimportant popular items. I had the piano taken to the famous Gerlice plain in Gömör County. The practising has not been at all to my taste; it's a nuisance, and I'd far rather have spent my time collecting as many more songs as possible. After spending every evening for 3 weeks in Slovakian villages, I have not been able to get down more than 150 songs; I phonographed 80.

Could you come to us for a few days at Christmas? I invite you to a song-collection excursion in the neighbouring villages. It's very interesting, especially the phonographing. Your knowledge of Russian (!) might be useful to us among the Slovakians.

I had your card from Paris. Since I have written a letter, I might have expected a letter in return.

In a few days I shall be sending a scolding to those negligent people who have so far failed to send in their subscription lists. Kindly accept your share of this reprimand together with this letter. I have to let people know that if these lists are not sent in very soon, we shall suffer a considerable loss through not fulfilling our

[1] Szöged = Szeged in local dialect.

agreement with the publisher. Permanent address: Pozsony, etc. From here I am going on to Békés County for more collecting.

Greetings from a zealous collector,

BÉLA

[Original in Hungarian]

37. TO HIS MOTHER, MRS. BÉLA BARTÓK—RÁKOSPALOTA

[21]

[Picture postcard: Greetings from Bánffy-Hunyad Ev. Church]

[*Bánffyhunyad, July* 5th, 1907]

I've found something for you, so you will be receiving a parcel—C.O.D. 32 Kr.—posted from here by the people at Körösfő. An advance of 20 Kr. on writing-desk must be sent to György Gyugyi Péntek at the end of this month. What joy! I've seen the same roses as those on my cabinets painted on the doorposts all the way from Hunyad to Körösfő.

In Körösfő, in the late afternoon there are always 2 or 3 women sitting, doing their embroidery in every doorway. What hard-working and unusual people they are! *Sahun sincs a turma, juhaim hol vadnak?* What is it?[1] I have been introduced to Gyugyi Péntek's people, and I'm now quite at home with them (his house consists of a kitchen and a very small workshop with a leaking roof).

It rains heavily every day, the heat is bearable, and the local folk costume is dazzling; in the streets of Bánffy-Hunyad the filth and litter is quite Moroccan without any of the amenities imported there for the sake of the Europeans.

B.

[Original in Hungarian]

38. TO ETELKA FREUND—ANNENHEIM AM OSSIACHER SEE

[1]

[Picture postcard: Greetings from Csík-Karczfalva]

[*July* 30th, 1907]

You ask me how I feel. Well, every now and again, I feel pretty bad.

I really never expected to have to endure quite so much trouble and torment. The result of our efforts is more or less satisfactory,

[1] The riddle for his mother in this excerpt from a folk-song is a Transylvanian dialect incomprehensible to her.

though it could have been better. The score is coming on—frequently in the most curious circumstances and the strangest places: in the parlours of pubs, in bootmakers' workshops, sometimes in the open air. When we first started out on this trip, there was not even the beauty of a landscape to compensate me; now the wide valley is closing in as we reach higher altitudes, and around Balánbánya I could imagine myself at Salzburg. My address, where letters will reach me for the next 12 days, is Gyergyószentmiklós, *Poste restante*.

Many greetings to you all from

B.

[Original in Hungarian]

39. TO STEFI GEYER

[1] *August* 16th, 1907

A dialogue in Gyergyó-Kilényfalva.

The traveller: (entering) God bless you!
The peasant woman: Jesus keep you!
T: Is your husband at home?
W: He's not at home; he's taken the waggon to bring hay from the field.
T: And how are you faring, I wonder?
W: Oh, we get along somehow, though we have our troubles, too: We have work, and plenty of it.
T: Well, well, you can cope with it somehow.
W: And what does the gentleman want? (To her little girl) Bring a chair for the gentleman!—Here's a chair, sit ye down. (To her daughter) Get the pigs in!
T: Now look here. I've come to ask you for something which, I think, you've never been asked for before.
W: ?
T: I've heard from your neighbour that you know all kinds of ancient folk-songs which you learnt from the old folks when you were a girl.
W: Me?! old songs?! You shouldn't poke fun at me, Sir. Old songs! Ha, ha!
T: Believe me, I'm not poking fun at you! I mean what I say! That's why I've made this long, long journey all the way from Budapest, specially to look for these very old songs which no one remembers except here!

W: And what are you going to do with those songs? Do you want to print them?

T: No indeed! What we want is to preserve the songs by writing them down. For if we don't write them down, then in years to come no one will know the songs that are being sung here now. You see, even now, the young people sing quite different songs; they don't care for the old ones and don't even learn them; and yet they are much prettier than the new ones, aren't they?! In 50 years no one will have heard of them if we don't write them down now.

W: Really? (Pause) Hmmm. Hahaha. No, I just can't believe it.

T: (Desperate) But look here, mother, at this little book. Do you see, I have written them all down. (He whistles a song) That was sung by the wife of Andrew Gegő (he whistles another), and Bálint Kosza's wife sang that one. Now! you know them, too, don't you?

W: Eh! my singing-days are past. What would an old woman be doing to sing such secular songs! I only know sacred songs now.

T: Come, you're not as old as all that. And the others, Stephen Csata's wife and Ignatius Hunyadi's wife, both told me that you know a great many.

W: Eh! my voice is not what it was . . .

T: (Chimes in) You don't need a strong voice; if you hum it faintly, that will be all right.

W: Why don't you ask the young men and girls, they know plenty of songs.

T: No! they only know new songs; and I don't need those because I've already got them all. In these parts there are such sad songs like this (whistling):

You know it? What are the words?

W: Long ago I heard that song, but I did not learn the words.

T: Don't you know any others like it?

W: I could think of one or two; but they don't come into one's mind very readily. When I want them, I can't remember a single one. Aye! There was a time when I knew a great many. But hard work is the devil, it takes the joy out of singing. When I was a girl . . .

T: Yes, yes. Now just think back a little, perhaps you will remember some old song.

W: (To her son) Come here! Take that to István Ábrán's wife; she is helping Felix György's wife. (She thinks for a long time) . . . One has just come into my mind.

T: (Brightening) Let's hear it, let's hear it!

W: But what shall I do? Just say the words?

T: No! Sing the tune, as it used to be sung.

W: (Breaks into a song) (Sings to the end)

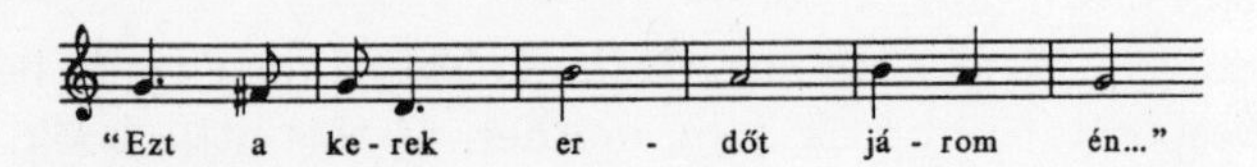
"Ezt a ke-rek er - dőt já - rom én..."

['I go around this wood . . . ']

Aye! that is a very old song.

T: I know, I know, it's very nice. But don't you know anything older? Just think a little.

W: Older than that? (She thinks . . . then suddenly to her daughters) For the love of God! Why did you let out the geese? This morning, when I closed the door, I said not to let them out only at midday! (She thinks a painful pause . . .) Now another has come into my mind.

T: ?

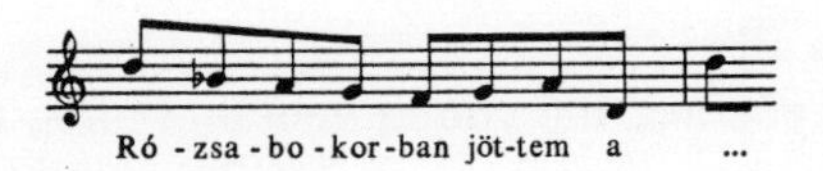
Ró - zsa - bo - kor - ban jöt-tem a ...

W: ['I was born in a rose bush . . . ']

T: (Interrupts) That's no good . . . It is not even old, and it's sung by the gentry.

W: No, no! We often used to sing it in the village. (To her children) Now you think, too, and maybe you'll remember something.

T: We don't want those that the children know. They are new songs. Only the very, very old ones!

W: Where did you say you came from, sir?

T: I've already told you, from Pest.

W: God help ye! Are you married?

T: No, I'm not.

W: Then you're only a youth.

T: Just so! But think a bit more. Don't you know 'The thief of the large mountain', 'Kata Kádár's song' or 'Where are you going to, you 3 orphans?'

W: (With devastating determination) No!!
T: Never heard them?
W: (In the same tone) No!! But I'll sing the gentleman another.
T: Let's hear it.
W: The song of Mary Magdalen . . .
T: I don't think that will do. It's a sacred song! (Privately cursing all the sacred songs in the world.)
W: Have you got this one:

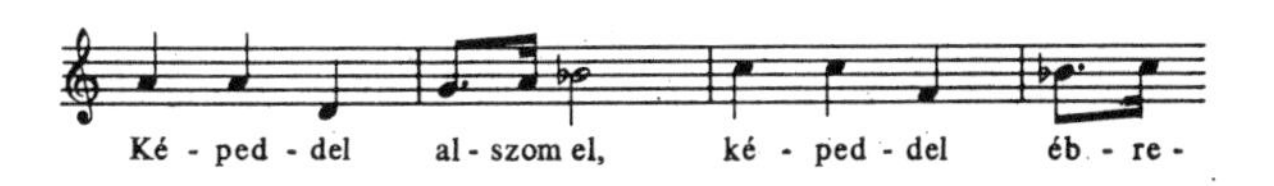

['I sleep and wake with your image . . . ']
T: (Bluntly) Yes, I have! (Clenching his teeth but preserving his friendliest tones) Now try some real, village song that no one in Hungary knows.
W: Well, is this one good? It's very old.

['This roll is round . . .']
T: They know that one, too, in Hungary. I've already got it.
W: But this one, the gentleman won't have put this one down yet . . . .

['I go around . . .']
T: But you began with that! I don't want it. (Giving up at last, he puts his book and pen back into his pocket.)
W: I know a lot of holy songs. The song of Mary Magdalen . . . .
T: (Defiantly silent.)
W: The gentleman has never heard anything more beautiful.
T: Do you know anyone who remembers the very, very old songs? Is your mother at home?
W: She's out working . . . If the gentleman were to come to our pig-killing feasts *(radina)* or listen when we are all working together *(kaláka)*, then he would hear plenty of songs. Oh, how we sing then!

T: Splendid! But it's now that I need a song. Is there anyone who would know such a singer?
W: Gyurka Sándor's wife lives round the corner of the street; she knows *so many*, she couldn't recite them all if you stayed all day.
T: Will she be at home now?
W: Oh, yes, she will be working at her loom. And her grandmother helps with the weaving, and she knows lots of old songs.
T: Then I will go to her.
W: Yes, the gentleman should go there. She knows a great deal, especially when she has had a drink or two.
T: How do I find her? This way?
W: No, not that way, keep on down the road. It's quicker.
T: Thank you, thank you. God bless you!
W: May God keep you!
T: (Departs downcast.)

And so *da capo al fine* from morning to night, Monday to Sunday (day after day)! I can't bear it any longer. Impossible!

Endurance, perseverance, patience . . . to hell with you all . . . I'm going home.

I can't do with this farce for more than 6 weeks at a stretch. Even in my dreams I hear: 'Jesus keep you . . . Is she at home? . . . She's gone mowing . . . holy songs . . . Round is the forest . . . it doesn't fit in my pocket.'

Terrible! Good-bye to you, high plateau of Gyergyó, I shall not see you again till Easter.

I shan't wear high boots nor see preserves till Christmas.

Your Gyergyószentmiklós card reached me at Tekerőpatak. On the way back I will look at the Szentdomokos post-office in case your letter has arrived.

Many greetings—still from Gyergyó.

BÉLA BARTÓK

[Original in Hungarian]

40. TO ETELKA FREUND—ANNENHEIM AM OSSIACHER SEE

[2]

[Picture postcard: Alps of Gyergyószentmiklós. Lake Gyilkos with Little-Czohárd]

[*August* 17th, 1907]

I have made a rather strange discovery while collecting folk-songs. I have found examples of Székely tunes which I had believed were now lost. The 4th movement of the Serenade is waiting to be orchestrated on this 800-metre-high plateau! Much work, much work! and many greetings.

B.

[Original in Hungarian]

41. TO STEFI GEYER—BUDAPEST

[2] *Vésztő, September* 6th, 1907

Dear Miss Stefi,
I caught a cold on Monday, but I've come here all the same. I was rash enough to make the journey on a wild, wet day—and all because, ever since last Sunday, I have been wondering whether your decision to write to me augured good news or bad. Perhaps you were only going to tell me a few jokes? Or had you something more serious to put on paper? Which part of my letter would you have thought about and commented on? These conjectures gave me such a headache, I had to do something about it as soon as possible—and there was almost a calamity. Your letter had arrived one day ahead of me, and as I had not told them I was coming, they had already sent it back to the post-office, re-addressed to Rákospalota.

'For life is so beautiful! There's so much beauty in nature—the arts—science . . . ' That is the most beautiful thing you have written to me so far. And why? Because it reflects my own view of life. It is one of man's weaknesses that we only recognize the correctness of judgments when they correspond with our own—a pardonable shortcoming.

I am infinitely grateful to you for your letter just because you put in those 4 or 5 lines which have given me the most intense delight. There may be some interest—even some charm—in exploring a conception of things which is quite alien to one's own. But to come upon a fellow human being—more, a friend—who shares, albeit in a different form, the ideas on which one's whole conception of the world is founded: that is one of the purest joys. It is evident from what you write that you have indeed failed to understand—or rather, you have misunderstood—my words about the lack of a purpose of existence. However, we must talk about that another time.

Suddenly, after those 4 or 5 delightful lines, you broach a weighty question such as we have never discussed as yet. But it had already occurred to me that there might come a day when we felt obliged to discuss this subject; and I am truly glad that this time, in contrast to what has always happened so far, the initiative has not had to come from me. I was absolutely convinced—although we have never talked about it—that you were 'godfearing'. It wasn't difficult for me to put two and two together. This makes it all the more difficult for me to touch on this subject. I am almost afraid to begin.

After giving these matters a great deal of thought, I have—almost in spite of myself—arrived at certain conclusions which may be summed up in the following—*corrected*—biblical assertions.

With amazing consistency, the Bible preaches the contrary of the truth learned in our existence on earth. For it isn't God who created man in his own image, after his likeness: *It is man who created God after his own likeness.* It is not the body that's mortal and the soul that's immortal, but the other way round: *The soul is transitory and the body (that is, matter) is everlasting!* Why are these false doctrines thrust upon so many millions of people—to ensure that they are accepted by the vast majority of people throughout their lives and can only be cast aside by a minority after a conflict that should be unnecessary. What purpose can this serve? If only they wouldn't teach anything! It is easier to till virgin soil than a land overgrown with weeds.

In accordance with this general scheme of things, I, too, have passed through a time of conflict. Until the age of 14, like everyone brought up to respect 'authority', I was a devoted Catholic. When, for political reasons, the institution of civil marriage was introduced in an attempt to curtail the authority of the Church, I was saddened, for I took such things deeply to heart. Between the ages of 15 and 16, in the divinity classes at school, we received exhaustive instruction in the history, ethics, rites and dogmas of the Church; as the divinity master was exceptionally zealous, we were taught even more, much more, than the prescribed syllabus. You cannot imagine in what minute detail each item was discussed. In the ethics classes, for instance, we had to discover how to answer questions like this: If a man's wife and parents all fall in the river, which of them does the Church require him to rescue first? We also learned the 'important' fact that if you had special permission from the bishop to eat meat on Fridays, then you must never eat fish on that day. We were given some examples of the mercy shown by the Church: e.g. that there is a papal decree forbidding believers, under pain of excommunication, to take heretics into their homes or to give them food. (I, for one, am now such a heretic.) The brilliant result of our divinity master's zeal was that since then I have ceased being a Catholic in principle. I left the issue of 'God' and the 'immortal soul' in abeyance—I could go neither forward nor back; I had to wait. At the age of 18, freed from the burden of school work, I found time for reading more serious literature. A few years later I was greatly influenced by my studies in astronomy, the works of a Danish writer, an acquaintance, and, above all, by my own meditations. By the time I had completed my 22nd year, I was a new man—an atheist. The two observations which I have stated above I once jotted down on the cover of one of my books—rather proudly, thinking it was the original expression of my own unique thought. (A few months ago, I came across the identical ideas in the works of an author who lived many years ago. There's hardly anything new under the sun!)

Greedily I devoured the literature of atheism. Today it seems a long time since I experienced that Renaissance, and whenever 'ungodly' writings come my way, I throw them out with contempt. It seems to me there is nothing to argue about. Why, it's all common knowledge, I think, and has been for centuries! There's nothing to make a fuss about! As if I had been an atheist for centuries, instead of for the last 4 years!

In several letters you have mentioned your lack of [religious] experience. Now you plead that you are no philosopher. But what is religion if not pure philosophy? Philosophy is the term used to describe any reasoned attempt to answer those questions to which the evidence of our senses cannot alone provide an answer. It is only natural that in this attempt we should make false assumptions, come to erroneous conclusions, and propound all manner of beliefs, sometimes interesting, sometimes merely fantastic.

Therefore, since you have 'no experience to speak of', whereas I have some, albeit slight, and since you are 'no philosopher' as yet, whereas I have already dabbled in that subject, I hope you will allow me to develop the two axioms I have already stated.

You have only to consider the history of mythologies to realize the truth of the first axiom. The Greeks would have us believe in gods who act and suffer in exactly the same way as mortals. This is why we find in their mythology an interest and a quality of imagination incomparably greater than anything to be discovered in that of the Jews. The Jehovah of the Old Testament is an obscure and mysterious Being who yet has the will to revenge himself, to reward men or punish them—all qualities which are intrinsically human and totally opposed to any conception of eternal values. When we come to the Holy Trinity of Christian mythology, we find a conception of something still more mysterious, something which even enslaves thought, itself 'a mystery'—we are told—'that mere wretched humans are unable to comprehend! Nor should they try to, for any attempt to prove such subjects is a mortal sin.' There's progress for you! This explains why the spiritual darkness of the Middle Ages persisted for so many centuries, and why we have had the utmost difficulty in emerging from it. Yet that mystical mumbo-jumbo is not even of Jesus's making, for, as a matter of fact, He was only a moralist and as such is responsible for one of the greatest works even though His teaching in a number of points is liable to give you something of a jolt.

Finally, our most recent conception of a deity is that of a bodiless, everlasting and omnipresent Spirit who has decreed all that has happened in the past, and who similarly ordains the future. What a muddled notion! How can we logically ascribe to an everlastingly omnipotent Being the finite functioning of a will?

The only evidence we can muster to prove this hypothesis is the existence of the universe. We say: 'Here is an ordered universe. It is impossible that it should have come into being by itself because nothing comes into being by itself, let alone a marvellously harmonious scheme of things like this.' Conclusion: It must have been created by such and such a Being—and then we proceed to define that Being, declaring that it has neither arms nor legs, that though it has no brain, it is nevertheless capable of thinking and exercising a will, etc. This is another example of our confused thinking. For if we agree that the processes of thought and the exercise of the will are functions of the brain (as indeed they are), then we must also admit that any Being without a brain is incapable of thought or the exercise of will. And we cannot conceive a Being capable of thought and willed action without being possessed of a brain. Such a supposition could never be proved. But if we consider it merely as a hypothesis, then we ought at least to employ a different terminology so as to avoid possible misunderstanding.

However, it is certainly foolish to put forward any audacious hypotheses about the origin of the universe, which are based on the mere fact of its existence. If I don't know how some object or other got into a place which I had carefully locked, I see no point in making up stories about how it may have come to be there. 'As it is utterly impossible to find out how this object came to be here, as it's an insoluble puzzle, therefore we can be certain beyond all doubt that it has been brought here by so and so.' Such reasoning would be absurd. And yet that's how people explain the universe. Why don't we simply say: *I can't explain the origin of its existence* and leave it at that?

And is it within the power of human beings, now or at any future time, to know the entire universe? No one will ever do that. For the universe is infinite, in time as well as in space. And mortal beings will never be able to conquer infinity. We have penetrated the firmament to a distance of 130 light-years and can determine the chemical composition and motion of fixed stars at that distance from the earth. But what is that distance compared with infinity? How dare we even attempt to determine the beginning of something so utterly unknown as the universe? At this point we must stop speculating, fold our hands and admit we are utterly helpless. Our thirst for knowledge will ensure that we come to know a little of it both in space and time; but such knowledge is only a fragment of the whole. And we cannot discuss—even in hypotheses—how something came into existence when we do not even know what that something is.

But man is both proud and stubborn. The idea of infinity he confronts with arrogance and even claims a share of it for himself. 'Man's soul is immortal,' he says. Let us not concern ourselves to define what we are to understand by the word 'soul'. Let us confine ourselves to an examination of what we mean when we say that this something we call soul is immortal. It means, doesn't it, that the soul has an infinite existence in time—but only in one direction! In time yet to come. Everybody must admit that when we look backwards in time, the soul is only too finite—it begins at birth! Now can you imagine something that is finite in one direction but infinite in the other?! It would be absurd! Anything that has a beginning must also have an end; that, I think, is a self-evident truth, one which cannot—and need not—be proved. It's axiomatic. And it is one of the principal proofs of the soul's mortality.

Let us, however, assume that the soul is immortal. What strange and crucial questions then arise—questions that nevertheless cannot be answered. When and where does the soul come into existence? When does a child acquire this parcel of immortality that we call the soul? Before birth, when still in the womb? And if this is the case, at what moment of its embryonic life? If at birth, at which precise moment? Or is it sometime after birth, and if so, at what age?

It would then be important to know, after all, whether an infant that died when 2 weeks old was possessed of a soul; whether a child that dies at birth has a soul; whether a pregnant woman bears within her one soul (her own) or two.

If we look upon the soul as some kind of essence of immortality, then we can have no physical test of its existence, and we can provide no answers to these questions.

And where does the soul begin? Why should an infant of two weeks have a 'soul' rather than an animal with a well-developed brain? The latter displays much greater intellectual capacity than such a wretched little human worm. Or is an absolutely incurable imbecile from birth granted a soul but not an intelligent animal? To this question many women would answer that they do in fact believe that even animals have souls. But how many of them? The snake, the stag-beetle, the snail, the earth-worm—do they all have souls?! Perhaps also the amoebae, the infusoria, the germs and microbes? And here we have already crossed the boundary into the vegetable kingdom: thus even the plants have souls. Maybe also the stones!! It's no use merely guessing—you have to draw a line somewhere if there is such a thing as an immortal soul. We must not be left in any doubt, must we, as to whether this or that soul, or 'animal spirit', is mortal or not.

What is the soul? It is the functioning of the brain and the nervous system. It develops by slow stages, from a pre-natal beginning (in conjunction with the development of the organs in question) and quite ceases to be at the moment of death. It is finite—mortal. The body, as matter, is 'immortal' indeed, for matter in this world is never lost; it only changes its form.

Human frailty has been the primary cause of our belief in gods.

In the beginning, man believed that everything in his environment which he could not understand and control must be an animate being capable of thought, able to exercise a will, and whose favour he must win. Thus he came to set up idols. He had little tin gods without number. When he began to find this rather cumbersome, and as his thinking became more advanced, he cut down the number of his gods. In this way pantheism developed into polytheism, which gave way to monotheism and finally—to atheism. Each was devoured by its successor. This accounts for the ease with which Christianity, with its splendid code of ethics, was able to supplant Graeco–Roman polytheism which in any case had already become corrupt. This easy victory would, I am sure, have scarcely been possible in the later stages of the development of Christianity when it became distorted into Catholicism.

It is perfectly understandable that the weaker man derives *inexpressible comfort* from being able to pray to a Powerful Being; he hopes that, in exchange, the Mighty One will spare him a few crumbs or scraps of the pig swill. But at the same time it is his inexpressible weakness.

And the reward in the hereafter, the damnation of the wicked, etc., all these are but human notions conceived to suit earthly circumstances; and much comfort they are to anyone in sore distress! That may be the reason why so many highly intelligent ecclesiastical personages simulate religious conviction: to help those weaker than themselves, who would fall into despair if they were robbed of their last remaining support—faith. Others, of course, pay lip service for the financial rewards – – –

Oh dear me, dear me. It's only a short time since I was still zealously bent on winning everyone over to atheism because freedom of thought alone can make one happy! And now I'm saying—let everyone do as he likes, it's no business of mine. But there's trouble in store for any pious person wanting to pick a quarrel with me and compel me by law to do this or that – – –

But this is not at all how I intended writing on this subject—I meant to employ a mild, melancholy key, avoiding all dissonance; and yet I've got carried away in the end. Mine is the domain of dissonances!

Though you wanted me to write on this subject, I must beg you to harbour no resentment against me for the way in which I've written; I would like you to feel towards me as you have always done in the past. And please, please, *do not feel sorry* for me on account of my views. That would indeed cause me distress. I hope you will comment on my lengthy discourse? I wonder how—in writing or in person? Is 10 to 12 kilometres a sufficient distance to justify our writing to each other? But if you ever do write to me, I wish you would not choose one of those moments when you are about to visit one of your cousins, and when 2/3 of your letter stays bottled up in your pen.

'I could fill a few more sheets with my scribbling, and I'd like to, but I can't. This evening I am going across to Buda.' What monumental, mammoth letters you write! In your handwriting, those 2 sentences fill just 2 lines!!

More about the purpose of life – – –

What I was referring to was an absolute, not a relative, purpose of life.

That is to say, on a small scale, everybody and every living thing—even mosquitoes and fleas—has an object in life. For instance, as far as I am concerned, it is, on however small a scale, to give a few people some minor pleasures; on a bigger scale, to work for the good of that set of corrupt demi-gentlemen we call the Hungarian intelligentsia by collecting folk-songs, etc., etc. In return, I am provided with a living, and my name will be included in the next edition of the encyclopaedia (so that I may be more get-at-able for all the would-be-academician, patronage-seeking ivory-ticklers that infest this country). The object in life and the reward are equally splendid.

But that is not what I am talking about. Life on this globe had a beginning at some time; consequently, it is bound to come to an en d—at some time. Already, our astronomers are making calculations tofind out when that millennium—rather calamitous for us to be sure—is likely to come. Blithely they work out their theories of how we shall all be finally destroyed. However, the way in which it happens is irrelevant; what counts is the certainty that it will happen. But before the day of total annihilation, the views, tastes and disposition of the social establishment are bound to be radically transformed. Those things we appreciate highly at the present time will be scorned at a later date, and vice versa.

In a thousand years, in 10 thousand years, I am sure that my whole work will have been lost without a trace; and maybe the entire Hungarian people and their language will have sunk into oblivion for ever. Or if not by then—well then, some time later. The same fate awaits the work of everyone of us. It would not be a pleasant thing to work with only this depressing thought in mind. To be able to work, one must have a zest for life, i.e. a keen interest in the living universe. One has to be filled with enthusiasm for the Trinity about which you write so eloquently in your letter; if I ever crossed myself, it would signify 'In the name of Nature, Art and Science . . . '

Isn't that enough?! Must you have the promised 'hereafter' as well? That's something I can't understand.

It's very strange, this making friends by letter. I wonder how we'll get on??!

You are 'no philosopher' as yet? Never mind! The important thing is that you should want to become one.

You are still green? Never mind! The important thing is that you should want to mature.

(You aren't as green as all that!)

Will you allow me to supply you with reading matter from time to time? (Something not too weighty as a start, just to bring you onto the right track; no middle-of-the-road stuff.) You needn't be afraid that reading will blight your youth; even if it were to shorten it, you would be amply compensated by all the pleasure you would get from it. (Not, of course, that reading ever does shorten youth!)

I could come round and see you about half-past twelve, Monday. I hope to get away from the Academy by then. If I can't come, I will send a wire about 10 a.m. It is quite certain that I shan't get a moment's peace all day because of the fuss connected with the entrance examinations on the following days. Now there you see one of my objects in life—to devote 2 or 3 days to the task of admitting new students.

It is one o'clock in the morning. At 6 a.m. I shall be on my way back. It seems I must have come to Vésztő for no other purpose than to intercept your letter and answer it from here.

Think about the 'Infinite'; and thinking, shudder and bow your head.

Greetings from
AN UNBELIEVER
(who is more honest than a great many believers.)

[Original in Hungarian]

42. TO STEFI GEYER—BUDAPEST

[3] *Wednesday*
[Middle of *September*]

Dear Miss Stefi,

By the time I had finished reading your letter, I was almost in tears—and that, as you can imagine, does not usually happen to me every day. Here is a case of human frailty! I anticipated that you might react like this, yet when you actually did so, I was upset. Why couldn't I read your letter with cold indifference? Why couldn't I put it down with a smile of contempt? Why should I be so affected by your reaction? So many 'Why's', and I must leave you to answer them—provided, of course, that you think them worthy of your consideration.

And yet I should add that it never occurred to me that you would write in precisely this way. I wouldn't have thought you capable of such dogmatism; that you believed in this or that just as you've been told to. Or maybe I am after all mistaken in thinking that you accept as true that clumsy fable about the Holy Trinity? There is a kind of holiness which can be entirely accounted for in terms of human qualities, and which is recognized by many thoughtful people. But to stick your head in the noose of dogmas! Surely you can't still be the slave of such notions! I must have got your letter all wrong, I am sure. If only you hadn't mentioned something about crossing oneself! Why is it necessary to have that kind of ceremony before you can communicate with a god? Even supposing that one could somehow manage to summon a belief in the existence of a god, it would still be absurd to think of him as a stickler for etiquette, as someone to whom mere words and gestures were as important as our thoughts.

I was very impressed by what you said about there not being enough time and opportunity in one span of life for us to win 'salvation'. I am sorry I made no comment in my last letter about the strange theory of the transmigration of souls.

Let us assume that there *does exist* a spirit, and that this spirit, after animating a number of physical bodies, in a succession of earthly existences, finally frees itself from matter. But how can we look on this as the continuous existence of one spirit only when there is no link of *memory* between one physical existence and the next?! Does that make sense?! Look, imagine that a man suffers a total loss of memory at the age of 20, and again at the age of 40. The life of this man would be divided into 3 completely independent parts. Such a complete loss of memory would not only mean that he would have to learn to write and speak all over again; he would also gradually have to learn to see, feel and move like any newborn human being. Would there be any point in regarding his life as a threefold but connected existence of one and the same soul? Would it not be truer to say that during the span of this man's life there are 3 periods when his brain has to go through a similar stage of development as it begins to function; for in each period of his life it is his brain which impels him to a fresh start. In fact, it would be rather as if here were the 3 separate lives of 3 independent but similar souls, not one human life. If we have no memory of any previous existence experienced by our own 'souls' before being born into our present life, then that is proof enough that our souls have not existed previously. *It is memory alone that gives our existence a dimension in time.*

It is all supposition and cannot be proved.

It would be very awkward if we were expected to believe in the existence of everything that has not yet been proved to be non-existent. On the contrary, one should believe only in those things which have been proved beyond doubt. It is best to refrain from discussing the various other theories that are put forward, for we are none of us clever enough to prove them, and all our argument is bound to be futile.

You are making a false comparison in your remarks on Reger. People who do not understand serious music show in other spheres, too, that compared with those who can appreciate serious music, their intellects are not so well developed. But one has to admit that the great majority of god-fearing folk are among the not so bright, whereas there is no such being as an atheist with an uncultivated mind. This means that cultivating the mind usually leads to atheism. Your comparison is wrong in other respects, too. It's hard to make comparisons within two such different fields as art and philosophy.

Any explanation of the rotation of the earth is something beyond the comprehension of the vast majority of mankind. However, there is a limited number of men who comprehend it very well, and who can produce evidence to prove the truth of their explanation. It is a different matter with the believers, who have no alternative but to insist on the truth of their thesis because this is the only way they have of explaining certain phenomena. When natural scientists are faced with a similar inability to account for the speed of light, electricity or heat, they put forward the theory that interplanetary space is filled with a substance—which they call ether—and that it is this substance which conducts the rays of light, etc. But the natural scientists make no claim for the truth of their theory, nor do they claim that their theory proves the truth of additional propositions. It is a kind of scientific fiction, a supposition that *this is how things might be*, since there is as yet no evidence to show that it is not so; and they look upon their own theory with suspicion, sifting the evidence, and as ready to disprove it as they were to advance it, for that is the scientific method. But when it comes to the idea of the existence of god—which is no less of a supposition—this is put forward as an incontrovertible truth, unquestioned alike by those who invented it and those amongst whom it was propagated. And this in spite of the fact that ordinary common sense tells us that it is a theory full of inherent contradictions and open to all kind of suspicions; as, for instance, the idea that an immortal being can be invested with mortal qualities . . .

Then, looking at evolution, we find that man *first* believed that the earth is fixed, and that only later did he come to the conclusion that it moves. Yet I have never met anyone who, as a child, did not imagine in his surroundings some kind of power to think but ceased to do so in later years. Please note the difference in development!!

Why are you such a very weak person, and why are you afraid of reading and learning?! This is what drives me to despair. Do you not credit yourself with sufficient strength to be able to retain your faith?

Isn't any work more interesting when we know how it came to be conceived, and who most influenced the author? Do you mean to say that you wouldn't have the courage to read Nietzsche's *Zarathustra*, even though you would be intrigued by Strauss's?!

Would you still refuse to accept books from me even if I only gave you books in which there is merely a total lack of reference to god—or at least only pious reference?!

I have just read a chapter of Rousseau's *Émile* in which he tries to prove the existence of god. It would show you what modern *theism* is. Of course, it provoked me to constant disagreement.

I do not see why you should condemn suicide as such a cowardly act! It's quite the contrary.

As long as I have some interest in the world, and as long as I feel bound in duty to live on for some person's sake, I will certainly not commit this 'cowardly act'. If I were to die, it would cause the death of my poor, dear mother. It would not be such a crushing blow to my sister, though she does love me and would even weep over my death. As long as my mother is alive, and as long as I have some interest in the world, I will not commit suicide. But beyond that? Once I have no responsibility towards *any* living person, once I live all by myself (never '*wavering*' even then)—why should suicide be a cowardly act? It's true, of course, that it would not be a deed of great daring, but it could not be dismissed as an act of cowardly indifference – – –

I would never attempt to talk you out of your faith, distressed though I am by your present state of mind. Come the first moment of crisis, you would relapse, I am sure – – –

Yes, let us drop the subject; we may discuss it again—at some later date, maybe, but not now.

After reading your letter, I sat down to the piano—I have a sad misgiving that I shall never find any consolation in life save in music. And yet – – –

For some time, I have been in a very strange mood, going from one extreme to the other. One letter from you, a line, even a word—and I am in a transport of joy, the next brings me almost to tears, it hurts so. What is to be the end of it all? And when? It is as if I am in a state of spiritual intoxication all the time. Just what one needs for work (composing)!

I am now in the frame of mind when I might do all kinds of 'foolish things'. You were quite right to describe my recent, impatient, departure in this way.

Incidentally, there was no risk of your letter getting lost. The worst would have been that it was delayed—by a day.

Even my pen seems to repudiate atheism—it gave up as I was writing. Well, I'll see you again tomorrow, Thursday. I have arranged my affairs so badly that I am not likely to arrive before 1 o'clock. But I shall be bringing quite a number of things with me. So that you don't feel obliged to pity me, I hereby declare in all sincerity that I am not in the least troubled by my lack of 'faith', and that I cannot even conceive of myself as a believer. It is not for 23 (twenty-three) but for 2 or 3 (two or three) days that I'll be busy at the Conservatory. There is a very apt word in Hungarian to describe a mentally deranged person—*lelkibeteg* ['soul-sick']. 'He has a sickness of the soul', they say, meaning that his mind functions in a disorderly way, until finally it will not function at all. Those who coined this word were no believers in the immortality of the soul.

Many greetings,
BÉLA

In spite of our ban, this subject is bound to crop up a good many times yet, I am afraid. Don't you agree?

We have one trait in common—that we are both better at writing than at talking – – – More about this some other time.

[Original in Hungarian]

43. TO GYULA SEBESTYÉN—BUDAPEST

Rákospalota, October 9th, 1907
Mária u. 15.

Dear Dr. Sebestyén,

At last I am able to send you the 23 selected Székely ballads.[1] If you should want to get in touch with me, please write to me at the Royal Hungarian Conservatory (Liszt tér). You can send the proofs there, too.

Yours very sincerely,
BÉLA BARTÓK

[1] As an example we quote from Bartók's first folk-song publication *Székely Ballads* (Székely balladák) one of the characteristic melodies that indicates the ornamentations (No. 12c); the same tune from the same phonograph recording in Bartók's later notation is to be found in the volume entitled *The Hungarian Folk-Song* (A magyar népdal) No. 21. The latter is so much more delicately shaded, and follows the original melody's previously unobserved turns, ornamentations and melodicand rhythmical variations so much more faithfully that visually one can hardly picture these to be notations of one and the same song. The foreword of 'A magyar népdal' is dated October 1921: there are some 12 or 13 years between the two notations.

[Original in Hungarian]

44. TO ETELKA FREUND—BUDAPEST

[3]
[Picture postcard: Kaiser Huldigungs-Festzug Wien 1908. Tiroler Schützen mit ihren historischen Fahnen]

Baden, June 28th, 1908

Busoni was very pleased with the piano pieces. '*Endlich etwas wirklich neues*', he said. Tomorrow I'm going to play all 14 of them at his piano-class. He has given me a very nice letter of recommendation for Messrs. Breitkopf & Härtel. We shall see how much it's really worth.

Greetings,
B. BARTÓK

[Original in Hungarian]

45. TO ETELKA FREUND—VITZNAU AM VIERWALDSTÄTTER SEE

[4]
[Picture postcard: Landesmuseum in Zürich. Zimmer aus Biasca]

[*Zurich, July* 20th, 1908]

I had a very bad time at Lucerne but don't worry about that now. Things are not too good here either; perhaps it'll be better in France. I've thought of two very good titles, but I can't translate them into German: 'Slowly Struggling Forward' for the 2nd piece. How would you say that in German? And for the B major piece: 'Red Dawn at Whitsun'. As there is no word for 'dawn' in German, I'll use the international term 'aurore'. Please send a good German translation of the first title to me, *Poste restante*, Genève.

Yours,
BARTÓK

[Original in Hungarian]

46. TO ETELKA FREUND—VITZNAU AM VIERWALDSTÄTTER SEE

[5]
[Picture postcard: Glacier d'Argentières et Aiguille du Chardonnet]

Argentières, July 27th, 1908

It's beautiful here! At last, no rows of 'Grand Hotels', no hordes of idle, time-wasting Englishmen, no network of cogwheel-railways ready to take you anywhere; here (well! *time is money*) poor yearning mortals can see Nature undefiled. This is far from the case in dusty Chamonix to which Baedeker awards 38 stars, only here in calm, quiet little Argentières where, thank God, the English millionaires don't come—for '*it just isn't done*'. Yes, that's how it is!

[Original in Hungarian]

47. TO ISTVÁN THOMÁN—UNGVÁR

[5]
[Picture postcard: Genève et la Rade]

[*Geneva*] *July* 31st, 1908

No getting away from it, Chamonix is in France; it just happens that Baedeker includes it in his guide to Switzerland. It's more beautiful here than in Switzerland which I find over-civilized. By the way, I didn't stay in Chamonix proper; Argentières, some 10 kilometres away, and to which the railway has only recently penetrated, is much nicer.

Greetings
B.

[Original in Hungarian]

48. TO ETELKA FREUND—VITZNAU AM VIERWALDSTÄTTER SEE

[6]
[Picture postcard: Genève—Jardin anglais]

Geneva, July 31st, 1908

Thanks for your suggestions; I choose *qualvolle*. That's quite good, I think. Breitkopf & Härtel write: '*wir sind überhäuft mit Arbeiten, so dass wir Werke, die wir gerne verlegen möchten, zurückweisen müssen. Ausserdem sind Ihre Kl-Stücke zu schwer (!) und zu modern um beim Publikum*' . . . etc., etc.

B.

[Original in Hungarian]

49. TO ETELKA FREUND—VITZNAU AM VIERWALDSTÄTTER SEE

[7]
[Picture postcard: Beaufort et Vallée de Roselend]

[*Albertville, Savoie, August* 11th, 1908]

I have experienced joy again (the joy of discovery): today for the first time I saw a genuine folk-garment here—a tricot-like man's coat, with flowers etc. embroidered on it in black cotton in various stitches. The food you get here for 5 francs a day is as good as that in the best hotels. True, one side of the house where I'm staying looks rather like a ruin on which someone has put a curse, and on the other side there are not only the rooms but also a pub, a butcher's shop and—a stable. But *ça ne fait rien,* you can't have everything.

[Original in Hungarian]

50. TO ETELKA FREUND—VITZNAU AM VIERWALDSTÄTTER SEE

[8]
[Picture postcard: Avignon. Le Pont Saint-Bénézech (XIIe et XVIe siècles)]

Les Saintes Maries, September 2nd, 1908

At last, via Lyon, Vienna, Valence and Avignon, I have reached the *ne plus ultra* of my desires: the sea. It's only the little Mediterranean Sea, but a *sea* it is nevertheless. Now I'm in the village of Les Saintes Maries, not far from Arles. It's wonderful! I walked for 7 hours without meeting a soul. Here I have bathed in the sea for the first time, walked barefoot for the first time and seen a mirage for the first time. For these three 'first-times' it's been well worth making such a long detour.

Sur le pont d'A - vi - gnon, tout le monde y pas - se,
Sur le pont d'A - vi - gnon, on y dan - se tous en rond.

(Children's song from Southern France. My own annotation.[1])

[Original in Hungarian]

51. TO ETELKA FREUND—VITZNAU AM VIERWALDSTÄTTER SEE

[9]
[Picture postcard: Combe de Savoie. Conflans et le Massif des Bauges]

[Chambéry, September 6th, 1908]

Please, do write to me in Budapest *(Teréz körút 17),* giving the translation of *Slowly Struggling Forward.* I've just received the proofs

[1] Bartók wrote the music and text of the song on the picture side of the card.

of those pieces, and now when I need the translation, it isn't here. Alas, it's completely gone out of my head, and the postcard on which you wrote it, has been travelling as 'slow goods' for the last 10 days, and God only knows when it will arrive. The Leipzig people were responsible for a marvellous printing error: 'Tót lepények tánca'!!![1]

–Vale–

[Original in Hungarian]

52. TO ETELKA FREUND—VITZNAU AM VIERWALDSTÄTTER SEE

[10]

[Picture postcard: Costumes de la Savoie. Sainte-Foy-Tarentaise]

[*Chambéry, September* 6th[2], 1908]

It's the woman marked with an X who did not want to give me anything to eat! Thanks to her I can say that there's not so much difference between Savoie and Csík County after all. But whereas no one ever mentions Csík County in any of the *Führer durch* ... Baedeker describes this woman's restaurant as: *bon!* (That's how reliable it is!)

En route for home, *September* 5th.

[Original in Hungarian]

53. TO IRMA FREUND—BUDAPEST

[Picture postcard: The Hundred-Year-Old Wooden Bridge at Torda]

Torockó, October 7th, 1908

Yesterday I went along the Torda Gorge; today I'm making merry at Torockó below Székelykő. In some ways this famous Székelykő reminds me of the Grand Salève, except that there's no *funiculaire* here! Of all the villages in Hungary which I've visited so far, this one is certainly the most beautifully situated.

To say nothing of those yellow-red forests – – –

[1] Slovak Lads' Dance. *Legény* = lad, *lepény* = pie.
[2] Date on stamp.

[Original in Hungarian]

54. TO ETELKA FREUND—BUDAPEST

[11] [About *December* 21st, 1908]

As you perhaps know, my Suite has been dropped from the programme (because Kerner is ill—or so they say). Ergo – –! Busoni has wired to ask if I'd like to conduct (!!) the Scherzo of my 2nd Suite on January 2. I think it would be decidedly better if he conducted it! It's bad luck that the parts aren't ready yet, and I shall only know this evening whether they'll be ready in time.

Greetings,

B.

[Original in Hungarian]

55. TO ETELKA FREUND—BUDAPEST

[12] *Vésztő, Christmas Eve* [*December* 24th, 1908]

I'm going to Berlin, and I shall be conducting. For immediately after receiving my first wire, Busoni put out a poster, advertising that I was to conduct my own work.

The copyist has promised the parts for Monday—for certain.

On Tuesday they will already be rehearsing in Berlin; I don't know if it will be in the morning or in the afternoon, but I think it's to be in the Beethoven Saal. I can't get there before a quarter past eleven that morning. I don't know if it will upset things if I'm late.

I hope everything will be all right, and that Busoni won't find all the to-do about the agreements too unpleasant.

Greetings,

BARTÓK.

[Original in Hungarian]

56. TO ISTVÁN THOMÁN—BUDAPEST

[6] *Berlin, January* 3rd [1909]

Isn't it a wonderful experience to conduct an orchestra which responds exactly to what one wants!

The effect on the audience was much the same as that of the

waltz in Budapest. Two camps; hisses on the one side, a storm of enthusiastic applause on the other, and I had 5 curtain calls. Oskar Fried was there, too, and he says he would like to perform the entire *Suite*. We're going to talk about it today.

The orchestra is splendid; everything sounded wonderful.

Many greetings,

BÉLA.

[Original in Hungarian]

57. TO ETELKA FREUND—BUDAPEST

[13]

[Postcard] [*Budapest, January* 28th, 1909]

I am happy to announce that the quartet got itself finished yesterday and would be pleased to visit you on Saturday evening (in my company). Would you be kind enough to receive it? If not, then perhaps Sunday, after lunch. I think I'll be able to telephone you tomorrow afternoon or in the early evening; if I can't, would you please reply by letter.

Greetings,

BARTÓK.

[Original in Hungarian]

58. TO ETELKA FREUND—BUDAPEST

[14]

[Picture postcard: Grand Hotel Black Eagle, Nagyvárad]

July 17th, [1909]

A piece of news worth communicating: my quartet is to be published by Rózsavölgyi & Co. in the autumn. It seems they were greatly impressed by their having sold 40 copies of my rhapsody abroad (while only 4 or 5 have been sold at home so far); hence their courage. Actually, it is rather surprising.

I often walk about barefoot (something I couldn't do anywhere on the Rigi, could I?), bask in the sun (ditto), get tanned, but all over (ditto), and now I'm off to work with the Wallachs.

[Original in Hungarian]

59. TO ISTVÁN THOMÁN—UNGVÁR

[Picture postcard: District of Biharfüred. Galbina: Eskimo-Ice Cave]
[*Beszterce-Marosludas, August* 31st, 1909]

I had wanted to pass the summer at Belényes, in the country that is, but this proved to be such a trial and a trouble that I couldn't stand it for more than 14 days. Since then, I've been roaming about; first in Budapest, then in Steiermark, and at present I'm doing collecting work in the Mezőség district. The Wallachian songs are the most exotic I've ever heard:

The many melismas are striking, I've heard real coloratura arias. This summer I've collected 25 Hungarian, 20 Slovak and 320 Rumanian songs!

Greetings,
B.

[Original in Hungarian]

60. TO ETELKA FREUND—BUDAPEST

[15]
[Picture postcard] [*Beszterce-Marosludas, August* 31st, 1909]

A peasant violinist played this tune and similar ones in the 3rd position on a violin tied with string. Interesting enough? I fell ill among the Wallachs of Belényes, so I left them to visit the Wallachs of the Mezőség district—and I've also been in Steiermark (not quite Ajkfalu). I got your postcard only quite recently, after a lot of delays.

Mezőkoók, August 31st, 1909

[Original in Hungarian]

61. TO ETELKA FREUND—BUDAPEST

[16]
[Picture postcard: Munich, Marienplatz]

[*January* 5th, 1910]

I was ill just before I started my trip, so I couldn't pay you a visit. Alas, I haven't anything good to report to you from Paris; Busoni only wrote to d'Indy and a music professor called Philipp. D'Indy turned me down completely: *il faut choisir les thèmes* --- that was really all he had to say. For instance, in the 3rd movement of the 2nd Suite he didn't feel any key or form!! etc., etc. The others, Risler for example, rather half-heartedly, promised me all kinds of things —that's to say, nothing. My meeting with d'Indy was very like when a celebrated professor condescends to receive a beginner and kindly gives him a few hints. *Enfin!* I have had enough of that, and I'm not looking for more.

Greetings till we meet again, from
B.

[Original in German]

62. TO RUDOLF GANZ

Budapest, Teréz körút 17. IV. 23.[1]
[Beginning of 1910]

Dear Mr. Ganz,
Your kind lines (just received) have given me real pleasure, especially as I have had to endure an unbelievable number of attacks all provoked by these very piano pieces—here in Budapest as well as abroad. Besides these, I have only 4 other piano pieces, including a scherzo which Busoni in fact knows but hasn't yet played. Incidentally there is hardly anything new in these 4 pieces, and they should be looked upon only as the promising work of a student, since I wrote them when I was 21.

My publishers sent the 2 volumes of piano pieces to the *Signale* in January. I would be exceedingly happy if *you* were to write about them, but I am afraid Herr Leichtentritt has got ahead of you in this, since a friend of mine has already approached him. After what he wrote about the Berlin performance of my orchestral scherzo, which he referred to as a confused work by a beginner with very

[1] 23. IV. 17. Teréz boulevard: 23 for apartment; IV for floor; 17 for house.

little talent, I cannot entertain much hope of a favourable judgment.

I wonder if you could perhaps advise me as to whom I might send these pieces. I mean, naturally, only musicians who are really interested in and enthusiastic about this sort of thing. To send the pieces at random to so-called good musicians would not be much help. For hardly more than one in a hundred will find any pleasure in these works, and I have to be thankful if they are not labelled as products of frenzy or insanity as has often occurred.

As it happens, I don't know anything by Ravel yet; I shall certainly order his latest piano pieces.

And now may I add that I had already heard of you before I received your letter. I often meet Etelka Freund who has a very high opinion of you as an artist. And in Berlin Dohnányi has also spoken about you in the most flattering terms. So I was all the more pleased to have aroused your interest, and now I hope that it will be possible to welcome you here next winter. If you have selected any of my compositions, would you please let me know?

With kind regards,

Yours sincerely,
BÉLA BARTÓK

[Original in Hungarian]

63. TO SÁNDOR KOVÁCS—PARIS

[1] [*Budapest, February* 18th, 1910]
[Postcard]

Dear Mr. Kovács,
Kodály will send the information you want in about 4 or 5 days. For my part, in a few days I'll be sending some folk-songs to Expert—part of my MS. collection, also the *For Children* book and our 20 folk-songs. Maybe he'll find this interesting now—not only from a scholarly point of view.

Perhaps we ought to have the biographical data inserted in the programme and not into the *conférence*.

It's only necessary to include year of birth, where we studied, and present positions. (1881 for me, 1883 for Kodály, 1877 for Dohnányi; and all of us studied in Budapest only.) Kodály would prefer us to put in the programme only movements 2 and 3 of his sonata.

I'll send you the titles and the order of my pieces by March 1. I don't think this will be too late. At the same time I'll let you know the address of some people to be invited. Have you any plans for getting the newspapers to come and show an interest and, above all, to write something? And if we have anything of a success, we ought to have someone to notify the Budapest papers. Shouldn't we have an advance notice put in the papers here beforehand?

Greetings,
BARTÓK

[Original in Hungarian]

64. TO SÁNDOR KOVÁCS—PARIS

[2] [*Budapest*] *February* 21st, [1910]
[Postcard]

Dear Mr. Kovács,
Please let me know, by return if possible, whether there will be M. songs in the programme or not; if there are, I shall try to get someone here to write about them, but I would need the exact programme. I shall play the following pieces:

a) from the *14 Bagatelles*: (1) C major, (2) D flat major, (3) C major, (4) D minor, (5) G minor, (6) B major, (7) D sharp minor, (9) E flat major, (10) C major, (11) A flat minor, (12) B minor, (13) *Ma mie qui danse*.

b) *Fantaisie*
Danse roumaine } manuscript

It occurs to me that Szendy's bagpipe piece would be good, too, after the 5 aphorisms. But this cannot be decided until after I've heard what Szendy has to say about it tomorrow, when I'll write again. May I also ask you to book a room for me in due course in one of the nearby hotels—but there's time enough for that. Best wishes for the success of your concert.

Greetings,
BARTÓK

[Original in Hungarian]

65. TO SÁNDOR KOVÁCS—PARIS

[3] [*Budapest, March* 5th, 1910]
[Postcard]

I'll go to see Ecorcheville with pleasure. And by the way, I'd also like to have a good talk with Expert (perhaps during Sunday).

I asked for the full names because of the press notices. But you forgot to let me know what Expert's job is. So will you please write this to Kodály (Áldás u. 11); and he will go to see your brother-in-law with all the exact data. I'd like to ask if you could also write about this to your brother-in-law—or isn't that possible?

Let's hope that lots of *musicians* come to the concert, that's the main thing. It would be advisable, perhaps, to invite Pierre Aubry, too. So good-bye till Thursday 9 p.m., at the railway station, on the platform.

B.

[Original in Hungarian]

66. TO SÁNDOR KOVÁCS—PARIS

[4] [After *March* 19th, 1910]

Dear Mr. Kovács,
I had to wait till my concerts were over before writing to thank you for the reviews you sent. (Though the 3 lines in the *Écho de Paris* were scarcely worth the trouble of cutting them out.) I wonder if only Ecorcheville's paper will deal with us, or if there will be notices in other musical journals, too? Now I want to ask you to do something for me; I left behind a pair of grey house-shoes (sort of sandals) and the first movement of the Kodály sonata; will you please be so kind as to send them to me, together with the Mihalovich songs. But only when you have the score of my rhapsody (which Risler has now). I'm going to write to Risler now, telling him that you will be fetching the score; so then you could do this in the first week of April or so. By that time you will have perhaps been able to get the pictures of Strasbourg Cathedral as well, so that all this could be sent in one parcel. Also, will you please let me know how much we owe you, so that I can collect the money from my colleagues and send it on to you.

Kodály had an immense success. It was a really sensational evening, for a hitherto quite unknown man emerged from it, as one of the first order. Rózsavölgyi immediately tried to get his quartet and piano pieces. (It's a notable event in this country when 2 quartets appear within a year.) Another interesting piece of news: my rhapsody for orchestra and Kodály's quartet have been accepted by the Allgem. Deutscher Musikverein for its *Musikfest* in Zurich.

The generally expressed view is that Kodály's music is much more gentle and humane than my own. The Waldbauers played beautifully, like a first-class string quartet. However, this music gave a headache to Hubay & Co.

I enclose the results of Lendvay's activities. The Rózsavölgyis also notified the papers about our reception in Paris, of course only mentioning the items in which they have an interest. If another musical journal prints something, you'll send it along, won't you? It is a strange thing that Villermose[1] does not mention Weiner. Is it possible that he hasn't heard anything by him? I would very much like to see your publications; if they were ready by the end of April, I could perhaps get one or two of them played.

Szendy wasn't here, so I haven't been able to speak to him about anything yet. G. Molnár happened to be present at Mihalovich's place just when I was describing what happened in Paris; he made a long face and quickly tried to change the subject.

Greetings,
BARTÓK

[Original in Hungarian]

67. TO SÁNDOR KOVÁCS—PARIS

[5] [*Budapest, April,* 1910]

Dear Mr. Kovács,
It is terrible how unreliable the French are. You were actually present, weren't you, when we agreed, or rather discussed, with Ecorcheville, the long notice they were going to publish about us. And after all, isn't that something in which we have a common interest? Furthermore, it was on that same occasion that we decided I was to write an article on musical folklore and even agreed on the length (15 pages!). Finally, we agreed which of Kodály's works Ecorcheville was to publish (viz. that small piece in B flat minor), and that I would get my publishers to let me assign him one small piece, etc. On the strength of this, and for this purpose, I sent Ecorcheville a whole packet of stuff complete with a letter.

But if the French are so forgetful, I think it is not worth starting anything with them. It is interesting that an unknown gentleman from S.A. Újhely should have sent me an article by Ecorcheville, from what paper I do not know. Do you know anything about it?

Mihalovich is not at home, so I can't talk to him about his Symphony in C sharp minor. I'll be meeting Weiner in the next few days.

[1] *Vuillermoz* is the correct spelling.

Kodály's pieces for the piano are to be published by Rózsavölgyi; I am not doing anything about publishing the *Rumanian Dance* at the moment as I'm not yet sure what to publish with it.

I'll send the 15 Kr. as soon as I've collected it.

Please be so good as to let me have the score of the Rhapsody as soon as possible. I need it urgently for the performance at Zurich. A few days ago I wrote to Risler to say that you would be collecting it.

Greetings from
Bartók

[Original in Hungarian]

68. TO SÁNDOR KOVÁCS—PARIS

[6] [*Budapest, April,* 1910]

Dear Mr. Kovács,
I have received the parcel, thank you. What am I to do with the Zágon songs? Shall I just look them through? And then where should I send them?

I'm sending the money by today's post. There has been a slight hitch: they forgot to put the name of the street on the parcel to Ecorcheville, and so he still hasn't got it. But it's all being put right now. All the necessary photographs will be collected and sent to you by Kodály. My quartet will be sent to you by Rózsavölgyi. I left a message for Weiner about this. I don't know if there's anything he can do about it. The Kodály quartet comes out in 5 weeks' time.

If Szántó knows that it was *we* who did not want him to appear on March 12 and plays our pieces none the less, he must be a rare idealist. *Eh bien!* we shall see.

Now I have some requests:

(1) Could I get Ecorcheville's article (in *Figaro)*? Perhaps you could ask him for a copy.

(2) Would you kindly ask him whether he received my letter and the parcel that was held up for so long?

(3) Was there anything about the Hungarian concert in the April issue of S.I.M., or are they waiting for your article?

What about the Scarlatti, etc., publications?

Greetings from
Bartók

[Original in Hungarian]

69. TO SÁNDOR KOVÁCS—PARIS

[7] [*Budapest, April* 21st, 1910]
[Postcard]

Dear Mr. Kovács,
Poor Mihalovich is in hospital with a serious fracture. I have been to see him twice, but I couldn't get any detailed information from him. And nobody else knows anything. All that I can tell you is what I've taken from an encyclopaedia: 1842 (Slovenia!), studied at Leipzig under Hauptmann. His opera *Hagbarth und Signe* was first performed in the Court Theatre at Dresden, then in Budapest (in the '80s); *Toldi* was performed in 1893; minor works (orchestra): *The Mermaids, The Ship of Horrors, Hero and Leander, La ronde du Sabbath.* He composed 4 symphonies. *Voilà tout!*

Do we get any copies of the number in which this appears?

Greetings from
B.

[Original in French]

70. TO DUMITRU G. KIRIAC—BUCHAREST

[1] *Budapest, Teréz körút 17. IV. 23.,*
April 29th, 1910

Dear Sir,
Allow me to introduce myself: I am Professor at the Royal Academy of Music in Budapest. For the last 4 or 5 years I have been studying the folklore of our country by collecting folk-songs. When I had collected numbers of Hungarian and Slovakian tunes, I went to Transylvania to look for Rumanian folk-songs, of which I found at least 400 in the neighbourhood of Beiuș (Bihar) and about 200 in other parts of the country. At first I used to take a Rumanian student with me to write down the songs, but now I can do this myself, and I think my rendering of the local dialect is more accurate—my companion often used to modify it (the practice of those who want above all things to correct the people).

As I am acquainted with your mixed choruses and think that you are the only one in Rumania concerned as a true artist with folk-music, I am now sending you a selection from my Bihar collection. I would willingly present my entire Rumanian collection to a public library in Bucharest as well as anything I may collect in the future. Perhaps it would be possible to collaborate with a Rumanian philologist and have them printed.

I should let you know that I do all my collecting for the Ethnographical Museum in Budapest, which reimburses my travelling expenses. My method is to use a phonograph (first taking down the melody and text, and then, as it were, verifying my notations with the aid of the phonograph). I consider it of the utmost importance to take phonogrammes of the folk-songs, for, as you know, there are some *glissandos* and *rubatos* which cannot be written out exactly.

If the Academy of Science in Bucharest attaches any importance to these phonogrammes, I could make two copies of each song: one for Budapest and one for Bucharest. In that case the expenses would have to be shared, half being paid by Budapest, and half by Bucharest (at present everything is paid for by our Museum alone). This would not amount to much, as a phonogramme of one cylinder containing 2 songs (each of 2 verses) costs about 1.50 francs to which you have to add the price of the cylinder (1.10 francs), so that each song would cost 1.85 francs in all.

It is true that we are rather far apart, which might give rise to some difficulties with regard to communications and payments; so this is no more than a tentative proposal. But I will in any case let you have a copy of my Rumanian collection if you will let me know where to send it for preservation.

Now I must give you some explanation of the signs used:

1. = *glissando*, to the note marked.
2. All the *melismas* are marked with ⁀⁀⁀.
3. As you know, among the people, lines of 7 syllables are often completed if necessary by adding 'ma', 'le' or 're', while in the case of 8 syllables the lines are shortened by . . .

[Continuation missing]

[Original in Hungarian]

71. TO ETELKA FREUND—BUDAPEST

[17]
[Picture postcard: Brunnen und die Mythen]

[*Zurich, May* 31st, 1910]

It's not possible to give a brief account of all that we've experienced recently. As a matter of fact, even the quality of our success could not be expressed in a few words. For the time being, suffice it to say that Kodály's quartet was particularly well received by the audience. For us, the most important impression was meeting Delius.

I'll tell you more—when I see you. Till then,

Greetings.

[Original in German]

72. TO FREDERICK DELIUS—PARIS

[1] *Budapest, Teréz körút 17.*
June 7th, 1910

Dear Mr. Delius,
I am afraid that you may not get this letter and my Suite before you go away. But after all, the Suite can wait, and the letter will perhaps be forwarded to you. I find it difficult to express adequately what a pleasure it was—I should almost say an experience—to make your acquaintance. And that is leaving music aside, simply as I saw you as a human being! I am afraid you may find it unnatural for me to write about these things which you must sense, anyhow, from my way of talking to you, but I simply cannot refrain from saying it explicitly. I am very much alone here apart from my one friend, Kodály; I have nobody to talk to, and I have never before met anyone to whom from the very first I could feel so close. This was something which made my time at the Zurich Festival one of the most beautiful periods of my life.

Now you will be going to your Norwegians again, or perhaps you are already there. I'm afraid I cannot leave town this summer, and so I can only yearn from here for those romantic regions you told me about. Could I have news of you sometimes? And I would very much like to know if the Suite made a favourable impression on you.

With warmest greetings,

Yours,
BÉLA BARTÓK

[Original in German]

73. TO FREDERICK DELIUS—DRESDEN

[2] *Budapest, Teréz körút 17. IV. 23.*
[1910]

Dear Mr. Delius,
We have had nothing but misfortune since I received your letter. My wife has been, and still is, ill, though on the way to recovery.

I couldn't write before we were over our troubles, otherwise my letter would have sounded too sad. I was very pleased to have your honest opinion—I, too, find the last movement the weakest, rather lacking in invention; and parts of the scherzo, too, are artificial and don't sound well. But, in some respects, I prefer the first movement to the third. What in this suite was intended as a contradiction of the commonplace recurred in the little piano pieces written somewhat later as a consequence of the peculiar mood I was in at the time, one which will probably never recur. I think the language of these piano pieces is less deliberate and strained than that of the Suite. Since writing them, I have regained some inner 'harmony', so that, today, I am not in need of the contradictory accumulation of dissonances which express that particular mood. This may be the consequence of allowing myself to become more and more influenced by folk-music. The business of the American copyright of our works is indeed unfortunate. God knows what peculiar motives strangers might ascribe to us for using your name. Because in print it looks a bit worse than I imagined. I am now quite seriously considering whether it wouldn't be possible to acquire some other citizenship which would secure the copyright of my compositions in America.

I have great pleasure in letting you know that your *Brigg Fair* is to be played here, in February, under a relatively good conductor. (For we have many conductors, but bad ones, and how bad!) For the following season I would like to suggest something by Grainger to him—for the simple reason that I would like to hear it. But then I don't know how to get the scores, whether the composer would give his consent, what to choose, etc. Please do give me your advice. If you have the opportunity, I would be glad if you could speak about me to Grainger; I would like to write to him on the subject of folklore, and I wouldn't like to approach him as a complete stranger. I would very much like to be able to accept your invitation, but we poor music teachers are so very much tied down—the school year lasts from the beginning of Sept. to the middle of June. If only they would give me the job of compiling a scientific collection of folk-songs, I would apply myself to that with the greatest enthusiasm. But teaching the piano to untalented youngsters who look upon music as a means of earning their living is truly not a thing I can feel any enthusiasm for. However, ours is a poor State unable to make much of a contribution to the solution of scientific and artistic problems. (I may say that my own motive for collecting folk-songs is really not 'the thirst for scientific knowledge'). We felt very sorry that you had to stay in a sanatorium—I can imagine that living in a sanatorium must be a very disagreeable experience. Let us hope you won't have any more need of it for a while.

Would you be interested in making the acquaintance (on paper) of Rumanian folk-music? If you have the time for it, I would be glad to send you some pieces from my collection to look at. And in March, please do keep your promise to pay us a visit, so that I can introduce you to that peculiarly oriental music of the Rumanian villages in all its vivid reality. We would enjoy that to be sure.

With warmest greetings,

Yours,
BÉLA BARTÓK

[Original in German]

74. TO FREDERICK DELIUS—DRESDEN

[3]

Budapest, Teréz körút 17. IV. 23.
[Autumn?] 1910

Dear Mr. Delius,

It had not occurred to me that you were ill and in a sanatorium again. Are you still suffering from the same illness you had in the summer? Two and a half years ago Kodály was in the same sanatorium, which he didn't care for much—the atmosphere wasn't free enough for him. However, he didn't go there because of any particular illness, only to build up his strength.

I hasten to send you some of our Rumanian melodies; perhaps you will still be in Dresden when the parcel arrives. Please keep this copy. I am curious as to what impression this very distinctive music will make on you; of course one must hear the originals, or an imitation, to get the right mood. The bagpipe tunes particularly lose much of their grotesque individuality if they are only read. But then, you may have heard tunes played on the bagpipe quite often, so that you will easily be able to allow for anything lost in the transcription.

I am wondering whether, when you come to Budapest, in March, you will be well enough to go on an excursion into the country. It will be a great pity if we can't, but you must of course take too much care of yourself rather than too little.

Please write soon with news that your health has improved. Wishing you that, with warmest greetings,

Bartók

I will send the score to the address given.

[Original in Hungarian]

75. TO ETELKA FREUND—BUDAPEST

[18]

[Picture postcard: Csetátja. Rock fortress]

Topánfalva, January 4th, 1911

The scenery here is magnificent—I wouldn't even mind if we had no success on this trip. We're making our way on foot, by sledge and sometimes by waggon—through pine forests and deep snow-drifts, and across rushing streams. All this is completely new to me; never before have I seen wild wooded regions in winter. It is as good as a winter trip to Semmering or the Tátra Mountains. I've found a lot of instrumental music; one or two peasant violinists in every village; and girls and women who blow the alpine horn (a wooden horn nearly 3 metres long).

[Original in German]

76. TO FREDERICK DELIUS

[4]

[Picture postcard: Stephansdom, Wien]

[After *February* 17th, 1911]

We are just about to return home to Budapest, after hearing the *Lebensmesse* by which we were deeply impressed. Our friendly greetings to all of you.

Z. Kodály (and wife) whom you met, among others, at the Zurich concert.

Bartók

[Original in Hungarian]

77. TO THE TURÓCSZENTMÁRTON PRINTING COMPANY LIMITED

Budapest, Teréz körút 17.
February 25th, 1911

Last June I offered you my manuscript collection of about 400 Slovakian folk-songs as a continuation of the *Slov. Spevy*[1] series. In your reply you asked to look through my collection, and for a statement of my terms.

I am only now able to give you an answer, and for the moment I am sending you 134 songs from Nyitra County, which will be just enough for a further volume.

The publication of the *Slov. Spevy* is such a wonderful cultural undertaking that it deserves everybody's support. For this reason I put my whole collection at your disposal free for the purpose of publication; I only ask for 4 or 5 complimentary copies of each volume and two copies of the 2½ volumes already published (if still available). Although I already have one copy of the latter, I should like to write a more intensive study on Slovakian folk-songs, and to simplify this task, I need 2 copies that I can cut up.

Most of the songs enclosed come from Drázovce, a village in Nyitra. I have carefully compared the material with the melodies and texts already published in the *Slov. Spev.* so that, as far as the melodies are concerned, this material is quite new, with the possible exception of one or two songs which are variants of some already printed in the *Slov. Sp.* I have carefully marked, by means of numbers, all the variations of text and melody. The abbreviations on the upper left corner of the sheets (phonogr. coll., etc.) refer to the number of the phonograph cylinders in the Budapest Museum of Folklore, on which I recorded the songs in question. It would be a good thing to publish this, too.

To make the checking easier, I have transposed every melody to end on . Of course you could change this if you wanted; and similarly the key and time signatures could be put in.

As the songs in the earlier volume were arranged in this order (according to villages), I should like the same method to be used in the next volume.

[1] Slovakian Songs.

Perhaps it would be better to keep the customary Italian expressions for the tempo (as in the 1st volume). The *Slov. Spevy* is such an important collection that there are few that can be compared with it; and in future years it will be referred to by foreign experts who will have difficulty in understanding the Slovakian tempo markings.

I should like to do the proof-reading of the music myself, but, of course, the editor will have to be responsible for correcting the text.

It is really marvellous that without assistance from the State, and just with amateur collectors, you have managed, single-handed, to publish such a beautiful collection; we have nothing to compare with this in Hungary, nor in Croatia; as for the Rumanians, nothing at all has been published, not even in Rumania itself.

The number of songs which could still be collected is quite incredible; it seems that in this country our richest source of folk-songs is amongst the Slovakians. In nearly every village they know different songs.

By the time you have published those 400, I shall probably have collected many more; and one of my colleagues, Zoltán Kodály, who has the additional qualification of speaking excellent Slovakian, has also started collecting and will gladly put his material at your disposal.

Other parts of my collection are: 80–90 songs from Tőkésújfalu and Felsőlefánt (Nyitra) and some 200 from four little villages (Ratkó-Bisztró, Fillér, Gerlice and Krokava) in Gömör County.

If, for any reason, you are unable to publish this material, I beg you to return it as soon as possible. I await your reply.

Yours sincerely,
BÉLA BARTÓK
Professor at the Royal Hungarian Academy of Music.

[Original in Hungarian]

78. TO JÁNOS BUȘIȚIA—BELÉNYES

[1] [*March*, 1911]

Dear Professor,
Thank you for taking so much trouble! Now I would like to know where to send the Monday concert ticket for your wife; also, where

we can meet, and, after you're out of quarantine, when you can come and see us; for I have so much to do in the near future (rehearsals, etc.) that I must know in advance when you are coming. Well, I must say, the newspapers are certainly the place to look if you want to be sure of what's really happened! Some examples: at a pupils' concert in January, *Ernő* Keresztély was to have played a Liszt rhapsody, but his hand was painful, and so another pupil of mine, *Renée* Engel, performed a Brahms rhapsody instead. The next day two newspapers wrote that 'finally, Ernő Keresztély played Liszt's rhapsody with a technique which was a credit to his teacher'!! Then five years ago my piano quintet was to have been played for the first time by an ensemble, but they couldn't learn it, so they played Schubert's quintet. The next day the paper *Az Újság* was loud with praise for the first performance of my composition which, they said, was 'bubbling with Hungarianisms'. And on another occasion Kreisler, the great violinist, was hoping to make his first appearance in Budapest, but the concert had to be cancelled at the last minute for lack of interest. The following day most of the papers gave out that Kreisler was a mediocre violinist not worth listening to!!! So you can't rely on the newspapers to get even the externals right, and as for the essence.

Greetings, Yours sincerely,

BARTÓK

[Original in German]

79. TO FREDERICK DELIUS—PARIS

[5] *Budapest, Teréz-körút 17. IV. 23.*
March 27th [1911]

Dear Mr. Delius,

Just imagine, immediately after getting home from Vienna, I fell ill; and then something even worse happened to me: they asked me to play Liszt's Concerto in E flat major here, so I had to start practising again and make my fingers come alive after several months without practising. But it's all over and done with now, so I can write to let you know what it was that moved me most in the Mass. It was '*Der alte Mittag*' and '*O Mensch, gieb acht*'. I wonder if you feel the same about it. Both parts, in their simplicity and poetry, are deeply affecting. Then we were very interested in the wordless choruses. We had never heard anything like that before. I think you are the first to have attempted such a thing. I believe this field offers many possibilities—quite remarkable effects could be obtained. What a pity that nothing came of the planned concert in Budapest by the Vienna Choral Society. I've heard that *Brigg Fair* was given a rather confused performance here. In this respect things here are quite impossible. Some of us are at present trying to get together a permanent first-class concert orchestra. With our present arrangements, we can never rely on having a worthy orchestral performance.

If we do not succeed in our plans, I shall have to give up all hope, for many years to come, of hearing my things performed (the compositions I plan writing), for I prefer no concert at all to a poor one from which it is impossible for either the audience or the composer to learn anything. I have now started a difficult job—that is to say a one-acter. I haven't written any songs before—you can well imagine how much the text bothered me at times—in the beginning. But it's going better now. And I think the music will be rather to your liking. I am going to Paris this summer (around June 20). I wonder whether you'll still be at home then? I should very much like to show you what I'm doing.

I haven't yet sent the 2nd Suite to Elberfeld. I now have a new work for orchestra (in 2 movements). If you are still in France when I arrive, I would like to discuss with you which of these would be more appropriate for Elberfeld.

And how are you? Have you found the tranquillity necessary for work? And what are you working on?

I'm so afraid that you'll again answer me from some sanatorium, so please, do set my mind at ease as soon as possible.

Many greetings,

Yours sincerely,
BARTÓK

[Original in German]

80. TO FREDERICK DELIUS—GREZ-SUR-LOING

[6] [*Rákoskeresztúr*, Middle of *July*, 1911]

Dear Mr. Delius,
I am very much afraid I have arrived too late to find you at Grez. But if you are still there, please let me know if I may come and visit you on Friday or Saturday. My address in Paris is:

Hôtel des Voyageurs, 93 B^{d}. Strasbourg.

I can find out all about the trains from the railway timetable, but to find your house I will need your exact address.

Should this letter not reach you at home, please write a few lines to me in Hungary (my address is not Budapest, etc., anymore, but *Rákoskeresztúr nyaraló, Hongrie)*. Let me know how you are, and about your stay in England where, I understand, your opera was performed.

I was too busy to get away before the middle of July. And in spite of all I have not managed to finish the compositions I mentioned to you recently, so I have come to Paris empty-handed. All good wishes till we meet again—perhaps quite soon.

Many greetings,

Yours,
BÉLA BARTÓK

[Original in Hungarian]

81. TO JÁNOS BUŞIŢIA—BELÉNYES

[2] [*Budapest, December* 18th, 1911]

Dear Professor,

It's really scandalous, finding such an incompetent fellow in the ministry. I'll write once more to the one who 'dealt with' the affair at the time (very nicely too!), and also to another official; then perhaps we'll really get the matter settled at last.

Just imagine, the day before yesterday I received a letter from the Rumanian Academy asking for my collection, in order to publish it.

I am very pleased about this!

It seems the Rumanians care much more about their folk-songs than the Hungarians. When, I wonder, can we hope for such enterprise in Budapest?

I only wish I knew more Rumanian!

I have had the temerity to have 2 boxes of cylinders sent to your address. Do please take charge of them! Although I don't intend to collect at Belényes, it is from there that I'll be taking them to the villages. I don't think I'll get to Belényes until after our New Year; till then I shall be working in the area of Magyarcséke and Drágcséke, making use of the letters of recommendation I received last year.

Many greetings till we meet again. BÉLA BARTÓK

Please, give my kindest regards to your wife.

[Original in Rumanian]

82. TO JÁNOS BUȘIȚIA—BELÉNYES

[3] *Rákoskeresztúri-nyaraló,*[1] *January,* 1912

Dear Professor,

Thank you for taking so much trouble over me. But I must tell you something: it was too much. With you I felt better than a king; I think your wife must have taken a great deal of trouble to prepare lunches of a sort I never have at home. You shouldn't do such things! Please give me ordinary meals; it distresses me to know that anyone is putting himself out for me.

Now I have a request that I hope you will grant me. As I said I want to go to the Élesd district; would you please be so good as to write me some introductions to the following villages: Tötös, and then those situated along the highroad from Mezőtelegd–Élesd–Tötös–Kis Báród–Nagy Báród to Csucsa; and those along the road from Élesd–Esküllő–Szászfalva–Vársonkolyos to Brátka; only six or seven (I've only ten days).

It doesn't matter if the villages are not next to each other. But if you can't get so many introductions for me, perhaps the priest from Tötös might be able to give them to me. Please write to the priest that I shall arrive at Tötös on 28/15[2] (Sunday) January in the afternoon.

I didn't fare very well in Cociuba at first. I went to the inn—they couldn't put me up; I went to the priest—he was at a funeral; I went to the notary—he was out hunting; I went to the teacher—he was at the funeral with the priest. Finally I found the new teacher, who didn't know anything or anybody, since he had been in the village only a few months to his home.

But in the end I collected a lot of songs, and I *saw* the *Turca* dance and other dances—they were really very beautiful; and the priest came and invited me.

I'm sending you a book of poems by Ady who is our youngest poet but the most respected since Petőfi and Arany. I suggest that you read those particularly on pages 30, 34, 38, 43, 44, 49, 88, 106, 115. The first one says that Hungarians, Rumanians and Slavs in this country should all be united, since they are kindred in misery. We've never had a poet who would dare to write such things. I shan't need the book for some months.

[1] Villa at Rákoskeresztúr.

[2] The date (15) is according to the Greek-Orthodox calendar.

You will be amused by all the mistakes I've made, but never mind: this is my first attempt.

Greetings,
BARTÓK

[Original in German]

83. TO ERICH MORITZ VON HORNBOSTEL—BERLIN

[*Rákoskeresztúr*] 22. 5. 1912

Dear Sir,
Please allow me to introduce myself. I am Professor at the Royal Hungarian Conservatory in Budapest, and I devote a large part of my spare time to collecting folk-music. I have so far handed over to the Ethnographical Museum in Budapest nearly 1000 phonograph cylinder recordings. I have heard about your own work from several of my countrymen, among them Dr. Solymossy, who has also given me your publications.

I am now writing to you on behalf of the Director of our Ethnographical Museum, Mr. V. Semayer.

We understand that in your Phonogramme Archives copies of phonograph recordings are made for the purpose of exchange with other institutes. Our Museum would also like to take part in this kind of exchange agreement with other institutes. We do not, however, know where or how such copies can be made, nor their cost.

We now ask you to be so kind as to give us some information about these things.

Alternatively, I could perhaps call on you on June 19th, 20th or 21st, when I expect to be in Berlin, and we could then discuss this together?

Yours faithfully,
BÉLA BARTÓK

[PS.] My address is: *Rákoskeresztúr* (Hungary).

[Original in Hungarian]

84. TO JÁNOS BUȘIȚIA—BELÉNYES

[4]

[Picture postcard: Parti Fra Raftsund, Lofoten]

Svolvaer, 12. 7. 1912

I salute you from one of the highlights of my trip! Did I remember to tell you that Kiriac came to Budapest for the day to ask my advice about taking phonograph records, the best machine, etc., etc.?

The Academy of Bucharest has commissioned him to record the folk-songs of Rumania. I warned him most emphatically not to record any teachers' versions of the songs, and I advised him to go to the most remote places. Whether he takes my advice or not we'll know from the results.

BARTÓK

[Original mixed in Hungarian and French]

85. TO MRS. ZOLTÁN KODÁLY *née* EMMA SÁNDOR—BUDAPEST

[Postcard]

Monday [*September* 9th, 1912]

Quite an extraordinary event occurred today: we had sunshine for 3 (three) minutes. Three minutes!! Everybody was deeply affected by the sight of this rare phenomenon!

On Thursday I'm going to see Zoltán; I want to sleep there because we'll be so busy with the folk-songs.

Will you be home by next week? As I'm going down to Pozsony next Friday for 4 or 5 days, I could come and see you Thursday night.

BÉLA BARTÓK

[Original in Hungarian]

86. TO JÁNOS BUŞIŢIA—BELÉNYES

[5] [Probably: *November–December*, 1912]

Dear Professor,
I wanted to answer your kind letter ages ago and tell you what a lot of interesting material I found in Torontál County. Now it is only because I need your help with it (another request!) that I've overcome my laziness in letter-writing. South Hungary turns out to be a particular nest of ballads. We had already heard one or two ballads here and there from young people, when, suddenly, at Petrovosel (a purely Rumanian village in spite of its Serbian name) an old pointsman dictated 7 long ballads at one go, just as if he was reading them out. I was notating for 2½ hours without a break; I could hardly keep it up. And the old man just went on and on, dictating – – – At first I thought perhaps he had learned them all from some calendar as ballads already collected and published by somebody else. But then it became more and more obvious that these were as yet

unrecorded and unpublished pieces. When I got home, I looked up various collections, and it turned out that 5 of the ballads were variants of previously published ballads, but 2 of them were entirely unknown. One of the latter, a ballad of 222 lines, is a real masterpiece in the genre. True, it has a very distant relative among the Székely ballads which, however, is much more laconic. I am enclosing my original notes of it, which will perhaps be of interest to you. Note, here and there I've given the dialect spelling: ş[1] instead of ci (cs)[2]; ci (cs) instead of t' (ty)[3], i.e., şe = *ce* (we); şiňe = *cine*' (who); ciňe = *tine* (thee in the accusative). There is also a Turkish word: *socac* = street; you may not know it. One characteristic thing: in South Torontál everyone says *pre* instead of *pe*.

I also discovered in the same village a primitive instrument:

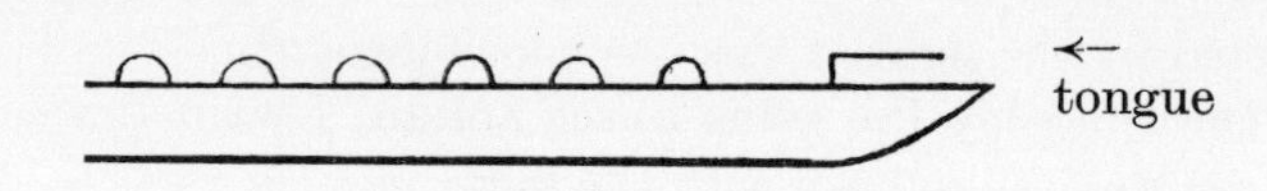

(⌒⌒⌒⌒⌒⌒ mark the place of the holes)

a long reed-whistle, with six holes and a cut-in tongue. A kind of primitive oboe! It actually gives a whistle-like sound, just like any ordinary pipe (or bagpipe), but it has no bag. It is blown directly from the mouth. There is only one old man in the village who can play it. It is called *cărabă*; however, that's also the name given to the ordinary bagpipe in these parts. It's rather interesting that this old man with the *cărabă* is also a quack-doctor and his healing rites include blowing a certain melody *(pentru beteșug)* on his instrument.

Finally, I made another interesting discovery: songs imploring rain *(dodoloaie)*. In times of drought, gipsy children go singing them from house to house, one of them all decked out with sprays of leaves. When the song comes to an end, the people living in the house sprinkle the child with water. The song goes something like this:

Paparugă rugă
Ja ieși de ňe udă
Cu-o ulcută nouă
S'o umplăm de rouă

Norii ňi se lasă
Ploaie ňi se varsă
etc.

[1] *sh* in English.
[2] *ch* as in the word church.
[3] A soft *t* as in the word Tuesday.

Meantime I learned that they have the same custom in Hunyad County, but that there it is the Rumanian villagers themselves who do it.

Now, I should like to know whether there is anything like this to be found in Bihar County; if so, I would later like to include one or two versions of it in the volume.

And so this is what I want to ask you to do for me: will you please question all your pupils (those who come from the Belényes district, especially the area between Belényes and Vaskóh) as to whether this custom exists there; if by chance they know the song, make them recite (or, maybe, sing) it; and, please, would you kindly take down both the words and the melody. For the melody is usually quite simple, and anyone who can play an instrument is quite capable of taking it down. In addition, you could ask the following questions:

1. Do they still dance the *Turca?*

2. When someone has died, do members of the family sing *at dawn* the dirge beginning: *Zorilor, surorilor?*

3. When do they sing the other, ordinary dirge?

(Vai Tănasa meu = *Vaîet după morții.*
Cum te-ai îndurat și m'ai le'sat, etc.)

And who sings it? (At what time of day, in the room or in the street, by paid mourning women or members of the bereaved family?)

4. Do the peasants, at Sunday dances, dance the *ardeleana* or some round dance (what is it called?; or do they dance the *Danțul mărunțel* and the *poarga românească* only, to the exclusion of all others? Do they know any solo dance for men? I'm afraid that when I was collecting in those districts, I did not acquire sufficiently accurate information, partly because at that time I knew even less of the language than I know now, but also because I had less knowledge of the subject.

It's true, of course, that I discovered an incredible number of dances in Torontál, e.g.:

hora	round dance	ardeleana (= *rară* = *larga)*
accion		pre loc (= *pre picioare* = *de doi)*
florica		pe sucite (= *învârtitî* = *de întoarsă)*
brău		(These 3 are danced one after the other.)

Then *poșovaica; dudureanca* (danced by 2 girls and a boy); *pupița* (2 boys squatting on their heels); *crucea*, pre bât, călușul (a man's solo dance, with 1 or 2 sticks); *judecată; babaleuca*.

And who is to know how many more there may be still undiscovered among them! Have you ever heard of those emphasized?

Let me ask you then once more—so that we can make Volume I as good as possible—do please be so good as to make a thorough investigation. Maybe, if he can find the time, your music teacher there could give a hand in taking down the tunes.

The trip to Máramaros I've postponed until Easter. I'm in touch with the assistant priest, Bîrlea, who has offered to accompany me everywhere. So I shan't need any other introductions, I hope. What we are planning is to publish, in the same volume as my collection, his own collection of texts and the material (about 200 tunes) recorded on the phonograph by Brediceanu in Máramaros County last year.

The material for the Torontál volume will be ready in a month's time when I'll send it to Professor Pável. I am so pleased that he has taken on the work. I am certain he will do it very well.

Many greetings,

BÉLA BARTÓK

[Original in Hungarian]

87. TO SÁMUEL BOBÁL—EGYHÁZMARÓT

[1] *Rákoskeresztúr, December* 16th, 1912

Dear Father Bobál,
Thank you very much for your kind lines. I am very pleased to accept your invitation and expect to arrive at Egeg-Szalatnya on January 2 by the evening train. I would like to stay with you on the 3rd, 4th and 5th, leaving for home on the 6th, at 3 p.m. I would prefer to work in fewer villages, perhaps even concentrating on one single village where I could be all the more thorough, rather than having to work more superficially in a number of places. I think the most we could find time for in those 3½ days in addition to Egyházmarót would be Lissó.

I wonder if I might ask you to copy for me in an exercise-book the texts you have collected so far, numbering the songs and, in each case, indicating the name of the person who knows it? In this way we would save a great deal of time, as I wouldn't then have to write down so many texts myself.

May I add that the best way to collect is for me to go into a peasant home where there is a gathering of good singers, friends, neighbours, etc.; first one person sings a song, then, another; phonographing, too, puts them in the right mood (for I immediately have the song just recorded played back to them). In this way we may draw from them a number of songs which even you, Father, haven't succeeded in getting so far.

For when peasants are asked to sing in a manor house, a school or a priest's house, etc., they feel embarrassed, are ashamed of themselves and can no longer call to mind some of the things they might remember in other circumstances.

It's a pity I cannot be there by Jan. 1, but I shall still be engaged elsewhere on that date.

These 3½ days will probably not give us enough time to cover the whole neighbourhood; in which case I would go there again in the middle of Jan. and maybe make another visit after Easter (in case Lent is not an appropriate time for such activities).

The *fujara*[1] interests me very much. I have already come across an instrument like that in Gömör County; it was called *fujera* there. As for Slovak bagpipers, I met one in the Ipolyság region 2 years ago.

Wedding songs are very important; and so are those with jocular texts, which often have a characteristic melody of their own.

I will, in any case, write to you once more before coming; and if I can manage it, I'll come a few days before the date fixed. (I may wire instead of writing.)

Just one thing more: I wonder if you would be so kind as to provide some sort of blanket for the coach in case we have very cold weather.

Many thanks for your trouble.

Yours very sincerely,
BÉLA BARTÓK

[Original in Hungarian]

88. TO GÉZA VILMOS ZÁGON—PARIS

[1] [*Budapest*, *April*, 1913]

Dear Mr. Zágon,
I write to ask a great favour of you, and I will have to lead up to my request by giving you a long explanation:

This summer—in June and July, to be more exact—I want to go to Algeria; to be more precise, it is the region of Biskra to which I want to go first, then to the 'Grande Kabylie', to collect Arab and Berber music (with a phonograph, of course). I have applied to our

[1] An instrument resembling a flute.

Ministry of Culture, asking them to obtain for me an official letter of introduction from the French Ministry of the Interior to the Algerian authorities. But the Ministry of Culture informs me that the French will give no such thing to us (for political reasons!). And indeed, the application was handed in to the Foreign Ministry, in the middle of Feb., and we've heard nothing since, so there's not much hope of our getting it. It occurs to me that perhaps I could get a card of accreditation from one of the Budapest newspapers (like the ones which special correspondents have when they travel to far-off places, battlefields, etc.). I've been advised to ask someone living in Paris about this. Would Laloy or Calvocoressi be able to do something for me? Have they any connections with the papers? What I have in mind is this: I would, 'formally', be the correspondent of a Paris paper *(Mercure de France* or any other *revue musicale)*, which would send me, also 'formally', to Algeria, to make a survey of the present position in regard to Arab and Berber folk-music. And as their correspondent, they would supply me with the kind of certificate with which such correspondents are usually provided to ensure that they receive official support. Could you please make enquiries amongst those who would know about all this, either personally or on the phone? Would something like this be possible? If it turns out that it is possible, but that Laloy and Calvocoressi are not themselves able to get such a document for me, could Jean Marnold get it through the *Revue de France*? If need be, I would myself write to the appropriate people, although it would be a bit difficult for me to write all this in French. I imagine it would be much simpler if you would not mind speaking for me to Laloy or Calvocoressi, as you are probably in touch with them. If neither of these two can do anything for me but believe that Marnold might have some influence, I would write to Jean Marnold myself.

What about the affair of the ballet?

When the Rózsavölgyi people sent the material, did they enclose one of my visiting-cards on which I had made notes about the dancers, or rather the lack of dancers?

Would you kindly send your reply to Rákoskeresztúr.

Many greetings,
BÉLA BARTÓK

N. B. The expenses of the trip will be met in part by the Ethnographical Museum to which I have to hand over the material.

However, I would gladly allow some of the material to be published in the *Revue* to help in this way—that is, if they would like to.

[Original in Hungarian]

89. TO GÉZA VILMOS ZÁGON—PARIS

[2] [*Budapest, May* 3rd, 1913]
[Postcard]

Dear Mr. Zágon,
Many thanks for your kindness. This sort of application has to be made through official channels in this order: first the heads of the appropriate authority (the Ministry of Culture in this case), then the Foreign Ministry, then the embassies, who finally approach the corresponding authority in the foreign country. You can't change that, try as you may. I know no one in an official position in Vienna, so I have no means of finding out the number of the file that may have been sent to Paris. A letter of introduction from a Paris periodical would probably carry less weight, but if you could procure that for me instead, I would be very satisfied. So would you kindly make enquiries please; I could always write personally to anyone interested, should that be necessary. I'd also be glad if you would mention me to your acquaintance in Algiers; I might find it helpful. In the first half of June I'll be in the region of Biskra, then either in or near Algiers. The heat does not worry me. The maximum temperature ever registered at Biskra (in the shade) was 48 centigrade. But it's not likely to be so high in June. Also, I can rest during the hottest time of day and do my work in the morning and evening. As we have temperatures of 40 centigrade (in the shade) in Hungary, too, and I can stand it quite well, and indeed like it, I am not at all worried by the heat. I'll speak to Rozsnyai about sending *For Children*. I forgot it. Best wishes for your success, and awaiting your early reply,

Yours,
BARTÓK

[Original in Hungarian]

90. TO SÁMUEL BOBÁL—EGYHÁZMARÓT

[2] [After *May* 8th and before *June* 3rd, 1913]

Dear Father Bobál,
I have been so very busy that, alas, I have had to cancel my second collecting trip. What is more, I haven't been able to copy out the

January collection either. I'm now completely exhausted and am about to set out for a long holiday. I'll be back in August, when I will arrange and copy out everything we've collected so far; then, during the autumn and the next school-year, I'll be able to continue with the research in your region altogether more energetically.

Meantime, the manuscript of my songs which I sent to Turócszentmárton has been returned safely. I have collected about 450 melodies already. The new material from Egyházmarót will probably provide another 100 melodies. That makes 550. My present hope is to go on collecting for some years to come, until I've accumulated 2 or 3 thousand; then I would like to send all the material, scientifically arranged, to Prague, for publication. I should be very glad if you would be willing to arrange or check through the texts, so that the work would then appear under both our names.

We could talk this over and go into it in more detail in the autumn, when we meet for our next collecting trip.

I'm afraid we won't get a *fujara* player! Yet it's very important that we should. Where did that man from Csábrágsomos go to? Perhaps we could go in search of him.

Wishing you and your wife a pleasant summer,

Yours very sincerely,
BÉLA BARTÓK

[Original in Hungarian]

91. TO GÉZA VILMOS ZÁGON—PARIS

[3]

[Picture postcard: Vieux Biskra. Une Rue]

[*Biskra, June* 19th, 1913]

For 8 days now I have been doing collecting work in the oases villages—thanks to the letter of introduction—the work is going more easily than in Hungary. The Arabs accompany almost all their songs with percussion instruments; sometimes in a very complicated rhythm (it is chiefly varying accentuations of equal bar lengths that produce the different rhythmic patterns). This is the most pronounced difference between their singing and ours. Apart from this, there are many primitive melodies (confined to three adjoining notes of the scale), and the compass of a fifth is hardly ever exceeded. None of their original string instruments have survived (they have the violin instead); their wind instruments have quite peculiar scales.

Greetings,
Bartók.
Regards,
Márta Bartók

[Original in Hungarian]

92. TO KÁLMÁN D'ISOZ—BUDAPEST

[Picture postcard: Biskra. Le Marché]

Biskra, June 19th, 1913

Allow me to thank you once again for your kind intervention on my behalf. At the 11th hour I received everything, even the letter of introduction from the Gouverneur d'Algérie, which I've already found very useful here.

I have found lots of interesting things for the Museum; and I will be able to bring home even more if I can endure the heat which is unrelentingly oppressive.

Greetings to you.

Yours sincerely,
Béla Bartók

[Original in Hungarian]

93. TO GÉZA VILMOS ZÁGON—SAINT-MALO

[4] *Vésztő, August* 22nd, 1913

Dear Mr. Zágon,

Your letter has been sent on to me, and I have only now received it after some delay.

Your scheme is a truly splendid one from the business point of view; the money that would have to be put into it is negligible when one considers how much profit could be made.

There is, however, an immense disadvantage in having me as a partner in the scheme, namely that a year ago sentence of death was officially pronounced on me as a composer. Either those people are right, in which case I am an untalented bungler; or I am right, and it's they who are the idiots. In either event, this means that between myself and them (that is, our musical leaders: Hubay, etc.) there can be no discussion of music, still less any joint action.

It therefore follows that since the official world of music has put me to death, you can no longer speak of my 'prestige' – – – Therefore I have resigned myself to write for my writing-desk only.

So far as appearances abroad are concerned, all my efforts during the last 8 years have proved to be in vain. I got tired of it, and a year ago I stopped pressing for that, too.

If they want to perform something somewhere, they can take my published works and perform them without me; if they ask for a manuscript with some definite intention, I'll give it with pleasure. But I shall never take any steps myself; I've had enough of that during the last 8 years.

My public appearances are confined to *one sole field*: I will do anything to further my research work in musical folklore! I have to be personally active in this field, for nothing can be achieved in any other way; while neither recognition nor public appearances are required for composing.

If I had any 'prestige', I would gladly support your cause, or rather make a common cause of yours and mine, and work for it. But as things are, this is impossible.

So I am not the door to knock on.

The door is: Mihalovich.

The Ministry asks his opinion about everything to do with music. And you might get Hubay to support you, and even enlist the help of Mihalovich, if he thinks that by doing so he could have some of his compositions performed in Paris every year. In that case, of course, the younger generation would be sent empty away!

The Opera House does not want to perform my opera at all. However, they've so far defied official opinion, by asking me for an hour-long ballet.

I am so disgusted with Budapest performances that I don't feel at all interested. The whole thing is hardly likely to add to my reputation, nor to my income!

So I am now officially engaged in collecting folk-songs and revising the Czerny études (the latter only for reasons of finance, of course); but I do all my composing as a private individual, exclusively for family use.

May I add, by way of consolation, that for me to support your cause could only do you harm. Anything I support is pre-judged as suspect by official musical circles—and rightly so from their point of view.

Many greetings. Yours sincerely,

BARTÓK

[Original in Hungarian]

94. TO ION BÎRLEA—MÁRAMAROSSZIGET

[Probably: *October*, 1913]

[..]
instead of *fo, zină*, etc., I would put *fost, vine*. In the appendix, of course, you would publish all these words in their literary form.

Finally, could I ask you to be so good as to translate into Rumanian the list of Hungarian titles between the melodies and to write out, on a separate piece of paper, next to the number of each melody, a translation of the term written beside it. If you can't understand some of the other musical terms, write to me, and I'll explain. (I have marked in *green* pencil the words I would like to have translated, so that you can find them more easily.)

As far as the numbering of the melodies is concerned, let me add that, e.g., when indicating 28^b; 28^c; 28^d; etc., 28 must be omitted, with the letters only appearing at the corresponding place. On the other hand, in references to them, the Arabic numerals must, of course, be cited, too.

I have written the Petrova texts out in full underneath the melodies, so that you can copy them from there (corrected), just as was done with the texts of the tunes received from those two lads in Jód (I collected these 2 years ago at Belényes).

Beneath the other tunes I have written out some lines to show how the text goes on; this is to help you to find the continuation in your version.

Could you also please let me know the following:

The age of Mărie Ardelean (singer at Visó).

The name of the director at Visó.

The age of Ileană Zubășcu (singer at Dragomérfalva).

The age of Mária Cocian (singer at Glód).

The age of Dumitru Bercia (flautist at Dragomérfalva).

Why is the *bârsănească* dance we heard at Jód called by this name? How and when is it danced and by whom? (Is it also performed at Jód?)

Your wife also sang two tunes. How should we mark these? What name should we put beside them, and what should we give as her occupation *(preoteasă)?*

Finally, one more request which several people have asked me to make (the Museum of Ethnography, among others): Could you procure, or order, from a tinker or some other likely villagers, perhaps by asking the priests at Glód or Poieni: 2 tin-horns, 2 bass-horns, 3 *fluer mare*, a *trişcă*, 3 *tilincă cu dup* and 3 *tilincă fără dup?* (They could be second-hand instruments; in fact that would be even better.)

As for the price, a few Kr. more or less won't matter. The whole consignment could be given to a Jewish shopkeeper in the village, asking him to pack it carefully in straw and sacking and send it by cart as express goods to *Rákoshegy* station. As for the money to pay for the instruments and the packing, I could send it to you, or perhaps to the priest at Poieni or Glód. We would be most grateful if you could do this for us.

Just imagine, the other day I had to go to the National Museum, and while I was there, they showed me a number of things, including a huge collection of Rumanian songs which they said they had just received. Well, when I looked at it carefully, I found it was Filimon's collection.

I don't know if I told you about my African trip when I last wrote. It was very interesting, I must say, chiefly because the work brought me into close contact with the natives.

The sheiks were most obliging; they simply ordered people to come in and sing. One very striking thing: there was no trace of shame in these people, not even in the women. Though in one or two places I collected songs from women 'under police surveillance', as respectable women are forbidden to speak with strange men.

Next summer (in July) I'll be going there again, and even to the Kabyls. This is a Berber tribe in the mountainous coastal region. I have already bought a Kabyl grammar.

Finally, may I ask you once more not to insert anything in ink into my collection, and the corrections should also be done in pencil, very faintly.

Looking forward to hearing from you, and with all good wishes to you and all your family,

BARTÓK

When you return the collection, please send it as a registered packet (valued at, say, 300 Kr.).

[Original in Hungarian]

95. TO SÁMUEL BOBÁL—EGYHÁZMARÓT

[3] [*Rákoskeresztúr, November* 3rd, 1913]

Dear Father Bobál,
After several weeks of back-breaking work, I have at last succeeded in making a fair copy of all the 180 songs.

I am now sending them to you, arranged in the order in which I collected them. Will you kindly insert, wherever possible, the name and age of the singer from whom we obtained the song (after the name of the locality, thus: Žuža Šlajber, 14; in Slovak spelling, of course).

Also, would you kindly complete the missing texts (with some of them, if you remember, we agreed that you would find out how the unfinished song continued), and perhaps you could correct the ones I have written out. But please leave the dialect forms as they are (e.g. *son* instead of *som*, etc.; then, the 'v' is often dropped; also, *diovča*, etc., etc.); correct only any obviously meaningless passages, wrong interpretations or mere spelling mistakes. It is especially the use of the 'i' and the 'y' I am uncertain about.

The individual pieces can be put in alphabetical order if this will help you to find texts not yet sung.

My plan is to compile a 'monography' of folk-music from the 2 Maróts, i.e., to make a complete survey of the melodies known there, regardless of whether I myself know them or not—or rather, regardless of whether they are Hungarian tunes or not.

So now I want to take down the young girls' songs we rejected last time. Please instruct my tireless girl singers to keep everything in mind that I haven't yet recorded because I want to note them all.

It is, actually, a tremendously exciting question, just how many melodies are 'hidden' among these 500 or so people, considering that during only 3 days of collecting we found as many as 180, apart from the ones we rejected. And it is precisely your own enthusiastic co-operation and interest which has made the 2 Marót villages such appropriate places for preparing a monography like this.

I could come on November 21 (Friday) in the evening, just as before. Couldn't one now take the shorter coach-road (I forget which station it starts from)? I would leave at dawn on the 25th.

If I have time, we could go over to Lissó, but it's doubtful that the Maról people's inexhaustible abundance of material will leave time for this.

I plan to make another collecting trip in the middle of January, and two more after Easter, to the *fujara* people or to other upper regions.

Ask the girls to note down the texts of any children's games (those with a tune). Also any jocular texts. I only hope that the indecent parts of the text won't deter people from singing the songs, for it is precisely these melodies that are so characteristic. (NB. Maybe I could collect these by myself.)

Looking forward to hearing from you, and with many greetings,

Yours sincerely,
BÉLA BARTÓK

[Original in French]

96. TO DUMITRU G. KIRIAC—BUCHAREST

[2] *Rákoskeresztúr, December* 18th, 1913

Dear Sir,
Many thanks for your letter. It gave me great pleasure to hear that M. Ravel feels sympathetically towards me and my work. Knowing his interest in folk-songs, I am sending him a copy of my Bihar collection, in which he may find something to inspire him.

You are partly right in your criticism of the classification of the Bihar collection. I very much regret that the letter, in which you give your reasons, has been lost!

However, the principle of the classification—of which, thank God, I am not the author, and which I am therefore free to praise without reserve—is good. Its practical usefulness is demonstrated more clearly every day when classifying the simple melodies of 4 lines. The task of making a Complete Edition of Hungarian Folk-Songs (containing approximately 5,000 songs) has been given to me and my colleague Zoltán Kodály (a first-rate musician), and in classifying them we have used Ilmari Krohn's system, with some slight modifications of our own. In order to be able to compare them with the songs of our neighbours, the Slovaks, I have classified about 3,000 Slovakian songs by the same method. And it is remarkable, I can tell you, to what a degree, through mere mechanical classification, the relation between the variants becomes clear. By this system of classification one can pick out any tune from a large collection with the greatest ease.

Bartók recording Slovak folk-songs at Darázs, Nyitra County, 1908

The manuscript of Székely Songs, *1932*

Béla Bartók in the summer of 1912

Ion Bîrlea, Bartók's assistant during his song-collecting tour of Máramaros County, March 1913

When it comes to the popular songs of Rumania, the situation is a bit different. With the Slovaks, and even more with ourselves, the distinction between the categories is a little blurred, while the Rumanians have kept the categories intact. Consequently, one must first pick out the melodies which belong together in one category (in this way one identifies the various categories such as the *colinda*, the funeral songs, the dance tunes and the *doina*). Once the categories have been made, the melodies within each category can be subdivided into 3 groups: songs of two lines, three lines and four lines. Most of the songs in the Mărămureș collection (and also in the Banat collection) belong to this last group, and these in turn can then be classified according to the last notes of the lines.

Unfortunately I omitted to make the subdivisions into *colinda*, *doina*, *bocete*, etc.; this is the fault in the classification of my Bihar collection. It happened because I had only just begun to study Rumanian folk-songs—I didn't realize how important it is to differentiate between the categories of *colinda* and *doina*, etc.

In the Mărămureș collection I have eliminated this error. You will see that the groupings are systematic, and that the variations merge into each other.

I am enclosing a copy of my letter to the Rumanian Academy, asking for the music to be engraved and not printed; I also enclose 2 engraved proof-sheets which will enable you to see what I have in mind. I really do not know how one can solve the problem of *type-setting* the glissando symbols shown below:

The problem cannot be solved correctly in any other way (i.e. by the conventional symbol). Otherwise the symbols would have to be replaced by innumerable explanations on every page! The number of pages would be decreased if engravings were used, and consequently the fee, too, but, to balance this, we should have only half the trouble in proof-reading than we had with the Bihar collection.

Would you please speak immediately in favour of this proposal: engraving is incomparably more practical and more beautiful than printing.

I hope that a volume of your collection will appear in the near future; it will be of great interest to us!

With best wishes to you,

My respects to Mme Kiriac! BÉLA BARTÓK

[Original in Hungarian]

97. TO IMRE WALDBAUER—PARIS

[Postcard]

[*Budapest, June* 15th, 1914]

I am arriving Sunday (21st), at 8.25 a.m. (maybe together with *Mrs.* Kodály); I'll leave my bag at the station, then come to you at your flat—it will be 10 o'clock by the time I get there. If you have found accommodation for me, all right; if not, I'll look for something during the day. I should add that I won't be staying in Paris for more than a week, as my business will be soon settled. A boarding-house wouldn't do, only a room. I'll bring plenty of scores—also Arab cylinders. About the latter, I wrote to Calvocoressi and have had a reply, too. I should like to see him on Sunday afternoon or Monday, so that we can discuss the rest. (He has spoken to Tiersot, to whom I'll have to show the collection.) I'll write to Calvocoressi again, asking him to reply to me at your address, letting me know when I can see him.

Till then, greetings,
BARTÓK.

[Original in Hungarian]

98. TO SÁMUEL BOBÁL—EGYHÁZMARÓT

[4] *Rákoskeresztúr (Teréz u. 28.)*
October 30th [1914 ?]

Dear Father Bobál,
It must be 3 or 4 weeks now since I wrote asking you to return the manuscript I left with you. It seems that, in these troubled times, my letter has gone astray. Please, would you be so kind as to let me have the fair copy of the manuscript of my first Marót collection, marked A, B, C, etc., together with the school exercise-books of Lissó. I'd like to have all this beside me, at home, before conditions get even more chaotic.

I also belong to the age-group which is to be called up for military service. There's a good chance that I shall be rejected on health grounds. But nowadays there's no knowing anything in advance.

How are you all? Is the baby coming on well? Is everyone very sad at Marót because of the war? I am so sorry for those good little women, my singers, for they are all sure to have somebody involved in the war. I wonder if I'll ever collect songs there again!

I should be very glad to have a few lines letting me know how things are with you.

Many greetings to you and all your family, I remain,

Yours sincerely,
BÉLA BARTÓK

[Original in Hungarian]

99. TO JÁNOS BUȘIȚIA—BELÉNYES

[6] [*Budapest*] *May* 20th [1915]

Dear Professor,
I am really ashamed of having delayed for so long replying to your charming letter of January. Meanwhile, your letter-card has arrived, too. My long silence has been due to the fact that every now and then I am thrown into a state of depression by the war—a condition which, in my case, alternates with a kind of devil-may-care attitude. In all my thinking there is a *ceterum censeo:* nothing matters, but to remain good friends with Rumania; it would be a grievous thing to me to see my beloved Transylvania devastated, besides greatly hindering my prospect of finishing, or rather continuing, my work.

In fact I can't hold out much hope for work of this kind; the future seems gloomy indeed!

I'm tremendously interested to learn how you are managing at Nagyvárad, whether you are busy and, first and foremost, whether you are sure you won't be dragged away to the front-line. Fortunately, you would always be able to find a good friend to look after your children—that would be one thing less to worry about.

You wouldn't imagine that in times like this I would find it possible to go on collecting folk-songs, would you? Well, I do!

Communications have been too disrupted for me to venture into Rumanian regions; but I have been collecting among the Slovaks, first in my own locality (Rákoskeresztúr), and then in Zólyom County, for a week around Easter!

The amazing thing about it was that one could go on collecting exactly as in times of peace; the peasants are so merry and light-hearted, one might think they didn't have a thought about the war.

Which just shows how quickly some heartaches can be cured! In August they were certainly doing enough moaning and groaning because their friends and relations had to go off to the war; now they've already quite got over their sorrow.

I've been rejected as unfit for service (lack of stamina); they're quite right, too, with only 45 kg. to help me along I would find it a bit of an effort to do big marches or quick advances (or retreats?), and with a great load on my back, too.

I have even found the time—and ability—to do some composing: it seems that the Muses are not silent in modern war.

But, of course, we keep repeating every day: 'If only it were over!' How far are we from that?!

You won't put off answering for as long as I did, will you?

Greetings and best wishes from both of us

Yours,
BARTÓK.

[Original in Hungarian]

100. TO THE BOARD OF DIRECTORS OF THE BUDAPEST PHILHARMONIC SOCIETY

Rákoskeresztúr, December 10th, 1915

Sirs,

As I did not want to cause a scene at the celebrations, I didn't protest when, on the occasion of your Gala concert in Vienna, you committed the barbarity of performing my 1st Suite in truncated form. However, I learn from the newspapers that you have done so again in Budapest, and I must therefore raise my voice in protest. It is generally accepted as improper and impermissible to omit movements from sonatas or symphonic compositions when these are played at a serious concert. This sort of thing can only be countenanced at 'zoo' concerts or 'young people's concerts' with anthology-type programmes. My own composition, to which I now refer, is not only symphonic: there is such a close thematic connection between the movements that certain bars of some of the movements cannot be understood unless one has already heard the preceding movements.

In these circumstances I have to inform you that I should be greatly obliged if you would never play any of my pieces again. I feel all the more entitled to make this request since the deplorable state of Budapest's musical life has forced me to forego all public appearances as a composer during the last 4 years and to withhold all my works written since then from public appearance.

BÉLA BARTÓK.

[Original in Hungarian]

101. TO HIS MOTHER, MRS. BÉLA BARTÓK—POZSONY

[22] *Budapest, March* 21st, 1917

D[ear] M.,
My letter—written, sealed, addressed and stamped—I left at Emma's on Tuesday. I hope they have posted it. Now I'm writing again because, in the meantime, I have received your letter-card. I am joyfully awaiting the promised parcel. In return I shall give you a very special present for Easter. Something really scarce; something that isn't to be had at all. You mustn't blame Tango—he's the best conductor I've ever worked with. He told me that the only reason he, at that time, refused to take on this performance was that it needed 30 rehearsals, and they still had to produce *Violanta* and Ábrányi's opera, and heaven knows what else. Plus the rehearsals for 5 postponed philharmonic concerts! That's what he said! And now *Violanta* and everything else has been cancelled, and the philharmonic orchestra is holding its concerts without rehearsals! 'His Excellency' has promised Tango that he can have his 30 rehearsals. Just think of it—30 rehearsals! So far Tango has proved magnificent. His refusing to conduct the work, unless he's given the opportunity to study it in detail first, is the finest thing a conductor could do. You can imagine anyone else, less gifted and with less preparation, would have done it on 5 or 6 rehearsals—and how! God protect us from that! Tango has also said that he is very pleased to have the opportunity to conduct a Hungarian work for once but went on to say that he would not have conducted anyone else's work, only mine. On Tuesday, when I gave him the score, he said, '*Ik werde eine Woge ganz krank sein von Studium*'[1] (meaning that he was getting down to work in earnest). He will spend *3 weeks* studying the score! (Kerner does not even bother to glance at it; it's only when he starts rehearsing that he really begins to get to know the work.)

Therefore: praised be Tango,
for ever and ever,
Amen.

[1] I shall be ill for a week studying it.

102. TO JÁNOS BUȘIȚIA—BELÉNYES

[7] *Budapest, May* 6th, 1917

Dear Professor,
Of course I haven't forgotten you; on the contrary, you and your family have been much in my thoughts as a result of the sad events of last autumn. I have often wanted to write to you (though nowadays a man cannot even write as his heart dictates). But the last 18 months have brought me more troubles than I've had during the rest of my life.

The steadily worsening world situation which, it seems, has ruined my career (collecting folk-songs, I mean), for the most beautiful regions of all, Eastern Europe and the Balkans, are completely ravaged—this in itself has depressed me enough. How my heart bled when I heard that the inhabitants of Fogaras, etc., had left their homes to go with the Rumanian army. Will they ever come back again, and if they do, what sort of condition will they be in?! Shall I ever be able to do any collecting there?! How I grieved for the Székelys of Csík and Gyergyó, for I was there, too. Later, of course, it came out that it was not the 'enemy' who caused them so much suffering but—but I'd rather not write it; anyway, you know who. To add to all these worries, my wife and son went to visit a relative, an army doctor in Marosvásárhely, just at the time when the place was invaded by the Rumanians. They escaped with the army, and for 3 weeks I had no news of them. At last, after much difficulty, my father-in-law managed, with the assistance of the country police, to get in touch with them by telephone.

It was probably this alarming experience which brought on my wife's illness—an infection of the lung—for which she had to be treated in Újtátrafüred for 2 months. Hungarian sanatoriums are miserable places; what she needed was the strict régime of a place like Davos, but no one can get to those places nowadays. She is still not fully recovered, and I don't know what will happen. At Keresztúr there is neither butter nor milk nor anything else. She is coming home for the time being, and we shall see how we get on. With so many troubles on my mind I only just managed to finish a one-act ballet for the Opera House. It would have been a big job even in peace time, with all these troubles. And when, with great difficulty, I had got it done, then the real struggle began: you've no idea what a senseless and frustrating battle I've had with the Opera House. What is the Royal Hungarian Opera House anyway?! An Augean stable; a dumping-ground for every kind of rubbish; the seat of all disorder; the pinnacle of confusion, where only one man is respected and has the right to make decisions, however trivial they may be: the Government Deputy; but this otherwise well-disposed V.C.P.C.[1] hardly ever looks in at the theatre. Now the first night is May 12th; and this is the last week of rehearsals. People are already sharpening their claws against me.

But I won't go on; I have written quite enough in this key. I long to hear some Rumanian song or speech; do you think it would be possible to go somewhere in Bihar, say to the Mareles or some such place, for a few weeks this summer? Of course, there will be the same difficulty about food wherever one goes.

Please write me a long letter, I'll be sure to read it and answer it more quickly than I answered your postcard, for by that time I shall have finished rehearsing at the Opera. It will reach me more quickly if addressed to the Conservatory; otherwise my home address is Rákoskeresztúr.

With kindest regards,

Yours,
BÉLA BARTÓK

[Original in Hungarian]

103. TO JÁNOS BUȘIȚIA—BELÉNYES

[8] [*Rákoskeresztúr, August,* 1917]

Dear Professor,
I have been wanting to write to you for a long time, but this time it's I who have been ill again. I've been laid low with some kind of 'flu' for a week or so; now I'm out of bed, but I still feel rather weak. Tango has probably written to you, so I won't comment on his health now.

I should be so pleased if you would accept, in a spirit of friendship, these 3 Hungarian books which I am sending you as tokens of a happier Hungarian–Rumanian relationship in the future. This friendship for the moment—as a result of Apponyi's 'blessed' activities—is delayed, but its time will come when the long-bearded old men have gone, and their place has been taken by the young

[1] Veritable Confidential Privy Councillor.

people of today, the people of *Világ*, *Nyugat* and—*Ma* (!)[1] get their chance. (I don't know exactly what has been going on, for I only read the newspapers once in a while; however, it seems that there has been another scandal in government circles about something or other.)

But to get back to the books:

I am sending you the 2 Balázs books, primarily, so that you can put in some advance study on the texts of *Bluebeard* and *The Wooden Prince*. Secondly, because the other two mystery plays are also worth reading; and thirdly, the drawings of the puppet play are very good, even though I don't like the text itself very much. (I find it rather commonplace, like so many of the verses in picture-books for children.)

On the other hand, I'm sending you the Móricz book because it is the best Hungarian novel to have been written so far, and indeed a very fine work by any standards. One is of course reminded, in more ways than one, of the greatest novelists (Flaubert, Dostoevski), which is a pity in so far as this makes it seem less original. Nevertheless, it is in many ways a very individual and therefore a valuable book. The author is a master of style and characterization. There is a quality of feverish excitement in the narrative and, if I remember correctly, the whole book covers the events of only 1½ days.

The writer is a Hungarian from Szatmár County, coming from a Reformed Church family, and it was his stories about peasants which first brought him fame. It is curious that this book, which is not about peasants, should be his best work.

I have not yet been able to get the Berény picture I promised you, for I hardly ever go to Budapest these days. But it isn't urgent, is it?

Besides a number of French books, I am now reading some Rumanian books, too, namely, the novels *Străin in țara lui*[2] (Rădulescu-Niger) and *Din bătrăni*[3] (Slavici). And in September I plan to get down to studying Rumanian grammar once again. I wonder if I'll be distracted by outward circumstances again as so often in the past!

I am enclosing some Hungarian folk-songs (soldiers' songs from

[1] See Notes (it is a play on words as the title of the review *Ma* means today).
[2] A Stranger in His Own Land.
[3] About Old People.

my soldiers' collection) among which there are one or two of real musical merit. I recommend you particularly to look at those marked with an X.

Thank you once more for all the kindness, consideration and assistance you gave us, especially poor Tango. All good wishes until our next meeting—which we now have grounds for hoping will be in the not too distant future.

Yours sincerely,
BARTÓK

[Original in Hungarian]

104. TO JÁNOS BUȘIȚIA—BELÉNYES

[9] *Rákoskeresztúr (Teréz u. 28.)*
January 28th, 1918

Dear Professor,
I'm afraid I have been a long time in answering your last letter. My time has been taken up with various things, including the Vienna Concert I told you about when I last wrote. Unfortunately the Rumanian dance series could not be included in the programme, as it would have made it too long. And so the only examples of the soldiers' songs of Hungary were the Hungarian and Slovakian songs. The King was not present—only the Queen—and you can imagine what a galaxy of *Gotterhalte* backers, gem and decoration wearers and musical ignoramuses were present. But all that is of no account; what is good is that at last there was an opportunity for 'real' Hungarian folk-songs to be heard by those few Viennese musicians who accidentally dropped into that company of pluto-aristocrats. Our tenor, Székelyhidy, sang the Hungarian songs very well (I accompanied him on the piano); the Slovakian songs (for men's chorus) were marvellously rendered by the Männergesangverein of Vienna (with the texts, of course, translated into German).

Needless to say, the generals who organized the concert produced some very peculiar things. For example, instead of 'Franz Joseph makes me fade away', the performers had to sing 'I am fading away in sorrow (!!).' Then, only German and Hungarian was permitted (dualism); and so the Slovakian songs had to be sung in German, which was clearly a legal offence against us, as the Slovaks are living in Hungary and not in Austria, and therefore, if they had to be translated at all, the songs should have been given in Hungarian. Then in the programme they were only allowed to mention *oester-*

reichische and *ungarische Lieder*. Thus the Slovakian songs (and it would have been the same with the Rumanian if there had been any) were listed as *ungarische Lieder*, and it was only at the end of the printed text that there was a note: *deutsche Übersetzung aus dem Slovakischen*. In short, it was all very bureaucratic and typically brass hat. But what do we care!

The brighter side of the affair is that the greater part of the programme is to be published in Vienna; also 100 Hungarian soldiers' songs (without accompaniment), and even more some time later.

My work of orchestrating the *Rumanian Folk Dances* was not in vain, after all, because they are going to be played in Budapest in Feb.—I think on the 9th. What a pity that you can't come, for you'd certainly enjoy hearing these Rumanian songs in a Budapest concert hall. Originally I transcribed these tunes for the piano, for two hands (very simply, as if for use in schools), and they are about to be printed in this form in Vienna where the Universal Edition is publishing them. I wanted them to be a surprise, but there is one thing I can't do without asking: I have dedicated this book of music to you as follows: *Domnului Prof. Joan Bușiția*. Have you any objection, and is it right like this? (I think it's simple enough for me not to have got it wrong.) It will be published in 3 languages: German, Hungarian and Rumanian.

The same publishing house is going to bring out 20 *colinda* songs in a piano arrangement for two hands, and I shall have to provide an appendix giving the first lines of the texts. Would you be kind enough to look over and correct—but preserving the dialect—the enclosed Rumanian verses? But please use only pencil markings; and would you also please translate into Rumanian the parts underlined in red. This work is not so very urgent; it will be all right if I get it back in 2 or 3 weeks.

The Ministry of War would like to repeat that Viennese concert in Budapest, but they've been given to understand by certain 'official' circles that only Hungarian songs may be sung in Budapest. The War Ministry which had commissioned me to arrange the programme for the Budapest concert is furious. When I was in Vienna, I had said that it was indeed possible to have a few Austrian songs—a fair enough exchange—and that on the Hungarian side some Slovakian, Rumanian and possibly Croatian songs might be given alongside the Hungarian ones. If the Budapest people do not accept my proposed programme, I shall withdraw from the whole business. They can get on with it by themselves as best they can. Here it is supposed to be a performance of the soldiers' songs of the Army, and this is actually the title of the concert, so it would be quite insupportable and unjust to pass over the various nationalities in silence. Well, that's the way things are in Hungary!—I am shocked to read in the press that more and more regulations are being made. A fine business, I must say! What about the State assistance which you mentioned in your last letter—what happened? And is there any other news from Belényes? The first night of *Bluebeard* is about to be postponed indefinitely, perhaps till May! That's the way they always treat me at the Opera!

Thanking you, in anticipation, for your kindness,
with best wishes,

Yours sincerely,
BÉLA BARTÓK

[PS.] I can't get a photograph of Berény's picture because the negative is missing. But now an older photo of it is coming out in *Ma*, and I can send you a copy of that.

[Original in Hungarian]

105. TO JÁNOS BUȘIȚIA—BELÉNYES[1]

[10] *Rákoskeresztúr, September* 14th, 1918

Dear Professor,
It really isn't nice of me to have given no sign of life for so long. But first of all I waited so as to be able to forward the *Rumanian Dances* —in vain, alas, for they haven't appeared to this day. In the second place I have been busy, doing all sorts of things—travelling, doing collecting work, etc. And thirdly, I've been extremely lazy about letter-writing. (Admitting one's faults means that one is half-way to rectifying them.)

I hear that you've been telling everyone in Belényes that I bought chocolate for a French lady. The truth is that I was eating the chocolate, but, naturally, offered some to the lady, too; I may say I bought it for my son—as there was nothing else to be bought—and of

[1] See Note for the explanation of the music example attached to the letter.

course he was very pleased to get the remains! The woman was a pleasant travelling companion inasmuch as I had the opportunity of talking to her in French, until, finally, I got tired—just to hear someone speaking good French is a pleasure in itself, quite apart from the subject of the discourse. I may add that she turned out to be a perfidious snake; she knew my wife and her family quite well and had seen my son once—and all this, God only knows why, she carefully concealed until the very end of our journey. Never trust a woman!

After a week at home, I went to spend a fortnight in lordly splendour with the Kohners. 3 footmen and a parlourmaid served at dinner, and there were 2 manservants and a chambermaid to tidy my room. Coaches, horses, food, baths, cigarettes, wine, real coffee—plenty of everything and everything of the best. And these people have such a gift for enjoying their affluence that one almost forgets to be angry at the unequal distribution of wealth. The guests came and went as though it were an hotel. We took books from the library and went for walks in the immense park of which, I'm pleased to say, only the area near the house had been mown and raked and generally over-cultivated; but the further one penetrated, the wilder it became, and eventually ended in the natural woodland typical of the lowlands. The park is well supplied with benches which no one ever uses. They have 4 women to do the laundry, and they are kept busy, washing, mangling and ironing all day long. And this tremendous display of luxury and labour is all for the benefit of the Kohner couple and their 3 children! N.B. They have a town house in Budapest as well, and another house on their estate in Hont County. Conversation ranged over a score of subjects such as music, literature, the Jewish problem, religion, the Bolshevist movement, commerce, trade, etc., etc., all this, of course, from the landowners' and capitalists' point of view.

The Baron went out hunting each morning and came home every day with a bag of 25 to 30 partridges. He knows quite a lot about music, is very fond of it, plays the violin himself, actually rather well, all things considered. He is very friendly with painters (the family are fond of Adolf Fényes who was also there for a few days); one of the Baron's daughters paints and was a student of Adolf Fényes's; his other daughter goes to the university. He lost his only son in the war.

As for me, I spent most of my time in the laundry of course; I collected lots of songs from the washerwomen, looking on as they ironed all the frilled shirts, lace petticoats and drawers. I can vouch for the quality of the family's underwear, too!

One evening barefooted peasant girls gathered outside the house to perform a farewell dance in accordance with the old customs. They even asked 'his Honour' for a dance!

As soon as I got home, I set to work. Bródy did not send the libretto, so I have begun to set Menyhért Lengyel's libretto to music.

They are getting on with the setting of my works, but there's some delay over the printing.

How is Bujor? His last escapade was to slip through the gate in the darkness and accompany me to the station, where he created a scene with his notoriously friendly manners; finally, after expending a good deal of energy in the attempt, I managed to drive him away. Did he get home safely?

May I ask you to be so kind as to send me a postcard sometime, giving me Headmaster Nutz's Christian name? About the middle of Oct. I would like to write to him about a possible trip to Szatmár in the middle of Nov.

With best regards,

Yours,
BÉLA BARTÓK

[Original in Hungarian]

106. TO JÁNOS BUȘIȚIA—BELÉNYES

[11] *January* 31st, 1919

Dear Professor,
It is with a feeling of dismay and grief that we have learned of the terrible sorrow which has overtaken you, for which consoling words cannot be found. I ask only this: please continue to believe that there are still ways in which you can serve your country and thus, indirectly, mankind as a whole. After all, it is honest, strong, uncompromising men like you who are most needed everywhere. May this knowledge give you strength to bear your grief. This is the one thing we can wish you.

The same danger lurked about us, too, but, for the time being, we have recovered from the illness without any major consequences. But I was left with inflammation of the middle ear, which was very painful and continued to torture me for a good many weeks. Torments of the soul were also added to my bodily pains.

I have made exhaustive enquiries about selling the piano and have come to the following conclusion. You can ask six times its original price. At present, for instance, a new Wirth piano (a make which is inferior to the Bösendorfer) costs 10,000 Kr.; and a second-hand one of the same make and in good condition, 6,000 Kr. Your piano is in perfectly good condition, so you should get at least 6,000 Kr. for it if you bought it for 1,000 Kr. Or more, if the original price was higher.

I also have a request to make: will you please take charge of the cylinders that were left with the Mareles if, for any reason, you think they are not safe with them (for instance, if riots were expected, etc.). There is an alphorn recording among them which is quite unique. It would be a great pity if it perished.

I'm sending the *Rumanian Dances* and the *Colindas* by today's post; I couldn't send them before because of our various troubles.

Do send me your news from time to time; it would interest me to know how things work out for you in the new world; and how Rumanian–Hungarian friendship develops generally. And our work of collecting Rumanian songs?!

As for me, they actually did want to put me in charge of the Opera House, but thank God, nothing came of it. It wouldn't have suited me anyway. Now I'm awaiting my appointment to the Museum where I think I would be very much in my element.

Many greetings,
BÉLA BARTÓK

[Original in Hungarian]

107. ZOLTÁN KODÁLY — TO THE MINISTER OF CULTURE, BUDAPEST

[Draft] [Early *September*, 1919]

Sir,
I have the honour of submitting to Your Excellency a request from Professor B[éla] B[artók] to be granted 6 months leave of absence, a request which has my full support.

It is vital to our national cultural prospects that B., our most eminent composer, with a reputation throughout Europe, should regain as soon as possible his full capacity for work. In this connection, I believe it would be right to take into consideration the fact that, although he has often suffered from indifferent health, Bartók has never, in the course of twelve and a half years in his post, asked to be granted a prolonged leave. During the last 10 to 20 years, in addition to discharging his duties on the staff of the Academy, he has been active as a composer, recital pianist and ethnographer; nor is it merely that he has worked so hard in these different fields; it is rather that his work is of such unusual significance that he is entitled to a period of rest, quite apart from the fact that the physical strain and serious privations of recent years and months have now dangerously impaired his health.

There would be no particular difficulty in arranging for his duties to be discharged, since most of his pupils graduated at the end of the past academic year, while 4 or 5 pupils still studying under him could without any difficulty be transferred.

Although he is not asking for an allowance, I would consider it only fair to give him the sum usually granted in such cases.[1]

I remain, with respect,

Yours faithfully,
ZOLTÁN KODÁLY
Deputy Director

[1] Kodály left out this paragraph in the final letter.

[Original in Hungarian]

108. TO HIS MOTHER, MRS. BÉLA BARTÓK—POZSONY

[23] *October* 23rd, 1919

Dear Mama and Aunt Irma,

[. . .] Dohnányi has been given a year's leave (!) with the result that 14 teachers went on strike; after a few days, 2 of them turned blackleg, then the rest also resumed their duties. And now the whole affair is fizzling out. There was to have been a disciplinary investigation into the activities of Zoltán and the others, but it's always being postponed—it is evident that the whole business was a farce. They continue to draw their full salaries, of course, only they do no work. In a word, they come off better than the teachers against whom no disciplinary action has been taken. As for me, I keep waiting and waiting. So long as we remain isolated and continue to find ourselves in what amounts to a state of siege, it will be impossible to do anything. But I have been making what enquiries I can in 3 different countries about the chances of making a living. For in this country, though one can make a living, for the next 10 years at least it will not be possible to do any work, i.e. the kind of work I am interested in (studying folk-music). In other words, if I have a chance to do this kind of work abroad, I see no point in staying here; and if it's impossible to make a living from this kind of work abroad either, it would still be better to teach music, in Vienna say, than in Budapest; for there at least they have good musical institutions (orchestras, opera, etc.), whereas everything is being ruined here because our best musicians, our only ones—Tango, Dohnányi, etc.—are being hounded out of their posts.

In short, I am not badly off here, and I'm not being persecuted (not because they have no cause to—they have no qualms about acting without good cause nowadays—but because they dare not). The 3 other countries are: Transylvania, Vienna and Germany. A university professor who has 'emigrated' to Germany has taken with him a German translation of all my papers on folk-music (they deal with Hungarian, Rumanian and Arab folk-music), and he is trying to do something for me there. The pleasantest place for me to go to would be Transylvania—it would feel more or less like Hungary to me; of all the territories that lay within the former boundaries of Hungary, that was the one I liked best, anyway. I have just heard something very interesting: Tango has received

A page from the score of The Wooden Prince, *completed in 1917*

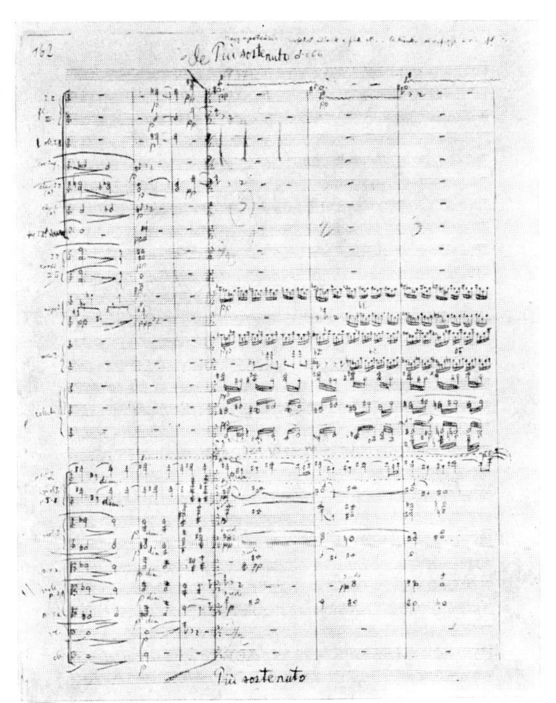

An unfinished portrait of Bartók by Ion Bușiția, 1917

A pencil-study of Bartók in 1922 by Márton Hosszú

Caricature of Béla Bartók from the October 22, 1924 issue of Rampa *(Bucharest)*

an invitation from the Rumanian Minister of Culture to take up a post in Rumania and Transylvania. An army officer was given the job of handing over the invitation, and to make Tango more interested, he dropped a hint that I, too, intended to settle in Transylvania (!!). Tango has now gone there to look over the place. I shall be curious to know what he thinks of it, and I'm anxiously awaiting his return.

Don't worry about us: we have by now managed to get hold of 2 tons of logs—it will do for now; there's enough to heat room and kitchen for about 4 months. Few people, either in Budapest or in Vienna, can afford greater luxury than that nowadays.

[Original in Hungarian]

109. TO HIS MOTHER, MRS. BÉLA BARTÓK—POZSONY

[24] *November* 28th, 1919

Dear Mama and Aunt Irma,
Here's another letter from me, a hasty and brief one, just so that you aren't left without news for too long.

1. I tried to get a passport to Pozsony, but the Hungarian authorities rejected my application with the enigmatic comment, 'It is quite impossible just now; we will give you our decision next week.' Just what decision will be made, and just what goes on in the minds of these new administrators of authority is quite beyond the power of ordinary mortals to fathom. But I fear they are hatching some wild scheme, though Heaven knows what it is. Well, we shall see.

2. You ask about my own situation. I have nothing particular to report. My leave continues until the end of Dec., then I shall ask for an extension, which, I suppose, they will be only too glad to allow me. Mr. Hubay has made his festive entry into the halls of the National Academy of Music (with an *Einzugsmarsch* which was probably self-provided for the occasion). He is now busy giving interviews to the representatives of every kind of newspaper and handing out statements right and left. Some 2 weeks ago, for instance, one of his pronouncements appeared in the columns of *Budapesti Hirlap*. 'I certainly count on having the support of Dohnányi and Bartók in my great work.' And the other day, in *Az Ujság*, he made a statement to the effect that I could not be expected to show an interest in piano-teaching; that some sort of post would have to be

created specially for me to make it possible for me to add to our national heritage of music in perfect freedom, as and when I could. That's all I know, as I haven't, of course, met Hubay as yet. Still, it should be enough to convince you that no one is persecuting me or stirring up trouble against me personally. You know, of course, that I have for a long time now wanted to give up teaching and do some other kind of work, e.g. in a museum. Hubay and his friends are equally well aware of this fact and must have in mind something like that. However, I'm going ahead with my own plans, quite apart from this possibility, but I will not give up my post, of course, until I have secured something that is absolutely certain and decidedly preferable elsewhere. When I say 'preferable', I do not mean from the point of view of income but as regards opportunities of work. For the prevailing conditions in this country are so wretched that, even with the best will in the world, it is very doubtful whether the government could afford to allocate money to buy, say, 600 phonograph cylinders a year and meet the cost of collecting and recording. Before the war they would have cost 3 francs per cylinder, i.e. a total of 1800 francs; the current rate is twenty times that amount, so-that each cylinder would now cost $3\times 20 = 60$ Kr. making a total of $1800\times 20 = 36{,}000$ Kr., which means one would have to raise a round sum of forty thousand Kr.!! That's our biggest obstacle! For the time being, of course, we can only wait.

We are very grateful for the sugar. We watched spellbound as the glistening, white lumps came into sight—we hadn't seen anything so marvellous for years. The little one was also delighted with the sweets. He now helps me with the arrangement of the folk-songs; he can indicate the cadences in each line of the melody with numbers as well as the number of syllables in each line of the text, and the compass of the melody! And he does it quite well, though mechanically, of course.

Nothing more has been done about taking disciplinary action against Zoltán and the others. They are awaiting developments with equanimity, of course, and continue to draw their full salaries while doing no work. All work at the Museum of Ethnography is at a standstill because of the coal shortage.

III

THE YEARS OF ACHIEVEMENT

1920–1926

This period reflects a beneficial 'crisis'—long meditation and sudden awakening—in the creative life of Béla Bartók. These are the years in which he struggled for a new, more balanced style. For instance his piano cycle written in 1920, *Improvisations on Hungarian Peasant Songs*, rests on such an integral, coherent, deliberately planned design that its title (Improvisations!) might almost seem ironical, as does the title *Allegro Barbaro* composed nine years earlier, in 1911. His two *Sonatas for Violin* (1921 and 1922) stand out as bold experiments and are clearly the product of the most intense concentration. The première of the *Dance Suite* for major orchestra in Budapest, on November 19th, 1923 (also the first night of Kodály's *Psalmus Hungaricus*), has become an important date in the history of Hungarian music, the symbol of the awakening of Hungarian intellectual life after the ravages of the First World War. The Slovak folk-song cycle entitled *Village Scenes*, composed in 1924 for female voice and piano, was dedicated to Ditta. A change had come over Bartók's whole life; he had to make a new beginning in every sense, for it was at this time that he obtained a divorce from his first wife, Márta Ziegler, after a marriage lasting fourteen years—their separation having been agreed by mutual consent—and in the summer of 1923 he married one of his pupils, Ditta Pásztory.

In the 'years of awakening' Bartók composed relatively few works. Strangely enough, in the year 1925 he wrote nothing at all.

However, in 1926—as in the years between 1908 and 1911—a considerable amount of piano music was composed: *Sonata for Piano*, the cycle *Out of Doors*, *Nine Small Pieces for Piano*, the *First Piano Concerto;* and the first pieces of the lengthy *Mikrokosmos* series also date from this period. This outburst of productivity recalls the memorable pianistic effusion of the year 1908; yet this musical explosion was also the preparation for a great synthesis. In these compositions his ideal of style, which in earlier years he had found in the work of Beethoven, was now enriched by the strictness of form, counterpoint and linear technique characteristic of the music of Bach, as manifested for the first time in the *Nine Small Pieces for Piano*, Nos 1–4, Dialogues.

From 1920 onwards he went on concert tours to Germany, Czechoslovakia, Rumania (Transylvania, formerly Hungarian territory), England, France and the Netherlands. As a result of these tours, which he was pressed to undertake for financial reasons, the world of music became acquainted with Bartók's personality as a composer and pianist. In the next period, comprising the years 1928 and 1929, he travelled still farther, giving concerts in the United States as well as in the Soviet Union.

During the years 1920 to 1926, Bartók established relations with concert bureaux and broadcasting corporations, with foreign artists and Hungarian musicians living abroad, and with violinists and conductors.

[Original in Hungarian]

110. TO GYULA WLASSICS—BUDAPEST

[1] *Rákoskeresztúr, February* 3rd, 1920

Your Honour,
I have only just learned that 'membership of the Directory' is one of the charges now being made against Zoltán Kodály for disciplinary investigations of which you are chairman. Having myself participated in the executive functions of that body in precisely the same way as Kodály, I must protest against his bearing alone any responsibility, either for the mere fact of former membership or for anything else he may have done to which objection is now raised. I request you to have this letter read out before the disciplinary commission and to have it put on record.

Yours respectfully,
BÉLA BARTÓK

[Original in Hungarian]

111. TO THE EDITOR-IN-CHIEF OF 'SZÓZAT'—BUDAPEST

Budapest, February 20th, 1920

Dear Sir,
I have been named in certain newspapers as one of the members of the newly formed Musical Council. I feel obliged to inform you that, on the contrary, I have received no official approach on this matter; nor would I wish to be a member of any musical council from which the greatest musicians of the country are excluded. I ask you to be kind enough to publish this statement in your columns.

Thanking you in anticipation for your kindness, I am,

Yours respectfully,
BÉLA BARTÓK

[Original in Hungarian]

112. TO GÉZA RÉVÉSZ—ROSTOCK

[1] *Vésztő, August* 22nd, 1920

Dear Friend,

You will appreciate that I have only just received your letter of July 15. It is my intention to write to Hornbostel immediately, without waiting for his letter to arrive, for the postcard makes quite clear what it is that he wants and the information he needs. It would be meaningless, of course, to publish anything without giving musical examples.

If you only knew what a wind you sowed by giving the article about Hunyad folk-music to Einstein, I don't know if it would make you laugh or cry. I was attacked savagely about it in May; the battle raged in 2 or 3 newspapers; Mr. Hubay, too, considered it his duty to air his views and show how well-informed he is. I also made a statement—*senza sordino!*—and finally the Ethnographic Society took *my* side!

Of course, I'm not worried about these things. My trouble is that, from Sept. on, it seems as if I'll have to start teaching again, and that there seems to be no end to all our miseries.

As regards earning a living, I have no difficulty—thanks to my Berlin trip I've had a ten-thousand-word article with musical examples accepted by the *Musical Quarterly* of New York, which will mean 120 dollars approximately. (It seems one shouldn't go to Berlin but rather to America.) But there's all the difference between 'earning a living' and 'living'; and as long as only the first is possible, there's bound to be trouble.

We are living in Budapest now, gratis, in two rooms in a flat, which we were given simply as a favour. Gyopár utca 2.

So Ani is in Rostock, too; or do you only mean that she *has been* there?

You will perhaps be interested to learn that Kodály has been restored to his position as a professor. So they didn't dare, after all——

But, of course, that doesn't in the least alter the basic situation.

Alas, I have no plans either; it would be too difficult to explain in a letter why this is so.

We are always hoping to hear from you, so do please write occasionally. With best regards,

Yours,
BARTÓK

[Original in Hungarian]

113. TO JÁNOS BUȘIȚIA—BELÉNYES

[12] *Budapest, I. Gyopár u. 2.*
May 8th, 1921

Dear Professor,
At last some news of you! No, we certainly didn't receive the two letters you mention—only the last one, dated April 21. For my part, I haven't even tried to write, for we all knew that postal communications between the two countries had been suspended.

It has been an eventful period for us. We have had some pleasant experiences, but mostly bad ones about which, of course, I cannot write.

In a nutshell: we couldn't go on staying at Rákoskeresztúr, so we had to accept the invitation when one of our acquaintances kindly offered us two rooms in his villa in Budapest (at the above address). Although we have everything we need here, we have no household of our own; and in spite of this, living expenses for the three of us are twice my year's salary. So I have to devote all my spare time to money-making. I play the piano at concerts, write articles for foreign periodicals, and I'm writing books about the folk-music of Hungary and other countries, etc. It is obvious that, in these circumstances, I have no time for composing, even if I were in the right mood for it. But my mood is far from right—and no wonder. The fact is, I am homeless: it is impossible to get any kind of a flat, and even if I could find one, I wouldn't be able to afford it. And I am hopelessly cut off from the one thing which is as necessary to me as fresh air is to other people—the possibility of going on with my studies of folk-music in the countryside. There's no time or money for it! It now seems that nowhere in the world is there any real interest in this work. I've made every attempt to find some opening, and I would have gone *anywhere* I was invited if there had been the opportunity of going on with this sort of work.

Yet at this moment my compositions are arousing interest abroad. In November I was the subject of a 12-page (approx.) article in a London music periodical in which the writer placed me in the ranks of the world's greatest composers, not merely the greatest living composers but of all time. The most important musical journal in Paris, the *Revue Musicale* also had a nice, 10-page article about me in March; and two other English periodicals and an Italian one will also be writing about my works. I am negotiating my own articles with 1 Italian, 2 English, 1 French and 2 American musical journals. The best of the music periodicals printed in German (it is actually Austrian), the *Anbruch* of Vienna, published a whole 'Bartók' number – – – all this, however, is but a moral victory. And anyhow, even if they were to make me the High Pope of Music, it would be no help to me so long as I remain cut off from peasant music.

I may add that I have no cause for complaint against my compatriots either. Some of them may not have acted fairly towards me; but others have tried to make up for this with all the more zeal, so that this year, for instance, two composer's evenings were devoted to my works, and I have signed contracts to write 3 books (about Hungarian, Slovak and Rumanian peasant music). And, a few days ago, I signed an agreement with our Opera House for something I began some time ago – – – so people are trying to help me, but they haven't much power either. And they are unable to do anything about the basic trouble. I am very glad to have your invitation for a summer holiday. I would gladly go, for I very much need a breath of mountain air which I haven't enjoyed since 1918. But now it's a question of money. Please let me know exactly how much it would cost per day to have a holiday either at Biharfüred or some other place.

I could afford 200 to 250 Hungarian Kr. a day for a few weeks; the Hungarian Kr. has substantially improved in value lately, so it should be possible to manage that. By the way, I spent Easter in Pozsony, visiting my mother, and I also made enquiries there about the possibilities of summer holidays in some Slovak village in the mountains. But I won't know about that before May.

You say that at Örvényes the cylinders are eagerly waiting to be filled by the collectors.

But no one is allowed to take phonographs across the frontier, neither one way nor the other! They wouldn't even let me bring my own note-books through! The most I could hope for would be to procure some special permits from heaven knows how many different authorities, and that only after I don't know how many weeks of running around for them! No, the curtain has been drawn over that work. My only regret is for 2 cylinders of the Örvényes recordings. These are entirely unique—the alphorn of Bihar, of which there are no other recordings in existence. If only I had a phonograph to help me to note them down! For there's no possibility of getting those 2 cylinders home: they would be confiscated at the frontier. I wonder if I could get a phonograph from somewhere just to do that. Once I had taken down the notes, I would gladly give up all claim to the cylinders.

I would be very glad if we could arrange to have our trip to Bihar this summer; I have so much to tell you, and I would also be tremendously interested to see what conditions are like there. So I am looking forward to an early reply, and meantime send you my best wishes.

BÉLA BARTÓK

[Original in Hungarian]

114. TO GÉZA RÉVÉSZ—AMSTERDAM

[From Mrs. Béla Bartók, *née* Márta Ziegler]

[2] *Budapest, March* 3rd, 1922

Dear Professor,

I believe your sister wrote to tell you that she had phoned me on the very day that we received your letter to B.; so you will know that it is because B. has been on a tour in Transylvania that he hasn't been able to answer you yet. Now, he is not only very busy (he has to get the visas and go on with his practising), but he is also tired after his trip; that is why I'm writing for him.

It would be very difficult to arrange the lecture you write about. It isn't that the material isn't there, but that it hasn't been sorted out, and now there is no time to arrange it, for B. leaves for London on the 8th. However, he would be pleased to go to Holland, and we are wondering if it wouldn't be possible to arrange a *concert* for him? It is like this: He'll be in Paris till April 12; then his Frankfurt première has been fixed for April 30, and his composer's evening for April 24 (he has to be in Frankfurt by April 20); thus he would have 8 days between leaving Paris and the date when he has to be in Frankfurt—just time enough for a trip to Holland. Otherwise, he would have to spend this period in some cheaper German town.

The following questions now arise: could a concert be arranged? If so, could a sum be secured to cover his travelling expenses—a rather substantial sum, for he would have to go through Belgium.

The programme for the concert would include only items for the piano. It might perhaps be possible to include four simple Székely folk-songs (with B. accompanying); they are not difficult, we have a German translation at our disposal, and they can be sung by a man or a woman, it doesn't matter; a mezzo-soprano or a baritone would be the best, but the songs could be transposed if necessary. B. could send them from England sometime during March.

Please send your reply to all this to London, addressing the letter to Jelly Arányi (18 Elm Park Gardens, London S.W. 10.). B. won't be living there, but all his letters are being sent to that address. Actually he won't have a permanent address, as he'll be the guest of a different family every week.

Your letter gave me great pleasure; it's very rare for someone to take matters in hand like this and do everything so thoroughly. And B. is very grateful for your invitation and happy to think that he will meet you—he only regrets that you won't be coming to Frankfurt. Couldn't you manage that even now? His new Sonata for piano and violin (composed this autumn) is also to be heard there, as well as his new pieces for the piano, composed last year. (The Sonata is not possible for Amsterdam, as B. cannot spare the copy because of Frankfurt.)

You see, I, for instance, would be only *too pleased* to go if I could. But it's impossible. I'm not complaining—as long as I am well, I don't complain. Anyway, I'll have enough to keep myself busy here: while B. is away, we're going to move into a new flat. You ask me how I am. Quite well, except that I seem to have lost something of my former resilience. Well, there's nothing to be done about that; I'm growing older. And even rubber will go if it's stretched too often.

With all good wishes—and my thanks for helping B.

MÁRTA BARTÓK

[Original in Hungarian]

115. TO GÉZA RÉVÉSZ—AMSTERDAM

[3] [*Budapest*] *March* 9th, 1922

[*Postcard* from Mrs. Béla Bartók, *née* Márta Ziegler]

Dear Professor,

This is only a postscript to my recent letter. B. wonders if you would be so kind as to enquire what he would need to go from Paris to Holland? A Dutch visa? Or only a few lines such as you sent to B. for the consul here? For B. has not tried to get a visa to Holland here, as he wasn't sure whether the concert in Amsterdam could be arranged or not. Please write to him to London about this; to the address I gave you in my letter.

B. left yesterday morning—I do so hope he will have a successful trip!

All good wishes,
MÁRTA BARTÓK

PS. Egon Kornstein has just this very minute telephoned to tell me that some kind of concert was organized for them in Amsterdam through their impresario there; so we're going to send him B.'s address in London at once, so that they can write to each other direct. This in no way interferes with your plans, I hope?

[Original in Hungarian]

116. TO HIS MOTHER, MRS. BÉLA BARTÓK—POZSONY

[25] *Aberystwyth, March* 16th, 1922

Dear Mother and Aunt Irma,

Here I am, on the west coast of England, or rather, of Wales. The 2 huge windows of my room look out over the sea—down below the waves roar, and it is marvellously sunny. Aberystwyth is a little university town with a pop. of 10,000, and it's here that I am playing tonight. The day before yesterday, I gave a 'private recital' in London, at the Hungarian 'Minister's' (or Consul's?) residence; it was arranged by the Arányis. Although it was not open to the public, *The Times* printed a review on the following day, and a very favourable one, too. My arrival had already been reported—in the *Daily Telegraph* and the *Daily Mail*, and in 2 music periodicals. People had shown a good deal of interest before I arrived, and I had a very warm welcome. My public recital in London has been arranged for March 24th; the concert agent is bearing the risk. My private recital, the day before yesterday, brought in about £30; I have to give 2 more performances in private houses (at £10 each); here in Aberystwyth, I'll earn £15 (of which I receive £10 net). As my fare here and back will not come to more than £15, and as I am staying here as the guest of a very friendly couple (I haven't been spending money on anything at all so far) and expect to receive a total of 1,500 francs in Paris, it looks as if I shall be able to bring lots of money home with me. Part of the money I will leave with you on my way home—that is, I will cash the cheque there [Pozsony]. The day before yesterday, I met a man named Lobkovitz who is something or other at the Czech Legation; I'll pay him a visit, in case he's able to help me get a Czech visa. If the worst comes to the worst, I'll come and see you on a transit visa which one can get without difficulties, and in that case I'll stop over for 24 hours (you are allowed to do that). On April 3rd I leave for Paris.

And now I'm off to a rehearsal (I am also to play a Beethoven trio here).

Much love,
B.

[Original in Hungarian]

117. TO HIS MOTHER, MRS. BÉLA BARTÓK—POZSONY

[26] *London, March* 20th, 1922

Dear Mother and Aunt Irma,
Your letter arrived the day before yesterday. I shall probably not need the certificate; I am trying to get a visa here—the man I mentioned in my letter the other day, Lobkovitz (he's a prince), tells me that I can get one for a long stay.

It's quite astounding that my first private recital (March 14th) has had so much space given to it in the press; *The Times* devoted a second article to it—I am enclosing it with this letter: try and take it to A.—there may be someone there who could translate it for you. It is quite something that the papers are treating my coming here as some exceptional event. I would really never have hoped for this. I meet an awful lot of people, so that I am getting quite confused. Last night, I went to a frightfully 'distinguished' party (i.e. all musicians and critics) given by a rich woman, a singer. I played there, too. Today I lunched with some French people. I have to speak first French, then English (sometimes German); I falter away as best I can, but I get all mixed up by having to keep changing from one language to another.

I have no idea yet when I shall come to Pozsony. Maybe only after the first performance in Frankfurt.

L.
B.

Yesterday I was interviewed by the *Pall Mall Gazette* (an evening paper). Tomorrow I'm to be photographed for the papers.

[Original in Hungarian]

118. TO GÉZA RÉVÉSZ—AMSTERDAM

[4]

c/o Miss Jelly Arányi,
[18 Elm Park Gardens, S.W. 10.]
London, March 22nd, 1922

My dear Friend,
I hasten to reply to your letter which arrived today.

I'm very pleased that you have succeeded in arranging the concert. The earliest date on which I could leave Paris is Apr. 10. I cannot put off my business there to a later date. It would be best to fix the date of the concert for Apr. 19, 20, 21 or at the very latest the 22nd. If none of these dates is possible, April 12 would be all right for me, or anything in between (though I'm afraid this period would not be very suitable because of the Easter holidays).

Jelly Arányi, the violinist, with whom I have already played my new violin Sonata here, and who will be with me again on April 8 in Paris, is also ready and willing, gratis and without any reimbursement of travelling expenses, etc., to play this Sonata (which, by the way, she does magnificently) with me in Amsterdam. I am tremendously pleased about this, for it will enable me to draw up a more interesting programme.

I don't know anything about the Kornstein plan for a concert—nor about Fenyves's appearance here.

I'll post the four Székely Songs from here on the 25th. Would you be so kind as to let me know, as soon as possible, the date finally agreed for the concert. I should like to know something definite about it while I'm still here (I leave on April 3). My address will remain as above. I cannot at the moment write more fully about my English tour; I can only say that the newspapers have given me a lot of space, *The Times* carried a long article about my Sonata and a photograph of me, etc.

Here is the programme:

I. a. Ungarische Bauerntänze
  b. 1. Burlesque (. . . un peu gris . . .) aus op. 8c
  c. Abend am Lande
  d. Bärentanz
  e. Allegro barbaro
  f. 1. Nénie
  g. 3. Burlesque (aus op. 8c)

II. 4 ungarische Volkslieder mit Klavierbegleitung
III. Sonate für Viol. und Kl. (op. 21)
Allegro appassionato–Adagio–Allegro vivace
IV. a. 8 Improvisationen über ungarische Volksmelodien (op. 20)
b. Suite (op. 14)
Allegretto–Scherzo–Allegro vivace–Sostenuto
c. 1. Rumänischer Tanz (aus op. 8a)

Could you also find a room for me in an *inexpensive* hotel, and one for Jelly Arányi (a double bedroom for her, as she is travelling with her mother), and to write me in Paris, giving the name of the hotel (I'll send you my address in Paris later).

Many greetings,
BÉLA BARTÓK

N. B. We should much prefer Apr. 18[1], 20, 21[2] or 22 rather than the 12th. I think this would suit you better, too.

[Original in Hungarian]

119. TO HIS MOTHER, MRS. BÉLA BARTÓK—BUDAPEST

[27] *Paris, April* 15th, 1922

Dear Mama,
I've received your postcard. I'm afraid it's rather long since I wrote, but I just couldn't. My recital on the 8th went off well. Afterwards I was invited to a dinner at Prunières', which was attended by over half the 'leading composers of the world'—that is, Ravel, Szymanowski, Stravinsky—as well as a few young (notorious) Frenchmen whom you would not know. Most of them were very enthusiastic about the Sonata for violin, and not less so about Jelly's playing, for she 'excelled herself' that evening. N.B. the concert was at 5 p.m., and the Sonata was performed once again after dinner at Prunières' for the benefit of the select company I've just mentioned. Prunières says I must come to Paris again next year, and he will try to get me about 3,000 francs' worth of engagements. (That would leave me 1,500 francs net profit.) Today I shall be dining with Hungarians, including the Hungarian *ambassadeur* in Paris. There have been fewer press notices here—something has appeared (or will

[1] Insertion encircled in pencil.
[2] Encircled in pencil.

appear), in 4 newspapers all told. For instance, on Easter Monday there will be a long article in *Le Temps* (perhaps you can get hold of a copy somewhere). Tomorrow I leave for Frankfurt—you can write to me there c/o Eugen Szenkár, Beethovenstrasse 50/a, Frankfurt am Main. I shall only be there until the 26th, and then on to Pozsony (because, unfortunately, the first performance has been postponed until May 6th, and I can't possibly stay on there until then).

L.
B.

[Original in Hungarian]

120. TO HIS MOTHER, MRS. BÉLA BARTÓK

[28] *Kassa, April* 5th, 1923

Dear Mother and Aunt Irma,
At last—after every kind of calamity—we succeeded in giving our concert here. We only got our visas in the most roundabout fashion. Then 20 minutes before the opening some officials came and wanted to stop the concert because permission from this or that *ministerstvo* had not been obtained; but in the end they graciously allowed us to proceed—on this one occasion only.

The platform was so shaky that the chair, the piano and the music-stand began to dance about whenever anyone moved. There was hardly enough room to put a chair on it for the man who turned the pages for me; so that I kept on hitting him in the stomach with my left elbow. The steps up to the platform were missing; they improvised one with a chair and a well-scrubbed kitchen-stool; these, Waldbauer and I climbed up and down to the delight of the audience. The programme was full of mistakes (because they'd lost one of my letters): it said Brahms's D minor Sonata, and, instead of Handel, the *Bear's Dance* and Rumanian peasant dances. The platform was badly lit, the poor fellow who turned the pages for me could hardly read the notes; during my Sonata, Imre also had to have his pages turned four times, and every time there was a loud creaking from the man's footsteps, and the platform shuddered alarmingly. In one part of the Sonata, Imre forgot to remove the mute.—The violin sounded fainter and fainter and fainter—and still he didn't notice anything; there was a *fermata* during which he could have removed the thing, but he didn't—and he was getting dangerously near to an *f*, in fact an *ff*. My God, I wondered, what's going to happen here! And at last I had to shout at him: 'Take off your mute!'

To crown all, the page-turner finally knocked my music off the stand and had to pick it up from the floor. By that time I was near to bursting with laughter. Never have I had such a concert. But the hall was full; there was plenty of applause; my total earnings after deducting all expenses were 1,400 Czech Kr.; and, on the whole, it was not very tiring. I've no idea who sent this letter on which I am now filling up the blank spaces.

Now I must go to bed; we start for home at 12 tomorrow, arriving at Pest at 7 p.m.—By the way, they want me to give a concert here next year, too—a solo recital.

Love,
B.

[Original in Hungarian]

121. TO HIS MOTHER, MRS. BÉLA BARTÓK

[29]
[Picture postcard]

Malvern Wells, May 4th, 1923

In England you can give recitals at beauty spots like this village. I am playing here today—at a girls' school!!

I shall be in England till the 13th, for I am being kept busier than I expected—which is, of course, a good thing in every respect.

[Original in Hungarian]

122. TO GÉZA RÉVÉSZ — AMSTERDAM

[5]
[A joint letter from Bartók and his wife, Márta Ziegler]

[From Bartók] *Budapest, Szilágyi tér 4.*
27. 5. 1923.

Dear Friend,
I have succeeded in bringing the parcels here: we visited your father-in-law to give him his share, but he was not at home, so we left the things there[1].

The Rózsavölgyis have sent the scores to your address (in 2 separate parcels); among them is a separate, complimentary copy of the *Ady Songs* for you from me.

It is perhaps unnecessary for me to send detailed accounts. The

[1] '. . . so we left the things there . . .'—subsequent insertion made by Mrs. Bartók.

sum total (postage included) amounts to 63,102 Kr. which is equivalent to 31 florins.

So that you now have 56 florins of mine.

There really was quite a row in the newspapers about the dedication of the *Ady Songs;* it even seemed at one moment that things were about to take a serious turn (official proceedings, etc.), but things have calmed down for the time being—perhaps for good.

[From Mrs. Bartók]

I am now finishing off this letter because I want to thank you very much indeed for the wonderful coffee. And I would also like to show how repentant I am, for when I first caught sight of the coffee, I despised the Dutch a little for having roasted it so black; however, as soon as we had drunk the first cup, there was nothing for it but to ask forgiveness from the Dutch for my having been so unjust!

Béla arrived home rather tired but well pleased with his trip; he is especially pleased by the prospect of an English edition. So am I. Nothing special happened here while he was away; little Béla is very well, growing up to be strong and studying hard. I am quite all right too.

We all send every good wish to each one of you—kisses for little Juca, and please tell her that I have read her fairy-tale and liked it very much, especially when the little boy says: 'Now you should laugh, *please!*'

MÁRTA BARTÓK

And thank you very much for being so kind to Béla; he always mentions you with warm affection!

[Original in Hungarian]

123. GYULA WLASSICS—TO BÉLA BARTÓK

[Draft] [Before *October* 1st, 1923]

My dear and honoured Friend,

When *The Miraculous Mandarin* had to be dropped from our programme for last season, we hoped that you would be able to finish the work of orchestration in time for us to produce this new work in the Opera House during the coming season. I was very sorry to learn that you have again been prevented from finishing this work because of all the many engagements to which you are committed as a teacher or in your other capacities as a bread-winner.

One of the great artistic ambitions of the Opera House is to produce once again your magnificent, world-famous works; but as it has been publicly announced that their performance would be followed by a scandal in the press, we cannot, despite our best intentions, foresee any possibility of this at present. In our opinion, the best solution would be to break the ice with a performance of *The Miraculous Mandarin*. The performance of this new piece would greatly facilitate the revival of your two masterpieces that were postponed; for we expect it to be so successful and to be acclaimed so enthusiastically, both in the press and by the public, that all opposition to the author of the libretto would be completely silenced.

As a friendly gesture, in token of my sincere admiration for your work, may I offer you an advance which would relieve you of financial worries for the few months necessary for finishing the orchestration of *The Miraculous Mandarin?*

In my opinion, if you were to get down to work immediately, we could be ready with the orchestral parts by the end of December, and meanwhile the piano score, which they already have at their disposal, could be used for the company's rehearsals, so that the première could take place in the first months of 1924.

Please rest assured that we would give the production our devoted attention, respecting your artistic intentions and asking your advice in everything, from the choice of a conductor down to the last detail.

Please do me the honour of calling on me, so that we can talk things over as soon as possible. I am so confident of the outcome of this production that I'm sure it will enable the Opera House henceforth to fulfil, unhindered, its most important function—the propagation throughout Europe of new Hungarian music.

Urgently awaiting your reply, I am

Yours respectfully and sincerely,
GYULA WLASSICS

[Original in Hungarian]

124. GYULA WLASSICS—TO BÉLA BARTÓK

Royal Hungarian Opera House
Re No. 1516/923

His Honour
Béla Bartók
Professor at the Royal National Conservatory,
composer, etc.
Szilágyi tér 4
Budapest

Budapest, October 1st, 1923

Honoured Sir,
When *The Miraculous Mandarin* had to be dropped from last year's programme, we confidently expected that you would be able to finish

the work of orchestration in the course of the summer, and that we should be in a position to perform your cherished work this season. I have been disappointed to learn—albeit at second-hand, since I could obtain no direct information—that our expectations have not been fulfilled. You, Sir, will appreciate with what feelings of regret I find myself unable, at present, for reasons outside my control, to carry out my intention of including your earlier, esteemed works, *The Wooden Prince* and *Bluebeard's Castle* in our repertoire. At the same time, I can assure you that, once we have removed the obstacles with which you are already familiar—and we now have reason to be more hopeful of doing this—I will seek ways and means at the very earliest possible moment of putting back into the repertoire of the Roy. Hung. Opera House your very precious works which are so much appreciated not only personally by myself but also by the majority of the art-loving and discerning public; and I will produce them with the utmost care and devotion.

However, until I am able to put my good intentions into practice, I earnestly request you, at whatever cost, to finish the orchestration of *The Miraculous Mandarin* and to be so kind as to let us have the complete work, so that we should be in a position to perform it in the middle of the 1924–25 season. If your financial circumstances prevent you from accomplishing whatever yet remains to be done, I need hardly emphasize that I will gladly try to meet any wish you may have for the payment of a larger advance on the performing fees; I should also be only too pleased if I can help you in any other way.

I await your reply with eager anticipation and, meantime, would like to convey my warmest good wishes.

Yours respectfully and sincerely,
GYULA WLASSICS
Chief Director

[Original in German]

125. TO EDWARD JOSEPH DENT

Budapest, Szilágyi tér 4.
October 2nd, 1923

Dear Mr. Dent,
I am gladly prepared to sit on the Society's jury next year. However, there are two things I must mention. In the first place, I can only make the trip to Zurich for the session if all my travelling expenses are reimbursed. In the second place, if I should be offered unpostponable engagements, at present unforeseen, for the end of

February, then I should be unable to take part. For, as you perhaps know, my circumstances are not very favourable at present, so that it is imperative for me to give concerts or do anything else which brings in money. So if the Society would like to have me as one of the judges, I am ready and willing to participate, provided I could withdraw should there arise any such eventuality as I have mentioned.

It would of course make things much easier for me if I could send my vote by post. Would it not be possible to do this?

I look forward to hearing from you.

Yours sincerely,
BÉLA BARTÓK

[Original in Hungarian]

126. GYULA WLASSICS—TO BÉLA BARTÓK

Royal Hungarian Opera House
Re No. 712/924

His Honour
Béla Bartók
Professor at the Royal National Conservatory,
composer, etc.
Szilágyi tér 4,
Budapest

Budapest, May 27th, 1924

Honoured Sir,

Before coming to the end of our current season at the Opera House, I should like to conclude my arrangements for next season's artistic programme by enriching our repertoire with a production of your *Miraculous Mandarin.*

However, we have, I'm afraid, only the libretto and the piano score of this work in our possession so far.

Before we can start rehearsing, we would have to have the parts copied, and as this should be completed sometime during the summer, I beg you to be so kind as to send us the score as soon as possible.

An early reply would be much appreciated. Meantime I remain,

Yours respectfully and sincerely,
GYULA WLASSICS
Chief Director

[Original in Hungarian]

127. TO GYULA WLASSICS—BUDAPEST

[2] *Budapest, Szilágyi tér 4.*
June 5th, 1924

Dear Sir,
In reply to your letter received at the beginning of this week, I have to inform you that although I have not yet been able to finish *The Miraculous Mandarin,* I have at last managed to begin writing the score so that I shall be in a position to deliver the first half to the Opera House, ready for copying, around July 15, and the second half, around August 15.

Yours respectfully,
BÉLA BARTÓK

[Original in Hungarian]

128. TO JÁNOS BUȘIȚIA—DELÉNYES

[13] *Budapest, Szilágyi tér 4.*
May 15th, 1925

My dear Friend,
I am writing to ask a great favour. I am preparing for the press my collection of Rumanian *colindas,* and I find that I forgot to take down the names of some Rumanian villages; would you be so good as to insert these in the enclosed list and, if possible, return the list within a few weeks?

I think I told you, at the time, for whom I'm preparing this collection for the press. When I was in Bucharest, in the autumn, it turned out that, actually, the most they can do at the moment is to purchase the material; there's no money for printing it, and it is quite uncertain when they will be able to give it to the printers. The head of the Music Department of a British publishing house, the Oxford University Press, was here recently; he would like to publish this collection in London. He is going to talk to the Bucharest people about it. This solution would be very much to my liking, and I think the people in Bucharest would like it, too. For the Oxford Univ. Press is a firm known throughout the world; and everyone takes notice of its publications.

You know, don't you, that since I last saw you, I have been awarded the 1st class of the order of merit known as *Bene Merenti!* What do you say to that? After the Rumanian tour I had very little work to take me abroad—I'm afraid the concert season was very poor this time. I only went to Prague and Brno; and in March I did an Italian tour which took me right down to Palermo. There's no need for me to tell you what a beautiful trip it was.

How are you? Getting ready to go up to Stâna once again? I'll never get there again, it seems; it's impossible this year anyway.

Best wishes,
BARTÓK.

[Original in Hungarian]

129. TO JENŐ TAKÁCS—BREMEN

[1] *Budapest, Szilágyi tér 4.*
December 31st, 1925

Dear Sir,
I am sorry I have not replied to your letter earlier; however, in reply to your postcard, I think the Zagreb programme is entirely satisfactory, and so is your project for Bremen. What we must be careful to avoid is any attempt to put on such works as my two Sonatas for violin or the piano Études and improvisations in places where the level of music appreciation is as low as it is in Hungarian country towns. Such works would merely rouse antagonism in an audience which has not been trained to listen.

Finally, as far as the performing fees are concerned, there is absolutely nothing I can do about this, as it is handled solely by the Gesellschaft der Autoren, Komponisten und Musikverleger.

Yours faithfully,
BÉLA BARTÓK

[Original in German]

130. TO CONSTANTIN BRĂILOIU—BUCHAREST

[1] *Budapest, Szilágyi tér 4.*
May 6th, 1926

Dear Mr. Brăiloiu,
A few days ago I sent you two copies of Tibolt Schmidt's article about Rumanian *colinda* texts. It also contains some unknown texts from Schmidt's collection, namely on pp. 11, 12, 14, 15, 16, 17, 18, 19, 20, 21, 22, 23, 24, 25, 31, 33, 34, 37, 39, 40, 48 and 49 (No. 1), 50, 51. It seems that this booklet is unknown in Bucharest, so I sent you two copies so that you could keep one for yourself and donate the other to a library. I find I have yet another spare copy

which I could also send to you if you would like it. The remaining texts in the article are quoted from various publications.

The manuscript of my *colinda* collection, now ready for the press (with preface, introductions, annotations, etc.), I at last handed in, on April 29, to the Rumanian Legation here; they said they would send it to Bucharest within a fortnight. I should be very grateful if you could let me know when the manuscript arrives and confirm that nothing is missing.

It contains:

1.	Preface and Introduction to the music examples	28 pages
2.	Music examples (on music-paper)	56 pages
3.	Annotations to the melodies	11 pages
4.	Introduction to the Texts	
5.	Annotations to Texts	
6.	List of refrains	27 pages
7.	List of localities, performers	
8.	Texts	501 separate pages

and an additional two pages of 'Instructions' for the printers.

I should also be very grateful if you would let me have your comments on that part of the 'Introduction to the music examples' in which I set out certain rules concerning the metrics of the texts (pp. 3–5?), and if you would draw my attention to any errors I may have made.

As I say, the manuscript is ready for the press as is the copy which I have sent to London. There is only one difference between the two, namely that in the 'Texts' of the Bucharest copy i and u figure throughout, instead of the semi-vowels ĭ and ŭ. (You'll find a note about this in the 'Introduction to the Texts', under the heading '*Orthography*'; I write there that I have also used ĭ and ŭ signs!) So if the material is ever printed from the Bucharest copy, *either* these semi-vowel (or mute) i's and u's would have to be changed into ĭ's and ŭ's, *or* the corresponding remark would have to be deleted from the 'Introduction to the Texts'. N. B. In the London copy I've used ĭ and ŭ throughout.

I had a letter from the London publishers recently, in which they assure me again that they want to bring out the work. I told you when I was in Bucharest about my conversation with Goga, didn't I? Now he has in fact been made Minister (not Min. of Culture but at least of the Interior); so that perhaps there may be a possibility now of publishing the work in Rumanian, too. In my opinion, the English publishers would be able to produce it for a comparatively moderate sum. For the 'Music examples', the 'Texts' and the two lists could be used for both editions; so one would have to engrave, or set up, these parts only once. Only the Rumanian version of the parts marked 1, 3, 4 and 5 in the manuscript would have to be set up separately, i.e. scarcely more than 40 pages when printed. Hence, it would be reasonable to write from Bucharest to the publishers in London to ask under what conditions they would be prepared to bring out a Rumanian edition parallel with the English one. If they are prepared to come to an agreement, one would only have to send to London the Rumanian translation of the parts in question. Here is the address of the publishers:

Mr. Hubert J. Foss,
Oxford University Press,
Amen House, Warwick Square,
London, E.C.4.

I have written to you, on this occasion, in German, as I find it easier; but it goes without saying that you can write to me in French, just as before! Can I hope to see you in Budapest?

Many greetings,

Yours sincerely,
BÉLA BARTÓK

[Original in German]

131. TO CONSTANTIN BRĂILOIU—BUCHAREST

[2] *Budapest, Szilágyi tér 4.*
June 27th, 1926

Dear Mr. Brăiloiu,
As I did not receive your letter from Cluj until June 14, there was no way of getting a reply to you before you yourself would probably have left for Zurich. So I was hoping that when you went to Zurich, you would visit me on your way; alas, nothing came of it.

In answer to your query about the publication of my *colinda* collection by the Societatea Compozitorilor, I can only answer that it would make me very happy indeed if that Society were to bring out this work.

I gladly comply with your request for the corrected form of the melodies you marked; you will find these in the present letter.[1]

[1] Brăiloiu had asked Bartók for the corrected forms of a few songs of the

I no longer possess the entirely correct form of the *colinda* entitled 'Întreabă și 'ntreaba', as I have sent the two manuscripts, corrected for press, to London and Bucharest, respectively. However, you can easily find it in the copy at Bucharest (for it must undoubtedly have arrived there by now), under No. [—]

I shall be leaving Budapest on July 5, returning sometime towards the middle of August. Till then my address is:

László major
Orosháza, Hungary

Many greetings,
Yours sincerely,
BÉLA BARTÓK

Bihar collection, Bartók quotes these at the end of the letter published here (on the third page of the letter paper). In this volume we make a comparison of these 1926 variants with the notations to be found in the original 1913 edition. On the following pages we have quoted the original notations on the left side, and the new, more accurate variants on the right. In this manner it is possible for us to make very interesting comparisons.

[1913]

Colindul Copiilor

Vivo
Leleşd (Lelesd)
1
Ler Doamne Sfân-tă Ma-ri e, Dom-ni Domn.

F. 691 a.
Andante
Crişţior (Kristyor)
5
Du-su-s'a (etc.)
rit.
lunga
poco allargando

Rubato
Dragoneşd (Drágánfalva)
32
lunga

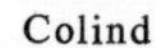
Colind

F. 885 b.
Poco allegro
Câmp.
33
gliss.

Poco rubato
Leleşd
49

[1926]

32 *unchanged*

49 *unchanged*

F. 694 a.
Molto rubato
Crişţior
131
gliss.
gliss.

F. 672 b.
Poco lento, rubato
Delan
134

F. 733 b.
Sostenuto
Şebiş
163

Colind

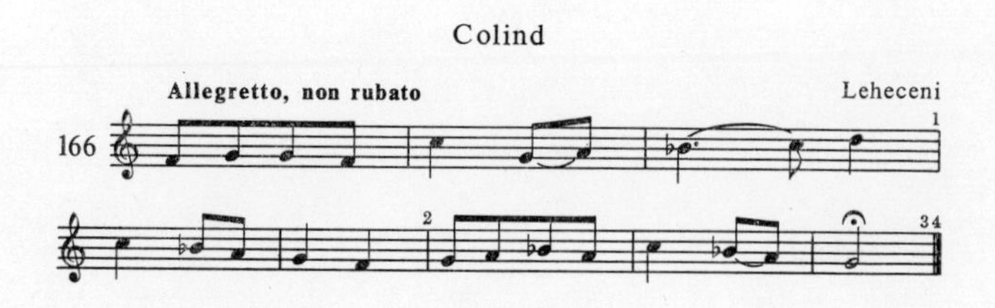
Allegretto, non rubato
Leheceni
166

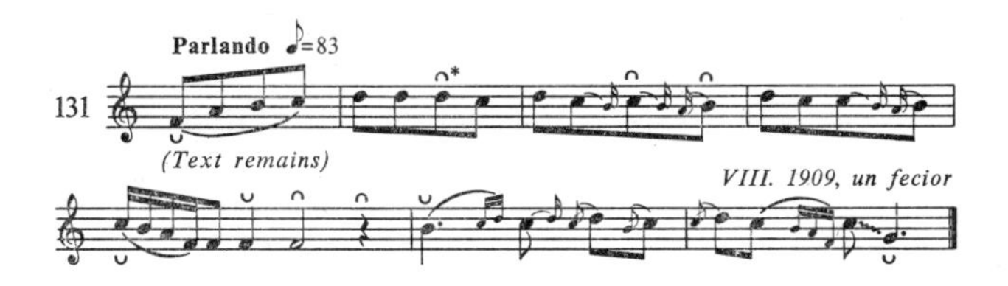

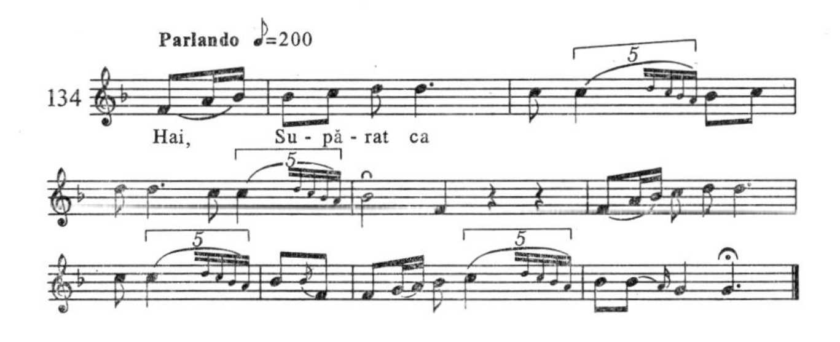

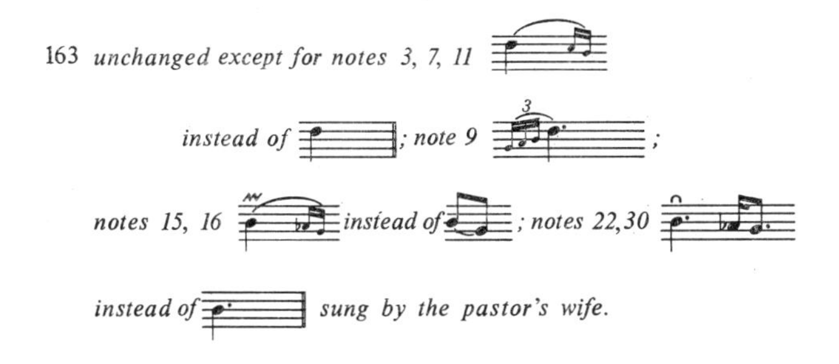

166 *unchanged*

* Bartók's explanatory indications include signs of an elongation of slight value ⌒ (♪, ♪) and of a slight shortening ◡ (♪, ♪)

(Page LXXI point 2 of 'A Magyar Népdal' (The Hungarian Folk-Song), and page XXXII point 5 of the volume of *colinda*).

[1913]

Cântec de Mireasă

F. 698 b.

Andante rubato

Cristior

177

F. 684 a.

Molto largo, non rubato

Leheceni

195

Bocet (vaet)

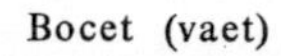

F. 674 c.

Quasi recitativo

Delan

199

Colind

F. 737 a.

Andante molto

Şebiş

207

[1926]

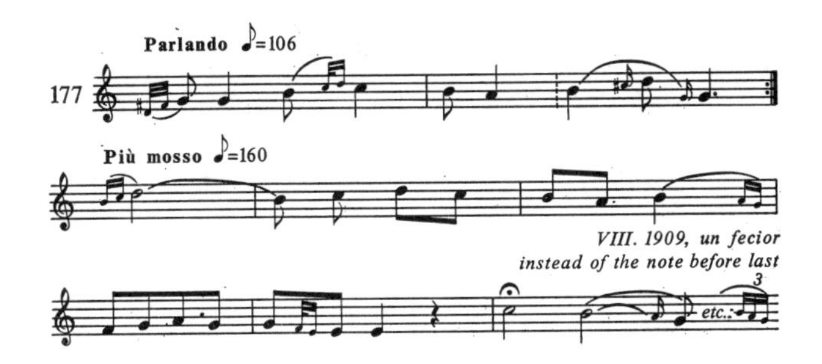

195 VIII. 1909, fete. **Tempo giusto** ♪=94

unchanged except for notes 14, 15 [music] *instead of*

[music] ; *last note* [music]

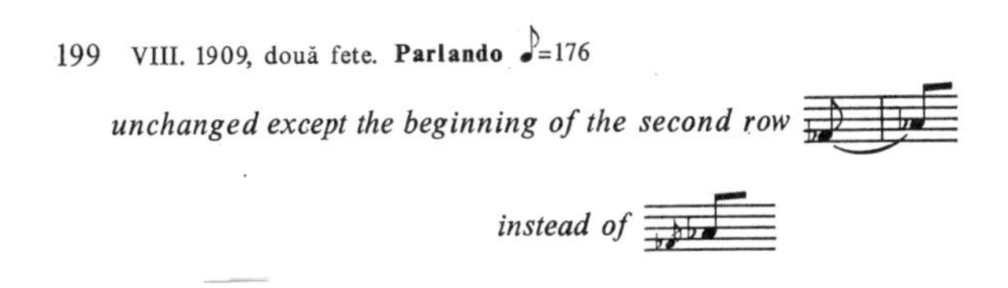

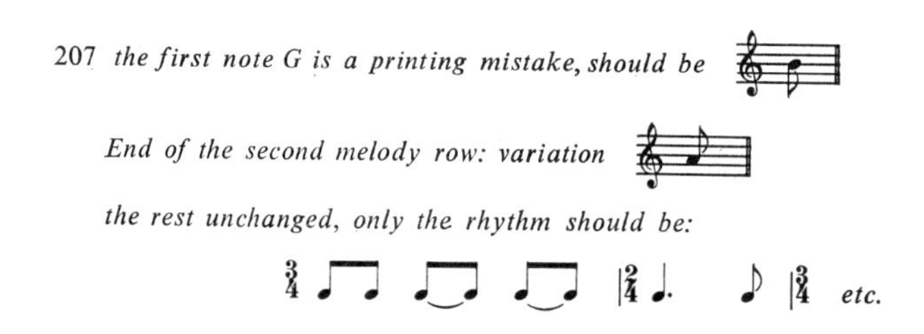

[Original in Hungarian]

132. TO ANTAL FLEISCHER—JUDENDORF BEI GRAZ

[1]
[Postcard: Pension Edelweiss]

Courmayeur, July 26th, 1926

Dear Mr. Fleischer,
It is only after some considerable delay that I have received your letter, as it was first sent on to Békés County and then here. Alas, I can't accept the Barcelona engagement, for it would take up too much of my time, quite out of proportion to the net profit. If my time were my own, this would be no great matter; but as I can't devote more than 5 or 6 weeks a year to concerts, I have to be very careful to avoid any unnecessary loss of time. I dare not risk posting from here the Barcelona letter which you enclosed; you may have left Judendorf by the time this letter gets there, and in the end it might get lost while being forwarded from one place to the next. On August 5 I'll be in Budapest again, and I will immediately send the letter to your address at the Opera House.

Yours very sincerely,
BÉLA BARTÓK

IV

AT THE HEIGHT OF HIS CAREER

1927–1940

During the period from 1927 to 40 Bartók's compositions showed a marked increase and power; he composed prolifically and successfully.

The compositions of this period manifest explosive force: the *First* and the *Second Rhapsody for Violin and Piano*, of the *First Rhapsody* even a version for 'cello and piano; *Twenty Hungarian Folk-Songs* for voice and piano accompaniment; the *Cantata Profana* for tenor and baritone soli, double chorus and orchestra; the *Second Piano Concerto*. In these years he undertook still more extensive concert tours. After 1933 he avoided Germany but frequently visited England, France, Switzerland, the Netherlands and on several occasions Italy, although, as explained in the letters addressed to Frau Müller-Widmann, the political system of the latter country was distasteful to him.

From his earlier letters we know that around the year 1912 Bartók made no public appearances in Budapest. This withdrawal was repeated: in the years 1930–34 he gave no concerts in Budapest and for a few more years played no composition of his own at his recitals. His programmes were made up chiefly of the works of Bach, Mozart and Beethoven. Hungarian official organizations and musical associations behaved offensively towards Bartók on a number of occasions. One scandalous episode involved the cancellation of a performance of *The Miraculous Mandarin*, planned for his fiftieth birthday. Again, in 1935, he was to be officially honoured—for the *First Suite for Orchestra* written thirty years earlier, in a youthful, romantic style. Angered, Bartók refused this honour in an open letter (see Letter No. 187).

In 1936 Bartók visited Turkey to collect folk-songs.

It should be noted here that very little of the folk-music collected was made known to the public during Bartók's life, and even today, more than two decades after his death, there has been no serious attempt to remedy this state of affairs. Thus the inspiring sources, to which we owe his art, have remained hidden from his contemporaries to this day. The indifference of Bartók's compatriots to Hungarian folk-music is a startling reflection on the period. The fact that in 1935 he had to publish his collection of Rumanian *colindas* at his own expense in Vienna is no less painful. Efforts to have the volume published failed both in Britain and in Rumania. The frustrations Bartók experienced with his collection of Slovak tunes is an illustration of what happens when the difficulties inherent in this type of publication—intellectual, linguistic and technical—are aggravated by chauvinist narrow-mindedness. (Publication of this collection began at Bratislava in 1959.)

Together with the simplicity of folk-music, the world of children was also of absorbing interest to someone of Bartók's complex artistic personality. In the 1930s he finished several series in which he developed and summarized an earlier series *For Children* written in his first great creative period. The *Forty-four Duets for Violin* (1931), the *Twenty-seven Two and Three-part Choruses for Children's and Female Choirs* (1935), and also the cycle *Mikrokosmos*, including 153 piano pieces (1926–39), are not transcriptions of folk-songs but expressions in miniature of Bartók's poetic world which found its pure source of inspiration in folk-music, as expressed in his superb composition, the *Cantata Profana*.

Three works commissioned in Basle were composed in this important period, namely *Music for Strings, Percussion and Celesta* (1936), *Sonata for Two Pianos and Percussion* (1937) and *Divertimento for String Orchestra* (1939). It was also at this time that he wrote *Contrasts for Violin, Clarinet and Piano* (1938) for József Szigeti and Benny Goodman, and his major *Violin Concerto* (1937–38) for Zoltán Székely. These works were produced just before the outbreak of the Second World War, in an atmosphere of growing tension.

His new string quartets, the Third, 1927, the Fourth, 1928, the Fifth, 1934, the Sixth, 1939, are masterpieces which mark an important stage in the development of his art; they embrace and mirror the years of Bartók's mature creative period; through them we gain an insight into the composer's vision of the world. Constituting as they do a unity, they may indeed be said to belong to the most significant compositions of the century.

The letters of this period, notwithstanding the complexity of their subject-matter, actually deal with a single theme: Bartók's struggle to achieve the aim he had set himself.

[Original in Hungarian]

133. TO ANTAL FLEISCHER—BARCELONA

[2]

[Picture postcard: 'Hotel Roma', Vicenza, Corso P. Umberto]

Budapest, Szilágyi tér 4
March 12th, 1927

Dear Sir,

I am sorry I was not able to meet you before you left. You did take the parts and the scores with you, didn't you? I am not going to Paris; I leave Budapest on the 20th in the afternoon and arrive in Barcelona on the 23rd, at 7.55 a.m.; would you please be so kind as to book a room for me in the Victoria Hotel, a simple one if possible.

Many greetings till we meet again,

Yours,
BÉLA BARTÓK

[Original in Hungarian]

134. TO HIS MOTHER, MRS. BÉLA BARTÓK

[30]

[Picture postcard] *Philadelphia, December* 30th, 1927
(=City of Brotherly Love)

Dear Mother, Aunt Irma and Elza,

My New Year greetings come to you from this city of 2 million people. Although New York is five times as big, there is a maddening hubbub here, too.

Everywhere indoors—rooms, corridors, vestibules and railway carriages—is quite frightfully overheated. Even the taxis are heated. I am by now half-boiled in this enervating indoor-climate. Then these people consume enormous quantities of ice or rather iced water: all drinks are iced, colder than anything people drink in Hungary, even in high summer. But that's something I'm not taking to. Everything is all right so far; the only depressing thing is lack of news: all I've had is one letter from D., dated December 11th. Perhaps you could write once in a while, too.

A Happy New Year to you; love and kisses, B.

Leaving for California on Jan. 2nd, and will be at the farthest point from you about Jan. 11th (in Los Angeles)—the time difference between you and me will then be 9 hours. When you are going to bed, I shall just be getting up!

[Original in Hungarian]

135. TO HIS MOTHER, MRS. BÉLA BARTÓK

[31]
[Picture postcard: Beverly Hills, California]

La Puella de Nuestra Señora la Reina de Los Angeles, January 9th, 1928

Here I am, on the coast of the Seventh Sea. And I am actually living by the seashore, in a private bungalow. The Pacific Ocean thunders outside and sometimes during the night even makes my bed shake. Yesterday I wrote D. a long account of the strange world I have found here.

My love to all of you,

BÉLA

[Original in Hungarian]

136. TO HIS MOTHER, MRS. BÉLA BARTÓK

[32] *Seattle, January* 18th, 1928

(I live somewhere here on the eleventh floor. Four elevators run up and down. No stairway to be seen.)[1]

Dear Mother, Aunt Irma and Elza!
Thank heavens I am again 'facing homewards'. I have already played in Portland (yesterday), and today I said good-bye to the 'far West' and started back for the East.

Yesterday I sent you a card from Portland, I wonder if you will get it before or after this letter.

It has really been very interesting to come so far, but now I have had enough. It is not at all tiring, this travelling to and fro; on the contrary, one gets lazy from 'doing nothing'. Sitting for days in the train, sitting around in hotels, waiting to get away, waiting for the concert to start—in these circumstances it's impossible to get into

[1] On the letterhead of the Seattle Hotel (The Olympic) Bartók drew an arrow to the building.

the mood for creative work. A few weeks are all right, but then one gets tired of it.

Everywhere the people are very friendly: they take me for drives; they want to show me all the sights; it makes them sad if the weather prevents them from doing so. They show a lot of interest, they want to progress with the times, but sometimes it is hard for them. These towns are so new, and the various cultural movements are only just taking shape. Seattle was a little place with a population of 3,000 in 1880. Today it has 400,000. The growth of Los Angeles is even more surprising: fifty years ago there were 10,000 or 20,000 inhabitants, now there are nearly 1½ million. This country is so enormous, and yet how uniform everything is! I have travelled as far as Madrid to Moscow and find exactly similar hotel furnishings, buildings, people and meals to those where I started. Apropos of food! I had pork chops for lunch today (in the dining-car), garnished with things that I can warmly recommend to Emil. They were quite ordinary pork chops, with mashed potatoes, hot beetroot, unpeeled apples cut in slices and *sprinkled with paprika*, and a large cup of white coffee! Apparently, I was supposed to eat the whole lot at once because they brought it all together, even the paprika-powdered apple, and the pork chop came on the same plate!

In Los Angeles I ate *avocado (advocate)*. This is a fruit the same size and colour as a cucumber, and soft as butter, so that it can be spread on bread. It tastes something like almonds, but not so sweet. It is one of the ingredients of the famous fruit salad (lettuce + apples + celery + pineapple + raw tomatoes + mayonnaise).

The enclosed picture of the Pacific Ocean was taken in Santa Monica (near Los Angeles). I was only able to see Santa Catalina from a distance—it lies in the sea 30 kms. away—and saw Santa Barbara from the train. I arrived in San Francisco at 8 p.m. and went immediately to a Chinese theatre. It was strange to be wandering about alone in the Chinese quarter in the evening; everything was Chinese, all the people and the signs in the street. I found the Great China Theatre very quickly (luckily its name was written in English as well as Chinese). This is the most interesting thing I have seen in this country so far. I stayed in the theatre till midnight and would so much have liked to stay to the end, but it was not possible. Heaven knows how long a play lasts there! I was the only white man there apart from one attendant. The audience was largely made up of men; there were a few women and a crowd of children of all ages.

I am writing this letter in the train between Portland and Denver; the journey takes 48 hours. Denver is in the very middle of the Continent.

Lots of kisses for all of you, BÉLA

Pro Musica, Portland Chapter
Presents
Bela Bartok
Hungarian Composer-Pianist
Tuesday Evening, January 17, 1928
Eight thirty o'clock
Little Theatre, Studio Building
West Park and Taylor

PROGRAM

TEN-MINUTE ADDRESS IN ENGLISH

I. BARTOK *a)* Suite, op. 14 (1916)
Allegretto
Scherzo
Allegro molto
Sostenuto
b) Rumanian Christmas Songs (1915)

II. KODALY *a)* Epitaphe (from op. 11) (1918)
Allegro molto (from op. 3) (1909)
BARTOK *b)* Sonata (1926)
Allegro moderato
Sostenuto e pesante
Allegro molto

III. BARTOK *a)* Burlesque, 2 (un peu gris)
b) Dirge, 1
c) Bear dance (1908–10)
d) Evening in the country
e) Allegro barbaro

Mr. Bartok uses the Baldwin Piano.
The Mason & Hamlin is the official Piano of Pro Musica, Inc.

Here's a programme for you. The 'ten-minute address'[1] is, of course, given by me. I daresay it takes 15 minutes. Already I have rattled

[1] Original text in English.

off 4 times 'Ladies and Gentlemen, etc.'[1] I shall know it by heart soon. I sit down at a small table and fire away. It's wonderful! Yet they listen quite seriously right to the end and say they can understand me. I find this set speech terribly boring; I would like to make some changes now and then, to make it sound different, but that would be beyond me.

People like the last item (group) best of all, of course—the *Bear Dance* has made people gay everywhere so far.

I shall be giving this address and play the same programme 5 times more. That's one good thing here: they demand very short programmes; for instance, the whole thing, address and all, takes exactly one and a half hours, which is really not too tiring.

Since beginning this letter I have had my supper—what do you think they gave me? Small candied gherkins! And Indian corn cake! Did you know that everyone here eats popcorn? Only they pop it over some electric machine.

Good night! Tonight at last I have to put my watch on again one hour, and so the difference between my time and yours will have been reduced to *only* 8 hours.

[Original in Hungarian]

137. TO HIS SON, PÉTER BARTÓK—BUDAPEST

[Picture postcard: Greetings from California:
A Gorgeous Bird is the Pelican
Whose Bill can Hold more than his Bellican,
He can put in his Beak, Food enough for a week,
But I'll be Blest if I can see how in Hellican.]

Szent Pál[2], *January* 24th, 1928

Dear Péter,
Yesterday I got Ma's letter (of January 3rd) in Kansas City, Missouri (*not* in Kansas City, Kansas!!). I'll answer it tomorrow if these St. Paul people let me. It's ghastly cold in St. Paul, but the people are friendly. I'll be on my way again the day after tomorrow.

[. . . . .][3]

(This verse is not for you to learn, Péter!) No more now—just kisses from your

FATHER

[1] Original text in English.
[2] St. Paul.
[3] Here follows a Hungarian translation of the Pelican verse on the postcard.

[Original in Hungarian]

138. TO THE MATICA SLOVENSKÁ—TURÓCSZENTMÁRTON

[1] *Budapest, Szilágyi tér 4.*
May 16th, 1928

Dear Sirs,

I am pleased to inform you that I have at last succeeded in finishing the final section of the work, so I can now hand it over to you or your representative at any time. I shall most probably be staying in Budapest during the whole of the next few months; all the same, would you be so kind as to give me 8 or 10 days' notice before the date on which you require the work. I wonder if we couldn't make the arrangements—if it is convenient to you—through your Legation here?

This last section contains 400 (four hundred) pages, making 3,150 Czech crowns according to the terms of the contract, if I have calculated correctly.

The task of completing the work has been delayed for various reasons including the fact that, having received from you the 3 copies of the last *Slov. Spevy* booklet, I inserted the material from it into the last third of the work now ready to be handed over, and also into the first two-thirds which I gave in some time ago. I'm enclosing a list of the tunes for insertion into these earlier sections, with the exact indication of where each tune should be inserted. Will you please be so kind as to insert the numbers of these tunes at the indicated points in the material I have already handed over. With this list I am also sending you 4 further tunes (collected by myself and Kodály) which were accidentally omitted from the section already handed over, and which have to be inserted. Will you please paste them into the appropriate places in the manuscript already handed in.

All that remains to be done now are a few appendices and the list of contents; this I am unable to do until I have the proofs, and I shall need to have the galley proofs in 5 copies for it. I shall return one set of proofs with my corrections; as to the other four, I need these for compiling the statistical tables of the appendices. But when it gets to the second proof stage, I shall only need one copy. The first appendix would contain a table of place-names indicating where the tunes were found, also the names of the performers. I would like to add to this a few photographs (of the performers) which I myself took at the time; I think their publication could only make the book more interesting.

The second appendix would give a survey of the texts, including variants. The third would be a comment on the tunes which are of foreign origin (as required by one of the clauses in the contract).

I would like to have a fourth appendix listing the tunes in previously published collections and arrangements, in order to indicate where they can be found in each of my own books. As there are approx. 8,000 tunes to be listed, this appendix would amount to forty pages of print (the numbers of approx. 200 tunes would go on each page if small print were to be used). So that this extensive—but, in my opinion, most useful—list could not be printed without your agreement, for there's no mention of this in our contract.

I shall look forward to hearing from you, and meantime remain,

Yours very sincerely,
BÉLA BARTÓK

[Original in Hungarian]

139. TO FRIGYES REINER—WESTPORT (CONN.)

Budapest, October 29th, 1928

My dear Friend,

Many thanks for the congratulations cabled jointly by you and Murray! Don't think, however, that you were first with the news: you were outstripped by the paper *Az Est* which, on the afternoon of Oct. 2, reported that I had won 6,000 dollars! I read this with suspicion and calmed down a little only when I got your cable in the evening and was able to say to myself that, after all, I really had won something. Within a few days I had learned from foreign newspapers that at least four of us had won something; who had won how much we couldn't discover from the many conflicting reports. So I waited patiently until, at last, a few days ago, the letter from Philadelphia arrived, telling me exactly what had happened (and including the cheque of course). There's no need for me to stress the fact that the money 'came in handy'; we are able to breathe more freely now, to say nothing of the publicity we've had. You can hardly imagine what a sensation this created in Budapest. Six thousand dollars! I told everybody, from the very outset, that it just couldn't be as much as that—but all to no effect; it is by now common knowledge that I have won 6,000. It has been such a long drawn out affair that I didn't count on winning anything, and only the day before I received the news I had sent the *Druckvorlage* to the Universal Edition in order that they might get it printed. As a result, my surprise was all the greater and so much the more agreeable. After reading some official-sounding comments about the four works only the other day in the *Musical Courier*, I'm actually beginning to feel astonished that I won anything at all!

I have been wanting to write you in any case, but I didn't know where you were. At last, someone told me last autumn that you were conducting in Cincinnati this season, too. I am sorry that the Budapest proposition came to nothing, although who knows whether you would have been able to bear it here. As regards membership of the Upper House[1], this is the one thing that—in my opinion—you shouldn't have asked for. This question wasn't brought up in the winter when we talked the matter over, so that I don't know if you really made it one of your conditions.

I've played my piano concerto a few times since I came home; the performances have been as diverse as the receptions!

The Budapest performance was conscientious enough, considering how things are here (though the brass instruments simply hadn't the required volume); the Berlin performance—under Kleiber—had lots of life, but the orchestra had a few misadventures. Of course, not one of the European performances came up to the standard of precision shown in Cincinnati. The Concerto is to be performed in Amsterdam next week (with Monteux! It seems Mengelberg doesn't feel like it); I wonder what it will be like there.

Every good wish to both of you from

Your friend,
BARTÓK

PS. Meanwhile I have written another string quartet, a much longer one this time; there are 5 movements (would there by any chance be another competition somewhere?!!)

[Original in Hungarian]

140. TO JÓZSEF SZIGETI

[1] *Budapest, III., Kavics u. 10.*
Phone number on the envelope[2]
[*October–November*, 1928]

My dear Friend,
I hope you'll allow me to address you in this way. When I was in America, I had already thought of suggesting it to you, but in that mad bustling country there isn't even time for a quiet talk!

[1] 'House of Lords'.
[2] Envelope missing

What I want to say is that I simply have to talk to you. I expect to arrive in Budapest from Holland on Nov. 12, at 1.10 p.m.; I could be at your disposal that afternoon or the next day (Tuesday) in the morning, any time and anywhere; or on Tuesday between 3 and 6 p.m. at the Academy of Music, or maybe in the evening, before or after your concert; or else on the 14th, at any time of day and anywhere, provided you are still in Budapest.

You see, I've written a minor (12-minute) composition for you (based on folk dances); and I want to talk to you about one or two points. And then, I should like you to give me some information about Russia.

So please give me a ring, so that we can fix a time.

Till then, all good wishes,

Yours,
Bartók

[Original in English]

141. TO OXFORD UNIVERSITY PRESS—LONDON

[1] *Budapest, III., Kavics u. 10.*
17 *November*, 1928.
new adress [*sic*]: KAVICS U. 10.

Dear Mr. Foss,
please will you kindly let me know your intentions about the Roumanian Christmas-songs as soon as possible. (Mr. Bianu, the president of the Academia Română in Bucarest, told me at Prague that the Academia Română would be very glad to publish that collection.)

Before making any agreement with them, I must have your decision. If you can not publish it, let me know it—I know the difficulties and shall not be 'fâché' at all. But if you decide to publish it, we must make an agreement (contract) containing the date before which the work must appear.

If it can not [be] published by you, you may give me back the manuscript next March (4th and 5th) when I shall be in London.

(Bucarest *[sic]* has an other copy of the manuscript.)

I hope to see you there at that occasion and remain,

with kind regards,
yours very sincerely,
Béla Bartók

[Original in Hungarian]

142. TO MRS. BARTÓK, *née* DITTA PÁSZTORY—BUDAPEST

[1] *Moscow, January* 2nd, 1929

My dearest Ditta,

I'm trying to write to you before the end of today; I have a 7 hours' wait here, so there's plenty of time. I wonder when you'll get this! I arrived here in real Russian weather; Moscow looks just as one knows it from pictures: the roofs loaded with snow, so that they seem ready to cave in, and little one-horse sledges tinkling everywhere. It is not so terribly cold; only about 10°C. And this cold isn't so disagreeable as that of, for instance, New York or Chicago. I got here without any trouble to speak of—except that my money is dwindling rapidly because everything is so expensive; to mention one example only: a ¼ of an hour's ride by car costs 5 r. (=13 pengős), and so on. So as not to have to idle away these 7 hours at a railway station, I took the advice of the person who came for me and went to a hotel (7 r.=18 pengős). I haven't seen much yet, of course—the train was comfortable enough. I sent a postcard from Warsaw, one to Mother, too. You would surely receive those in good time. I'll be leaving tonight for Kharkov.

All my love, BÉLA

Maupassant is right when he says that one ought to come here in the middle of winter (just as one ought to go to Africa at the height of summer); it is then that the country is at its most characteristic.

[Original in Hungarian]

143. TO MRS. BARTÓK, *née* DITTA PÁSZTORY—BUDAPEST

[2] *Kharkov, January* 7th, 1929

My dear Ditta,

Well, the first 2 concerts are safely over, though, actually, one of them was cancelled. This is what happened: as soon as I arrived, I was met with the news that the first concert would be held here on the 6th, the next one, on the 9th in Kiev, and the third one, on the 14th in Odessa. These unhappy people had completely forgotten that I had to be in Leningrad on the 12th, although the Ithma had written to them at least four times about it! In their first shock of dismay, they tried to organize another concert here in Kharkov on the 5th, instead of the one in Kiev, and telegraphed to alter the date of the one in Odessa to the 9th. However, the Kharkov concert couldn't be held on the 5th after all, so there are only 2 concerts altogether in the Ukraine. They will pay for 3, nevertheless, because it's all their fault.—The first thing I did was to go to the travel bureau to enquire how to get from Odessa to Leningrad. I was told that if I leave on the 10th, I can't arrive there until the morning of the 13th, yet according to my contract, I must be there by the 12th. Well then, some frantic wires were sent off to Leningrad, and the reply came that I simply had to be there on the 12th. It almost seemed that Odessa would have to be cancelled, too, when someone discovered, and made himself responsible for the truth of it, that there was a direct train from Odessa on the 10th, which would get me to Leningrad on the 12th, in the evening. So that was how we amused ourselves for some days, hovering about in constant uncertainty. But apart from this, they are very charming people, and they have loaded me with scores and folk-song publications (I shall have plenty to drag home with me). The audience also proved to be very enthusiastic at the end of the concert; they shouted, *bis! bis!* (encore! encore!), and there were 3 encores. After the concert we went to a 'lordly' mansion now owned by some Ukrainian People's Commissariat, where a banquet was held in my honour to seal the Hungaro–Ukrainian friendship. There were speeches, for which I, too, had to give thanks in return; then there was also a concert afterwards: they played among other things, the 3rd movement of my 1st String Quartet, and quite passably.—I have been to the theatre twice; the first time I saw *The Barber of Seville*, with the strangest arrangement and stage-setting. The sets, which move from time to time, are strongly in the Constructivist style. The whole production has the flavour of a revue, but it is very lively. Having movable sets is a clever idea which could be used to good effect in many new theatrical productions.— Then I've seen a new building, a real skyscraper built in the new style similar to that of Dessau, a grouping of undecorated blocks. There is plenty of lively activity, this much I have seen so far. Life goes on quite normally, but their way of life is entirely different from ours. The main meal is between 4 and 5. Supper is called tea, and they eat it late at night. My only trouble is that I keep on thinking so much about home and remembering that, once again, I left everything unsettled: when Péter is to be taken to Szőllős, when you will leave for the Tátra mountains, and things like that. And when I am likely to hear from you, and when you'll get this letter! I sent a postcard from Moscow, and one from here (registered); this is the third time I've written. A year ago I was in Los Angeles!

All my love, BÉLA

[Original in Hungarian]

144. TO MRS. BARTÓK, *née* DITTA PÁSZTORY—BUDAPEST

[3]

[Picture postcard: Le poète Gogol (illustre habitué du Café Greco)]

[The small portrait of the poet seen on the right of this photograph was painted by Paul Swedomsky and was donated to the Café Greco by the Russian colony which, on the occasion of the poet's fiftieth anniversary in 1902, tacked up at his favourite place, and below his portrait, a parchment square with the signatures of all the donors.]

Rome, April 12th, 1929

Dear Ditta,

We're writing from this café which used to be frequented by Gogol.

All my love,
B.

Kindest regards from

JÓZSEF SZIGETI

Poor Szigeti was quite shocked because the audience was rather noisy during my violin sonata. He has never experienced such a thing before, but I'm pretty hardened in this respect.

(The Zoltán Székelys are also here!!)

[Original in German]

145. MICHAEL D. CALVOCORESSI — LONDON

Berlin, December 11th, 1929

Dear Calvocoressi,

Enclosed you'll find the German draft of the Appendix I mentioned; I hope you won't have much trouble with it.

On November 30, I returned pp. 81 to 176 of the proof, and I would like to make the following comments:

1. *Komitat* is the German form; the right word is actually 'county', isn't it? Here it means *département*. I don't think it's good to use the German word, I should use 'county' or some other English term.

2. p. 97: Brünn is the German name; as there isn't an English version, should one use the Czech *Brno*?

3. p. 98: Turócszentmárton and Rózsahegy are Hungarian place-names. Shall we use them or the official Slovak names: Turčiansky Svätý Martin and Ružomberok?

4. p. 99: Appendix III is completely *unnecessary!* (This was an unfortunate idea on the part of the German publishers, and there's no necessity to take it over in the English edition.) The enclosed new Appendix should be substituted for Appendix III.

5. p. 113: *pandur* or *pandour??* The Oxford Dictionary gives the latter.

6. *Bíró* originally meant 'judge'. But then, it also means—and much more often—*Dorfrichter, Dorfschulze, Schultheiss,* something like a 'mayor of a village',[1] who is no 'judge'[2] at all! Is there a suitable English word? A *bíró* in the village is a peasant who has been elected for a term of several years as the official who undertakes certain administrative duties in the village.

All good wishes,
Yours,
BÉLA BARTÓK

[Original in Hungarian]

146. TO ERNŐ SÜDY—BÉKÉSCSABA

[1] *Budapest, III. Kavics u. 10.*
May 17th, 1930

Dear Mr. Südy,
I have no great hope that this letter will produce results; still, it's worth making the attempt.

Monsieur Robert Schmitz is to give concerts in Europe in the coming season, and he would like to play in Hungary, too. He is the president of 'Pro musica' of New York, the association which arranged tours for Ravel, Milhaud, etc., and which also made possible my own American tour. This association was the first to sponsor a performance of *Psalmus Hungaricus* in New York. As you can see from the text of the enclosed letter, Kodály and myself are on the 'Advisory Board'.[3] This is M. Schmitz's connection with Hungarian

[1] 'mayor of a village' original text in English.
[2] 'Judge': original text in English.
[3] 'Advisory Board': original text in English

musical culture. Apart from this, he is an excellent pianist, well known in Western Europe and the U.S.A. He was on a world tour last winter. What I would like to ask you is whether Békéscsaba could engage him for a concert next winter, for a fee of some hundred pengős. I don't know if it would count as an attraction or the opposite if I mention that he can offer such delicacies as music by Milhaud or Poulenc. Items, that is, which neither I nor any of the other artists making the trip to Békéscsaba have at our command.

Awaiting your kind reply (and asking you to return the enclosed letter),

Yours sincerely,
BÉLA BARTÓK

[Original in German]

147. TO OCTAVIAN BEU—BUCHAREST

[1] *Budapest, III. Kavics u. 10.*
November 5th, 1930

Dear Sir,

I am sorry I have not been able to answer your letter of October 27th before now.

1. I began collecting Rumanian folk music in the summer of 1918, in the same place.

2. Unfortunately, I am unable to give you the exact number of the phonogr. cylinders, still less the different groups into which they are divided (indicating the latter would involve me in at least a week's work!).

I recorded Rum. folk-music on approximately 800 cylinders. About half of these cylinders are the property of the Ethnogr. Department of the Hung. National Museum, and they are in fact stored there.

3. I am enclosing a list of my works (before 1923), indicating the year of composition.

(1) About the *Hungarian Folk Melodies,* some of them have been published (Univ. Edition) in J. Szigeti's transcription for violin and piano.

(2) These have also been published for small orchestra (my transcription), for string orchestra (Willner's transcription) and for violin + piano (transcription by Z. Székely).

From 1923 on (Universal Edition):

1924. 5 Village Scenes for 1 voice + piano.
Of these, Nos. 3, 4 and 5 under the title Three Village Scenes for 8 women's voices + chamber orchestra.

1924. Four Old Hungarian Folk-Songs for men's voices.
1926. Sonata for the piano.
Out of Doors (5 piano pieces).
9 small piano pieces.
Concerto for piano + orch.
1927. 3rd String Quartet.
1916. (1)—1927 (2, 3). Three Rondos for the piano.
1928. 4th String Quartet.
1928. 2 Rhapsodies for violin & piano, alternatively, for viol. + orchestra (with Rumanian folk-dance tunes incorporated).
1929. Hungarian Folk-Songs for mixed voices.
1929. 20 Hungarian Folk-Songs for voice + piano.
1930. Cantata Profana for mixed choir, with tenor & baritone solos and orchestra (to a Rumanian *colinda* text from my own collection) (manuscript, unperformed as yet).

N.B. Incidentally, I don't know whether you want this complete list or only the list of those of my works in which I have utilized Rumanian folk-music motifs!

4. I have two additional books: *Volksmusik der Rumänen von Mărămureș*, München, Drei Maskenverlag, 1923; *Das Ungarische Volkslied*, Berlin, Walter de Gruyter & Co., 1925.

5. Kodály's article appeared in the *Revue Musicale*, in 1921 (and not in *La Musique* as you write). Other articles: Cecil Gray: 'B. B.' (*Sackbut*, 1920, London); M. D. Calvocoressi: 'B. B., an Introduction' (*The Monthly Musical Record*, 1922, London); A. Coeuroy: 'B. B. and the Balkans' (*Eolus*, New York, 1929) (I haven't seen this); Cecil Gray: *A Survey of Contemporary Music* (Oxford University Press, London, 1924; a section of it: 'B. B.'); I am not including any Hungarian articles here.

Finally, 2 booklets have come out recently: E. von der Nüll: *B. B. A Contribution to the Morphology of the New Music*, Halle, 1930; E. Haraszty: *B. B.* (Budapest, 1930, in Hungarian).

I don't know if you are aware that there is an as yet unpublished rhapsody by Liszt in which the themes are probably of Rumanian origin; it is in the Liszt Museum in Weimar, in a so-called 'Collection Volume' which includes also the first drafts of the 15 Hung. rhapsodies. It was in that that he utilized themes he had heard in Szatmár County (Satu Mare). I think this work has not yet been included in Breitkopf & Härtel's comprehensive edition.

To Octavian Beu NOVEMBER 1930

I enclose two photos for you and will be glad to hear from you when and where they are published. I shall be playing in London on the evening of the 26th, so I'm afraid I won't be able to hear your lecture.

Yours sincerely,
BÉLA BARTÓK

N. B. Wherever I have utilized folk-music in my compositions, I have always in some way indicated the fact. The absence of such a reference means that the theme is my own invention.

[Original in Hungarian]

148. BÉLA BALÁZS—TO BÉLA BARTÓK

Paris, November 15th, 1930

This is to declare that I do not wish my name to be mentioned in connection with the performances, in the Roy. Hung. Opera House of Budapest, of my ballet *The Wooden Prince* and my opera *Bluebeard's Castle.*

I also relinquish the fees due to me from these performances in favour of Béla Bartók, and I am simultaneously notifying our publishers, Universal Edition, Vienna, Austria, of this fact.

This surrender of the right to use my name and to claim my fees is valid until revocation and, for the present, until January 1, 1933.

BÉLA BALÁZS

[Original in Hungarian]

149. TO MIKLÓS RADNAI—BUDAPEST

Budapest, III. Kavics u. 10.
November 21st, 1930

Dear Sir,
Enclosed please find Béla Balázs's statement which we discussed in the course of our last conversation. Will you kindly acknowledge receipt of this and also let me know if the matter has now been settled.

Yours faithfully,
BÉLA BARTÓK

[Original in Hungarian]

150. TO HIS MOTHER, MRS. BÉLA BARTÓK—POZSONY

[33]
[Picture postcard: Freiburg i. Br., Schwabentor]

Freiburg, December 6th, 1930

Dear Mother, Aunt Irma and Elza (if she is still with you?!)! I found your postcard here. It is true that I've had a big enough success in London; but it's been a long time coming—overdue by about 24 years. The morning after the day after tomorrow, I leave for home. About time, too, for I've had just about enough of this roving around!

Much love,
BÉLA

[Original in Hungarian]

151. MIKLÓS RADNAI—TO BÉLA BARTÓK

Budapest, December 10th, 1930

Dear Sir,
I gratefully acknowledge receipt of Béla Balázs's statement which I hope will now enable me to solve the problems connected with the performance of these two of your works.
I am, Sir, with respect,

Yours very sincerely,
RADNAI
Director

[Original in German]

152. TO OCTAVIAN BEU—BUCHAREST

[2]

Between Berlin and Budapest,
January 10th, 1931

Dear Sir,
Please forgive me for the delay in answering your letter of December 3, but I have been very busy giving concerts during this period. First of all, I wish to let you know my observations concerning your essay on my works of Rumanian character.

Page 1. 1) At Nagyszentmiklós, during childhood, I had no opportunity whatever to hear Rumanian folk-music.

I do not understand the word *coricultură* and do not find it anywhere in the dictionary. It should be *agricultură* (agriculture)!!

Third line from the bottom: Instead of 'Bistrița' it should be 'Nagyszőllős' (now belonging to Ruthenia).

Last line: 'he became acquainted' would be more correct than *se împrietenise cu*[1].

Page 2. appr. in the middle: what does *tresătura* mean? I can't find it in the dictionary. 2. There is possibly some misunderstanding here on your part. Liszt voiced an unfavourable opinion on Hungarian 'peasant' music (in which he was wrong, not having had any opportunity—as I have tried to prove—to look into the matter thoroughly); I, in contrast, have expressed myself unfavourably about 'Hungarian art music in "folk" style' (in any case only relatively unfavourably, whereas Liszt considers Hungarian peasant music totally worthless; for I in my book, page 2, say that our peasant music is incomparably more valuable than our 'folk'-style art music); by *chansons populaires hongroises* Liszt, in his book, means Hungarian peasant music (which does not figure in the repertoire of the Gypsies), this is completely clear from the context.

The passage should read something like this: 'Despite Liszt's low opinion of Hungarian peasant music,* *Bartók începe în anul 1905,* etc. *bis colaborator și prieten*[2], because the knowledge of the Hungarian "folk"-style art music familiar from the repertoire of the Gypsies did not satisfy him.'

Page 4. 3) The same as I said above; neither at Nagyszentmiklós nor at Beszterce or Nagyszőllős did I receive any folkloristic musical impressions. The whole paragraph should be deleted.

4. Point 1) and 3) are all right; but I don't know what to do with point 2). What compositions would you list in group 2)? I would suggest that you set up two groups only:

1. (your Group 1) works which use folk-songs as themes,

2. (your Group 3) works with original themes which are imitations or evocations of Rumanian, etc., folk melodies.

In No. 1 there are in any case works to be found where varied forms of the folk tunes are given in addition to the original, but in my view this is unimportant; moreover, these works (2–3) contain not Rumanian but Hungarian folk melodies.

Page 5. 5) *compositorul român*[3].

[1] Became friendly with.

[2] In 1905 etc. Bartók begins, as collaborator and friend.

[3] Rumanian composer.

My views are as follows: I consider myself a Hungarian composer. The fact that the melodies in some of my own original compositions were inspired by or based on Rumanian folk-songs is no justification for classing me as a *compositorul român*; such a label would have no more truth than the word 'Hungarian' applied to Brahms, or Schubert, and is as inappropriate as if one were to speak of Debussy, as a Spanish composer because their works were inspired by themes of Hungarian or Spanish origin. In my opinion it would be better for you and other scholars to give up these labels and confine yourself to remarking that 'here or there, in this or that composition, there are themes of Rumanian inspiration'. If your view were correct, I could just as easily be called a 'Slovak composer'; and then I should be a composer of three nationalities! As I'm being so frank, I should like to give you some idea of what I think about all this.

My creative work, just because it arises from 3 sources (Hungarian, Rumanian, Slovakian), might be regarded as the embodiment of the very concept of integration so much emphasized in Hungary today. Of course I do not write this for you to make it public; you will yourself beware of doing so, for such ideas are not for the Rumanian press. I only mention it as a possible point of view which I encountered about 10 years ago, when I was attacked in the most violent manner by our chauvinists as a musical Scotus Viator. My own idea, however—of which I have been fully conscious since I found myself as a composer—is the brotherhood of peoples, brotherhood in spite of all wars and conflicts. I try—to the best of my ability—to serve this idea in my music; therefore I don't reject any influence, be it Slovakian, Rumanian, Arabic or from any other source. The source must only be clean, fresh and healthy! Owing to my—let us say geographical—position it is the Hungarian source that is nearest to me, and therefore the Hungarian influence is the strongest. Whether my style—notwithstanding its various sources—has a Hungarian character or not (and that is the point)—is for others to judge, not for me. For my own part, I certainly feel that it has. For character and milieu must somehow harmonize with each other.

Page 5. second half: *trei mari lucrări*[1] are the books about 1) Bihor, 2) Mărămureș, 3) *colindas; lucrarea mic*[2] is the study on Hunedioara.

Page 6. 6) *nicidecum*.[3] True enough, I do so express myself in the

[1] Three great works.
[2] Small work.
[3] In no way.

Bihor preface, but the collections of ensuing years have proved that this is not quite correct, for isolated Gypsy musicians can be found who play in just the same peasant fashion as their peasant colleagues.

Page 7. 7) This must be corrected: What is meant here is that *colinda* texts are not sung to *doina* melodies, nor *vice versa*, but in six-syllable *colinda* melodies and six-syllable *colinda* texts on the one hand, and in eight-syllable *colinda* melodies and eight-syllable *colinda* texts on the other, no close connection between melody and text is shown.

Page 8. 8) Instead of *209 melodii*, it should be '365 melodies (in 209 variant groups)'.

9) Mistake! There are even bigger *colecție particulară de folclor muzical*[1]; for instance the Moravian collector Plicka told me that he noted down *8000* Slovakian melodies in the post-war years in Slovakia.

Page 10. 10) 'Emil Haraszti'. I must inform you that Haraszti is a stupid and, in addition, a malicious man *who, moreover, understands as much of music as a hen does of the ABC*![2] I would advise you for your own sake not to quote him. Of course he understands how to make use of what he hears or reads from others, so that his limitations are not so obvious at first.

Page 11. 11) H. here is talking through his hat (*hasból beszél, ahogy azt magyarán mondják*)[3] ; more of this later.

Page 13. The Dance Suite cannot very well be listed here just like that; No. 1 is partly, and No. 4 entirely of an Oriental (Arab) character; the *ritornell* and No. 2 are of Hungarian character; in No. 3 Hungarian, Rumanian and even Arab influences alternate; and the theme of No. 5 is so primitive that one can only speak of a primitive peasant character here, and any classification according to nationality must be abandoned.

The two Rhapsodies contain folk melodies from various sources. I intentionally did not indicate any source here, so I restrict myself to saying to you that No. 1 uses Rumanian and Hungarian melodies, No. 2 Rumanian, Hungarian and Ruthenian. H.'s chatter here is

[1] Partial collection of musical folklore.

[2] Bartók wrote this Hungarian saying in Hungarian in this German letter. It must be mentioned here that it was Emil Haraszti who first accused Bartók of being a 'musical Scotus Viator' (*Budapesti Hirlap*, February 27th, 1913).

[3] The Hungarian saying inserted in parentheses by Bartók means literally to talk out of his belly'.

partly false, partly correct, but then '*even a blind hen may chance to find a grain*!'[1] So I advise you not to go by H. but by me, and write 'partially' for both rhapsodies instead of *partea a duna*[2] and *partea întâia*[3]; this solution is perfectly correct; those who are interested may then guess.

In the Cantata Profana only the text is Rumanian; the thematic material is my own invention, nor is it an imitation of Rumanian folk-music, indeed much of it has no folk character. This work can only be mentioned as a 'setting to music of a Rumanian *colinda* text'. In general, I would advise you to arrange page 13 as follows:

1a) Arrangements of Rumanian folk melodies:
  1) No. 5 of the Sketches, op. 9 for piano,
  2) Rumanian Folk Dances (1915) for piano; transcribed by the composer for small orchestra; transcribed for violin and the piano by Z. Székely
  3) Rumanian Colindas (1915)
  4) Sonatina (1915)

1b) Works utilizing in part Rumanian folk melodies:
  1) Rhapsody No. 1
  2) Rhapsody No. 2
  } (1928); both for violin and piano, or violin and orchestra; No. 1 also transcribed by the composer for violoncello and piano

2a) Works with original thematic material, but of a completely Rumanian character:
  1) No. 6 of the Sketches, op. 9 for piano
  2) Two Rumanian Dances (1909)

2b) Works with original thematic material, partly of Rumanian character:
  Dance Suite (1923) (third movement, in part) for orchestra; piano transcription by the author

3) Setting to music of Rumanian texts:
  Cantata Profana (1930, manuscript) for etc.[4]

Page 14. In the bibliography, point 2 and 3, it would be right to insert the titles in the original language (German), too. In addition to these, I published a polemical essay in the issue for July–August, 1914, of *Convorbiri* ('Observări despre muzica poporală românească')[5].

[1] Quoted in Hungarian by Bartók.
[2] Second part.
[3] First part.
[4] See the rest of Bartók's remark in Notes (p. 410).
[5] Observations on Rumanian Folk Music.

I have a remark to add to your study on Liszt; I hope you won't take it amiss. You allege that Liszt cannot be considered Hungarian. Well, of what other nationality would he be then? He spoke French best, not German; his music is completely un-German; the name 'Liszt' appears to be a Slav word, in Hungarian orthography (List ⟨ = leaf ⟩ is a Western Slav family name); but he regarded himself as Hungarian. In such a complicated case we must go by Liszt's own view. That he did not know Hungarian can be attributed to the conditions of the time (the Germanizing influence of the Austrians); many of our magnates did not speak Hungarian either at that time (Eötvös, the writer, for example, only learnt Hungarian as a young man, in order to be able to write in this language.)

I don't know your assertion concerning Liszt's XIIth Rhapsody, so I cannot say anything about it.

I *don't* know the theme of Brahms's op. 21 as a Rumanian *colinda;* I only know that this melody was very widespread as a Hungarian song. However, even if it occurs as a Rumanian *colinda* melody, too (one would have to know where and to what extent), it is still no proof, and, indeed, improbable that it originated on Rumanian soil. In any case, the melody is not characteristic of Rumanian *colinda* melodies or Hungarian peasant melodies. I should think rather that either we took it over from the material of our northwestern neighbours, or that it had originated here under northwestern influence, and that we passed it on to Rumanian territory. In any case, one must be very cautious with statements of this sort, for the strangest cases of melody-migration and melody-crossing occur.

There is nothing Rumanian in Kodály's works; Chován's manuscripts can perhaps be acquired through his publishers: Károly Rozsnyai, Budapest, Múzeum körút 15.—E. Poldini's address is Bergerot, près Vevey, Suisse.

You ask from me, in addition,

1. a preface, 2. a page of manuscript, 3. photographs.

1. What sort of preface do you have in mind? A scientific essay? In this case you could perhaps use (with the publishers' permission) an abridged version of my essay that appeared in the *Musical Encyclopaedia*. Or something different?

2. It is a little difficult to send a manuscript. It would be better if you had a negative of a page made here in Budapest.

3. You could obtain a good photo at Dénes Rónai's, Budapest,

IV., Váci utca 17. (Alas, I only have a single copy of it, which I cannot part with.) You should ask for a glossy copy which is cheaper, too. *One* photo would be quite enough. In addition, I am sending you a glossy print of an older photo, in photostat. Enclosed the picture you wanted.

I hope I've not forgotten to answer any question. It would be good if you sent me the second (extended) version of your essay, so that no errors creep in.

Yours sincerely,
Béla Bartók

PS. 1. I am now going away again and shall return about the 10th, when I shall be staying in Budapest for some time, so I shall be able to look through the second version within a couple of days.

2. By the same post I am sending you your essay and the photograph.

* The original French text should be quoted in the footnote.

[Original in English]

153. TO THE OXFORD UNIVERSITY PRESS—LONDON

[2] *Budapest, III. Kavics u. 10.*
16. *February* 1931.

Oxford University Press (Music Dept.)
Amen House
Warwick Square, London, E.C.4.

Sir,
would you be so kind as to return my manuscript of the Roumanian Christmas-Songs to me immediately. When—after a certain time (in five, ten or twenty years)—you will be ready to publish it, you may get it from me once more, but—for the moment—I must have it at my disposal.

Yours sincerely,
Béla Bartók

[Original in German]

154. TO CONSTANTIN BRĂILOIU—BUCHAREST

[3] *Budapest, III. Kavics u. 10.*
February 22nd, 1931

Dear Mr. Brăiloiu,

Your wire arrived after a delay of 24 hours (it was addressed to KAICZ instead of 'Kavics' Street!)

1. In the middle of January, I received a letter from a Mr. Tamașiu, whom I have never met, informing me that my 'friends and adherents' are planning a festival of 3 concerts (in Arad, Timișoara and Bucharest), and that they also plan to erect a memorial tablet at N.szentmiklós, in March—all this with me participating. To which I answered:

2. That I was not the one for such ceremonies; but if they wanted to organize 2 concerts (in Arad and Timișoara), *without festivities*, then, of course, I might participate; but that I was afraid I could not spare the time to go to Bucharest for a third concert (nor, as had been suggested, for 2 additional concerts in Oradea and Cluj). So far as the memorial tablet was concerned, would they, please, drop the idea, as I did not take kindly to the thought of squeezing money out of people for such a thing. As for the concerts, they should negotiate with my agents, 'Studio', Budapest.

To which Mr. Tamașiu replied:

3. That the cost of the mem. tablet was trifling, and, anyway, the money had already been collected; that the little town of Nagyszentmiklós had been notified, and everyone was so glad, etc., so would I be so kind as to give my consent. To which I answered:

4. All right, I had nothing against it if things really stood as Mr. T. indicated. However, I could only participate in the business of the memorial tablet if the text was *also* in Hungarian.

So that was the gist of our correspondence. However, no contract for the 2 concerts has arrived as yet; Mr. Tamașiu has kept obstinately silent for 2 or 3 weeks now, which, in any case, seems a bit suspicious.

So my principal demands were: no festivities in Arad and Timiș.; 2 concerts only; a bilingual memorial tablet.

But now I'm really curious to know what they wanted from you!

Be cautious, in any case; I don't know these people, and, as I've already said, the contract is still outstanding, although the concerts were planned for March 12 and 13 (I am not available for a later date). Meantime, I have posted to you my reply about the *colinda* publication; did you get the letter?

With all good wishes,

Yours sincerely,
BÉLA BARTÓK

[Original in Hungarian]

155. TO LÁSZLÓ POLLATSEK [PATAKI]—BUDAPEST

[Postcard]

Budapest, February 23rd, 1931

Dear Mr. Pollatsek,

1. The *4 Nénies* have no opus number, at least not in my copy; I can't understand how an opus number could have got on to other copies! Incidentally, at the outset I wanted to mark the *4 Nénies* with the opus number *9a.* (and the *Esquisses, 9b.*). The numbering was accidentally omitted.

2. The scale of the *Slovak Boys' Dance* is C D E flat F G *A flat* B flat ('A' only in bars 8 and 9, and in the penultimate accompanying chord, so the '*A flat*' can be considered predominant), which is an *Aeolian scale.* At the very most, one could speak of a scale that is partly 'Aeolian' and—on account of the 'a'—partly '*Dorian*'; but in no case could it be Mixolydian. An *Evening with the Székelys* cannot be considered anything but Aeolian, with the *F sharp* figuring everywhere in the accompaniment. I don't understand how you could have thought of a Phrygian scale in this instance?!

3. Both the 1st and the 2nd Rhapsody were originally written for violin + piano (or orchestra), later I transcribed the 1st for the cello, too; or to be more exact, I had always imagined it, from the very outset, both for violin + piano and for cello + piano; but it wasn't until sometime later that the cello + piano version was written out. This is shown, incidentally, by the fact that the 1st Rhaps. is dedicated to a *violinist*!

Yours faithfully,
BÉLA BARTÓK

[Original in Hungarian]

156. TO THE PRESIDIUM OF THE SIMC
[SOCIÉTÉ INTERNATIONALE DE LA MUSIQUE CONTEMPORAINE]

[*Budapest,* Middle of *May,* 1931]

Draft Resolution

1. It is with profound dismay and indignation that the UMZE learns of the grave insult suffered by A. T. It assures him of its full

sympathy and support, and salutes him with the utmost respect and affection.

2. The UMZE notes with anxiety that outside authorities are more and more frequently interfering in an aggressive manner with the activities of artists and no longer shrink back even before the world-wide esteem of a Toscanini. For this reason it considers that the time has come to raise the problem of defence.

It is therefore addressing a circular letter to all sections of the SIMC, asking them to formulate for the Oxford session to be held in July appropriate proposals for the protection of the integrity and autonomy of the arts. It requests the Central Presidium to make preparations for the discussion and to approach other musical—and possibly artistic and literary—organizations, in this matter, so that it will be possible to establish a suitable world organization for the protection of the freedom of the arts.

BÉLA BARTÓK

[Original in English]

157. TO THE OXFORD UNIVERSITY PRESS—LONDON

[3]

Budapest, III. Kavics u. 10.
20th *Mai [sic]* 1931.
[Correctly: 30th *May*]

Dear Mr. Foss,
in possession of your letter of the 20th Mai *[sic]* I want to assure you, that I highly appreciate your sacrifices you made in publishing my book; I know very well it is a bad business for you. But all the more I desired the publication as perfect as possible: the greater the sacrifice, the better should be the work done. Or else the sacrifice is not worth while. After your last letter, nevertheless, I hope we shall finish this matter with a mutual understanding.

But in connection with what you are saying on page 2 (last 10 lines) of your last letter, would you be so kind as to consider this: every human being is subject to mistakes; therefore, I asked you (in Dec. 1929) to send me *second* (for *me:* second; for the printing office perhaps *third*) proofs, in order to have opportunity to revise them again (for the case, I have omitted to correct some faults in the 1. proof; and—of course—to control if my suggestions, regarding the 1. proofs, have been duly put in execution).

I am now waiting for the Ms. of the errata slip (I postponed my journey till 8. June); I am very well disposed to omit corrections of minor importance or of unidiomatic character. So I hope, the friendly settlement of this business will be secured.

Roumanian Songs.

You are saying in your last letter: 'The translation into English of your text is lying on my table.' Please tell me as soon as possible: the translation of *how many numbers* (No) of the song-texts have you there on your table? They ought to go from No 1. to No 141. However, Mr. Milford returned me only No 1.– to No 105f. The original rumanian *[sic]* Ms. of the song-texts going from No 105g—to No 105x and from No 106—No 141, therefore, seem *to be lost*. The question is: have you the translation of No 1—No 105f only or have you the translation of the following No 105g—to No 105x and No 106—to No 141 also??!

The frequently found remark 'unintelligible' of the English translator must not puzzle you: in very ancient peasant song-texts there are plenty of words, the meaning of which is unknown even to the peasant-singers.

Of course M. Brăiloiu has the complete duplicate of the whole Ms. (music included). If you want to purchase sheets of the printed music-part from him, please write him directly and—if possible—immediately. Do please the same concerning the copy of the introduction and notes (possibly also of the song-texts from No 105g—to No 141) which you want to obtain from him.—Myself, I shall be very glad to see those X-mas songs published by you, for they represent a material of the highest value not only for musicologues and musicians, but—the song-texts—for the explorers of ancient Eastern culture and folklore. So I want to help you in every way; but for getting another copy of the missing Ms. parts the best advice I can give you, is to have it made in Bucarest *[sic]* by Mr. Brăiloiu (Strada Solon 6). For me to make another copy of it here from my note-books would mean a hard work of many hundred hours—at present an almost impossible task for me!

Yours very sincerely,
BÉLA BARTÓK

My best greetings to Mr. Calvocoressi; I hope he does not mind my remarks about the translation; he ought to understand my motto *exactitude above all*!

[Original in English]

158. TO THE OXFORD UNIVERSITY PRESS

[4] *Budapest, III. Kavics u. 10.*
31. *Mai [sic]* 1931

Dear Mr. Foss,
you will find here enclosed a letter of Mr. Brăiloiu, adressed *[sic]* to me.

The translation of the red-marked parts of it is this:

'Will you, please, ask the gentlemen in London'(—he means the Oxf. Un. Press—) 'to write directly to me (for, I am obliged to have their direct answer, owing to administrativ[e] causes), and to tell me how many copies of the music-part they want; then, to tell me if they would not perhaps *want to have copies of the rumanian* [sic] *song-text-part too.*'

My opinion is, it would be very advantageous both for you and for Mr. Brăiloiu, if the rumanian *[sic]* song-text-part could be made also on a basis of cooperation between the Oxf. Un. Pr. and Mr. Brăiloiu (or Societatea Compositorilor Români). In this case (if you accept his proposal concerning the supplying of the ruman. *[sic]* song-text-part too), your edition would have the followings parts:

1. Introduction to the music-part (translation into English)
2. Notes to the music-part (translation into English)
3. Music-part (supplied by Mr. Brăiloiu)
4. Introduction to the song-text-part } (translation
5. Notes to the song-text-part } into English)
6. Song-texts in original Rumanian (supplied by Mr. Brăiloiu)
7. English translation of the song-texts.

I hope you got my letter of yesterday.

Yours very sincerely
BÉLA BARTÓK

Please turn!

After having finished this letter, your letter of 28 May arrived (with the copy of your letter and of Mr. Brăiloiu's letter).

It remains now for you only to inform Mr. Brăiloiu,

1) how many copies you want;
2) if you want also copies of the song-texts part in Rumanian;
3) if the seize *[sic]* and types of the music-part of my Hungarian book will suite *[sic]* you also for the rumanian *[sic]* book;

4) What kind of letter-types you want to have for the rumanian [*sic*] song-texts part if it will be supplied too by Mr. Brăiloiu;
5) What kind of paper you want to have for the copies.

As I know, Mr. Brăiloiu wants to have made the work in *Prague*, not in Rumania.

[Original in Hungarian]

159. TO HIS MOTHER, MRS. BÉLA BARTÓK—BUDAPEST

[34] *Geneva, July* 9th, 1931

Dear Mother and Aunt Irma, we finished this morning. I am going to pack this afternoon and will be leaving in the evening, as I have to be in Mondsee tomorrow night. I meant to write you a letter, but it was impossible here—the meetings were protracted, and then I was obliged to go here and there. Tomorrow, on the way, or at Mondsee, I will give you an account of things; it's quite interesting. Today I had to get off a couple of urgent letters: one to Berlin; the other—to Cairo, to my friend Mustafa Rida Bey who lives there, in Queen Nazli Street! I talked a great deal with Th. Mann; his wife was here, too. Your postcard of July 7th arrived safely today, while your letter of the 4th was handed to me the day before yesterday, just as I was reading my proposal (in German, worse luck!). It was subsequently reshaped into a heavily trimmed resolution. The result, for the time being—nil. The other resolutions, too, will most probably share the same fate. The greatest benefit has been in providing these 20 to 25 people with an opportunity for getting together, meeting and talking with one another. I'll do my best to write the letter as soon as possible, and I'll post it from Mondsee. When will D. get there? and who will be with her?

Much love,
B.

[Original in Hungarian]

160. TO HIS MOTHER, MRS. BÉLA BARTÓK—BUDAPEST

[35] *Mondsee, July* 13th, 1931

Dear Mother and Aunt Irma,
For the moment I am not writing about Mondsee; I am going back in a week, so that I can give you a full account of what happened in Geneva.

On Monday the first thing I did was to go to the Hungarian Legation. B. was away on holiday, so I spoke to his chief, the Minister, P. (his title is rather that of *chargé d'affaires*). I asked what he thought about the Toscanini application. He would have shaken his head vigorously, had he not been a diplomat, but, as it was, he only advised me politely not to hand it in for the time being and to get to know a little more from the members of the committee first. Then we went together to the building of the League of Nations where he personally wanted to introduce me to some important people. This took place in one of the Council Chambers where everyone's place at the big table was already indicated; on the table there were also blank sheets of paper, ready for use, League of Nations pencils, a large folder with publications, and most important—the post which had just arrived, but which, to my great regret, I could not open for a long time. On my right the famous Čapek took his place, on the left, Gilbert Murray, English university professor. What a lot of faces—until I got to know whom they belonged to, I always asked Čapek to tell me who was speaking. The translators sat in the middle of the room, and along the 4 walls there were various League of Nations officials and other employees, journalists, and later on even some guests. Mr. Murray opened the meeting in English. He had hardly finished speaking, when the interpreter for the English speeches jumped up and virtually raced through an improvised translation. The interpreters amazed me more than anything. They take down the speeches in shorthand, so that they are able to give an immediate translation, almost without stopping for breath. And some, for instance, the German interpreter, spoke and gesticulated with such 'deep conviction' that he might have been giving voice to his own most sacred beliefs; sometimes he was so carried away that he did not even look at his notes. This apeing of the orators was really comical, especially when in one of his 'speeches' he contradicted his 'previous speech', the first having been made by one speaker, and the second, by the opposing speaker.

On Murray's recommendation, Destrée, the former Belgian Minister of Education, was elected president, to everybody's satisfaction. (I wonder what would have happened if I, for instance, had made an opposing nomination of our friend Čapek for this honour!) Destrée called upon everybody to speak in whatever language he wanted to (but, of course, an interpreter had to be available!). After his speech it appeared that nobody wanted to have the French speeches translated into English (the official languages of the League of Nations are French and English, and at anyone's request both languages have to be equally respected). Well, French 'was understood perfectly' by everyone, thank goodness, because this shortened the time of discussion by half: with the exception of perhaps 3 men, everybody spoke French, except those who made their contributions in German. Otherwise the German speeches would have had to be translated not only into French but into English as well. The interpreters must also have been very pleased about this; they could bite their nails and read the whole time. But whenever an English or German word was to be heard, they snatched up their pencils.

I nearly expired with the effort of so much concentration, as I found it difficult to follow some of the speakers, especially at the beginning. Of course they all began slowly, but then they got more and more heated, so that the tempo became quicker and quicker. The Wallachian Oprescu I understood perfectly. It soon became evident that those who spoke the most were the above-mentioned Wallachian, the Italian Ojetti (a journalist, I believe), Paul Valéry, the French poet (60 yrs. old), Focillon, a French art historian, and a Swiss, Reynold (I don't know what he is). First they spoke on general questions: there was a proposal that we should declare what we regard as the proper attitude to be adopted in these times, what our conception of modern man is, etc. After many *für* and *wider* which followed every serious proposal, a subcommittee was set up by the President, composed of the man who made the proposal and those who had commented most. Between the sittings this committee was to prepare a draft resolution, which would then be submitted to the full meeting for acceptance or modification. Then they made up the *ordre du jour* (agenda) for the afternoon and the next day, etc. The *ordre* was that after the general business had been dealt with, specific subjects should be discussed, such as literature, music and art. I forgot to say that the President gave an account of the dissolved *sous-commission*, the forerunner of the *comité*, and told us what it had achieved (so that these items need not be raised again, that was the main point). A number of decisions had been reached on the subject of folk art and the question of artistic translations (see the Prague Peasant Art Congress in which I took part 3 years ago). But with regard to music, they had nothing to show for their work; so now they are awaiting from me—as the only musician member—proposals of any kind; only let me propose, and they will accept.

I explained that I could only propose things that would cost a lot of money; they answered that it did not matter. So far so good; so I went ahead and that evening drafted something (about gramophone records), which I read out the next day—in German. Čapek had also had similar ideas, so we discussed them together. A subcommittee was formed, we drafted a resolution, which was of course far different from the original and of no practical use, but it needed no money. I will give you the details when I get home.

Here are some more examples of what went on: The English 'Poet Laureate' complained that poems are not *recited* often enough in public, and when they are, they are badly recited; Valéry added that this is insufficiently taught in schools. Decision: the broadcasting companies should be asked to give more recitals and to ensure that the poems are well recited. (Nothing practical will come of this either!) Another decision: The film companies should be asked to show an 'educational' film after each ordinary one. (They, of course, will not care a straw about us or the whole League of Nations; they will go on doing what brings them the greatest profit.)

It was very amusing to see one speaker's reactions to another. They all began by saying that they had heard the proposal made by the previous speaker with the greatest pleasure and enjoyment, that the ideas were excellent, but that this wasn't quite accurate, and needed slight changes before being put into practice, or that something else was incorrect—in the end it turned out that nothing said by the preceding speaker was any good. However, politeness is the prime consideration. One thing you can be quite sure about, and that is that there will never be any violence in this Comité.

Thomas Mann spoke several times, always in German: his speeches were shrewd and very interesting.

Every day at about 5 o'clock there was a friendly rattling of tea things; the League of Nations maids laid out the china on a table brought in from the League of Nations kitchen (not the witches' kitchen) but possibly from a nearby restaurant, cakes, tea and other drinks. The President then said: *Je vous donne la liberté pour dix minutes*—and the free tea began.

One afternoon an Italian speech was in full swing, when there was a sudden interruption by the President who said: *Voici Madame X*. (I could not catch the name.) At this, as if at a command, we all stood up to greet an attractive-looking princess, or whoever she was—an elderly woman wearing a wide-brimmed hat; the President addressed her as follows: 'We are very touched and honoured by your visit and feel sad that your late husband cannot see us all here together' (at that it began to dawn on me), etc. She turned out to be Mrs. Wilson (the widow of the American Peace President). She said a few words in English, thanking him for receiving her so warmly and sat down among the audience.

There was an official luncheon and one dinner. The Secretary of the Commission gave the luncheon, the President gave the dinner. Luncheon was in a hotel—it was excellent; dinner, in the President's beautiful flat—not so good. Neither was unpleasant because I talked to people who interested me. At dinner I sat next to Mrs. Thomas Mann. I also talked a lot with Thomas Mann. Nini Roll-Anker, the Norwegian authoress, came over to pay her compliments, saying this book was so nice and that one so charming. A Nini could not act otherwise. They got me to play the inevitable *Evening with the Székelys* and the *Bear Dance;* the former was at the request of the Wallachian Oprescu who had heard me play it—in Kolozsvár when he was there as professor at the University.

There was another luncheon, at the Hungarian Minister's: only me and X., the plenipotentiary Hungarian delegate, and his wife (an awful woman). The Minister's wife is an American; she speaks only American but behaves like a native Hungarian. Then there were such cunningly contrived delicacies for lunch, I can hardly remember when I ate anything to equal them. There were 5 or 6 wine glasses at each place of expensive Venetian glass, with dolphin-shaped stems. Before lunch delicious cocktails (brandy), at the end of the meal—Tokay (this, of course, is as it should be at the Hungarian Minister's). Nevertheless, the lunch wasn't pleasant; what with the horrid screeching of Mme X. and these smooth and cunning diplomats—there's no getting away from it, they are an artificial crowd, quite different from artists.

The Geneva hotel was good, quiet, simple and with a family atmosphere—a kind of boarding-house, not too expensive.

Well, that's what happened at Geneva.

And now for Mondsee: I did not expect much from this American School, and in truth it proved to be a farce.

I arrived on Friday evening. The *Generalsekretär* was waiting for me, and we arranged that I should see my pupils at 10 o'clock the next morning. I asked how many? Well, about 6, said he (instead of 8). When I arrived next day I found—1 (say 'one') pupil. Where were the others!? Well, 2, who *had already paid,* had not yet arrived; they were gadding about somewhere in Europe. As for the others:

some had withdrawn, some just didn't exist. However, Mrs. P., the school organizer, and Mrs. C., the assistant organizer, also wanted to study with me—both of them old hags. It is all the same to me, I said, but I must get the money for 8 lessons even if I teach only one pupil.

This week, by degrees, more pupils have come rolling up—and this is how things are at the moment: I have 3 regular pupils (1 pianist, not bad; 1 composer, satisfactory; 1 pupil still studying harmony, dubious—all 3 girls) and the two old hags! A sixth wanted to study harmony with me, but he did not even know his scales, so I drew the line at that!!

The Viennese Weingarten has gone back to Vienna because not a single pupil reported to him. However, everybody says that this year the school is marvellous; it is just beginning to prosper. In which case I can't imagine what it must have been like last year if it was worse than now. There is a violin teacher from Berlin; he has one pupil!—Already I am giving them all much more individual attention, in fact I give 8 lessons per week. They do pay; today they kindly sent me a cheque for 496 Austrian Schillings, for this week's 8 lessons.

D. hopes to write soon about other things such as bathing, walking, the *Gasthof* and the food. I must finish this letter now: I am very sorry that you have been kept waiting so long, but better late than never; and it would really have been difficult to produce so much news at an earlier date, whether in Geneva or even here!

Much love,
BÉLA

[Original in Hungarian]

161. TO IMRE WEISSHAUS [PÁL ARMA]—DESSAU

Mondsee, Gasthof Koflerbräu
August 4th, 1931

Your parcel has arrived, and as soon as I have looked over the quartet, I'll tell you what I think of it. I received your previous letter, though it's true that it had been held up a great deal on the way. I asked the Róths about the letter you sent them, and they say they didn't get it, and will you send the work to their address here?

As for my Dessau concert, in principle I'm all for making an appearance like that from time to time. There are only two snags. The first is that, as far as I can judge at present, I shall not get to

Berlin, or anywhere near Dessau, next year. The second is the problem of what I should actually play. There wouldn't be much sense in playing any of my earlier works in this *fortschrittlich gesinnt* milieu. And as for my Sonata, I have already played it there. True, the audience has probably changed since then and would now be composed of people who did not hear my concert at the time. And it is also true that it does no one any harm to hear such works twice.

So let us say I would play the Sonata (13 min.), improvisation (10 min.), 2 or 3 items from *Out of Doors* and a few of the *9 Little Piano Pieces* (10 + 8 min.); that would make 41 mins. altogether. Anything else??

To sum up: I cannot promise anything for certain; but if I do play, then the concert must be quite private and intimate in character, with no question of critics being present, wearing evening dress nor playing by heart.

It is a very queer set-up here at the Mondsee conservatory. Only 2 pupils registered, instead of the minimum of 8. From sheer necessity, Mrs. Carter 'enrolled' a few days later (for the piano faculty!); so did Mrs. Peeples (for composition, but after a few lessons she also switched over to the piano); I was left wondering when Mr. Kienzl would 'enrol' for 'atonal composition' or some such thing. As for me, I am giving 8 lessons to these 4 pupils, of course; how they'll settle the financial side of the problem between themselves is none of my business. Weingarten left sadly, not a single pupil having registered with him. To be frank, the only tutors who have any pupils are those who actually recruited their own over here, in America (Mrs. Lévinne has 10, and a singer also has about that number). The whole thing doesn't make sense! Which, by the way, I suspected before I came.

I will be writing again, and meantime we send both of you our best wishes.

béla bartók
(it now occurs to me that I should have used capitals!)

[*Original in German*]

62. TO MAX ROSTAL—BERLIN

Budapest, III. Kavics u. 10.
November 6th, 1931

Dear Sir,

I am very sorry that I haven't been able to reply earlier; in order to be able to do so I had to study thoroughly the tempo and MM signs, especially of the first Quartet, and I've only now found the necessary time. Let's hope you will have an opportunity to play the works in other places, too, so that when you do so, you will be able to consider the contents of this letter; but perhaps it won't reach you in time.

Quartet I. In the first movement, the MM sign is indeed quite impossible and incomprehensible, and in the 3rd movement, too, I find many misplaced MM figures. I should add at this point that in my earlier works MM signs are very often inexact, or rather they do not correspond to the correct tempo. The only explanation I can think of is that I metronomized too hastily at the time, and perhaps my metronome was working imperfectly. I have phonogrammes made 20 years ago of some of my piano pieces played by myself, and they show that I play them today in exactly the same tempo as I did then. Now I use a balance metronome which, of course, cannot show any considerable differences from the correct oscillation number Let me give you all the tempi exactly.

1st movement. Tempo, ♪ = 60 (actually, fluctuating from 56 to 63);
last crotchet before *6*: poco rit., at *6* a tempo;
4th bar after *6*: poco rit. (calando);
5th bar after *6*: a tempo (♪ = 70, here and there also 76);
from the 3rd bar on after *8*: poco a poco più tranquillo;
5th bar after *8*: a tempo (♪ = 66);
2nd–5th crotchets before *10*: rit;
2nd bar after *10*: poco rit.;
11: a tempo (♪ = 63);
from the 7th bar after *11*: poco stringendo;
9th bar after *11*: ♪ = 72
11th bar after *11*: ♪ = 80
13th bar after *11*: ♪ = 60

2nd movement. The MM figures are generally right (the da below are converted from 𝅗𝅥. to ♩)
1: ♩ = 138; *3*: ♩ = 132; *5*: ♩ = 138 (in the 5th bar befo *6* viola and violoncello the 3rd quaver is B and not C)
3rd bar after *11*: ♩ = 120; 9th bar after *11*: ♩ = 112; *1* ♩ = 144; *13*: ♩ = 152; *14*: ♩ = 162–168; *16*: ♩ = 138; arou *18* sempre più agitato; from the 4th bar on before *19*: ♩ = 15 *20*: ♩ = 120, etc. (no divergence till the end of the movemen 3 bars before the end: ritardando.

Introduzione. 6th bar, 2nd violin: full note (not half)

3rd movement. *1* to *3* somewhat *quicker*, except the 6th and 10th bar after *1* and the 4th bar after *2*, which are approximately in the main tempo. The half bar before *4:* definite and moderate ritardando; *11*: adagio (♩ = 108); 2nd bar before *12*: più adagio (♩ = 80); from the 5th bar after *13*: accelerando, till: *14*: vivo, 𝅗𝅥 = 116; 10th bar after *14*: 𝅗𝅥 = 100; 12th bar after *14*: poco string., 13th bar: tornado al; 14th bar: tempo (𝅗𝅥 = 92) 5th bar after *16*: meno mosso, 𝅗𝅥 = 88. 9th bar 1st viol.: *p;* 10th bar 1st viol.: poco *f*, *25*: più mosso: 𝅗𝅥 = 100; 2nd bar before *27*: ancora più mosso, 𝅗𝅥 = 108. *28*: maestoso, 𝅗𝅥 = 92; 6th bar after *28*: 𝅗𝅥 = 80; 9th bar after *28*: 𝅗𝅥 = 80, 2nd bar before *30*: 𝅗𝅥 = 84; 3rd after *30*: rit. begins already here (hardly perceptible at first, of course); 6th bar after *30*: (rit.) molto; 7th bar after *30*: tempo I (*mosso*, 𝅗𝅥 = 100), *33*: 𝅗𝅥 = 104; 5th bar after *34*:

{ adagio; ♩ = 88 } then: { più largo; ♩ = 80 } then: { tempo I 𝅗𝅥 = 92 }

4th bar after *36*: accel. till *37*;

37: 𝅗𝅥 = 116; *38*: 𝅗𝅥 = 92;

5th bar before *39*: accel.; 3rd bar before *39*: 𝅗𝅥 = 116;

39: 𝅗𝅥 = 126; 5th bar after *39*: 𝅗𝅥 = 116; 7th bar after *39*: 𝅗𝅥 = 124; then: presto, 𝅗𝅥 = 126.

Quartet IV. While in Quartet I the tempo should be very elastic all through, in Quartet IV it is much more even and machine-like (except in the 3rd movement). But even here the chords, for instance, in the 37th bar of the 1st movement can and, indeed, should oe played more forcefully, making the tempo, of course, rather lrawn out. To indicate a change of tempo at this point (and in similar places) would be confusing; the tempo changes of itself, so to peak, if one correctly grasps and interprets the character of hese 'pesante' chords.

All the MM figures are *correct* here.

In the 2nd movement the main tempo should, if possible, be . = 98 or even quicker, not slower (of course with legato bowing... nd *in no case spiccato!*); from bar 78 to 101 (of the middle movement) 𝅗𝅥.: = 88 is better; from 102 on, the main tempo again. The 5th novement can perhaps be played somewhat quicker than indicated y the MM figures.

Best wishes,

Yours sincerely,
BÉLA BARTÓK

[Original in Hungarian]

163. TO JÁNOS BUȘIȚIA—BELÉNYES

[14] *Budapest, III. Kavics u. 10.*
December 20th, 1931

Dear Friend,
It is really not fair to reply so belatedly to your letter of congratulation, but I've been so busy and had so much trouble! Thank you very much for thinking of me, but let me tell you that even a decoration like this is not such a great thing as it would seem. For I am not the first Hungarian musician to have gained this distinction since the war; the first was Tivadar Szántó (formerly Smulevic), composer and pianist! József Szigeti, the violinist, also obtained it before me—but then, he deserves it. I, personally, would have been more pleased if, instead of bestowing a decoration on me, they would play my works more often in Paris—something which, I'm afraid, has happened very infrequently lately.

What do you say to this miserable state of affairs which now prevails, more or less, all over Central Europe?! In this country salaries and pensions are being reduced, and in your part of the world, as I understand it, they are settling things much more radically: they do not pay pensions at all. A fine prospect, indeed!

My Sonatina written for the piano has just come out in an arrangement for violin; I shall send you a copy, for, as you may remember Rumanian folk-dance melodies are incorporated in this piece. The part for violin is much easier than in Z. Székely's arrangement.

I have also written recently 44 short, easy duets for two violins in which I have incorporated Hungarian, Slovak, Rumanian, Serbian, Ruthenian and even Arab melodies. I would have liked t send you a copy of these too, but my publishers have dragged th business out for so long that they are hardly likely to appear befor the summer. Bungling everything, all along the line!

Someone in Nagyvárad wrote to me recently saying that yo had resigned from the 'iron guard' (that's what it's called if I re member rightly). We are all right so far as health is concerne but find it hard to put up with the extraordinary state of affairs i our country. The situation is actually much worse than it was im mediately after the war. Then we expected things to get better time went on, and things did improve to some extent! Now w cannot even hope for that. I have no personal worries at the m ment, but if things go on like this I certainly shall have. And I can even say 'if only I were in this or that other country', for everywhere there is the greatest uncertainty and economic anarchy! What a lot of wonderful things I might have achieved—I mean the collecting of folk-songs—but for the madness of the world.

All good wishes from

Béla Bartók

PS. 1. Do you know Drăgoi's *colinda* collection published recently? A good work.

2. I was elected to the League of Nations' Comité Internationale de Coopération Intellectuelle (intellectual co-operation) last year. We discussed many lofty notions there—the first session was in July; but what I'd like to say to those people is this: as long as one is unable to put the world in order economically and in other ways; as long as, for instance, currency restrictions make it difficult for even works of culture to pass the various frontiers, grandiose garrulity about 'intellectual co-operation' is completely useless. Even if I said it, it would, of course, be in vain – – – There were two delegates from Rumania on my Comité: Oprescu and Madame Vacarescu—do you know them?

Original in Hungarian]

.64. TO JENŐ TAKÁCS—CAIRO

2] *Budapest, May* 8th, 1932

New address: *II. Csalán út 27.*

)ear Mr. Takács,

'hank you for the photographs which arrived yesterday. I intended riting to you a long while ago, to thank you for acting as my guide nd for helping me in so many ways during my stay in Cairo. Howver, my hectic search for a new home and then the moving in has ıken up practically all my free time.

You may have heard that the Polnauers' emissary missed me at ıe railway station in Alexandria, although I did stare very hard t a young Polnauer-suspect as I passed him (it turned out later ıat he was actually my man). The cabbie kept saying something ›out *gumruk*. I said, 'All right, *gumruk*.' Only when I was on board, d I learn that it meant 'customs'. The fare was 19 piastres; I gave m 22, and he demanded 30. I told him to go and see a policeman he had any complaints, and walked away.

Next day we ran into bad weather, and our ship put in at Athens 12 hours late. The food which the Turks gave us was so bad that it upset my stomach, and I hereby caution everyone against Turkish ships! I had no other adventures. In Budapest I was surprised to be welcomed, not by winter, but by warm, spring breezes. This was a pleasant transition.

I hope you and your family will enjoy every happiness and success in your new country.

With all good wishes,
Yours sincerely,
BÉLA BARTÓK

[Original in English]

165. TO THE BRITISH BROADCASTING CORPORATION—LONDON

[1] *Budapest, II. Csalán út, 27.*
September 6th, 1933

B.B.C., Music Department,
London.

Dear Sir,
enclosed I return the contract for 8 Nov's engagement. I would be very pleased to know the date of the other engagement in your studio and in connexion with that of 8. Nov.

I am sending you some suggestions for the programm *[sic]* of the studio-appearance:

I. J. S. Bach: Suite in G minor .... 13'
Beethoven: Sonata E flat major, op. 31. No 3 .... 30'
II. Frescobaldi: Toccata in G major & Fuga in G minor (Transcription by B. Bartók) 8
Domenico Zipoli: Suite in B minor 6
Kodály: No 2 from piano pieces op. 11 3
Bartók: Sonata 13

As I am invited by the 'Active Music-Society' in Glasgow to com[e] and play [in] Glasgow on Nov. 10th, the best date for your Studi[o] engagement would be a few days before Nov 8.

Please, write me directly about this date and the programm *[sic* you selected for it (you may also select one piece from one and othe[r] pieces from the other).

Yours very sincerel[y]
BÉLA BARTÓK

[Original in English]

166. TO THE BRITISH BROADCASTING CORPORATION—LONDON

[2]

Budapest, II. Csalán út 27.
September 30th, 1933

Dear Mr. Tillett,
enclosed you will find the signed contract. Please, would you let me know directly and as soon as possible the items of the programm *[sic]* you have chosen, I sent you proposals a few weeks ago. Also, I should like to know the time of the orchestra rehearsals. I will leave Budapest probably on 29. Oct. already; would you please send me the permit of the Home-office in time. I will be in London from 5. Nov; my adress *[sic]* there will be 7 Sydney Place, S.W.7 (c/o Mr. Duncan Wilson).

Yours faithfully
BÉLA BARTÓK

[Original in English]

167. TO THE BRITISH BROADCASTING CORPORATION—LONDON

[3]

Budapest, II. Csalán út 27.
[About *October* 7th, 1933]

The British Broadc. Corp.
London.

Dear Sir,
I got your letter of 27th Sept.; I think this programme will not be too long, as I have 30 minutes at my disposal (9.0 to 9.30) and to *[sic]* items make 26 minutes only (13 minutes for Bach are counted without any repetitions). I enclose herewith the corrected programme; and, further, two pages with some additions to the score of my 2. piano-concerto, which I beg you to give to the leader of orch. who will conduct the work.
As always before, I will play Bechstein piano.
Waiting for the 'permit', I am yours very sincerely

BÉLA BARTÓK

[Original in Hungarian]

168. TO THE BOARD OF DIRECTORS OF THE MATICA SLOVENSKÁ—TURÓCSZENTMÁRTON

[2]

Budapest, II. Csalán út 27.
October 8th, 1933

Dear Sirs,
I received your letter dated September 29 somewhat belatedly, as it had been directed to my old address; for the last year and a half now I have been living at the above address.

The contents of your letter greatly startled me! I thought you had cleared things up long ago with Mr. Ballo. I very much regret that it is not he who will be continuing the work of preparing the texts for the press, for it is precisely in the task of revision that his expert knowledge has proved to be first-class. Of course, I myself must admit that he has been terribly slow so far in accomplishing this work: he always blamed you for this; now, however, it is you who blame him—for my part, I cannot form an opinion on the subject from this distance. I also agree that the fee he is asking is quite enormous! (I myself, e.g., didn't get more than a quarter of this for the whole manuscript, did I?)

However, let's get down to ways and means of solving the problem.

I would be pleased to prepare the manuscript for press on my own, provided that—as you suggest in your letter—'the Matica would check the Slovak text of the folk-songs'; I leave the conditions entirely to you. All I have to add in this connection is that this checking will have to be done in instalments, before giving the MS. to the printers; I'm afraid that whoever made the corrections on the text in red ink has deleted the peculiarities of dialect in nearly every instance and has substituted literary phraseology for the original words of the songs. This is a totally wrong and unacceptable standpoint. These passages will in every case have to be changed back just as Mr. Ballo did, very accurately and with an outstanding display of expert knowledge, in the first 100 song texts (already set up). Also, it will be essential to get someone to look through and correct the translation of the preface, notes, etc., for, according to Mr. Ballo—and about this we can unquestionably believe him—they contain many errors and mistranslations.

What you have to do now is this:

1. You must instruct the printers in Prague to complete the

2nd proofs of the melodies and texts that have already been engraved *right to the end* and to send them to me (for I received the 2nd proofs of the first 20 melodies at the end of July and since then have waited in vain for those of the remaining 80, although, as I say, *they were engraved (gestochen)* long ago). At the same time, you must inform the printers that you have entrusted me with the task of preparing the material for the press, and that they can correspond with me in German.

2. You must officially entrust me with this task and state exactly what the conditions are to be.

3. Regarding the portion of manuscript that has not yet been sent to the printers, you must send a section, equivalent to about 4 sheets, to whoever has been given the job of checking the song texts. He should then do a preliminary check, restoring the original text where necessary, and then forward them to me as quickly as possible (together with any questions he may wish to ask). I would clear up, by letter, any doubtful phrases, and then I would immediately send this section of the manuscript to the printers in Prague. In the meantime, the checker could be looking through the texts of the next section, and so on. What we need is to get things speeded up!

Christian names, for instance, will also have to be checked when the texts are revised! I give the singers' Christian names just as they were given to me (e.g. Liza, Zuza, etc.; to correct these names to Alžbeta, etc., is completely wrong; after all, this is not some official document of public administration but a publication of folklore).

I look forward to hearing from you in the near future! I'm very anxious not to be left without a word for weeks on end as has happened so often in the past! I must ask you to let me have an answer, if not by return, then at least very soon, especially about the 3 points listed above.

Yours faithfully,
BÉLA BARTÓK

[Original in English]

169. TO THE BRITISH BROADCASTING CORPORATION—LONDON

[4] *Budapest, II. Csalán út, 27.*
October 19th, 1933

Dear Sir,
I understand from a letter of the 'Konzertgesellschaft, Zürich', that the piano rehearsal will be held on the 6th of Nov. at 6 p.m. and the

orchestral rehearsal on the 7th at 11 A.M. and 8th at 12. Herewith I give you my London adress *[sic]* where I shall arrive on the 4th Nov.: c/o Mr. Duncan Wilson 7 Sydney Place, (London) SW 7.

I want to ask you again, to send me the permit of performance immediately, in case it still is necessary to have it at the landing. I start from Budapest on the 30th of October via Hook of Holland, and shall arrive in the harbour of Harwich on the 1st of Nov. at 6 A.M.

Yours very sincerely,
BÉLA BARTÓK

[Original in English]

170. TO THE BRITISH BROADCASTING CORPORATION—LONDON

[5] *Budapest, II. Csalán út, 27.*
[End of *October*, 1933]

To the
British Broadcasting Corporation, Music Department
London

Dear Sirs,
a few weeks ago, in answering your telegramm *[sic]*, I sent you a telegramm *[sic]* telling you that I accept 8. Nov., for the Queens Hall-engagement. Now, I should like to have settled this matter definitely, and also that of a Studio-engagement in connexion with the Queens Hall engagement. At the same time I give you the statement, that my *only* manager is the '*Konzertgesellschaft (Mr Walter Schulthess), Zürich, Pianohaus Jecklin, Pfauen, Switzerland*'; I have no more business at all with Mr. Paul Bechert.

Yours very sincerely,
BÉLA BARTÓK

[Original in Hungarian]

171. TO ERNŐ SÜDY—BÉKÉSCSABA

[2] *Budapest, II. Csalán út 27.*
January 20th, 1934

Dear Mr. Südy,
May I ask you to be patient for a few days about the question of the date, as negotiations are still going on with Temesvár and Bucharest; depending on what is settled in those places, the concert could be fixed for the 27th or the 23rd, or else on the 18th or 19th.

I am a bit surprised by what you write regarding the programme: we agreed at the time, that it was to be a *Hungarian–Slovak* evening; accordingly, I have drawn up the following programme:

1. Choral pieces (these are so short that it would be best to have them sung one immediately after the other; if, however, they do not want this, then the 2nd choral piece could be immediately after the interval).
2. *Village Scenes;* 5 Slovak folk-songs
3. 2 selections from the *Children* (one Hungarian, one Slovak)

– Interval –

4. From the *20 Hungarian Folk-Songs* (1929)
5. a) 3 rondos (on Slovak folk-songs)
   b) Ballad and old dance tunes from *Hungarian Peasant Songs*
6. Another selection from *20 Hungarian Folk-Songs*

By the way: I cannot play the 3 Études (!). I haven't played them—ever or anywhere—since 1918; and the piano Sonata would give the audience a fright, so there would be no sense in putting it in the programme. But to you (and anyone else who might be interested) I would gladly play it in private (before or after the concert).

I look forward to hearing from you about the programme. With all good wishes,

Yours sincerely,
BÉLA BARTÓK

[Original in English]

172. TO THE BRITISH BROADCASTING CORPORATION—LONDON

[6] *Budapest, II. Csalán út 27.*
9th *May*, 1934

To B.B.C.'s
Music department

Dear Sir,
today I received the permit. Let me know, please, the time and place of the rehearsals as soon as possible, in order that I may know, at what day I have to be in London. It seems there will be necessary also preliminary rehearsals with the singers and the piano (without orchestra)?

I suppose the concert is to be given in the studio, so that no evening dress is needed.

Answer me, please, directly on the above adresse *[sic]* (Budapest

II. CSALÁN ÚT, 27 which is my permanent adresse *[sic]* since *[sic]* 2 years) and not through Zürich.

I think it would be advisable to publish the english *[sic]* words of the Cantata in your radio paper.

Yours sincerely
BÉLA BARTÓK

[Original in English]

173. TO THE OXFORD UNIVERSITY PRESS—LONDON

[5] *Budapest, II. CSALÁN ÚT 27.*
9th *May*, 1934.

(Oxford) University Press
London
Amen House
Amen Corner

Dear Sir,
I am going to play in London on the 25th May (at B.B.C.). On this occasion I should like to come and see Mr. Foss or Mr. Milford and show them some proposals I have about those Rumanian-Xmas-song business. I whish *[sic]* especially to see those english *[sic]* translations of the words of these songs (from No 1 to No 105) you are in possession of, as you told me once.

You may answer me to Budapest (on the adresse *[sic]* shown above), as I am leaving Budapest the 20th only; or c/o B.B.C.

Yours very sincerely
BÉLA BARTÓK

[Original in English]

174. TO THE OXFORD UNIVERSITY PRESS—LONDON

[6] SOLDA, provincia Bolzano, Italy
Hotel ZEBRU
2. *July*, 1934.

Dear Mr. Foss,
a few days ago I sent you 95 type-written pages (the Introduction, explanations etc. in german *[sic]* of my 'Rumanian X-mas Songs') through Rózsavölgyi from Budapest. Please, would you give this to Mr. Calvocoressi—it is him you have probably appointed to translate it—as soon as possible; I would be very glad to have the english *[sic]* translation ready about September or October.

Also, I would be very pleased to have a word from you about the arrival of that type-written copy. Above adresse *[sic]* is to be used until 23. July when I am leaving for Venice; from 30. July I will be again in Budapest (II. CSALÁN ÚT, 27).

Yours very sincerely
BÉLA BARTÓK

PS. I have met Mr. Brăiloiu in Budapest a few weeks ago; in fact he has the english *[sic]* translation of the words of the Xmas songs (No 1 to No 105) you sent to him in his possession; he will send it to me to look it over.

The translation of No 105–141 you gave me is rather good.

[Original in Hungarian]

175. TO VINKO ŽGANEC—ZOMBOR

[1] *Budapest, II. Csalán út 27.*
October 27th, 1934

Dear Sir,
Please excuse me for being so late in thanking you for sending the ecclesiastical folk-songs of the Muraköz region. The reason for this long delay is that I have been waiting for the booklet containing my radio talks to appear (appropriately enlarged), as I wanted to send it to you in return—and this I have done today. At the same time, and in connection with this booklet, I would like to make a few observations (which will, perhaps, interest you), to prevent any misunderstanding as to the contents of this publication.

1. First of all, I beg you not to take amiss my statements about the Muraköz material. Please believe me when I say that in my studies I have not been, and never shall be, guided by any chauvinist bias; my sole aim is to search for the truth and to conduct my search with as much impartiality as is humanly possible. As the clearest proof of this I can point to my explicit statement in this booklet that approximately 38 per cent of the Hungarian material is of foreign, chiefly Slovak, origin, while only about 20 per cent of the Slovak material is of Hungarian origin (all this, of course, on the basis of the material collected so far; additional collecting might well change the picture). I should like to point out that there is nothing humiliating in the fact that one nation, or especially a small region such as the Muraköz, falls in one respect or another under

the influence of their neighbours on this side or that. The people of the Muraköz could still remain, and in fact have remained, Croatian, just as, for instance, the Slovenes have remained Slovenes, however much their folk music has been Germanized. My personal feelings in this matter can be summed up, broadly speaking, in this way: as a Hungarian, I'm tremendously interested that there has been in the Muraköz such a powerful infiltration of the old-style Hungarian melodies (belonging to group a); but from the general human point of view I would naturally be more pleased if this were not so—if, in fact, the material from the Muraköz had proved to be unique. Just as I am, for example, very pleased—and this, I think, can be read between the lines of my booklet—that the Rumanians of the Bihar region have been able from their own resources to produce something so marvellously different, musically speaking; and so on. The most pleasing thing of all would be if each country, each region, each county, even each village, could produce something of its own, original and unique. But this is impossible, for people—whether they speak the same language or not—come into contact with one another, influence one another - - - It is these interactions that we, as research workers, must endeavour to unravel with the utmost impartiality.

2. I hope the bitter irony in the last paragraph on p. 33 of my booklet will not be misunderstood. This irony—as the attentive reader and anyone acquainted with Hungarian conditions can instantly sense—is exclusively directed against the indifference, or rather the hostility, of my own compatriots. For 80 or perhaps 90 per cent of the Hungarian upper classes even now look upon me and my colleagues almost as traitors, simply because I study and propagate the music of the Hungarian village (instead of the art-music called 'Magyar songs'!). It was in order to shake people here out of this indifference that I described the plight of Hungarian folk music in such strong terms. And I have actually succeeded in arousing some interest in official circles, so that, at long last, we are this autumn in a position to begin the task, which will occupy us for several years, of preparing for the press the folk-song material of Hungary.

The Academy in Zagreb is deserving of the highest praise for having published your collection, for every item that is discovered ought to be published, regardless of its origin, whether autochthonous or suspected of being alien. Just as we include in our universal collection every melody found in Hungarian language territory, irrespective of its origin; with regard to those of alien origin, of course, there will be suitable references to known variants of other languages.

3. Lastly I should be very pleased if you did not take it amiss that in certain places I disagreed with your metrical division. The correctness of my view is supported by the fact that you yourself give three different metrical divisions to one and the same melody and text rhythm. For example, in the 1st Muraköz volume:

Obviously only one of the three can be correct, and that is the placing of bar lines in No. 200. Therefore, 201 and 203 would be correct as follows:

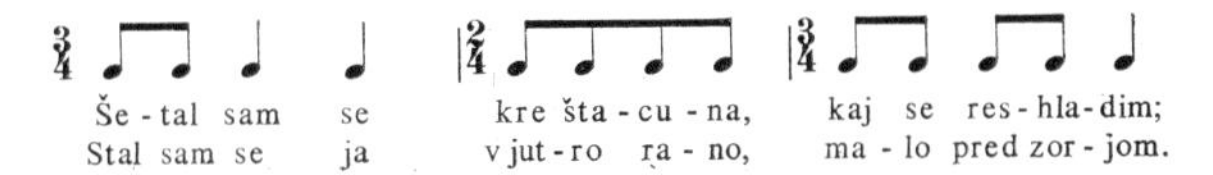

And there are more instances like these. Even more serious mistakes arise in connection with the 'new Hungarian' melodies because the prosodic rhythm of the eleven-syllable lines (whether in the Hungarian, Croatian, Slovak or Ruthenian languages) is the following:

If now, as the consequence of rubato performance, one or another value becomes lengthened in the melody, this must be shown as, at most, a prolongation of the bar, since the bar lines must always be placed after the 4th and 8th syllables; for instance:

or however else it may be. It is clear that only this can correspond to the rhythm of the *text lines*, and of course of the *music*.

4. In my booklet I was not able to give a detailed enumeration of the material because it was addressed to the general public which is not interested in the listing of too much data; apart from this,

my space was also limited. On the assumption that the matter will interest you, I list below the numbers of those melodies in your first Muraköz volume which are taken over from ancient pentatonic Hungarian melodies, and which you could not have ascertained at the time of the publication of your book:

6-syllable lines:

339–340 | * 55, 57, 58, 59, 60, 61, 63, 64, 65, 67, 68, 69, 70, 71, 72, 115, 414 | 126, 382b, 240–241 | 246, 254, 320, 215 | 314, 457 | 131, 256, 315 | 161, 162, 166 | 207, 318 | 208, 210, 213 | 290, 299, 333, 334 (335) | 222–226 | 332 | 168, 198 | 394 | 113 | 181, 177–180, 182–193, 197, 137–140, 204–206, 214, 247–251, 176 | 172–175, 321, 284, 66, 526, 527 | 149–150, 152–156, 167, 252–253 | 209, 211, 212 | 157 | 146–148 | 406–407 | 56, 74, 412 | 164, 135, 316, 382a, 127, 397, 319 | 516, 518 | 142–144, 227

7-syllable:

* 107, 109, 111 | 390 | 237–238 | 108 | 341, 343, 344 | 349, 375 | 194–195 | 464, 476–478, 416 | 388

8-syllable:

255, 469, 356, 323 | 262–264, 325, 291, 485, 486 | 265–267, 269 | 289, 300 | 420, 438 | 292, 295, 296 | 430, 239 | 293, 294 | 493, 494 | 563, 564

9-syllable and 11-syllable:
373, 501, 358, 297

Kolomejka-like:

11, 413 | 89, 92, 93 | 87, 45

* The pentatonic nature, or rather the Hungarian origin, of the 2 groups marked with asterisks is still doubtful.

Finally, I would like to ask you for information on one or two points:

How is the collecting activity proceeding in Yugoslavia at present? Could I study phonograph recordings somewhere? Is the phonograph used at all? Are there anywhere any major (unpublished) collections, noted down and in a state suitable for study, in Zagreb or Belgrade for instance? Is any major publication planned? I would be very interested to see such material, not from the Hungarian point of view, for, as one can see from Kuhač's and Kuba's great (Bosnian and Herzegovinian) collection (published in Sarajevo), with the exception of the items from Muraköz, there are hardly any points of contact. But it is with Rumanian folk music that I would like to compare it as thoroughly as possible; for I suspect, especially in the music of the Rumanians in the Bánát, a strong Southern Slav influence; what is more, I even think that the music of the Rumanians in the Bihar region came into existence as the result of the crossing of pentatonic and Southern Slav melodies. Unfortunately Kuhač and Kuba (and a few smaller publications on which I have also drawn) do not provide enough evidence to give a definitive answer to these questions. However, Kuba, for instance, noticed some highly interesting phenomena: e.g. syllable-clipping at the end of the lines and the splitting of syllables with pauses are things which also occur (though not so often) with the Rumanians, and which, in all probability, were general throughout the entire Balkan Peninsula (they are not found in Hungarian songs, and among the Slovaks only in one single melody have I observed an unmistakable example of syllable-splitting). Then, too, it would be very interesting to know, for instance, whether the so-called 'Bulgarian' type of rhythm occurs in the Serbo-Croatian language territory. For it does occur with the Rumanians, though only occasionally, and there is no more than a hint of it in the songs of the Hungarians of Transylvania. I suspect this to be a common characteristic of South-East Europe, and not peculiar to Bulgaria; it is merely—or so it would seem—that the Bulgarians have preserved it in the most intact form.

I would be very pleased to have some information on these points, and, of course, I am always ready to help you in similar ways.

Yours faithfully,
BÉLA BARTÓK

PS. I've written in Hungarian, for I believe you understand Hungarian. But if you find it difficult to write in Hungarian, you can write in German, French or English. In Croatian, unfortunately, I only understand the folk texts, but the literary language, hardly.

[Original in English]

176. TO THE OXFORD UNIVERSITY PRESS—LONDON

[7] *Budapest, II. Csalán út 27.*
2. *November* 1934.

Dear Mr. Foss,
at last I got the english *[sic]* translations of the X-mas songs from Budapest[1] Nr. 1–92 r is written with pencil and translated by Mr. X (his name does not appear in the manuscript) Nr. 87 l–141 is typed and translated by Mrs. Lucy Byng.

Now, Mrs. Byng's translation is very good indeed; only a few slight changes will be necessary, which probably I can do myself with the help of an american *[sic]* pupil of mine.

But Mr. X's translation is, I am sorry to say, quite impossible! He uses a XX century's middle-class every-day language which utterly destroys the beauty of those old poems. Luckily, there are a few numbers (from 87 l to 92 r)—I don't know why—translated by *both* of the translators, so you may judge them yourself. Here enclosed you find two examples.

By the way, Mrs. Byng's version is *always much nearer to the original,* for Mr. X. changed very often (but quite unnecessarily), the original meaning (apparently by intention).

Now what could be done? What is your opinion? Is Mr[s]. Byng still available? A little more than the half of the whole thing is—in Mrs. Byng's translation—acceptable; the other half should also be done by her. I can send you a copy of Nr. 1–84 k (there are now 4 copies of the words at our disposal); but first I must have your decision. I could also send you Mr. X.'s translation, may-be *[sic]* Mrs. Byng will find there some useful hints, but maybe—also—Mr. X's bad expressions would confuse her.

At the same time I ask you what happened in meantime with the introduction etc, I sent you end of June. Is it already translated in english *[sic]*, or has the work of its translation begun?

Expecting your answer I am yours very truly

BÉLA BARTÓK

[1] Bartók wrote erroneously Budapest instead of Bucharest.

[Typed text]	[Bartók's Handwriting. A few of his italics are not reproduced]
91 A. REFR. Lord!	
He prayed, he prayed.	He prayed and prayed
That which he prayed for	And God granted him
God did give to him.	All that he prayed for.
He gave him a place in Paradise	He gave him a good place in paradise,
5. Where he lived well,	Where everything is well provided for,
Where tables were spread	Where there are spread tables,
And white lights were burning.	Beautiful wax-lights burning,
Round the tables	And decorated chairs
Chairs were arranged.	All round the tables.
10. In the centre of the tables	In the centre of the tables
Flourished and grew an	A pearl apple-tree
Apple-tree of pearl,	Had grown,
Proudly bearing	All in lovely bloom,
Flowers of silver	With blossoms of silver
15. Apples of gold.	And apples of gold.
Through the mist overhead	When fine, drizzling rain,
Which swayed softly,	Began to evaporate,
The apple trees quivered,	The rising vapours
The apples fell down,	Shook the apples down
20. The tables were laden.	And loaded the table with them.
The dear God	The good Lord,
On a throne seated	Seated on an elevated chair,
Stretched forth a hand,	Put forth His hand
And took two apples,	And took two apples,
25. In His hand He held them	Lifted,
And smelt them,	And smelt them,
And spoke thus:	And then said:
– John, John,	– John, John,
Godfather Saint John!	Godfather, Saint John!
30. In order of time,	According to time,
Who is the elder?	Who comes first?
John, Saint John	Saint John replied,
Spoke thus:	Saying:
– In order of lordship	— As to rulership,
35. Thou art chief lord,	Thou art first,
In order of time	But as to time
I am the elder.	I take precedence,
Dost Thou know, Lord, or not,	For knowest Thou or knowest thou not,
That when Thou wast born	When thou wast born
40. Thou didst fall on the hearth	Thou dropped down on to the hearth,
And I lifted Thee up,	But I lifted thee up
It was I who baptised Thee	And baptised thee
And the name that I gave Thee	And gave thee the name of:
Was Lord of the Highest,	'Lord of the Highest,
45. Lord of Heaven	Ruler of Heaven
Lord of Earth.	And Earth.'

Another example (from Nr. 7 a):

'When Theodore heard this, he was very angry. He got his hounds ready and mounted his horse, setting out after the stag, whom he found sleeping, and immediately thought of shooting him in his sleep, but there would have been no pride, no honour in that. He therefore unleashed the pointers and let loose the hounds. The hounds barked at the stag and the pointers surrounded him' a.s.o.

(This sounds like a report from a newspaper!)

[Original in Hungarian]

177. TO VINKO ŽGANEC—ZOMBOR

[2] *Budapest, II. Csalán út 27.*
November 7th, 1934

Dear Sir,

The booklet I sent you has been returned from the Yugoslav frontier, stamped 'ZABRANJENO, INTERDITE'![1] I don't suppose the frontier guard read the booklet; it rather seems he has imposed an intellectual blockade. I shall try to find some other way of getting the pamphlet to you; meanwhile, I should be grateful if you would notify me as to whether you have at least received my registered letter.

Yours faithfully,
BÉLA BARTÓK

[Original in English]

178. TO THE OXFORD UNIVERSITY PRESS—LONDON

[8] *Budapest, II. Csalán út 27.*
3. *November* 1934.

Oxford University Press [stamped: 7. *Dec.* 1934.]
Amen house, Warwick square,
London.

Dear Sir,

a few weeks ago, I wrote a letter to Mr. Foss, telling him that the first half of the english *[sic]* translation of the Roumanian X-mas song-words are quite wrong in style and it would be preferable to get a new translation of this part by Mrs. Lucy Byng, if she is still at your disposal. I asked him about his opinion of this matter, but, untill *[sic]* now, no answer arrived.

[1] Prohibited.

Would you, please, let me know your decision; if you changed your mind so as not to publish the X-mas songs, will you kindly let me know it.

In that case, I would be very pleased to have returned the 'Introduction and Notes' I sent to you in Juin *[sic]*.

Yours very sincerely
Béla Bartók

[Original in French]

179. TO RAÏNA KATZAROVA—SOFIA

Budapest II. Csalán út 27.
February 27th, 1935

Dear Madam,
I am deeply sorry to have to tell you that I have been prevented from making my trip because of a breach of faith on the part of the Antonov Concert Office. At the last moment, 5 days before the 1st concert, they altered the conditions!

It would have interested me so much to make your acquaintance, to see how you work in the field of folk music, and perhaps go to some village to hear the peasants sing those extraordinary rhythms of theirs. But, alas, God—or rather Antonov—decreed otherwise.

I have already begun to study the 1st volume of the large edition. There are a number of questions I shall want to ask you, but I can only do that in a few months when I have done more work on the subject. With regard to the money you wanted to send me, I beg you to buy and send me Bulgarian books, till the sum is exhausted (postage included); for example, some middle-grade grammars used in the schools, some readers—say for the 2nd or 3rd elementary classes (perhaps with pictures); also, if there is any money left, some picture postcards and magazines. (Of course this is only if it can be done without much trouble: otherwise you could wait for some opportunity to send me the money, for example through Professor Fehér when he comes to Budapest.)

I have no need of a dictionary because I have an excellent one, the Weigand (Bulgarian–German).

With regard to the songs you ask for, I could send you (as a present) a volume of 20 Hungarian songs with simple and easy piano accompaniments, which was published by Kodály and myself.

Another collection (5 Slovak folk-songs), which you might care to have, would cost 3 or 4 Reichsmarks; but they are very difficult to sing and to accompany.

To Raïna Katzarova FEBRUARY 1935

Will you kindly send the enclosed letter to Prof. Fehér, as I do not know his address; it is to explain why I can't make my journey to Sofia.

Yours very sincerely,
BÉLA BARTÓK

[Original in Hungarian]

180. TO IMRE DEÁK—PASADENA (CAL.)

Budapest II. Csalán út 27.
March 5th, 1935

Dear Deáks,

I was very pleased indeed to learn that you have at last succeeded in reaching your goal—and that I can start my letter addressing you as above. Has settling in California turned out successfully for you? Here—as far as I am concerned—the main item of news is that I have not done any teaching in the school since Sept.; instead, I am commissioned by the Ministry to work on folk music at the Academy of Sciences—for which I am truly thankful.

I have a little request to make in connection with the following matter:

It so happens that I myself have to publish a certain scientific work on Rumanian folk music. It is a strictly scientific publication consisting of 3 sheets of introductory preface *in German* and 484 melodies. To cover at any rate part of the publishing expenses, I am trying to procure orders privately. Of course, as the work is of a scientific nature, only libraries and experts are likely to be interested in advance orders. Would it be at all possible for you to get some orders (university, state or town libraries if there are such over there)? Or perhaps you might commission someone who could be trusted to make the arrangements. The book will appear in about April; and then I will send out the prospectuses (the price will be 5 Sw. fr. = about $ 1.70).

Please don't be annoyed with me for troubling you with such things and, if you can't do anything because you don't know a sufficient number of people, write and say so quite frankly.

Professor Thomán has again been very ill; he has been in a sanatorium for some weeks and is now a little better. A few days ago, the Lipótváros Casino gave a benefit concert for him; all his pupils who have 'made their fortunes' collaborated (except Dohnányi who is still a convalescent).

With kindest regards to you both,

Yours sincerely,
BÉLA BARTÓK

[Original in Hungarian]

181. TO VINKO ŽGANEC—ZOMBOR

[3] *Budapest, II., Csalán út 27.*
July 3rd, 1935

Dear Sir,
I hope you will be so kind as to accept my apologies for not having answered your letter earlier. I hope, too, that you received the little booklet I sent you, maybe even two copies of it (for someone wanted to send you one from Prague). In the meantime, another collection has appeared *(Rumanian Colindas);* 2 or 3 weeks ago I had it sent to you from Vienna; I think the material will be of interest to you, as it has certain links with South-Slav folk music.

Thank you for the data in your letter. With regard to *Melodije iz Južne Srbije,* I already had it; but of the other *(Iz predratne Srbije)*, I had no knowledge. I immediately had it sent to me, had it copied and have already been studying it.

Of the Bulgarian publications, I have not only *Od Timok do Vita* but also the 2nd big volume by Stoin, and the Rodope volume too (and these two only came out about last Christmas).

In answer to your query, I mention below the following Hungarian folk-song publications:

1. Bartók, B., and Kodály, Z.: *Erdélyi magyarság* [Hungarians of Transylvania—Folk-Songs]: 150 melodies and texts, Budapest, 1921. Rózsavölgyi & Co. (Budapest, Szervita tér 5) distributors. (The price would be appr. 6 to 7 pengős).

2. Ecsedi, Dr. István: *Hortobágyi pásztor- és betyárnóták* [Shepherd and Outlaw Songs of the Hortobágy], Debrecen, 1927. 'Méliusz' bookshop. (150 pp., but 62 melodies only; the price can hardly be more than 3 or 4 pengős; this, too, can be ordered from Rózsavölgyi, provided it is not out of print. This was collected and published by dilettanti.)

I am surprised to read in your letter that Kuhač has still 4,000 unpublished melodies. These are surely in some library where they can be studied, aren't they? In my opinion it would be better not to publish these, Kuhač's notations being very defective but rather to use the money thus earmarked for new collecting activity, namely, collecting organized scientifically with all kinds of equipment (phonograph)!

Yours sincerely,
Béla Bartók

PS. An acquaintance of mine, just back from Prague, told me only today that when he was there, he heard your opera based on folk music material. I didn't even know you had written an opera!

[Original in English]

182. TO THE OXFORD UNIVERSITY PRESS—LONDON

[9] *Budapest, II., Csalán út 27.*
4. *July*, 1935

Dear Mr. Foss,
beeing *[sic]* impossible a complete English edition of the Roumanian X-mas Songs, and having arisen some difficulties even in Bucarest, *[sic]* I decided to publish these tunes at my own expenses (with introduction etc. in German).

Of course, I could not afford to publish the complete words; so the publication is a complete one only from the musical point of vue *[sic]*.—I am sending you some prospectusses *[sic]* and (order-) postcards; perhaps some libraries or scientists will be interested in the book, so that you could do something for the propagation of it.

Yours very sincerely
BÉLA BARTÓK

[Original in English]

183. TO THE BRITISH BROADCASTING CORPORATION—LONDON

[7] *Budapest*, 10. *December* 1935

Dear Sir,
I hope you have been informed by my secretary, Mrs. Kossar, that I have been abroad from 2. Dec. untill *[sic]* 10. Dec.; this is the reason for returning the contracts later, than the date required by you.

Yours sincerely
BÉLA BARTÓK

PS. The programme form I am sending at the same time to the Midland Regional Director, Birmingham directly, according to your suggestion.

[Original in English]

184. TO THE BRITISH BROADCASTING CORPORATION—LONDON

[8] *Budapest, II., Csalán út 27.*
the 14. *December* 1935

B.B.C.
London

Dear Sir,
many thanks for your letter of 11th Dec. (AP/DW); I will be at your disposal Monday 6th Jan. 10 a.m. and 7th *10.20 a.m.* for the orchestral rehearsals, but with the 4th Jan. there is a difficulty: I have on the same day an orchestral rehearsal in Utrecht (Holland). The earliest day I can be in London is 5th Jan. about 10 a.m.; being this day a Sunday, Sir Henry [Wood] will probably not be able to come to London for that piano rehearsal. What I may suggest is this: piano rehearsal the 6th Jan. at 9. a.m. (just before the 1. orchestral rehearsal); or if Sir Henry can come to London the 5th Jan. then on this day at any time from 11 a.m. Please let me know your decision as soon as possible. Could you send me the yellow 'permit' at the same time?

Yours very sincerely
Béla Bartók

[Original in Hungarian]

185. TO LÁSZLÓ RÁSONYI—ANKARA

[1] *Budapest, II., Csalán út 27.*
December 18th, 1935

Dear Professor,
Your letter addressed to the High School for Music has only just reached me, quite by accident. (I have not taught there for 1½ years and only send someone over to collect my salary from there once a month.)

1. I should very much like to visit you and to give a lecture, even if I do not make anything out of it financially. But it is important for me—because it costs me time—not to have any expenses with regard to the journey. Even the incidental expenses (such as visas, meals on the train and taxis, etc.) would amount to quite a large sum.

2. I *do* know that Hindemith was recently invited to Ankara by the Turkish Government to organize a High School for Music. I am on very friendly terms with him and hold him in high esteem; therefore we must at all costs avoid even the slightest suggestion that I might want to interfere with his work. But there is no need

for this to happen; he gives advice on the organization of music schools, and I should only give advice in relation to the collecting of folk-songs—something not in his line.

3. You might find it helpful to have other advisers from here, too, but I could not very well undertake such matters. I would even find it difficult to say *who* should go. Those who have managed in one way or another to find work are just the ones who presumably would not like to settle there permanently. Those who are 'unemployed', like Mátyás Seiber (composer and cellist), Iván Engel and Kentner (pianists), are for the most part Jewish; I do not know if this is a disadvantage there or not?! Sándor Veress has just come to my mind (he is one of our best young composers, a good pianist, and has also been engaged in collecting folk-songs). Of course, none of these has any money for travelling: perhaps their travelling expenses could also be paid?

I would like, if I may, to make certain suggestions:

Owing to my other work, I cannot start before the end of March, so that only April or May would be suitable. Would a 1½ hours lecture be all right, and in what language (German, French, perhaps English)? Which foreign language do they know? To illustrate my lecture, I could play one or two suitable small pieces on the piano; but it would be better if your Philharmonic Orchestra—assuming there is one—could also play some of our compositions, say one or two days after the lecture; I have a number of easy orchestral works, perhaps the *Háry* Suite by Kodály or his *Dances of Galánta* would not be too difficult. At a rough guess, the incidental expenses would come to at least 200 pengős (I suppose the journey will take 3 days). I cannot afford to spend so much on travelling. My idea is that it would be better for you to provide me with 2nd-class sleeping-car accommodation (a few years ago I travelled to Athens in this way, and it was quite comfortable), and to find me a room at a less elegant place (I don't like very luxurious hotels anyhow), and the difference could then be used for my minor expenses. Or couldn't I live in a private house, as the guest of some Turk? That is really what I would prefer; but of course, I don't know what it is like there, or whether such an arrangement is possible. I have yet another idea for procuring money. I am just preparing for press a short booklet of appr. 2½ or 3 sheets with the title *How and Why Should We Collect Folk Music* (this is to appear in Budapest in Hungarian). As you have asked me to answer precisely these questions, would it not be possible to buy the Turkish-language rights from me at our usual price (80 pengős per sheet)? I understand that the collecting of folk-songs has only just begun in Turkey; a small handbook of this nature might prove to be very useful to future Turkish collectors.

During my stay I would like to go on a little collecting trip, but for this a phonograph and phon. cylinders would be necessary. Is there one in your Museum, or does anyone else have one that could be used? Have they any unused cylinders? I could bring a phonograph, but they would have to order the cylinders (from Germany or possibly Pest).

Finally, I should like to say a few words about the subject of the lecture. In the first place, I would deal with the relations between the folk music (of Eastern Europe) and contemporary music in general; I should really say that I would speak almost exclusively on that subject. Because, for example, we do not actually know anything about the connections between Hungarian and Turkish folk music; the ancient Turkish music that has come my way has always been more Arabic in origin. Mahmud Raghib came to the conclusion that in the true Turkish folk music there are many pentatonic melodies; he sent some of these melodies to someone in Budapest, but there was too small a quantity of material for us to draw any conclusions. Now I see that Raghib has written in the *Musical Lexicon* (1931) as follows: 'In 1923 the Conservatory Darül-elhán was established in Istanbul as a centre for the modern Turkish folklore movement. A collection of folk-songs is being made with the aid of the phonograph. With regard to the publication of material, two volumes of songs and 13 song series including 1,000 folk-songs and 200 "art" songs have appeared to date, compiled by the writer.' (It is a pity that the folk-songs and the others have been mixed. Could I obtain a copy of those 1,000 folk-songs (perhaps by now there are even more), so that I can see what has been collected and how? (I do not need the 'art' songs—at the moment.) Another point: it would be essential for me to see the Centre of Folk Music in Istanbul on my way before giving my lecture, for I can only give useful advice when I know what has and what has not been done in this field to date.

Would you kindly answer all this before the end of Dec., if possible; I am going to England on Jan. 2nd and only return about Jan 21st.

Yours very sincerely,
Béla Bartók

PS. There is one thing that I absolutely don't want in this matter, and that is the financial assistance of the Hungarian Ministry of Culture. I have my pressing reason for this.

[Original in Hungarian]

186. TO VINKO ŽGANEC—ZOMBOR

[4] *Budapest, II., Csalán út 27.*
December 23rd, 1935

Dear Sir,
I have recently noted down some of my own Serbian and Bulgarian phonogr. recordings dated 1912, or rather I have revised my earlier, not altogether accurate, notations made from these recordings. I think the Serbian material will interest you, so I am sending you a copy of the notations. It's true that some of the Serbian pieces are well-known melodies, but nowhere have such accurate recordings and notations been published. In fact, I think this is the only Serbian material so far to have been taken down (with the greatest possible accuracy) from phonograph recordings; for, as far as I know, no phonograph has been used hitherto in your country for folk-song collecting; or at any rate, no material collected in this way has been published. The figures marked M.F. refer to cylinders owned by the National Museum in Budapest, the (sole) figure marked F. refers to a cylinder owned by myself.

Some parts of the texts I understand quite well; there are places, however, where I cannot find my way: the words I don't know I can't find in the dictionary. But it is quite possible that I have taken them down wrongly or that I don't hear them clearly in the phonograph recordings. I should be very grateful if you could write them down for me with the necessary corrections—if ever you have time, that is (it's not urgent).

For instance, is the last word on p. 9 perhaps 'NEĆE'? What does 'LUČE GUČE' mean on p. 10? And 'MA NO BI ĆE' on p. 11? I simply cannot get the sense of verses 2 and 3 of No. 21.

By the way, the method, in which the syllables are swallowed in the songs that are sung, is very interesting; this is that phenomenon first noticed and described by Kuba. Very valuable, in my opinion, are the bagpipe notations; bagpipe music so exactly taken down has not appeared so far, to my knowledge.

Permit me to add, for your information, that both villages now belong to Rumania (the majority of the inhabitants are Rumanians, the minority, Serbs).

Yours sincerely,
BÉLA BARTÓK

PS. Have any new publications of musical folklore appeared since last year on the territory of the S.H.S.?

[Original in Hungarian]

187. TO THE KISFALUDY SOCIETY—BUDAPEST

Budapest, December 29th, 1935

Dear Sirs,
I have read in today's paper that this year the Kisfaludy Society has awarded me the Greguss Medal for my 1st orchestral Suite (op. 3). In this connection I should like to make the following comments:

1. The statement made in the Notes giving reasons for the award, that the *first* Hungarian performance of this work in its entirety took place in November, 1929, is *incorrect*, since the work in its entirety was introduced to Budapest, thank God, in 1909 by Jenő Hubay, and on November 29th, 1920, by Antal Fleischer. I say 'thank God' because it would be odd if a work written in 1905, and of such excellence as to merit the Greguss Medal, should have had to wait for 24 years to be performed in Hungary, in its entirety.

2. But even if the above-mentioned statement were true—which it is not—the award itself cannot be justified. I am, it is true, very fond of that particular work of mine—it was in fact an outstanding achievement for a young man of 24. Nevertheless, in the period between 1929 and 1934, numerous works of greater merit and maturity were performed in Hungary, for instance *The Spinning Room* or the *Dances of Galánta*.

3. I should like to make the suggestion—unsolicited, yet in good faith—that you should seek, as a matter of urgency, another selector. How could the intrinsic merits of particular works be evaluated by a man who cannot even establish which works can come into consideration chronologically?

4. And lastly I take the liberty of declaring that I do not wish to accept the Greguss Medal, neither now, nor in the future, nor during my life-time, nor after my death.

I remain,

Yours faithfully,
BÉLA BARTÓK

[Original in English]

188. TO THE BRITISH BROADCASTING CORPORATION—LONDON

[9] *Santpoort (Holland), January* 13th, 1936
[Postcard]

Dear Mr Clark,
I am sorry that you have been abroad. Now, I will be again in London (coming from Birmingham) from next Sunday afternoon* untill *[sic]* Monday (20th) evening (19 p.m.) leaving for Harwich. I will stay at Mr. Duncan R. Wilson's, 7, Sydney place (Tel. Kensington 4070). Would you write me there or 'phone, where and when may I see you?

Yours very sincerely
BÉLA BARTÓK

* probably 4 or 5 p. m.

[Original in English]

189. TO THE BRITISH BROADCASTING CORPORATION—LONDON

[10] *Liverpool, January* 16th, 1936

Dear Mr. Clark, I hope you got my postcard from Holland. Now, I see that I have on Sunday (19th) a train at 11.45 a.m. arriving in London at 1.50, so I will be at 7, Sydney Place (Mr. Duncan Wilson's) already about ½ past two. I am at your disposal that day entirely; would you let me know where and when we could meet. For me, it would be better to meet you Sunday than Monday. You may write or 'phone to my London adresse *[sic]*, or write to Queen's Hotel, Birmingham, where I am staying untill *[sic]* Sunday morning,

Yours very sincerely
BARTÓK

[Original in Hungarian]

190. TO THE BUDAPEST DAILIES

[Through the intermediary of the Hungarian Academy of Sciences]
[*February* 3rd, 1936]

The lecturer considered 4 questions relating to F. Liszt.

The first question was that of the response of the general public to Liszt's compositions. In the lecturer's opinion, even today, the general public did not sufficiently appreciate Liszt's important works and preferred the less significant ones, e.g. the rhapsodies. According to the lecturer, the reason for this was that audiences lacked the capacity to see what was really essential in musical compositions and were unduly influenced by superficial elements. In other words, it was precisely that which is most valuable in Liszt's works that the general public did not like, while at the same time favouring that which is of least value.

The second question was that of the impact of Liszt's works on the further development of music as an art. In the lecturer's opinion, Liszt's œuvre was more important in this respect than Wagner's; not that Liszt's works were more perfect than Wagner's (for, actually, just the opposite was the case), but Wagner, the lecturer said, had exploited and developed to the full all the possibilities arising from his own inventiveness. On the other hand, much of Liszt's invention indicated possible developments which he himself failed to exploit, and which were only fully utilized by his successors.

The third question referred to Liszt's book *Gypsy Music in Hungary*, i.e. to the erroneous statement which this contains. According to the lecturer, Liszt was only partly to blame for his errors. These were more to be attributed to 19th-century conditions—a fundamentally false idea of musical folklore; the romantic fondness for excess in all things, for superfluous ornaments, for pathos and a corresponding disregard for classic simplicity. In addition, we could blame our grandfathers, too, who had not been able, or had not wanted, to help Liszt to find the truth: the truth of life in a Hungarian village.

The fourth question concerned our right to consider Ferenc Liszt a Hungarian. Here it was Liszt's own attitude which was decisive; for on countless occasions he had declared himself to be Hungarian. The whole world owed it to Ferenc Liszt to respect his wishes in this respect and not to go against them.

[Original in Hungarian]

191. TO JENŐ TAKÁCS—CAIRO

[3] *Budapest, II., Csalán út 27.*
[Postcard] *February* 16th, 1936

Dear Mr. Takács,
During almost the entire month of Jan. I was away from Budapest (in England, etc.), and so it is only now that I can answer your

question. No. 1 = a Slovak melody (with a characteristically 'Slovak rhythm contraction' in the inner lines; countless Slovak and Moravian variants are known). No. 2 = an inter-East European melody (the so-called 'pillow dance'), very generally known among the Hungarians, the Slovaks, the Rumanians, etc.: not typical of any of these peoples. No. 3 = a *South-Slav* melody (with a so-called half-close as a typical feature). No. 4 = The Train Goes to Kanizsa; this also belongs to the international East European jargon; countless Hungarian, Slovak, Ukrainian, Moravian, etc., variants are known; not typical of any of these peoples. No. 5 = a generally known *Hungarian melody* (more recent); fairly widespread with the neighbouring peoples, typical, nevertheless, of the *Hungarian* material and obviously originating from it.—I am glad you feel more or less settled. Of course, there are difficulties everywhere, and we are no exception, to be sure. The biggest trouble of all is that things continually get worse.

With all good wishes,

Yours sincerely,
BÉLA BARTÓK

These are the music examples mentioned in the letter:

1. Zelena Jelva

2. Ča se kadi?

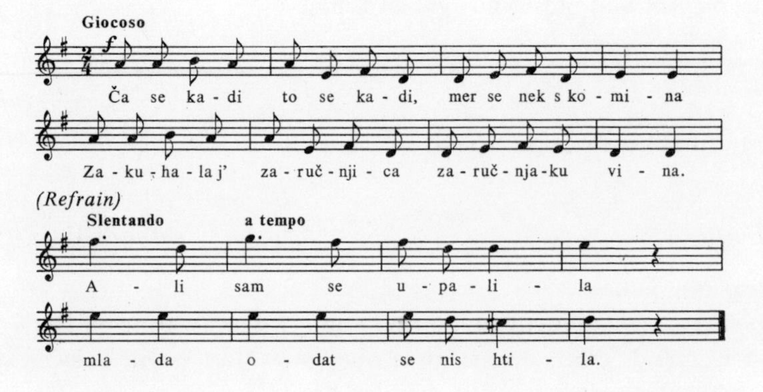

3. Oj Jelena

Lento (ma non troppo) rubato
Oj Je - le - na ja - bu - ka črlje - na, Oj Je - le - na ja - bu - ka črlje - na.

4. Marica rožica...

Presto
Ma - ri - ca ro - ži - ca ča - te pro - sim
Ze - le - nu ki - ti - cu ra - do no - sim
Ze - le - na je, Kod to tra - va
Ma - rí - ca ro - ži - ca ljù-bav pra - va.
etc.

5. Nemoj Majko tužna biti...

Mosso
calando rit.
Ne-moj majko tuž - na bi - ti što ja mo-ram u - boj i - ti;
Meno mosso
rit. poco
Più lento
Ne - moj maj - ko tuž - na bi - ti što ja mo-ram u - boj i - ti.

[Original in Hungarian]

192. TO LÁSZLÓ RÁSONYI—ANKARA

[2] [*Budapest*] *April* 16th, 1936

Dear Professor,

I was very pleased to have your letter. What you suggest would, of course, be a very satisfactory way of arranging things—but not this season. In Dec. I still had Apr. and May free, but in the meantime I have, of course, had to dispose of these two months as well, so that the situation is now as follows: on April 22, I have to play in Budapest; on May 2, in Temesvár; on May 6, in Kecskemét; on May 18, in Vienna; and at the end of May or the beginning of June there will be a session of the Comité des Arts et des Lettres de la Coopération Intellectuelle in Budapest, which I ought to take part in.

However, if I could reach a final agreement with the Halk Evi now, we could fix things up very satisfactorily for Oct. In fact, this would be a much better arrangement, for several reasons.

1. We could make better preparations: 2. By that time the gramophone records of Hungarian folk music would perhaps be ready, so that we could use them to illustrate the lectures. (Up to now there haven't been any of these, so I should have had no alternative but to play records from Bucharest or Cairo of Rumanian or Arab folk music, which would not be saying much for the situation in Hungary!)

At the moment, I most favour the following 'programme':

1. Three lectures, illustrated with gramophone records and the piano (as proposed: the lecture in Hungarian or German, interpreted into Turkish). The text of the lectures to be sent well in advance, say by the beginning of Sept.

2. Appearance with the Philharmonic Orchestra, with perhaps the following pieces:

a) Liszt: *Totentanz* (this being a Liszt year), for piano and orchestra
b) Bartók: *Rhapsody*, op. 1, for piano and orchestra
c) Bartók: *Hungarian Peasant Songs*
d) Bartók: *Hungarian Sketches*
} for orchestra only (they do not need a large orchestra)
e) One of Kodály's orchestral compositions

3. Collecting of Turkish folk music.

4. Arising from this, discussions with the persons concerned about tasks for the future.

Before going to Ankara, I should want without fail to spend a few days in Istanbul (I have already been invited to stay with someone there) to see for myself what the phonogramme archives there really contain.

We must, however, definitely reach an agreement in principle now, sometime in May; otherwise, I can't keep even October available. Once an agreement has been reached, we can then discuss the programme in greater detail.

I look forward to hearing from you further—as soon as possible.

With kind regards,

Yours sincerely,
BÉLA BARTÓK

PS. I met Hindemith in London, in January; we discussed, among other things, conditions in Turkey. He says the Turks do not much understand foreign languages. So that I don't know whether it's worth while to deliver my lectures in German or just stick to Hungarian. How many, roughly, of those who are likely to come and hear me will understand German or French?

[Original in German]

193. TO BRIGITTE SCHIFFER-OELSNER—CAIRO

July 14th, 1936

Dear Mrs. Schiffer-Oelsner,

Thank you very much indeed for sending me your excellent and thorough work. There is only one thing I regret: the absence of the texts of the songs. Was this totally impossible? Let me say that my little collection from the Biskra region suffers from the same defect (just like many of Hornbostel's publications and others too). Being wholly ignorant of the Arab language, I was totally incapable of putting down even a single line; my hope was to repair the omission on some future occasion—a hope which, alas, has never been fulfilled.—For I think that to determine the structure of the melodies sung, it is all important to know the subject-matter.

With all best wishes for the continued pursuit of your studies, I remain,

Yours sincerely,
BÉLA BARTÓK

[Original in Hungarian]

194. TO LÁSZLÓ RÁSONYI—MÁTRAFÜRED

[3] [*Budapest*] *August* 21st, 1936

Dear Professor,

I see that you will soon be going back to Turkey; you will keep your promise to visit me before you leave, won't you? For my part, I would welcome the opportunity to talk over various aspects of my trip and send a few messages to the halk-evis.

Except for Aug. 28 (when I shall not be in Budapest), I am at your disposal any day and any time; may I have the pleasure of welcoming you to my home? Or, if you would find it more convenient, we could meet at the Acad. of Sci., although I do not go there regularly now.

It would be nice if I could keep that little Turkish dictionary for some time.

I have struggled through the grammar; it's more difficult than I thought at first. All those verbal forms are rather difficult, especially the seemingly countless finite participles and infinitives. For the time being, I have given up trying to understand those tortuous sentences into which as much meaning has been compressed as would go into 10 sentences in any other language. Fortunately, these do not occur very frequently in folk-song texts; now I am going to buckle down to the corresponding part of the Kúnos collection.

I am enclosing a copy of the letter which I sent to Ankara about the middle of July; I have not, of course, had any reply yet. Please give me a few days' notice before you come, so that I can plan my work accordingly.

Yours very sincerely,
BÉLA BARTÓK

[Original in Hungarian]

195. TO HUGÓ KELEN—BUDAPEST

Budapest, September 28th, 1936

Dear Mr. Kelen,
It's impossible to alter anything there, to be sure! If it can't be managed otherwise, our dear father *must be left out,* lock, stock and barrel!![1]

Under the circumstances, sorrowful greetings from

BÉLA BARTÓK

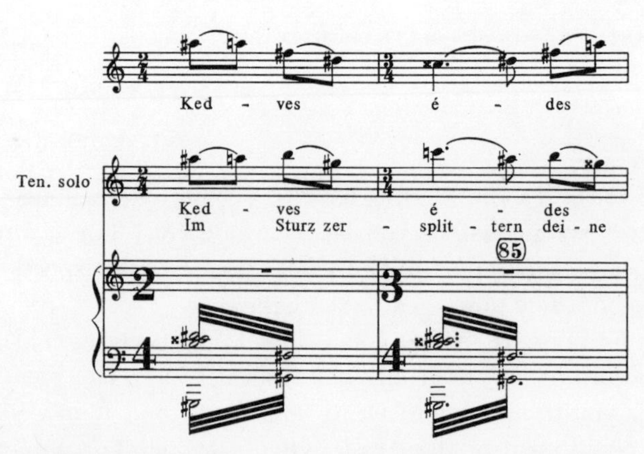

[1] The upper music example is the altered version Bartók after all prepared. For further explanation see note. (Editor)

[Original in Hungarian]

196. TO SÁNDOR ALBRECHT—POZSONY

[1]

[Postcard]

Ankara, Légation de Hongrie
November 15th, 1936

Dear Sanyi,[1]

I thought of you a great deal in Istanbul—wondering which streets you had walked in, and whether you had made the boat trip in the cistern of 1001 pillars.—I intend to go even farther than Ankara (with the phonograph), to Adana, near the Syrian border, among certain nomadic tribes.—They are building up the country in all kinds of ways, and there is a great deal of organized activity; there is a conservatory, too, but no pupils as yet. I hope you are all right (as for me, I was unwell here for some days).

All good wishes,

Yours,
BÉLA

[Original in Hungarian]

197. TO JÁNOS BUŞIŢIA—BELÉNYES

[15]

[Picture postcard: Ankara . . .]

Ankara, Légation de Hongrie
November 18th, 1936

My dear Friend, now I'm doing some collecting with the phonograph, deep in the heart of Asia Minor. It was in 1917 that I last worked with a phonograph, at Dumbraviţa de Codru. I wouldn't have thought then that the continuation [. . . . .] will be delayed and, what is more [. . . . .]

[Original in French]

198. TO AHMED ADNAN SAYGĬN—ISTANBUL

[1]

Budapest, II., Csalán út 29.[2]
January 2nd, 1937

Dear Mr. Adnan,

First, I would like you to know that I shall be giving a talk on the Radio on Jan. 11, 7.30 p.m. about my journey through Anatolia, with musical illustrations. Perhaps it will be possible for you to hear it. Then, I am eagerly awaiting the translations you promised;

[1] The Hungarian diminutive for Sándor (Alexander).

[2] The number of the house Bartók lived in was changed from 27 to 29.

I am already writing down the recordings. It is a most exhausting task, but at the same time very interesting. One quarter of the material has already been transcribed. Have you started transcribing some of the recordings? I am awaiting the photographs, too. It seems from the newspapers here that some great disaster has occurred at Adana! Could you give me details? I am most worried about the fate of our friends there!

As regards the copying of my recordings, this is the position now: I have found a firm which makes recordings on disc for its customers. The records, that is to say each side of them, plays for 3½ minutes (my cylinders 2½ minutes each), so that 3 cylinders correspond to approximately 1 record. The price of a record is 10 pengős (= 2½ [Turkish] pounds). As I have 65 cylinders, corresponding to about 25 records, the whole series will cost 250 pengős (= appr. 60 pounds). The weight of these 25 records will be a bit less than that of ordinary ones, so carriage and customs duties will not be very high. However, we must first make a test to see if the sound is satisfactory in copies made like this. The test will be made in a few days' time; I shall let you know with what result. By the way, if you come to Budapest in February (will you be coming?), you can judge for yourself the quality of these test copies and, at the same time, settle matters with the firm in question.

I have not forgotten about the publications I promised you, but I'm still waiting for one booklet to come out; I shall send you them all together.

You have been very accurate in taking down the words; so far I have only found mistakes in No. ... in which the singer made changes which have not been noted (and which, of course, I cannot understand).

Thank you once more for all your interest, and I shall look forward to hearing from you.

With my kindest regards,

Yours sincerely,
BÉLA BARTÓK

[Original in French]

199. TO AHMED ADNAN SAYGİN—ISTANBUL

[2] *Budapest, II., Csalán út 29.*
January 14th, 1937

Dear Mr. Adnan,

I think the best thing would be to send you the copy I mentioned in my previous letter. This copy, which you will receive in a few days' time, contains the melodies No. 41 (verses 4 to 6) and No. 1 on the one side, and No. 82 and No. 2 on the other. You will then be able to judge for yourself. Will you please, in any case, try to take down these 4 tunes; let me have the transcriptions, and I will give you my comments.

I should like to know whether you were able to listen to my talk on Jan. 11?

Enclosed you will find an article and the reproduction of a photograph, both published in our *Rádió-Élet*.

I'll be away until Febr. 13; I hope to have news from you by the time I get home.

Till then, all good wishes,

Yours sincerely,
Béla Bartók

[Original in German]

200. TO MME MÜLLER-WIDMANN—BASLE

[1] *Bruxelles, February* 3rd, 1937

Dear Mme Müller-Widmann,
First of all, thank you very much indeed for sending me the beautiful pictures—a memento of the happy days we had in Basle. But where did you get my Amsterdam address?! I thought I had forgotten to give it to you. Everything went well at Hilversum, also my lecture in Amsterdam; as for the latter, it was a novelty for me to be able to work with musical examples and a map (of Europe and Asia Minor) all projected on a screen. Meanwhile, I have had a little excursion to Paris where I played with Székely on the 30th; you probably couldn't pick this up (but never mind, we are due to play much the same programme from Hilversum on the 11th). In Paris the arrangements were very casual. There was only the announcer to welcome us to the studio, and at first he took Zoltán Székely to be the composer; then he confused our first names and very nearly announced us as Zoltán Bartók and Béla Székely; finally, he asked which country we actually came from and, to crown it all, he thought we were Czechs. There was no one at all in charge of the microphone, so we had to play just as we thought fit, quite at random.

Everything was entirely different in Brussels. First, there was a really excellent orchestra, and second, a highly efficient conductor. The way in which the members of the orchestra play at sight is quite astonishing. Unfortunately, the time allowed for rehearsing this huge programme (1½ hours of music) was extremely brief; in spite of this, everything went very well, only here and there the tempi were not quite true (and, unfortunately, I blundered a few times in the piano Concerto!!), for there was no time to discuss everything thoroughly. I met Herr Vogel several times; he also came to the rehearsals.

The programme was divided into two parts, the first for the French-language transmission and the second for the Flemish one. I wonder if you were able to pick it up. In Part 2 they gave *Village Scenes,* the 2nd Rhapsody for violin + orch. and the *Mandarin* music. I was delighted with the (terribly difficult) *Village Scenes* and the 2nd Rhaps., for I have never had the chance of hearing these 2 works performed satisfactorily.

Once more my warmest thanks to both of you for everything, I remain, with every good wish,

Sincerely yours,
BÉLA BARTÓK

Please tell Herr Beck when you have the chance that Mount Bonvin (near Montana) *is* 3000 m. high!

[Original in German]

201. TO MME MÜLLER-WIDMANN—BASLE

[2] *Budapest, II., Csalán út 29.*
May 24th, 1937

Dear Mme Müller-Widmann,
I will begin first with the matter of letters. There is a good side and a bad side to this question. To get letters is, for the most part, a pleasure to me, and especially such friendly ones as your own. But letter writing is my weak point; it is such a torture to me that as long as possible I go on putting it off from one day to the next. This aversion seems to come from having to write usually about tiresome or at best uninteresting and boring things: I have to argue with publishers and concert bureaux because everybody tries to cheat you, and people never do what they ought to do, fulfil their obligations or keep their promises, etc., etc.—In the case of letters such as this one, of course, it is quite different—here there are other obstacles: first lack of time in general, together with incredible arrears of work (for instance, part of my Arab collection of cylinders which I made in 1913!! I have still not written down); and secondly, the flood of disagreeable letters which I have to write every month

—so many that I can't count them. From every corner of Europe and North America people write to me, making the most amazing requests; I really ought to have a very clever secretary with a good understanding of Hungarian, German, English and French, who would be also capable of answering all these letters more or less unassisted. Unfortunately I cannot afford such an assistant even if one were to be found!

As to our travelling next summer, we—my wife and I—had really planned a journey, not to France but to the French part of Switzerland (to Fionnay, near Sembranches). From there I should have liked to go to Paris to take part in the meeting of the Comité des Lettres et des Arts, July 20th–23rd. But because of my recent illness ('flu and bronchitis), I have lost so much time that I must give up my visit to Paris (though, as a matter of fact, meetings of that kind are, in my opinion, completely purposeless, consisting of nothing but more or less elevated chatter, with not the slightest practical result). Because of all this, we have had to alter our plans completely—we will go somewhere in Carinthia, which will be a much less expensive journey. Even before your letter arrived, I had been wanting to write to you to ask about the hotels in Fionnay—then came our change of plans, and now unfortunately everything is different.—Why are you going to Paris? For the Music Festival perhaps? (I don't know at all when it will take place.) Or for the Exhibition? (which, it seems, will not be ready until the end of July.)—Originally we wanted to go to Italy (to the Dolomites), but my hatred of Italy has of late grown to such unnatural proportions that I simply cannot make up my mind to set foot in that country. This may seem a very strained and exaggerated point of view; but I have no wish, at least during my few weeks' holiday, to be continuously bothered by the aggressiveness of the Italians. Actually, they say that Austria has also been infected with the Nazi poison, but it is not so obvious there.

At the concert on May 7th I really did play some pieces from the *Mikrokosmos*. However, at this particular concert they were not so important as the children's choruses. It was a great experience for me when—at the rehearsal—I heard for the first time my little choruses coming from the lips of these children. I shall never forget this impression of the freshness and gaiety of the little ones' voices. There is something in the natural way these children from the suburban schools produce their voices, that reminds one of the unspoilt sound of peasant singing.

To Mme Müller-Widmann MAY 1937

I am sorry not to be able to come to Basle again this year. I wish you and your family everything good for the summer. With kindest regards to you all,

Yours,
BÉLA BARTÓK

[Original in Hungarian]

202. TO THE GOVERNORS OF THE ENGLISH-LANGUAGE RESIDENTIAL BOARDING SCHOOL—SÁROSPATAK

Budapest, II., Csalán út 29.
May 26th, 1937

Dear Sirs,
I wish to apply for a place for my son, Péter Bartók, in the 4th form of the English section of the Sárospatak Boarding School so that he may acquire a command of the English language. My son will be 13 yrs. old in July and will then have passed through the 3rd form of the Secondary School Teachers' Training Grammar School in Budapest. I would be glad to have information on the following points:

1. I have by me the prospectus of the Boarding School; it appears that an application must be sent in by June 10 and that, among other things, last year's report must be enclosed with it. As the school year does not end until June 19, it is impossible to obtain the report as early as June 10. What should we do, please?

2. What are the prospects of his being admitted?

3. I see from the prospectus that places will be allotted at the end of June. I imagine that if my son succeeds in his application, it will be necessary to send some kind of deposit on receipt of the notice. As neither I nor my wife will be in Budapest at that time, would it be possible for you to notify some other person whose name and address I would indicate in the application?

4. As my son has not previously studied English and would go straight into the 4th form, I should like to know if there is any way in which he could make up for what he has missed, so as to catch up with his classmates?

5. On which day of September does the school year begin?

I look forward to hearing from you on these points and would appreciate an early reply.

Yours faithfully,
BÉLA BARTÓK
Professor at the High School for Music

[Original in French]

203. TO AHMED ADNAN SAYGÏN—KADI KÖY

[3] *Budapest, II., Csalán út 29.*
June 20th, 1937
[*Heiligenblut, July* 7th, 1937]

Dear M. Adnan,

I am so sorry to have left you without news for such a long time. But it's always the same old tune: terribly busy, etc., etc.

First let me thank you for all that you sent me. I received first the translation of the text; your essay on notation (of the songs on the record sent from Budapest to Istanbul); and the photographs. And recently I received the rest of your notations.

For my part, I sent to you: 1. on May 18, those of my own works which I had promised you, namely (*a*) a study of the relations between the folk music of the Hungarians and that of the neighbouring peoples, (*b*) the collection entitled *Melodien der rumänischen Weihnachtslieder*, (*c*) my choruses. All this was sent off by registered printed matter to the address 'A. A. Saygïn, Konservatuarda Muallim, *Istanbul*, Konservatuar.' As, in your letter of May 27, you do not mention this consignment, I am a bit worried as to whether you have received it or not. The other parcel was sent off (registered) on June 16, this time to the address 'A. A. Saygïn, 127 Mühürdar caddesi, *Kadïköy* Istanbul.' This second parcel contains my transcriptions of cylinders Nos. 1 to 30 (approximately one half of all the cylinders). May I now ask you to go through the texts, the titles of the pieces, and the names of the villages, vilayets and singers; to correct the mistakes in spelling, if any; and to return all the material to me, let us say at the beginning of September (if convenient to you). *Please will you kindly add the translation of the texts on the cylinders Nos. 1 to 11.*

I've already finished transcribing cylinders Nos. 31 to 64; as soon as I get back the transcriptions of cylinders Nos. 1 to 30 with your comments, I'll let you have these and ask you to do the same with them.

As far as your first transcriptions are concerned, you can compare them now with my corresponding transcriptions and draw your conclusions. In my opinion, you should have used small notes in the *gruppetti* to indicate the sounds of lesser importance (those which sound, so to speak, less articulately, less forcefully); further, it seems to me that the values of the notes you have chosen are, generally speaking, too big; it would be more convenient to stay between the limits ♪ = 100—♪ = 200. In a few cases you did not notice all the small notes! Your notations of the song recorded on cylinder No. 53 doesn't seem to me to be well done; you will only be able to compare that one with my version when you receive the second batch of my notations.

I think your notation of Rije and Aydĭn has been more successful; but I would need the corresponding records to form a final opinion. You write that Director Zija Bey will bring them to me when he comes here. I shall not be in Budapest before September 8; should he arrive before that date, I wonder if he would be so good as to deposit the records with *Rózsavölgyi et Cie* (publishers of music), Szervita tér, *Budapest* (French spoken!).

Allow me to suggest yet another way by which you could improve your work in this field: our National Museum has just recorded some peasant music on 4 discs (songs sung by old peasants).

These records are on sale—and the notations (made by Kodály and myself) are enclosed with the records. Do try and persuade the Director of your Conservatory either to buy them or to offer our Museum 4 records of his collection in exchange. He would have to write to Count István Zichy (Director of the Museum), Történeti Múzeum, Múzeum körút, Budapest. Hearing these records and perusing the notation, you will be able to see for yourself (and if you wish, to imitate) the method of work we have adopted.

We have chosen the *sol* as final tone for practical reasons.

For the has—so far—been applicable to the melodies *of all the peoples*. One tone lower (e.g. *fa* or *re*) would be impossible for many West European melodies, for the latter often go down as far as the octave below the final. On the other hand, a tone higher would entail a number of inconveniences, with many Turkish and Hungarian melodies going up to the thirteenth degree above the final!

With the *sol* as final tone we have the following scale at our disposal for the melodies of the entire globe:

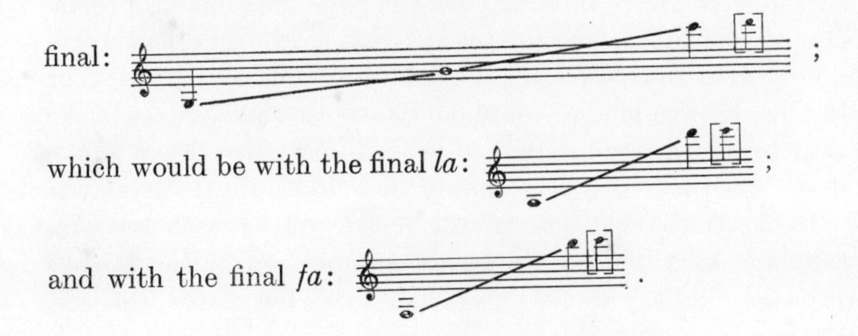
final: ;
which would be with the final *la*: ;
and with the final *fa*: .

So you see that the sol system is the most convenient one.

You ask me whether the 'improvisations' should be notated or not. You are right when you say that a genuine improvisation cannot be classed as a 'popular melody'. Nevertheless, if improvisations of this sort are current fashion with the peasant musicians in the villages, they should be collected, from the point of view of folklore. That is my own view and, as a matter of fact, I have collected such pieces myself (incidentally, they are very rare here). What you have to do in your country is to examine whether these improvisers really are villagers permanently living on the spot or just vagrant troubadours. In the latter case, their improvisations, too, must be looked upon with suspicion and caution.

Before finishing, there is something else I must mention. Rózsavölgyi, the publishers (mentioned earlier), are willing to bring out my Turkish collection. It would be a publication in three parts: I. Preface and annotations in French; II. The melodies with the texts; III. The French translation of the texts.—Would you allow me to make use of your translations in this Part III?

Now, while on vacation, I am studying the texts of my Turkish collection with the help of your translations. There are, however, a few places which I don't find clear enough. Then, it seems that, here and there, you have omitted to translate a line or a word. I will send you a list of these queries in September in the hope that you will clear them up.

I ask you once more to forgive my prolonged silence; truly I have been overwhelmed with work and all kinds of problems during the past season. But I have already taken steps to prevent this happening in the coming season. I should like to continue to keep in touch with you permanently, and I hope I'll be able to answer your communications in an acceptable space of time.

Thank you very much for the photos, some of which have come out remarkably well!

With all good wishes,

Yours sincerely,
BÉLA BARTÓK

PS. You have not sent me your compositions yet!

[Original in Hungarian]

204. TO GÉZA VOINOVICH—BUDAPEST

Budapest, September 14th, 1937

His Honour
Géza Voinovich
Secretary General
Hung. Acad. of Sciences
Budapest

Dear Sir,
I beg to submit, as requested, a report on the work that is being done in connection with the publication of the comprehensive collection of Hungarian folk-songs.

We have been engaged in preparing these for the press since September, 1934. During this time I have revised the transcriptions of all the phonograph cylinders, 1,026 in number. Meanwhile, Kodály has selected all relevant material from what is already in print. We have copied, and partly systematized, the song material—necessary for purposes of comparison—of the neighbouring peoples of Hungary (Bulgarians, Serbo-Croatians, Slovaks, Poles, Ukrainians).

The plan of work for the years ahead consists of: 1. final preparation for the press of the Hungarian material already revised; 2. comparison of the material thus arranged with the songs of the peoples listed above. This will in all probability take another 3 years. (Comparison with the German material is a separate task which can only be accomplished in the folk-song archives in Berlin, by someone sent to work there for a period of 3 to 4 months.) The total material for the press is estimated at about 12 thousand songs. In print this would amount to approximately 4 thousand quarto pages. The minimum cost for printing and paper would amount to 100 thousand pengős, quite possibly more.

We shall have all the material ready for the printers 3 years from now. It would be most helpful if over the next 3 years a certain sum could be set aside for the printing expenses, for it is hardly likely that such a sum would be forthcoming immediately when the time comes for handing in the material to the printers. Alternatively, instead of setting aside the money, it would also be possible for the Hung. Acad. of Sciences to purchase paper out of an annual allowance and keep this in reserve, for it is known that the major part of the cost of printing is accounted for by the price of paper. The continued rise in the price of paper is also a by no means negligible factor.

Yours faithfully,
Béla Bartók

[Original in French]

205. TO PAUL COLLAER—BRUXELLES

[1] *Amsterdam, January* 25th, 1938

Dear M. Collaer,
First of all, I beg you to be kind enough to forgive me for being so late in answering your letter of Nov. 8.—You can't imagine what a harassed life I lead in Budapest; it is only with the greatest difficulty that I can find time for correspondence.

I've given a good deal of thought to your request for a work (or, as you say, 'a page') for that symphonic concert to be held in May—it's going to be extremely difficult for me to do it. Nevertheless, I have had an idea (for 'a page' rather than an entire work)—next Sunday, after our concert, we can discuss how to realize it.

I am very interested to learn that you will play my 2nd Sonata. However, there are some difficulties over the 8 songs (which, if my information is correct, I am to accompany). I have only just this very minute learned the titles of these songs, and I haven't got the music with me. I shall have to practise them a bit, even before rehearsing with the singer, for it's quite a long time since I last played these accompaniments.

I shall arrive in Brussels (from Luxembourg) on Jan. 30, at 12.48, and will be staying at the Hotel Cosmopolite, near the Gare du Nord. I shall have my lunch immediately and be free at 2 p.m. Would you be so kind as to leave a message for me, indicating when I could go (between 2 p.m. and 5 p.m.) to the Radio to practise in a vacant room the accompaniment of these songs; of course, I shall also need the music; as I didn't know which of my songs had been selected, I couldn't bring them with me.

With kindest regards,

Yours sincerely,
Béla Bartók

[Original in Hungarian]

206. TO SÁNDOR ALBRECHT—POZSONY

[2] *En route, January* 31st, 1938

Dear Sanyi,

Don't be surprised that I haven't written to you for such a long time; I have so much to do and to arrange whenever I am in Budapest that it defies description; it's almost unbearable, really. I am very sorry that the Pozsony people didn't get a permit for me: it was just as well that I did not accept the invitation for the chamber-music festival to be held in August! They would like to have me as a guest of honour, of course, but do not grant permission for a concert; what a gang! I didn't even have time to do anything in that Sl. Mat. affair.—It has occurred to me meanwhile that I could, perhaps, have my entire Slovak collection copied in Budapest from the rough draft, and that this could hardly cost more than buying back the whole manuscript. But first I would have to take a good look at that rough draft at home and see if it wasn't a bit too rough! If I decide that this will be the solution, then you would have collected the *tromba* and *corno* all for nothing; and then we would have to think about ways and means of getting them to me. One way is a trouble, the other way is a trouble—and I have hundreds of other troubles as well; if I had not turned grey years ago, I would certainly do so now.

I am at the moment on my way home from a little money-making tour: for 3 weeks I have been touring in the few countries that have remained free. I even managed to get to little Luxembourg (they have a good radio orchestra). Only the beginning of my tour really interested me—I started off in Basle with a performance of my new work (which I think I mentioned to you some time ago) for 2 pianos and 2 groups of percussion instruments; my wife played the 2nd piano and held her own splendidly. The whole thing sounds quite unusual—but the Basle people liked it, anyway. What a pity we can't give it in Pozsony! Perhaps there isn't even a *Maschinenpauke* in Pozsony, which you simply must have for the performance. The timpanist in Basle was a real virtuoso.

I'll have a look at that rough draft as soon as I get home (at this moment, I'm sitting in the glorious 卐-country, not of my own choice, of course, but while waiting to change trains!), and then I'll write to you again. Till then, every good wish to you all, from

BÉLA

[Original in English]

207. TO WILHELMINE CREEL—TOKYO

[1] *Budapest, II. Csalán út 29.*
31st *January* 1938

Dear Mrs. Creel,
I fear you are very angry with [me] or disappointed because of my really too long silence. But you can hardly imagine how difficulte *[sic]* it is for me to find time and to gather my thought *[sic]* on correspondance *[sic]* (especially if it is to be done in a foreign language). In fact, (as a matter of fact) the accumulation of work I am expected to accomplish is really a terrible one. In that respect, my life is still worse than it was a year ago—and I have no help from anybody.

However, I was very much touched by your first letter and desired it so much to give you some suggestions: how to get on with your worries. But, of course, this task is a very difficult one for me: I don't know exactly all the circumstances giving your life so many difficulties.—I was very glad to see in your second letter, that your spirit is now in much better conditions. All I could have given you as an advice is this: you, as a musician should try to get on through the difficulties by giving yourself entirely to your art! Only, I don't like your beeing *[sic]* in that country where you now are (I hope you understand what I mean and why!). For the same reason I don't like that business with the music-revue. I don't want to get in touch with anybody of that country, unless they give me a declaration which they can not give! But I sent you three weeks ago some of my articles, and I give you the autorisation *[sic]* to use them or to publish them where ever *[sic]*, when ever *[sic]* and in whatever language you like. I give it to you because you told me in your letter that this business is very important for you.

We all are quite well. I had to compose two big works in the summer, but unhappily I could finish only one of them (a sonata for 2 pianos and percussion). The second one (a concerto for violin & orchestra) is not yet finished—having not finished it is a very opressing *[sic]* burden on me.

As for the 2 piano + percussion sonata, its world-premier has been given in Basel 2 weeks ago. My wife and myself played the 2 pianos—it had a 'tremendous' success. Mrs. Bartók played very well—this was her first public appearance in a foreign country. After that premier I had to go—alone—to Luxembourg, Brussels, Amsterdam, Haag *[sic]* and London and to accomplish there not very interesting works, only for sake of getting money!

How are you getting on with the Japanese language? Is it very interesting and—of course—very difficult? If I had more time, I would learn it with great pleasure (you know how fond I am of exotic languages).

Had you already occasion to play with an orchestra? Are conditions not rather disagreable *[sic]* (uncomfortable) there? Of course you have nothing to fear ennemy-aeroplans *[sic]*, but nevertheless – – – – – –

I will be always very much pleased to get news from you. Don't mind, please, my silence in the past (and in the future?) and let me have news from you.

Yours very sincerely,
BÉLA BARTÓK

[Original in Hungarian]

208. TO THE EDITOR OF 'AZ EST'—BUDAPEST

Budapest, II., Csalán út 29.
March 27th, 1938

I have just learned with some astonishment that in one of your numbers last week you again made reference to a matter which concerns me, and which, in view of my statement published in the *Pesti Napló* in November, we could rightly consider to be closed. Now you republish that statement of mine with an erroneous addition to the effect that I made this statement, or sent it, to German authorities.

You would greatly oblige me by printing a declaration by me to the effect that up to this day, i.e. March twenty-seventh, 1938, I have not made, or sent, any statement to German authorities.

I would like to know, by the way, the source from which you obtained this distorted information—and who it is who finds it to his interest to go on stirring up this matter.

Yours faithfully,
BÉLA BARTÓK

[Original in German]

209. TO MME MÜLLER-WIDMANN—BASLE

[3] *Budapest, April* 13th, 1938

Dear Mme Müller,
I was very pleased indeed to have your letter of sympathy. You are right, the days when Austria was attacked without warning were also dreadful days for us. I think it is quite superfluous to write about this catastrophe—you have very concisely and eloquently put into words the main issue. That is exactly how we feel. There is one thing I want to add, concerning what is at this moment—at least for us—the most terrible prospect. That is the imminent danger that Hungary will surrender to this regime of thieves and murderers. The only question is—when and how? And how I can then go on living in such a country or—which means the same thing—working, I simply cannot conceive. As a matter of fact, I would feel it my duty to emigrate, so long as that were possible. But—even in the most favourable circumstances—to have to earn my living in some foreign country (to start toiling at the age of 58, to begin, say, teaching, and to be wholly dependent on it) would be immensely difficult and would cause me such distress of mind that I can hardly bear to think of it. In that event I could achieve nothing, and in such conditions I could not do my proper and most important work anywhere else either. Consequently, it is exactly the same for me whether I go or stay.—And then I have my mother here: shall I abandon her altogether in her last years?—No, I cannot do that! So much for Hungary, where, unfortunately, nearly all of our 'educated' Christians are adherents of the Nazi regime; I feel quite ashamed of coming from this class.

I am no less alarmed by the question when (after the collapse of Czechoslovakia and Hungary) it will be the turn of, e.g., Switzerland (and then Belgium)? What is the situation really like there? However favourable it may be, there is always the possibility that a thousand people might be found who would suddenly ask Germany to march in!!

As regards my own affairs, I must say that things are not very good at the moment because not only my publishing house (U.E.) has gone Nazi (the proprietors and directors were simply turned out) but also the A.K.M., the Viennese society for performing rights, to which I belong (and Kodály, too), is also being 'nazified'. Only the day before yesterday I received the notorious questionnaire about grandfathers, etc., then: 'Are you of German blood, of kindred race, or non-Aryan?' Naturally neither I nor Kodály will fill in the form: our opinion is that such questions are wrong and illegal. Actually it's rather a pity, for we could give answers that would make fun of them; e.g., we could say that we are *non*-Aryans—because (according to my lexicon) in the last analysis 'Aryan' means 'Indo-European'; we Hungarians are Finno-Ugrians, or ethnically, we might possibly be northern Turks, that is we are a non-Indo-European people, and consequently non-Aryans. Another question runs like this:

'Where and when were you wounded?' Answer:

'On the 11th, 12th and 13th of March, 1938, in Vienna!'

But I'm afraid we cannot allow ourselves to joke like this, for we must insist on having nothing to do with this unlawful questionnaire, which therefore must remain unanswered.—The more unlawful the activities of the A.K.M., the better for us, and the easier it will be for us to get out of its clutches (otherwise we would have to remain in this prison for another 10—say ten—years according to one single unfortunate § in the statutes!). We have just learned that in the West European countries 2 powerful Societies of Composers would willingly admit us as members – – – – – – so we wait and hope for further irregular infringements of the statutes, and then we shall be justified in taking the necessary steps. As far as the U.E. is concerned, we have just heard of certain plans on the part of a very important foreign country to release us from them. Unfortunately, I cannot give you any more details, in fact, I must ask you not to talk about these two items of news (in these last 13 lines).

We were greatly touched by your offer of help! Actually there are 3 matters in which I would appreciate your assistance if this would not cause you too much inconvenience.

1. As far back as Nov. I noticed that Hungarian policy was being diverted from the right track: I then conceived the idea of putting at least the original manuscripts of my musical compositions in some safe place. As a matter of fact I was intending to talk about this as long ago as January, but there was no time for it because of the general hullabaloo. Well, now I ask you both, would you be so kind as to give shelter to my manuscripts? With no obligation to be responsible for them, of course: I would bear all the risk. These things do not take up much room: not more than a small suitcase.—

I should like to get someone (possibly Stefi Geyer) to take some of them to you, the rest I would bring myself some time.

2. (This has nothing to do with the crisis!) I have lost the copy of the rough German translation of my children's and women's choruses. Could you possibly ask Mr. Huber (I think this is the name of your daughters' singing teacher?) to let you borrow his copy for a short time, so that you could have 5 copies made at a typing agency? I, or Schulthess, will pay back whatever this costs (in June).

3. (This refers to a dispute I am having with the Association of German Writers and Composers.) I am sending you a file separately—registered—which will tell you what it is about. I have also sent this protest to Baden-Baden (where, to my sincere regret, it caused general consternation, but it is impossible to make exceptions) for—as you will see from the enclosed programme—they wanted to perform my *5 Hungarian Folk-Songs*, demoted by that Association of composers, the notorious Stagma, to the status of an 'arrangement'. I suppose someone, maybe Mr. Sacher himself, will attend this musical festival: could you send this file to him, so that he can look through it, and on my behalf ask him (or whoever happens to go to Baden-Baden) as follows: a) to inform me after the musical festival whether this composition of mine was performed there in spite of my protest; b) if the performance took place, to make it known to large circles that I had protested against it; c) if it was not performed, to let me know the reasons given for cancelling the performance.

Did you know that we're leaving for London in June to play the 2-piano Sonata on the 20th(?)? The Society there has engaged us for a fee of £50; before then, on the 11th, we are to play this composition on the Luxembourg Radio, so we shall still manage to make both ends meet somehow. On our journey back we'd like to go through Switzerland!

This letter has turned out to be a pretty long one—*beg your pardon*![1] All kind wishes from both of us to you and the Professor,

Yours sincerely,
Béla Bartók

PS. Please do not, for the time being, show the passage about the Stagma to any journalists. (That comes later—perhaps.)

[1] In English.

[Original in Hungarian]

210. IN ÁKOS WERESS'S KEEPSAKE ALBUM

Three timely wishes in May, 1938

Liberation from German { ideological / economic / cultural } influences

BÉLA BARTÓK

[Original in German]

211. TO MME MÜLLER-WIDMANN—BASLE

[4] *Budapest, May* 29th, 1938

Dear Mme Müller,
Here is the second consignment:
44 44 Duos for 2 viol. (draft and fair copy on transparent paper), Petite Suite for piano
41 20 Hungarian Folk-Songs, piano & voice, draft and fair copy
42 Hungarian Folk-Songs for mixed choir, draft and fair copy (on transparent paper)
40 2nd Rhapsody for viol. & orch.
2nd Rhapsody for viol. & piano
Alterations to these.
In the meantime, I have received your letter acknowledging the arrival of the first consignment.

I had two very nice days yesterday and the day before: 2 so-called 'Csángó' women were here from Moldavia (East Rumania): the Csángó people are the very easternmost of the Hungarians and have never really belonged to Hungary. There are about 20,000 of them, (linguistically) terribly oppressed (politically, too), but they have preserved a remarkable ancient language. All because of the horrible Rumanian oppression it is normally impossible to bring them to Budapest; it is only the Eucharistic World Congress which has now given us this opportunity. We have made some marvellous gramophone recordings. The two women (both illiterate!) sang songs, told fairy tales, and, with their remarkable accent and ancient costumes, were altogether charming. Only, the whole thing must be kept secret for the time being, and even for some time to come; and when it comes to publication, no names must be given, for it could easily happen that the Rumanian police would put those poor innocent creatures in prison for no other reason than that they recorded songs and fairy tales in their mother tongue. A wonderful world, isn't it?!

All good wishes, and perhaps *another* consignment in a week's time (in addition to the things to be brought along personally) from

Yours,
BÉLA BARTÓK

[Original in German]

212. TO MME MÜLLER-WIDMANN—DAVOS

[5] *Budapest, October* 9th, 1938

Dear Mme Müller,
We have learned with dismay that you are in Davos sanatorium! Please do write frequently and in detail (you probably—and alas!—have all too much time) about your life there, and how you feel; as you know, I like to receive letters, it is writing them that gives me trouble. Possibly, however, it will be only a temporary relapse; let us hope so since you write that you will be able to go home quite soon. In these unholy times it must have been particularly oppressive to be alone, among strangers.—I need not describe the way the events affected me.—And now the situation is in reality much worse than before. What a defeat for England and France—all the worse that it should be at the hands of a Hitler; and, moreover, in an affair in which—if one looks at it superficially—he seems to be 100 per cent in the right. And on top of that we, too, obtain justice through him.—You can't imagine to what extent this has strengthened his following in this country.—But, and this is the most important thing, I can hardly imagine any cooperation between the infamous Axis and the Western countries; the great settling of accounts must come, but later and under even more unfavourable circumstances. So that one must need think that it would have been preferable to have the painful operation now.—Did you read attentively Ch.'s big speech (after Godesberg or Gottesberg or Teufelsberg[1])? It is obvious from this speech that Herr H. twice bared his teeth on that occasion. In the course of the first talks, he told Ch.: if you will recognize the right of self-determination, I prom-

[1] Before the Munich agreement in the autumn of 1938, Hitler and Chamberlain met at Godesberg, Germany. Gottesberg = God's mountain, Teufelsberg = devil's mountain.

ise to negotiate its execution.—Then 6 days later, Ch. agrees to recognition of the right of self-determination, wants the negotiations to begin as he had been promised, and then to his dismay learns that negotiations are out of the question; instead, he gets an ultimatum. 'What do you mean by this?' he asks, whereupon that scoundrel answers, 'I only gave the promise because I was firmly convinced that you would not agree to recognition of the right of self-determination.' 'I never for a moment thought that Herr H. intentionally wanted to deceive me,' Ch. comments. A nice definition of deception.

And secondly: H. said, 'You had better be content with the terms of the ultimatum, for if I had taken military action, I would have imposed *quite different* frontiers' (i.e., he intended to march in without any respect for the Czechs' right of self-determination: that is, he intended to do *the same things* as the Western powers had done after a 4-year military campaign, and which he now so much resents).

Thus, the prestige and influence of this system based on lies will prevail in Europe to an even greater extent. One ought to go away somewhere—but where?! As regards the Czechs—just to look at the other side of the coin for a moment—they are not much better either. They used every kind of trick to try to deprive my mother of her citizenship and thus of her pension; they robbed my mother-in-law of a considerable part of her pension; and, throughout these last 4 or 5 years *I have not had permission* to appear publicly in Slovakia. When so many injustices can be enumerated by one single person, you can easily imagine what an immense number of them have been perpetrated in the course of these 20 years – – –

As for me, I have been working hard this summer. I have finished the Violin Concerto and two pieces (commissioned) for Szigeti and the American jazz clarinetist Benny Goodman (3 pieces, to be exact, 16 minutes altogether). As, however, these artists have exclusive rights to perform the works for 3 years, it will not be possible to hear them in Europe until then.

That business with the Vienna people has still not been settled; the composers' union has petered out in the meantime, i.e. has been swallowed up by the German association, Stagma. So much the better. Something quite remarkable has occurred: when the accounts of this association were made up in March, I received a sum amounting to about 1,000 Swiss francs and also, at the same time, a smaller sum (100). And now I have received this money *again* (the large sum, 1,000 fr., exactly the same as before), and there was no separate account attached. So that I got those March payments twice, in May and in June. Obviously, they not only sent me the same accounts 2× by mistake, they also paid the money out 2×, equally by mistake! For the time being I am keeping silent about it and will make enquiries only when I know that my English membership is completely in order. I am leading an even more retired life here, if that is possible; I do not feel like meeting people, everyone is suspected of Nazism. I work nearly 10 hours a day, exclusively on folk-music material; but I would have to work 20 hours to make real progress. A distressing situation—I would so very much like to finish this work before we are involved in the next world catastrophe that's hanging in the air. And, at this rate, it will take a few more years!

Two weeks ago, I really didn't know which I regretted more: my own and my family's ruin or the destruction of my entire work, etc., etc.—A war would of course ruin me, even if I wasn't hit by a bomb—and yet, I don't know if it wouldn't have been better to have it now than later!

So please write to us quite often, and we both hope that you'll soon be able to tell us that you've gone back to Basle.

With best wishes from us both,

BÉLA BARTÓK
DITTA BARTÓK

[Original polyglot][1]

213. TO MRS. ZOLTÁN SZÉKELY—AMSTERDAM(?)

[*Budapest*] *October* 24th, 1938

Dear Mien!

It is a shame que nous n'avons pas immédiatement répondu après avoir reçu les nouvelles, and that we did not shout forth in a letter: *evviva il Francesco Jacopo, vive le petit François Jacobe, éljen a kis Ferencjákob,* to everyone's joy and the happiness of his parents, hurrah! *živio! să traiască! Yasasĭn küçüh oğlunuz!* So now we are making up for it several times over and in a polyglot way.—Do not be annoyed by our delay.

Meantime, so much trouble has broken out all over the world, such unrest, such upheavals - - - - and now this shocking

[1] Romans indicate that this part of the letter was written in Hungarian.

change of front on the part of the Western countries. One ought to get away from here, from the neighbourhood of that pestilential country, far, far away, but where: to Greenland, Cape Colony, the Tierra del Fuego, the Fiji Islands, or somewhere even the Almighty has not heard of!

I got your letter. What Zoltán wrote is all right; he just forgot to answer one thing. But now it's all the same; soon—if nothing intervenes—we shall be going to Holland, and I shall meet him; *then we will talk it over.*

I am afraid you will not quite understand my very genuine Hungarian expressions but I can't help it: in writing to you my mind poures [sic] out the most colourful words – – – Et puis je n'ai pas voulu faire usage de questa maledetta lingua dei nostri vicini, que j'abhorre plus que jamais.

Our best wishes to you, to your little darling and to your husband.

A bientôt,
BÉLA

From my innermost heart I wish all three of you much joy and happiness.

DITTA

[Original in German]

214. TO HANS PRIEGNITZ—BERLIN

Budapest, II., Csalán út 29.
January 12th, 1939

Dear Sir,

I have received your letter of December 20th. Besides my first piano concerto of 1926, I have only one other, composed 1931–32, the score of which appeared a few years ago and may be bought and performed by anyone. There is no third piano concerto. With regard to the proposed performance of the first piano concerto on the German wireless, I should like to say that the orchestral part of this piano concerto is extraordinarily difficult, and if the conductor and the orchestra are not absolutely first class, and if there is no adequate time for rehearsals, it would be better to abandon the performance. I am, by the way, astonished that such 'degenerate' music should be selected for—of all things—a radio broadcast.

Yours faithfully,
BÉLA BARTÓK

[Original in English]

215. TO THE BOARD OF DIRECTORS OF THE MATICA SLOVENSKÁ—TURÓCSZENTMÁRTON

[3] *Budapest, II., Csalán u. 29.*
January 28th, 1939

For about a year I had intended to declare to you what follows:

1. The stipulations of our recent Agreement of about 6 or 7 years ago—in which I granted you a certain respiro—have been repeatedly violated by your further unjustified delaying and silence. In consequence a) you have definitely forfeited your right of publication of the folk-music material I have given respectively sold to you, b) you are obliged to return to me the manuscript I handed you for the purpose of publication, when I claim it, under the modalities laid down in our Contract in this respect.

2. I have repeatedly summoned you, both in writing and personally in the presence of your Representative, to make a statement as to what has happened to my phonographe-records *[sic]* handed to you, where are they and in what state? As it is your habit, you did not reply. In view of the fact that on page 245 of the publication 'Musique et Chansons populaires' (Institut International de Coopération Intellectuelle, Paris, 1934) the report of the 'Matica Slovenská' contains no allusion to these my phonograph-records, I cannot but presume that the statement of Mr. Ballo to the effect that this phonograph material has become useless under your 'careful' handling, is true. I may tell you: I shall not miss a single opportunity to make this shameful fact public. Had I but had the faintest idea of your utter incompetence in the handling of musical articles, I would have certainly refused to have any dealings with you.

3. Unless an answer to this letter is received by me not later than the 28th February 1939, I shall consider your silence as your agreement with its contents.

BÉLA BARTÓK

[Original in English]

216. TO DOROTHY PARRISH—HUNTINGDON

[1] *Budapest, II., Csalán u. 29.*
February 8, 1939.

Dear Miss Parrish,
it *is* a shame to have left you without a letter for such a long time, whereas you have so often given and so detailed accounts of your life

over there. This is also due to the fact that the very lugubrous *[sic]* political events of last year have on the one hand rather depressed me, and on the other, all the excitement and unpleasantness I had to put up with in this connection, robbed me of very much of my time. Just imagine: the publishers of practically all my works are *Viennese!*, the performing right society of composers to which I belonged was *Viennese*. The society protecting the mechanical rights of which I am unfortunately still member, is *Viennese!* Since that notorious Anschluss, all these have come to Germany. Now, I have a good number of reasons for not being particularly keen on being in any way connected with Germany. I did all in my strength to sever these 'sweet' links, but it was, respectively is by no means an easy matter. For these Germans cling to me like ticks. What efforts, what a lot of scribbling it required to become a member of the English Performing Right Society. In this I succeeded at long last, thank God! To get rid of the Universal Edition is a harder nut to crack: I failed in this so far. The fatal influence of the Germans is steadily growing in Hungary, the time seems not to be far, when we shall become quite a German colony (as Cecho-Slovakia *[sic]* for instance has actually been turned into one). I would like best to turn my back on the whole of Europe. But where am I to go? And should I go at all before the situation becomes insupportable, or had I better wait until the chaos is complete? 'All grave, practically unsolvable problems'—Mr. Mertens, the European representative of the Columbia Broadcasting, wrote to me last March regarding the proposed American tour. I replied at once, but heard nothing further from him since.

Otherwise, we are well (!!). A novel thing is that recently I am frequently playing in concerts compositions for two pianos with my wife. I myself have composed a Sonata for two pianos and percussion instruments, we have played it already in Basle, London, Amsterdam, Brussels, Luxembourg and of course in Budapest. We are again leaving next week to play it in Zurich and in Paris (at the latter place we are also giving Mozart's Concerto for two pianos with orchestra). Even though I be *[sic]* somewhat slack, write to me as frequently as you can. We both are very glad to have news from you and about your doings.

I have to thank you specially for the photo you sent us for Christmas: it *was* good of you to have remembered us in this form.

Very sincerely yours
BÉLA BARTÓK

[Original in French]

217. TO DENIJS DILLE—ANTWERP

Budapest, May 19th, 1939

Dear Mr. Dille,

I was very pleased to get your parcel—the two copies of your book and the list of works; thank you very much. Unfortunately, I am unable to give any opinion of your work, for I do not understand the language well enough; with the help of a dictionary I might possibly be able to discover what you have to say about my works. But such a procedure is a bit too complicated for the time being . . . It would be easier if I had a French or an English translation.

However, I like the plan of the book very much, and I am convinced I'll like its contents, too.

Allow me to send you a copy of my latest work (for clar., viol. + piano). The rights to public performance are reserved for Mr. Benny Goodman till November 1941! But you may read it, and—I hope—find it interesting.

With kindest regards,

Yours sincerely,
Béla Bartók

P.T.O.

The solution of the ő, ű problem seems acceptable (for lack of anything better); there are always difficulties at the printers with the 'exotic' letters; one really ought to have special types cast, but that is too costly. The same difficulty arises, incidentally, with the Rumanian letters ă, â!

[Original in Hungarian]

218. TO DEZSŐ ZÁDOR—UNGVÁR

[1] *Budapest, June* 24th, 1939

Dear Mr. Zádor,

Professor Molnár sent me your collection of Ruthenian folk-songs a few months ago. With your permission, I would like to have copied, for the MS. collection of the Hung. Acad. of Sciences, that part of your collection which is of peasant origin. I would therefore be glad if you could send me a statement to this effect. If you do give this consent, please inform me also which songs in your collection are from peasant singers.

Thanking you in advance for your trouble, I remain,

Yours faithfully,
BÉLA BARTÓK

[Original in Hungarian]

219. TO HIS SON BÉLA BARTÓK, JR.—OROSHÁZA, SZŐLLŐSPUSZTA

[1] *Châlet Aellen, Saanen,*
August 18th, 1939

My dear Son,

Once again the anniversary of your birthday has arrived. I hasten to congratulate you while you are still at Szőllős, as I hear that you will only be there until your birthday. At the same time I will give you a brief description of my life here.

Somehow I feel like a musician of olden times—the invited guest of a patron of the arts. For here I am, as you know, entirely the guest of the Sachers; they see to everything—from a distance. In a word, I am living alone—in an ethnographic object: a genuine peasant cottage. The furnishings are not in character, but so much the better, because they are the last word in comfort. They even had a piano brought from Berne for me. I had been notified that it would arrive on August 2nd at 10 o'clock, and, just imagine, it did not arrive at noon or sometime in the afternoon (as usually happens at home) but was actually here at 9.45. The janitor's wife cooks and cleans; she is a very nice and honest woman, and my wish is her command. Recently, even the weather has been favouring me—this is the 9th day that we've had beautifully clear skies, and not a drop of rain has fallen since the 9th. However, I can't take advantage of the weather to make excursions: I have to work. And for Sacher himself—on a commission (something for a string orchestra); in this respect also my position is like that of the old-time musician. Luckily the work went well, and I finished it in 15 days (a piece of about 25 minutes), I just finished it yesterday. Now I have another commission to fulfil, this time a string quartet for Z. Székely (i.e. for the 'New Hungarian Quartet'). Since 1934 virtually everything I have done has been commissioned.

The poor, peaceful, honest Swiss are being compelled to burn with war-fever. Their newspapers are full of military articles, they have taken defence measures on the more important passes, etc.—military preparedness. I saw this for myself on the Julier Pass; for example, boulders have been made into road-blocks against tanks, and such like attractions. It's the same in Holland—even in Scheveningen.—I do not like your going to Rumania—in such uncertain times it is unwise to go anywhere so unsafe. I am also worried about whether I shall be able to get home from here if this or that happens. Fortunately I can put this worry out of my mind if I have to—it does not disturb my work. Today the Sachers are coming to see me for a few hours. N.B., they do not own this house; after what happened last September, they rented it against all eventualities.—I hadn't read a newspaper for 2 weeks until I picked one up yesterday; the lapse of time was not perceptible, it was just as if I was reading one 2 weeks old. Nothing had happened in between (Thank God!).

My best wishes to you and everybody. If anything happens, think of me.

Much love from your
FATHER.

[Original in English]

220. TO DOROTHY PARRISH—HUNTINGDON

[2] *Budapest, II., Csalán út, 29.*
January 17th, 1940

Dear Miss Parrish,
thank you for your 2 letter[s], I got them both, as usually I am so very late in answering them, for different reasons. First, when the war broke out, I was at a loss, whether to go to America or not to go. In Nov., I decided not to go and have written a renouncing letter to the Library of Congress. Finally, in Dec., I changed again my standpoint (owing to Mr. Szigeti's persuasion), so I will go. Then I had to wait for engagement-dates, in order to know at what days I will be free.

Now, I know that you secured a concert and a lecture for your College, it is—if I am right, the Juniata-College, *Huntingdon*, Pennsylvania (but you are in *Duluth*, how is this?)

I am very glad to have the occasion to see you again! Of course, I am entirely at your disposal for those lessons you will have. The rather difficult question is that of the fee; considering the difference between the Hungarian and American pecuniary situation, perhaps $10 for lesson would not be too high for you?

I am in Huntingdon (or Duluth?) as you know, the 15th and 16th. The next engagement is at Harvard University in Cambridge the 22nd April. So I could stay in your town until 21st (if no new engagement will be fixed between 16th and 22nd), plenty of time for lessons. I could even manage it, to reserve time for lessons on the 15th and 16th.

As for works to study, you may choose whatever you like from all the works by Beethoven (excepted the last sonata, and the 'Hammerklavier'), by Mozart, Bach, Schubert, Chopin, Schumann, Debussy, and—Bartók! You will get this letter probably in the beginning of Febr. and will have more than 2 months to prepare works. (I forgot to mention Liszt: all works, excepted the most 'hackneyed',—is this the right expression?)

For the programm *[sic]* of my concert in Huntingdon, I would select of my older works (f.i. Mikrokosmos), and some of Kodály's works. I will send the detailed programm *[sic]* later through Mr. Schulhof.

We had and still have rather difficult times, not only because of the general situation, but also privately; but all these I will tell you when being there.

Excuse-me again for being so very late and please let me know the arrival of this letter.

Yours, very sincerely,
BÉLA BARTÓK

PS. 1. As I will arrive in the first days of April in New York, there I will have (from 3rd—to 8th) 7–8 days free.

2. Excuse-me for all this trouble: I could not find your letter of Dec. 12., but just now je viens de la retrouver. So I see, you are in Huntingdon (in Duluth probably only during the summer)—everything is clear now.

[Original in Hungarian]

221. TO DEZSŐ ZÁDOR—UNGVÁR

[2] *Budapest II., Csalán út 29.*
February 3rd, 1940

Dear Mr. Zádor,
Please forgive me—many times over—for this long delay; for I have to confess that the copying was finished in the autumn, and the manuscript could have been returned long ago!

Thank you, first of all, for your June letter and for permitting the copying. I had to put certain signs in pencil on the manuscript, to help the copyist, but these are very faint and can easily be erased. With regard to the pieces contributed by educated people, I solved this problem by incorporating into the copy the ones from the *ouchitelyi*[1] (and, fortunately, all this seems to be folk material), but left out everything coming from that 'professor' (all of which, with the exception of, perhaps, one single item, seems to consist of art songs).

What you say in your letter about the question of orthography made me very sad. It seems that nothing has been learned from the past in this country, and that they want to begin again exactly where, and in the same way as, they left off 25 years ago. It is clear that the phonetic spelling generally accepted 30 (40?) years ago is the only rational one!

I am at the same time returning the collection by registered book post, and I remain

Yours very sincerely,
BÉLA BARTÓK

[Original in German]

222. TO MME MÜLLER-WIDMANN—BASLE

[6] *Naples, April* 2nd, 1940

Dear Mrs. Müller,
I was very pleased indeed to have both your letters, especially the second. Yes, you are right, I have been too overwhelmed by grief to be able to write letters. Three and a half months have passed since I lost my mother, and I still feel as if it had just happened yesterday. It is difficult to describe my state of mind which, in any case, it might perhaps be difficult for others to understand – – –

However, it is the self-reproaches that are most difficult to endure—all the many things I should have done differently to make my mother's life easier and to comfort her in her last years. It's too late now, nothing can be repaired or set right again—nothing, never. Of course, it was all so confused and complicated; I was under pressure from so many contradictory motives at one and the same time. Last summer, for instance, I went to Saanen to be totally undisturbed, so that I could write 2 works as quickly as possible; I spent 3½ weeks there, the works got done, wholly or in part, and those 3½ weeks I took away from my mother. I can never make

[1] Teachers (Russian).

amends for this. I should not have done it – – – – And there were many similar things in the past – – – and none of this can be helped now.

These last months I have drowned myself in work which I've got through in a mechanical sort of way, some of it in connection with my trip to America; finally I fell ill (*not* as a consequence of the work, it was simply 'flu), and the trip had to be postponed. So it will be tomorrow when I leave Europe. The boat is due in New York on Apr. 11; my first (and most important) concert is with Szigeti in Washington on the 13th. If the boat does not arrive on time, the prospects for that concert would look bad. But this boat was my last chance. I had to try it.

There is no need to tell you how I feel about everything else; it is better not to refer to it. You can imagine how very embittered I am. There can be no point in writing letters full of lamentations—even though I do not approve of the '*keep smiling*'[1] attitude. On the other hand, it seems hypocritical to write letters and not complain at all. What a dilemma – – – – ! But please do write often, and let me know all about you and yours. It would do me good, even if I cannot reply every time.

I am so glad that things are still settled in your country—at least so far. However, even if nothing *foudroyant* happens, things are certainly going down with the rest of us, that's certain. All good wishes to you and all your family,

Yours,

BÉLA BARTÓK

I am due back in Budapest in seven weeks.

[Original in English]

223. TO DOROTHY PARRISH—HUNTINGDON

[3]

The Buckingham
101 West 57th Street
New York
May 17, 1940

Dear Dorothy,

thank you so much for your kind letter. Enclosed you will find the letter you asked for; I hope you will find it all right.

After so many troublesom *[sic]* days tomorrow I will try my voyage to Hungary, full of misgivings – – –

[1] In English.

There are plans (excepted concertising) to make it possible to me (and to my wife too, of course) to stay here longer, perhaps for several years. I am not authorised to give details, but I hope these plans can be turned in reality. So, if there will be still a possibility to come over next fall, I will stay here for a longer periode *[sic]*.—In the meantime, you will be already a 'menyecske' (= young married lady) and I send you my heartiest and best wishes for this new periode *[sic]* of your life.

Yours, very sincerely
BÉLA BARTÓK

PS. The dollars to Rózsavölgyi you may send by postal order or check or what it is called. You may ask in a post-office or in a bank.

*

I am very glad to state that Miss Dorothy Parrish studied with me in Budapest from 1935–1937. She achieved excellent results and proved to be a very serious and gifted musicien *[sic]*.

New York
May 16.
1940.

[Original in Hungarian]

224. TO GYULA KERTÉSZ—BUDAPEST

Budapest, July 14th, 1940

Dear Professor,
I have only just found time to occupy myself with the compilation mentioned in your letter of June 19th. The material sent comprises first and second proofs of 12 choruses, and only one set of proofs (first?) of another 11. (I have seen all these proofs already.) Missing are: 'Spring', 'Enchanting Song', 'I've No One in the World', 'Michaelmas Congratulation'. Do you want to leave these out?

In any case, I am now enclosing a scheme using all the material (27 choruses). If you want to leave any of them out, you can simply cross them out. But it would be better if you did the pagination. Please let me know if you want me to return the 23 proofs, and if not what I am to do with them.

I do not think that I can write a preface and annotations; for one thing, I haven't time, and apart from that, I wouldn't know what to write about or what to explain.

Owing to recent developments, I find it impossible to write more choruses or indeed anything at all—and this is probably how it will be for the rest of the year. What the future will bring—only Wotan (and his earthly deputy) knows. At the end of Sept. I have to go to America once again (if it's possible). My wife will be going with me, and we shall be staying for a longer period. It would be nice if these proofs could be done by then.

I have received the music-paper, and I sent a cheque to cover the cost about 5 weeks ago. Did you get it?

Yours very sincerely,
BÉLA BARTÓK

[Original in German]

225. TO MME MÜLLER-WIDMANN—BASLE

[7] *[Geneva] October* 14th, 1940

Dear Mrs. Müller,

I had hoped to write to you from Budapest, but the preparations for the voyage grew to such proportions that one could have gone mad. To make matters worse, 3 days before leaving we got a wire from Schulthess, notifying us that we had to start a day earlier, as the motor-coach would leave on the 15th instead of the 16th! And we also had a farewell concert in Budapest on October 8: I played Bach's Concerto in A major, my wife Mozart's (scarcely known) beautiful Concerto in F major—this was her first solo appearance, and she played beautifully—then we played Mozart's Concerto for 2 pianos, and finally I played from Mikrokosmos.

And now we are here, with sorrowful hearts, bidding farewell to you and your family—who knows for how long—perhaps for ever! It is hard, very hard to say farewell. And to see this wonderful country, your country, perhaps for the last time, wondering all the time: what sort of a future awaits it and all our friends who are here!

Mrs. Stefi Geyer came yesterday afternoon and was with us until this evening, helping us and seeing us off.

This voyage is, actually, like plunging into the unknown from what is known but unbearable. If only on account of my none too satisfactory state of health; I mean my periarthritis, still incompletely cured. God only knows how and for how long I'll be able to work over there.

But we have no choice; it isn't at all the question whether this has to happen; for it must happen.[1]

I send my thanks to you and your family for all the beauty, love and friendship you have bestowed upon me, and we send you every possible good wish for the future.

Yours,
BÉLA BARTÓK

[1] This paragraph in the original German: *('... es ist garnicht die Frage: muss es sein; denn es muss sein')* calls to mind the legendary motto of the last movement of Beethoven's F major *String Quartet* (op.135) where the Grave question '*Muss es sein?*' is answered in Allegro: '*Es muss sein!*' Above this Beethoven wrote: '*Der schwer gefasste Entschluss*'.

V

THE YEARS OF EXILE

1940–1945

On October 8th 1940, Bartók gave his farewell concert in Budapest and at the end of the same month arrived in the United States. It was in the season of 1927–28 that he had paid his first visit to America, and he had stayed there again in the spring of 1940. As a result of tragic developments this third visit was to be the last.

It was not long before Columbia University in New York conferred on him an honorary degree and offered him a post to arrange systematically its huge collection of recordings of Yugoslav folk music. As long as he was able to devote himself to it, this work fully occupied Bartók while he was in America and gave him much pleasure. Of his own earlier collections it was especially the Rumanian and Turkish material to which he gave most of his attention.

At the same time he went on long concert tours. But soon these had to be given up. Symptoms of the fatal disease, leukaemia, from which he would die within the space of a few years, had already been felt as early as the summer of 1941, and in a distressing form in April, 1942. His illness was promptly diagnosed by his physicians who, however, kept the patient in ignorance. Various treatments brought transient relief. For several years he had been unable to compose, the events of the Second World War and his personal problems in exile having broken his spirit. A visit from the conductor Koussevitzky who came to see him on his sick-bed roused him from the profoundest lethargy. It is to this stimulation that we owe the first major work composed in America in the summer of 1943, the *Concerto* for full orchestra. This was followed by the *Solo Sonata for Violin* commissioned by Yehudi Menuhin in the spring of 1944. Then came the *Third Piano Concerto* intended as a surprise for his wife, the last few bars of which he did not live to orchestrate. On September 26th, 1945, Béla Bartók died.

To the very last moments of his life his mind was filled with thoughts of new works.

Bartók's letters to his friends, József Szigeti and the Kecskemétis, are filled with zest for life. They provide yet further evidence that Bartók's untimely death was an irreparable loss to the world of music.

[Original in English]

226. TO DOROTHY PARRISH—HUNTINGDON

[4]

The Buckingham
101 West 57th Street
New York
November 30. 1940

Dear Dorothy,
excuse me for being so late in answering your letter of Nov. 10., but I had so much worry and trouble since I arrived to New York. And of course, we were very busy with our concerts-preparations. Therefore, the Thank-givings *[sic]* days would have been impossible for any lesson-givings.

I will be in Pittsburgh from Jan. 23 to 26. Before that, I have several weeks free, so I could come to Huntingdon for 2–3 days, before Jan. 23. (excepted if I get some new engagements, which is not very probable). Does this suite *[sic]* you?

The troubles and worries, mentioned above, began with our baggage (6 heavy trunks) which are still in Lisbon. We arrived in N.Y. only with clothes which we have been wearing. Evening dresses etc., all our linen, all our music being in our baggage, we had to buy all the articles absolutely necessary for our appearances. Besides, we had to send telegramms *[sic]*, cables, in order to investigate where our baggage may be (it had been retained in Spain, in that terrible country). At last, we got news about its arrival in Lisbon. Now a British permit was needed and has been sent by clipper to Lisbon. Since that we have no further news about the developpement *[sic]* of that dreary business.

In addition there were some other disappointments, too; so our time was until now not very agreeable.

Now we have been looking for a lodging in an appartment-house *[sic]* and will move on Dec. 7. Our new adress *[sic]* is 110-31 73 Road, Forest Hills (I presume, this is still in New York State).

Kind regards from Mrs. Bartók!

Expecting to see you in Jan. in Huntingdon
I am yours, very sincerely

BÉLA BARTÓK

1. (Tomorrow I am leaving for Cleveland, will be back on Dec. 8.)
2. (I sent the letter to Mr. Barone.)

[Original in Hungarian]

227. TO HIS SONS BÉLA AND PÉTER BARTÓK — BUDAPEST

[2] 110-31, 73 Road,|Forest Hills,|Long Island,|*N.Y.*|U.S.A.

(the address is written in 5 lines; we are staying in this flat till May 7th)

December 24th, 1940

Dear Béla and Péter,
I am writing two copies of this letter, one to each of you; the first I am sending to you, Béla, today, and the second, to Péter next week. When you get it, Béla, please show it to Aunt Irma and then forward it to Péter in case his copy has not yet arrived. And you, Péter, send yours to Béla if you don't get his.

With us it is now 1 o'clock in the afternoon, and with you it is Christmas Eve, and of course we are thinking very much of you—who is spending it where; we are thinking of past Christmas Eves, and—we are alone. It is bad that the post is so unreliable. Till now we have had only *one* letter from you, Péter (written at the end of Oct. and brought by clipper, about 4 weeks ago); and from you, Béla, we had a postcard 4 days ago from Kolozsvár, dated Nov. 1st; at the same time we got Elza's postcard from Pest, written at the end of Oct. (and a letter from Julis, written at the same time).

We have written about 3 letters from here to you, Péter, and about the same number to you, Béla; also I sent $250 by telegraph on Nov. 27th—that is the sum in dollars which I received from the National Bank. I wrote two letters about the business of my passport, asking you to go to the Min[istry] of the Int[erior] and press them about my passport extension; it went from the Hung. Consulate here; No. 5832. If it's been done, pay them the cost of a telegram to inform the Consulate here about it! Write to us only by air mail (as long as it's possible)—it takes 2 months to get a letter by boat!

On Dec. 7th, we moved into a furnished flat at the above address. It is 16 kilometres from the centre of New York, but the subway (express) station is in front of our gate, so that we can get to town any time for 5 cents in 20 minutes. There is a continuous and frequent train service night and day. It is much nicer to live here than in the centre. The streets are wide, we can also see forests, fields and lakes; there is a great deal of traffic, but it is not noisy, only the subway trains rumble every 5 minutes. We have shops and every kind of amenity. The heating system is so efficient that we have to shut off ¾ of the radiators. If there is no wind, we can always keep one of our bedroom windows open. We are beginning to become Americanized, e.g. with regard to food. In the morning grape-fruit, puffed *wheat* with cream, brown bread and butter, eggs or bacon or fish. In the afternoon, sometime between 2 and 4, coffee with bread and butter or something else (this is not American because the people here take a quick lunch at 1 o'clock); in the evening between 8 and 10, we have our main meal: raw carrots, lettuce, radishes, olives and other things with bread and butter, perhaps soup, meat, possibly pastry.—Cooking takes rather a long time; but there are all kinds of restaurants (though we have not tried them yet). We had some language difficulties with words like 'yeast' and 'caraway seeds', but now we have got over that, too. My head is bursting with new words of every kind: the names of subway stations and of streets; subway maps, scores of possibilities for changing from one line to another—all absolutely necessary for living here, but otherwise futile. We live on the sixth *floor*[1] (= 5th floor); there is no floor above us. The *lobby*[1] of the house is low but long and wide, heated, and furnished with sofas, small tables and lamps which are always lit. The letter-boxes for the tenants are there, and everyone goes down for his or her own mail. The janitor, Mr. Janosko, or rather *pán* Janoško, is a Slovakian from Kassa, who still knows Hungarian quite well (and also Slovakian of course), in spite of having been here for 30 years. For 12 years he has been a widower, 11 of his children are living, and all of them know only English. One of his sons-in-law—an official who works for a small electric company—took us for an outing to the seaside, in his comfortable 4-seater car. We went to his 4-roomed flat fitted with every modern convenience, and he offered me *kocsonya*[2] for lunch, prepared by

[1] In English.
[2] Meat in aspic.

Janoško. Such are the descendants of a janitor here! We had a certain amount of trouble in learning how to use various electric and gas appliances—cork-screws, tin-openers, etc., also with the means of transport; but we manage fairly well now. Only occasionally do we find ourselves in a difficulty, for instance, the last time we wanted to go to the southernmost part of New York. I did not know exactly where to change (the sign-posts are not exactly conspicuous enough, rather too few, and confusing), so that we travelled for 3 hours to and fro on the subway. At last, simply because we had no more time, we went home again, rather sheepishly and without having done what we set out to do—underground all the way back, of course.

On Nov. 25th I was 'doctorated'. It was some ceremony. Before it could take place, I had to be measured in yards, feet and inches, so that they would know the size of my head, width of my shoulders, etc., and send in the details. At the University we all had to put on our academic gowns and hoods and to march in solemnly two by two to the sound of discreet organ music. We had been given exact instructions. When my name was called, I had to stand up, when the president addressed me, I had to take off my gown, and when he came to the end of his speech, I had to proceed towards him, so that he could hand me my diploma, while the pink velvet sash of the Order of Music was placed on my back; and then I could go back and sit down. And that is exactly what happened. Fortunately those of us who were being honoured did not have to say anything. Someone, a kind of Dean, made a speech to the effect that it was a splendid thing that in this chaotic world Columbia University could give this honorary title to a son of the Hungarian Plains, to a son of France, to an English scholar and to a professor of the United States.

We have played a few times in New York; on Dec. 1st I set out on an 8-day tour of Cleveland and the surrounding district; it was there that I made the acquaintance of Oszkár Jászi. The Hungarians in Cleveland gave a large party: with gypsy music and *palotás*[1] (!!). Hungarians here, there and everywhere; but we cannot be happy about this because the 2nd generation already speaks the language brokenly.

We often think of you and anxiously await news of you, Aunt Irma and Elza. Who knows how long the post will continue to func-

[1] Romantic Hungarian national dance.

tion; or that there will not be something in the spring that will put an end to even our present means of communication, imperfect though it is.

To comply with the law, we reported at the Jamaica post office which is the nearest to us (4 or 5 stops on the subway, but farther out). We had to have our fingerprints taken in accordance with their rules and regulations (we washed our hands in benzine on the spot afterwards), and we had to take an oath; it took us 3 or 4 hours, there was such a crowd. The Americans had anticipated that there would be 3 million foreigners, but already 4 million have reported; it seems possible that the total number will be about 5 million.

On Dec. 9th we received a telegram from Lisbon, saying that our luggage would be put on board the Excambion on the 13th. The boat docked yesterday afternoon, but we still don't know whether the luggage has arrived or not; there was luggage belonging to 3,000 people on board and by midday we hadn't been able to find out anything. Tomorrow is a holiday, so we shall know nothing further until the next day. Isn't it infuriating?! For we thought that we should have everything by Christmas!

The things that mean most to us at the moment I cannot of course write about; but in the end it's just as well. Nobody knows anything for certain, and there is a lot of rumour. One thing is certain, and that is that the tone has changed all along the line.

Much love to you all.

DAD

It is now 6 o'clock, and for you Christmas Eve is already over. I wonder how everything was—for all of you. We have been thinking of home continuously since yesterday, almost every minute.

Love to everyone,

DITTA

I just want to add that on Oct. 30th, the day we arrived, we sent you this telegram, Béla:

'Arrived safely, tell everybody.'

It seems that you didn't get it!

We have no Christmas tree; there is one downstairs in the lobby of our house, with electric bulbs, as is the custom here; *pán* Janoško put it up and decorated it.

There are Christmas trees in the streets, squares, stores and at the railway stations, too.

[Original in English]

228. TO DOROTHY PARRISH—HUNTINGDON

[5] 110-31, 73 Road, Forest Hills,
Long Island, *N. Y.*
January 7, 1941.

Dear Dorothy,
thank you for your letter of Dec. 9.

Now I can tell you definitively *[sic]* that I will be able to stop at Huntingdon when going to Pittsburgh. I will leave New York Jan. 20th in the morning, will arrive in Huntingdon probably late in the afternoon (I don't know yet what trains are available, will let you know later the exact time of my arrival). I have to leave Huntingdon for Pittsburgh Jan. 22. (the best would be the same train I used last time, but it does not stop there!) in order to arrive in Pittsburgh in the evening. Next morning I have there my first rehearsal. I do not prefer a hotel at all, so you may choose the college guest room or the family house for living quarters, what best you think for me.

As for my practising, it would be enough for me: one hour on 20th, two on 21th *[sic]* and one on 22th *[sic]*. You may have 4–5 or 6 lesons *[sic]* with me, during those 40 and odd hours, as you like.

Our trunks have not yet arrived! It is simply awful! Dec. 9th we got a cable from Lisbon saying they will be shipped on Excambion Dec. 13th. Excambion arrived, no trunks on it. Since that time we can not get any explanations from Lisbon, why they have been not shipped, in spite of sending cables after cables (through Cook's Office and through private people). Now I am at a loss what to do in order to get news about my trunks from those damned people.

We thank you so much for your kind offer to help us, but for the moment that would not do. I will explain everything to you.

Unluck after unluck happens. The other day three of my records I used at my lectures dropped and have been broken. Now the gentleman (I forgot his name) in Huntingdon, who has a recording gramophone, made fortunately a copy of one of them for himself—of that one with violon *[sic]* accompanied by an other (pizzicato) string instrument (two Rumanian dances in irregular 'bulgarian') *[sic]*. Could he not make another or two copies after his copy? I would be very grateful if this could be done, for broken disks can not very well be adjusted, I believe. And this was such a beautiful and interesting record!

Would you write me a word about this copy?

Yours, very sincerely
BÉLA BARTÓK

[Original in English]

229. TO DOROTHY PARRISH—HUNTINGDON

[6] 110-31. 73 Road, Forest Hills,
Long Island, *N. Y.*
January 15, 1941.

Dear Dorothy,
thank you for your letter of Jan. 14. Now, there is a slight change in my plans, because on Jan. 20. there will be the world premiere performance of my 6. String Quartet in New York. It is rather important for me to be present at this performance, and also perhaps a duty towards my friend, the Kolisch quartet who will play the work.

So, I will leave New York Tuesday, Jan. 21. 10. a.m., arrive in Huntingdon at 4,26 p.m.; and will leave Huntingdon next day at 4,26 p.m. I will have 24 hours to spend there, and will be entirely at your disposal. So I can give you 4 or 5 lessons: one Tuesday before dinner, 1½ after dinner; one Wednesday before luncheon, 1½ after luncheon. Maybe I will have still one hour in the morning of Wednesday for practising.

I hope you don't mind this change!

Yours, very sincerely
BARTÓK

PS. I would be very glad to have a confirmation of this letter from you, in order to know that you will meet me at the station.

[Original in English]

230. TO WILHELMINE CREEL—SEATTLE

[2] *February* 1. 1941

Dear Mrs. Creel,
I was really very glad to get your letter of Dec. 23. (somebody told me already that you are there in Seattle). I got as well your letter

The manuscript of the English text of Cantata Profana *adapted by Bartók*

Once upon a time there
Was an aged man. He
Had nine handsome boys, they
Came to life through him. He
Has not taught them any
Trade nor handicraft:
Neither ploughing lands, nor
Herding cows and hogs, nor
Rearing horses, oxen.
Yet he has them taught to
Hunt in forest's dark.

Off they went to hunt in
Forests dark and wild.
There they hunted till they
Found a brook, a bridge and
Trace of wondrous deer.
Those they traced, hunted
So they've gotten lost and
Changed into stags.

Yet their father could not
Bear to stay at home: he
Took his bow and went to
Forests dark and wild.
There he found the brook and
Trace of wondrous deer.
After them he went and
To a spring he came:
There he saw nine stags.
On his knees at once he
Sank to aim at them.
Lo! the tallest stag, he
Spake to him these words:
"Dearest father mine! oh
Do not shoot at us!

Else we will thee seize by
Antlers tall and strong.
And we will thee throw from
Mountain slopes to slopes from
Mountain woods to woods, from
Rocks to rocks so fast:
Woe! thou wilt, dear father
On the ragged boulders
Break to smithereens."
Yet their father unto
Them he spake these words:
"Oh, my dearest boys, my
Children most beloved!
Come, oh come with me to
Your beloved mother!
Yearning is your mother
Woeful, sad, for you:
Lighted are the torches,
Laid the tables are, and
Full of wine the cups.
Cups are on the table,
Crying stands she there;
Cups replete with wine, yet
Sobbing sits she there."
But the tallest stag he
Spake to him these words and
Gave him answer thus:
"Father, dearest father
Go thou home, go home to
Our beloved mother!
Yet we shall not go!

We'll not go with you
Never shall our antlers
Enter gates and doors, but
Only woods and shrubs;
Never shall our bodies
Wear a shirt and coat, but
Only foliage;
Nevermore our feet shall
Walk on houses' floors, but
Only on the sward;
Nevermore our mouth shall
Drink from cups and jugs but
From the dearest springs.

Once upon a time there
Was an aged man, he
Had nine handsome boys.
Never has he taught them
Any handicraft, he
Taught them only how to
Hunt in forests dark.
There they roamed, hunted
All the year around, and
Changed into stags in
Forests dark and wild.
Never will their antlers
Enter gates and doors, but
Only woods and shrubs;
Never will their bodies
Wear a shirt and coat but
Only foliage;
Nevermore their feet will
Walk on houses' floors but
Only on the sward;
Nevermore their mouth will
Drink from cups and jugs but
From the dearest springs.

The composer's hands

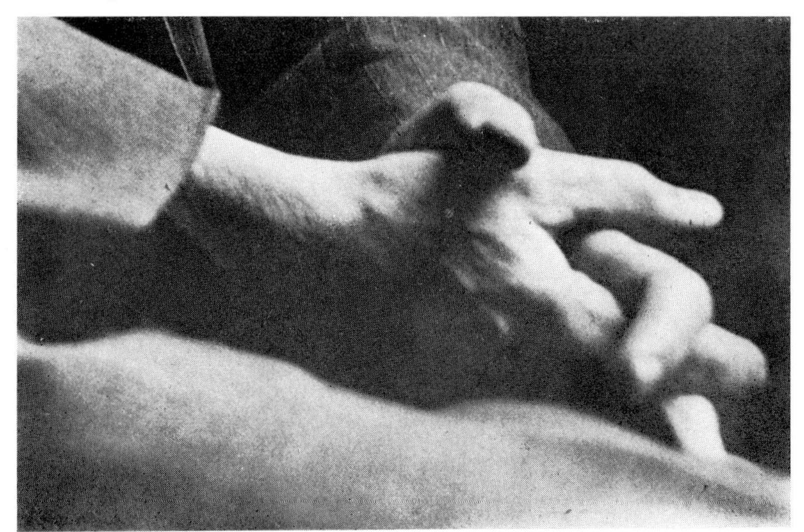

The manuscript of Bartók's last transcription,

the Ukranian folk-song 'I bought barley at the market'

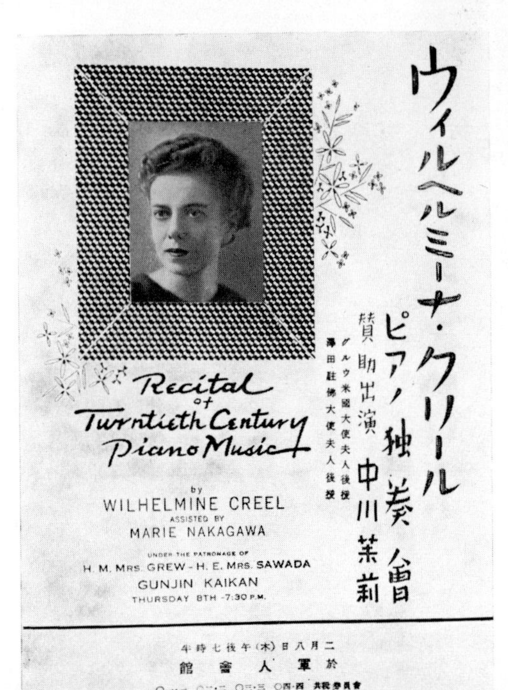

ウィルヘルミーナ・クリール
ピアノ独奏會
賛助出演 中川茉莉
グルウ米國大使夫人後援
澤田駐佛大使夫人後援
Recital of Twentieth Century Piano Music
by
WILHELMINE CREEL
ASSISTED BY
MARIE NAKAGAWA
UNDER THE PATRONAGE OF
H. M. MRS. GREW - H. E. MRS. SAWADA
GUNJIN KAIKAN
THURSDAY 8TH -7:30 P.M.
二月八日(木)午後七時半
於軍人會館

The title-page of a concert programme given by Mrs. Wilhelmine Creel in Japan, 8th February, 1940

Béla Bartók aged forty-five

sent me from Japan c/o Miss Parrish (—or, now, Mrs. Domonkos), I had never the idea to go to Japan! It will be indeed fine to meet again, in Seattle. We will arrive there on Febr. 28th at 5·30 p.m. (stay at Edmond Meany) and leave on March 5th 10·30 p.m. So if you want to play me and show the developement *[sic]* of your playing since the good old (how remote!) Budapest times, I will be at your disposal.

Mrs. Turner who says to be your friend, wrote me a letter about giving lessons to some pianists. In my reply I told her, my fee is 20$ for one hour. But of course, *this does not apply to you*. I mention this only, because I am afraid, she will tell you about it. Peter is not here! Kodály's *[sic]* are not here. But all about this and many other things we will tell you there.

Yours, very sincerely
BÉLA BARTÓK

PS. If you see Mr. Gombosi, give him my kind regards and greetings.

[Original in Hungarian]

231. TO HIS SON BÉLA BARTÓK, JR.—BUDAPEST

[3] *Jersey City, February* 11th, 1941

My dear Son,

Don't think from the above that we have moved here to live—it's only that our luggage has *arrived*!! It arrived yesterday, and we were told to come and collect it this morning, but at 12 o'clock it still hadn't been unloaded. They say we shall get it by 3 p.m. There would have been no sense in going home and coming back again—it takes $1\frac{1}{2}$ hours each way—so I went into a cafeteria to have lunch, wait, and write a letter. Though I have already paid the shipping company $43 (excess weight, charges and other expenses), I won't believe those ill-fated pieces of luggage are really there until I see them with my own eyes.

Your last letter, dated Dec. 28th, came at the beginning of Febr. You write that our letter of Nov. 10th is the last one to have reached you. Yet I wrote you often enough until about the end of Dec., on Nov. 20th I think, and on Nov. 30th and Dec. 15th. It's incredible that letters should take so long to reach you by air mail—always provided, of course, that they do not get lost on the way. On Jan.

29th, I again called at our Consulate: in view of the *vis major* (for, of course, they had heard nothing from Budapest) my passport was extended, but only until Aug. 7th. Again they advised me to cable you, which I did on Jan. 31st as follows: 'Request Ministry Interior urgent lifting exit restriction number 79706/940 ask ministry cable accordingly New York Consulate.' Did you receive the cable? If you did, and have taken these steps, then they must have raised difficulties. For this reason, I want you to know the following facts, so that you may make use of them, if need be, as a basis for further steps. I am making my request. 1. On about Nov. 7th or 8th, our New York Consulate dispatched the official request; on about Jan. 7th or 8th, a duplicate copy of same was also forwarded (again to the Ministry of the Interior), while I sent yet another copy to your address. It seems as if even official documents like this fail to reach their destination. 2. It was absolutely impossible for me to return, for what with the failure of my luggage to arrive and the fact that the cost of the return fare was much greater than I had foreseen, I found that I couldn't balance my budget, and I simply hadn't got $1,200 to pay for my return fare: I was living from one week to the next. 3. Columbia University of New York (after conferring on me an honorary degree last Nov.) in Jan. invited me to stay on as 'Visiting Associate in Music' for a 2nd term, to do certain work of musical scholarship (notation of recordings, etc.); this invitation will evidently be extended to cover the whole of the next academic year. It is therefore important for me to stay on here. N.B. our money has indeed shrunk considerably, but now that Columbia is paying me $1,500 for half a year, our situation has improved; but, of course, I shall have to work from now till next June to earn the money.

(At this point a man has just come to tell me that the luggage is outside.)

February 12th

So we have got our luggage; what's more, we managed to get it to our place yesterday and that evening got it all unpacked. Nothing has been lost, eaten by moths or pilfered by people. Well, we have got over that one.

Tomorrow we shall be setting out on a longer trip lasting 4 weeks, towards California. Stops: St. Louis, Denver, Provo (Utah State), San Francisco, Seattle, and, on the way back, Kansas City. That's not a great deal for four weeks, of course, but at least it won't be tiring. I don't start work at Columbia University until March 13th.

I am very concerned about the general trend of events. Here, for the time being, everything is all right, of course; but there are a lot of things about which I don't know what to do. I have no personal worries now that I have this university work, but, as I see it, the future is very uncertain. I did not like hearing that they have still (at the end of Dec.) not paid the pension! Can it be that they want to withhold it!? In Jan., as I told you in my last letter, some money is due from Magyar Kórus[1], a couple of hundred pengős approx., also something from Rózsavölgyi & Co. After that, I'm afraid there will be nothing until May–June, when money (possibly a few thousand) is due from the Hungarian Copyright Union, although then the payment of this, too, will have to be requested. Should you be in difficulty before then, you must go to Kodály (who, as you may remember, promised to help); then you would have to repay anything he lends you out of the money you receive in May–June. It's really fantastic that it should take so long for letters to get to you from here and from you to us. It's scarcely possible to make any arrangements, they are out of date by the time they reach you.

I will now write on a separate sheet to Aunt Irma, take it to her as soon as you get it.

Last week I had a letter from Elza, dated Dec. 31st.

We will write again during our tour.

Love to you all from
DAD

[Original in Hungarian]

232. TO HIS SON BÉLA BARTÓK, JR.—BUDAPEST

[Passages from a letter]
[4] *New York, April* 2nd, 1941

My dear Son,

. . . since March 27th I have been deriving a good deal of pleasure from my work on the Yugoslav material which I wrote to you about some time ago (the notation of the music of 1,600 folk epics from a collection consisting of many times that number in all; the material was collected 5 or 6 years ago by a Harvard professor on several thousand records). [. . .]

The former U.S. Minister in Budapest arrived here yesterday and —one may write about this perhaps—he spoke very favourably

[1] The name of a publishing firm.

and sympathetically about Hungary. This is to be understood as I put it.

Our biggest success so far was in Detroit—the audience seems to have been delighted with our programme.

Still to come is a 2 piano recital in Baltimore on the evening of Apr. 16th, and an address to be read by me the following day at Princeton (that's where the great Einstein is), and that will be the last of our public appearances this year.

. . . I have been unable so far to get used to: human beings ruminating like cows (every second person is chewing gum); railway carriages in semi-darkness; the cheque-book system.

[Original in English]

233. TO DOUGLAS MOORE—NEW YORK

110-31, 73 Road
Forest Hills, *N.Y.*
April 18, 1941

Dear Professor Moore:

I have been, as you know, working for a while on the Parry Yugoslav folk music collection. Besides transcribing a certain amount into musical notation, I have had an opportunity to familiarize myself with its contents.

This unique collection of over 2,600 phonograph records—to my knowledge the only collection of Yugoslav folk music on accoustical *[sic]* recordings—contains a very large mass of epic song accompanied by the gusle, a primitive one-string instrument. The style and musical treatment of these heroic songs is probably as close to that of the Homeric poems as any folk music style found today may be. While from the historical, literary, and musicological point of view this material is invaluable, from the musical-esthetic point of view the lyric songs or 'women's songs' and the instrumental pieces in the collection are more rewarding. The epic songs are carried by a mode of chanting which, while on the whole simple, varies somewhat from region to region and singer to singer. The chant itself is undoubtedly part of old European folk heritage, but the gusle accompaniment occasionally shows parallels with Arabic melodic treatment—probably due to an influence during the long Turkish occupation.

There are two ends in view according to which the collection ought to be studied. One is the transcription into musical notation of the most important samples of the epic material, to be incorporated into its literary and textual study at Harvard University. The other is the transcription of the other materials in the collection, for an inclusive picture of Yugoslav folk music. This latter could well result, as you once suggested, in a book on Yugoslav folk music. I estimate that transcribing those parts of the collection which are the most important in these two respects would take a year's time, not including my work during the current semester.

In view of my long-standing interest in the folk music of Eastern Europe and the Balkans, I was delighted to learn of the existence of such a singular collection in this country. The tragic European situation makes me wonder when if ever we shall have an opportunity to embark on similar field studies. Nothing would please me better than a chance to devote some more of my time to this highly interesting research so that the results could be brought before all those interested.

Sincerely yours,
BÉLA BARTÓK

[Original in Hungarian]

234. TO HIS SON BÉLA BARTÓK, JR.—BUDAPEST

[5]
[Passages from a letter]

3242, Cambridge Avenue
Bronx, *N.Y.*
May 7th, 1941

My dear Son,
. . . You ask, why did we have to move from Forest Hills. Well, because the place was unsuitable in every way. It was a large apartment house, and we were piano-played and radio-blasted from right and left; a lot of noise came in from the street night and day; every 5 minutes we heard the rumble of the subway which made the very walls shake. Lastly, it took more than an hour to get from there to Columbia. We were lucky in that the very first place we looked at in this part of the city proved to be perfectly suitable for us. This is a 3-apartment family house; we are in the middle; and the people living above and below are quiet. It is a garden-city district, peaceful, near a most lovely park with rocks, trees and lawns (rather like the Hill of Roses in Budapest).

We have five fine rooms and a sun-parlour (where we have put the two pianos), and for all this the monthly rent is $70. [. . .]

To his Son Béla MAY 1941

It is just as well I wasn't over there on March 25th, or I should have had to appear everywhere, and that—as you know—is something I dislike. Over here, I had no such worries, for apart from 5 people who cabled me greetings, nobody cared a damn about March 25th.

[Original in English]

235. C. P. WOOD—TO BÉLA BARTÓK
NEW YORK

[*Seattle*] *May* 22, 1941

Dear Mr. Bartók:
The Graduate Council of our university has been considering with favor my suggestion that you be offered an appointment as visiting lecturer on the Walker-Ames Foundation. This is a fund used to bring distinguished scholars to the University of Washington for varying periods up to nine months.

Such an appointment carries with it no fixed requirements of class teaching or public lectures, but gives opportunity for research and creative work which may be shared with any advanced students capable of profiting by it. I realize that you do not wish to teach composition, yet I believe your visit could be most stimulating to some of our young composers.

Perhaps you might conduct conferences or seminars for the study of certain selected music, modern or otherwise, as well as laying a groundwork for continuation in research on the primitive (Indian) music of our region. I should suppose that piano teaching would not come within the scope of the plan, but we should naturally welcome any recitals you might care to give on the campus.

If you are at all interested in the idea I should like to have you give me in reply some outline of what you think might be accomplished during your appointment. Financial arrangements would be made in the President's office, but I believe the sum of $300 per month has been mentioned.

I shall of course be very much pleased if these plans can be carried out, and the many friends you and Mrs. Bartok have made here will be delighted. Please give her my regards, and accept my thanks for the photograph.

Cordially yours,
CARL PAIGE WOOD

[Original in English]

236. H. W. HEINSHEIMER—TO C. P. WOOD
SEATTLE

[*New York*] *May* 29, 1941

Dear Mr. Wood:
I have to apologize that your letter of May 22nd addressed to Mr. Bartok has not been answered earlier. This is due to the fact that Mr. Andrew Schulhof, who made all these arrangements with you, is at present out of town and we hoped he would be back in time to discuss the whole matter with Mr. Bartok. However, it seems that he will not be back for another week or so, and I thought therefore we should not keep you waiting longer, and have asked Mr. Bartok to answer your letter directly.

Mr. Bartok, as a matter of fact, was very pleased with your suggestions and I am convinced that it will be easily possible to find a definite understanding. As you have already heard through Mr. Schulhof, Mr. Bartok's appointment at Columbia University has been extended for another year and will not be terminated before June 30th, 1942. This will give him time enough to travel and do his concert work, but of course he cannot accept another scholarship during the time of his association with Columbia University. However, after this will be over, he will be free to accept a position with your University either beginning in the summer 1942 and covering the Summer School as well, or beginning with the new term in October.

You will receive Mr. Bartok's letter within the next few days and I am looking forward with great anticipation to hearing from you in this matter.

Very sincerely yours,
H. W. HEINSHEIMER

[Original in English]

237. TO C. P. WOOD—SEATTLE

[1] [*New York*] *June* 9, 1941

Dear Professor Wood:
I was very pleased to receive your letter of May 22 and I am glad to say that the conditions mentioned suit me very well. I have been considering, however, the question of expenses in connection with a move to Seattle and travelling for myself, my wife, and boy which would be a substantial sum. Furthermore, the expenses regarding my furniture and rent etc. when considered in conjunction with

travelling, would reduce the emolument to a figure which would be rather below what I had in mind. I am wondering therefore whether some concession could not be made for me in connection with travelling and living expenses. I should be happy to hear from you in this regard.

As Mr. Heinsheimer has already notified you, I am now an Associate in Music at Columbia University and my engagement there continues until June 30, 1942. My work at the University of Washington would, therefore, only begin after that date. I presume that you have a vacation during July, August and September, so I could therefore begin in October and carry on for the next nine months. My plan of working would be as follows:

1. To transcribe all the recorded Indian material existing there. In this connection I would like to know approximately how many records (double or single-sided) or Edison cylinders there are.

2. To give one lecture weekly to students who might be interested in this work during the first six weeks, on the method of transcribing folk music from records. I could eventually extend these lectures to related subjects after the first six weeks such as 'How to collect folk music', 'How to study folk music scientifically'.

3. As conference and seminar work students themselves might try to transcribe folk music records under my guidance and supervision.

Yours very sincerely
BÉLA BARTÓK

[Original in English]

238. C. P. WOOD—TO DR. PADELFORD
SEATTLE

[*Seattle*] *June* 19, 1941

Dear Dr. Padelford:
Enclosed is a copy of a letter from Bela Bartok regarding the Walker-Ames appointment. The letter I showed you previously was from his agent.

I hope that the Graduate Council will confirm the appointment for 1942–43, and that some adjustment of the compensation such as Mr. Bartok requests can be made. I shall write him that I am turning the matter over to you with this recommendation.

Cordially yours,
CARL PAIGE WOOD

[Original in Hungarian]

239. TO HIS SON BÉLA BARTÓK, JR.—BUDAPEST

[6] 3242, Cambridge Avenue
Bronx, *N.Y.*
June 20th, 1941

My dear Son,
I have a bad conscience because—if I remember rightly—I haven't written to you for over a month. In my last letter, I enclosed an affidavit authorizing you to cash any payments made out to me. That must have been somewhere about May 10th! From time to time since then, I have become depressed by the frustrations I've encountered in personal and other matters; e.g. the long-drawn-out business of my request for a non-quota immigrant visa (required for Péter's entry into this country). I still haven't got it, in spite of constant pressure from a Washington solicitor (at least he says he's been pressing for it, and he's not doing it for love). It's true that the procedure is rather complicated, and I don't want to waste paper describing it, but I will just mention one or two points. I shall need a 'certificate of good conduct' from the New York police; 8 photographs; an affidavit from Columbia University stating that my income from them 'will not decrease'; and such-like rot. And even when I have obtained all these documents, I'll still have to go to Canada (!) and re-enter as the holder of a 'non-quota'. Otherwise we are all right, and we still like our apartment. It's about the same size as the one we had in Kavics utca. And compared with the annual rent of 4,000 pengős which I paid for that one the $840 a year I pay here, makes this one only very slightly more expensive.

Two good things have happened in the meantime: (1) Columbia University has extended my contract until June 30, 1942 (I may have written about that already). And secondly: At the Michigan University music festival next May (a big, annual affair) they intend to perform 5 or 6 of my choruses for children (those with orchestral accompaniment): they would be sung by 450 children, accompanied by the Philad. Orch. Their Director of Music heard a few of them in Budapest in 1937! Hence the idea.

Both copies of your letter arrived at an interval of one week (2 and 3 weeks ago, respectively). You handled the removal very well and ingeniously, and the journalist, too. Well, you know, do what you may, there is absolutely no defence against journalists' cooked-up stories. I can recall how one—some 12 to 14 years ago—

made out in his interview that the tramway along the Danube Embankment was an express train.—I see you have approached X's people about storing the piano. You obviously didn't know that my 'ties' with them were broken some 5 years ago, after X took back the piano he had lent to me free of charge. Since then, A. K. has been my man—I used to hire a piano from him for a very small fee. I wonder if you could have obtained one cheaper from him. However, the difference is obviously not great enough to warrant your trying to find out. Only I would like you to tell him some time (possibly ring him up) that I have remained loyal to them, that you did not know the position and had merely remembered what happened in the early days, etc.

I said I would write fully about my work at the University, but I am not now in the mood even for that. I will just give you a rough idea of things. It is not true, of course, that I have been invited to take up an appointment as a 'professor'. I do not give lectures regularly (so far there have been only 2 occasions, in 2 different faculties, when I have lectured about this or that—on the side, so to speak—and only because I was asked). The reason for inviting me here (apart from the fact that it would help me personally) was so that I could accomplish certain research work, that is, to study and transcribe this incomparable material on Yugoslav folk music. It is, in fact, this work which brought me here (as far as work is concerned, without taking into consideration my own feelings): material such as this can be found nowhere else in the world, and (apart from some Bulgarian material) this is what was so badly lacking to me over in Europe. I will have finished working on this material—or so I expect—by next summer. Afterwards, possibly at some other university, I could go on to transcribe some American Indian material (there is plenty of material which has not been worked on), but I don't feel very much inclined to do that: it is a field of study very remote from the folklore areas I have dealt with so far, and to start on it now would mean frittering away my energies.

Our prospect of breaking into the concert world is not very bright: either our agent is bad, or the circumstances are not favourable (and will become even less so in the near future, as a result of wartime atmosphere). In these circumstances we should then have to return to Hungary, no matter how the situation develops there. By that time things won't be much better even here. No one need feel gratified by our return—from any higher point of view—for it will not be much use to anyone. All it would mean is that, if things are bad everywhere, one prefers to be at home.

We haven't heard from Péter for four weeks: we should be very worried if we didn't think it quite possible that someone may have pinched one of his letters. When you write to us, please tell us about him as well: where has he in the end decided to go when the school-year is over?

[Original in English]

240. C. P. WOOD — TO BÉLA BARTÓK
NEW YORK

[*Seattle*] *June* 24, 1941

Dear Mr. Bartok:
I am sorry to hear that we are too late to engage you for the coming year. I have sent a copy of your letter to Dr. Padelford who is chairman of the Graduate Council in charge of the Walker-Ames appointments, and I have recommended that the appointment be held over until next year, and that if possible some adjustment be made in the compensation as you request.

I understand that the Council is to meet soon, and I hope we shall hear something favorable at the time.

Cordially yours,
CARL PAIGE WOOD

[Original in English]

241. C. P. WOOD — TO BÉLA BARTÓK
NEW YORK

[*Seattle*] *July* 1, 1941

Dear Mr. Bartok:
Dr. Padelford tells me that the Graduate Council and President Sieg are favorable to the idea of setting your appointment over until 1942.

They would like to know what you would consider adequate in the way of transportation expense. I do not imagine you would care to bring furniture out here for nine months' stay, other than books and music, unless you have some that you could not store with reasonable economy.

If you will give me some sort of estimate I will see how much can be obtained over the suggested sum of $3,000.

Cordially yours,
CARL PAIGE WOOD

[Original in English]

242. A. SCHULHOF—TO C. P. WOOD
SEATTLE

[*New York*] *August* 6, 1941

Dear Professor Wood:
I do not know whether Mr. Bartok has written to you in the meantime as he had promised. He is still on his vacation out of town. However, I sincerely hope that everything will be settled soon to the satisfaction of all people concerned.

Today I only want to let you know that Mr. Bartok will make a short coast to coast tour following his appearance with the Chicago Symphony Orchestra on November 21st, and that he will be in your vicinity probably around December 5th. I wonder whether it might not be possible for you to arrange for one or two lectures to be given by Mr. Bartok on Folklore Research at that time. In any case, I thought it important to let you know of this possibility and I would be thankful if you would consider this matter and let me have your reaction at an early opportunity.

With kindest regards and looking forward to hearing from you soon,

Most sincerely yours,
ANDREW SCHULHOF

[Original in English]

243. L. P. SIEG—TO BÉLA BARTÓK
NEW YORK

[*Seattle*] *August* 20, 1941

My dear Mr. Bartok,
I have been informed by Professor Carl Paige Wood of our School of Music that you have expressed a willingness to come to the University of Washington for the full academic year of 1942–1943.

On the strength of Professor Wood's recommendation and the approval of the Graduate Council, I herewith extend to you an invitation to come to the University at the beginning of the academic year October 1942, for a year's engagement, at a salary of $3,600, payable in ten payments. Your position will be Walker-Ames Lecturer in Music. Your duties, I believe, have been discussed with you by Professor Wood.

If you will write to me indicating your acceptance of this appointment, I shall lay it before the Board of Regents for their formal approval, concerning which, however, there need be no serious question.

Sincerely yours
L. P. SIEG
President

[Original in English]

244. C. P. WOOD—TO A. SCHULHOF
NEW YORK

[*Seattle*] *August* 21, 1941

Dear Mr. Schulhof:
President Sieg has just now written Mr. Bartok, offering him a research appointment on our Walker-Ames Foundation for the year 1942–1943. I imagine the work would be somewhat similar to his present work at Columbia, except that we should like to have a certain number of public appearances, either as lecturer or as pianist, and he should have some contact with advanced students.

In view of this I doubt whether we could arrange a lecture for him in December, particularly since that is a bad time for us, coming too near the Christmas vacation. It is conceivable that the Seattle Art Museum might consider the subject of folklore research to come within their field. The museum director is Dr. Richard Fuller.

Cordially yours,
CARL PAIGE WOOD

[Original in English]

245. TO C. P. WOOD—SEATTLE

[2] *Vermont*, Riverton, *August* 26., 1941

Dear Prof. Wood,
will you please excuse me for being so late in answering your letter of last month. When your letter arrived, my health was in a rather bad state, I had to undergo some medical examinations and after this to go for vacation and to have a complete rest for a while. So I could not gather the necessary datas *[sic]*. I told Mr. Schulhof all this asking him to let you know the reasons for the delay. I wonder if he complied with my request.

Although I am still detained here in this place and cannot yet acquire exact datas, I nevertheless don't want to delay my answer any more. So I will give you only approximate figures about the expenses in connection with our eventual settlement in Seattle for 9 months.

1. Railway tickets for two persons in sleeper to Seattle and back to New York. As roundtrip tickets cannot be used because of the long periode *[sic]* of 9 months, this would be probably 500 or 600 $.

2. Transportation of our personal belongings: these make about 700 lb. If I am right, 300 lb. are free baggage for two persons, so we have to consider the transportation fare (as checked baggage) fo 400 lb. to and fro, of course.

3. We have now in our New York apartment our own furniture. The storage of it would cost approximately 120 $ for a year.

Now, would you be so kind as to tell me wether *[sic]* these additional charges can be accepted by your University. In case of an affirmative answer, I again have a suggestion to make. Before doing that, I must give you a more detailed account concerning my appointment at the Columbia University.

My work there consists of transcribing and analysing the famous Milman Parry collection (records of Serbo-Croatian folkmusic). According to our estimates, this work should be finished until end of June, 1942. My appointment there expires at the same time, too. Now, there are unfortunately signs indicating that maybe I will not be able to finish it at this date; and it would be a pity to leave that work half-done. If the Columbia University appointment cannot be renewed for one more year, then, of course, I must leave it, as it will be.—But if I am not ready with the work and if the appointment can be prolongued *[sic]* for one more year, then it would be preferable to postpone the Seattle-appointment for one year, i.e. for 1943/44. My suggestion, therefore, is this: we should not take final decision before early spring, i.e. about February. At that time the situation will be clearer.

Yours, very sincerely
BÉLA BARTÓK

From Sept. 5. I will be again in New York (3242, Cambridge Avenue, Bronx, N. Y.)

[Original in English]

246. TO L. P. SIEG—SEATTLE

3242 Cambridge Avenue, Bronx
September 8. 1941

My dear Mr. Sieg:
many thanks for your communication of Aug. 20, 1941, received only this morning when I went the first time after my vacation to

the Columbia University offices. There were no instructions left there to forward mail (this has been done for my private address only).

I am very pleased with the conditions offered in your letter, which I accept. Having had no knowledge of your letter, I wrote to Prof. Wood on Aug. 26. The first part of that letter dealing with some extra charges is now of course to be regarded as void. In the second part, however, I suggested to postpone the final decision until Febr. or March 1942, owing to certain circumstances explained in the letter.

I would be very glad if this could be done.

Yours, very sincerely,
BÉLA BARTÓK

[Original in English]

247. A. SCHULHOF—TO C. P. WOOD
SEATTLE

[*New York*] *September* 20, 1941

Dear Dr. Wood:

At your suggestion I wrote some time ago to Mr. Richard E. Fuller, President and Director of the Seattle Art Museum, regarding a possible appearance of Bela Bartok with this institution. Today I received the following answer:

'Although I have heard high praise of Bela Bartok, his lecture falls essentially in the field of music rather than of art. At all events, however, our lecture schedule is already as extensive as our budget permits.'

I am sorry that nothing could be worked out in this matter.

I am still working hard to have Mr. Bartok accept your offer, instead of his continuing the work at Columbia University for another year, and I sincerely hope I shall be successful. Would you be kind enough to let me know the latest possible date on which you have to have his decision. I would also appreciate having some details in this matter, as I do not wish to bother Mr. Bartok too much and as I have to handle him in his own way. I would be most grateful for this and it would help matters a great deal.

Looking forward to seeing you in December during my forthcoming visit to Seattle,

Very sincerely yours,
ANDREW SCHULHOF

[Original in English]

248. L. P. SIEG—TO BÉLA BARTÓK
NEW YORK

[*Seattle*] *September* 22, 1941

My dear Mr. Bartok:

I have delayed answering your letter of September 8 until I could have opportunity to discuss the matter with Professor Wood.

It is entirely satisfactory to us to postpone final decision until the early part of 1942. In other words the offer which we made you will still hold good up to, say, March, 1942. I shall leave it that you will communicate with us as soon as possible after you have made your final decision.

Trusting that your final decision may be favorable, I am

Sincerely yours,
L. P. SIEG
President

[Original in English]

249. C. P. WOOD—TO A. SCHULHOF
NEW YORK

[*Seattle*] *September* 25, 1941

Dear Mr. Schulhof,

President Sieg has written Mr. Bartok that he may postpone his decision until, say, March of 1942. In other words the appointment will be kept open for him to accept for either 1942–3 or 1943–4.

I hope it will be the former, but he naturally wants to finish his work at Columbia if possible, and it does not greatly matter to us.

Sincerely yours,
CARL PAIGE WOOD

[Original in English]

250. A. SCHULHOF—TO C. P. WOOD
SEATTLE

[*New York*] *October* 1, 1941

Dear Dr. Wood:

I just heard from Mr. Bartok that he received a letter from Mr. Sieg, the president of your University, who was kind enough to give him more time for his decision regarding the appointment for Seattle. However, may I inform you that it now seems really quite definite that Mr. Bartok will be able to accept your kind invitation. As you will remember from our conversation, we have always been very much in favor of this project and shall certainly give you every possible support you may wish to have in this connection. The credit for having thought of this plan is naturally all yours.

I wish to inform you today that it is very likely that Mr. Bartok shall visit Seattle probably on Friday, November 28th, Saturday, November 29th and perhaps Sunday, the 30th. He is rather anxious to meet you, the president Dr. Sieg, and all the important people connected with his future work, and he would also like to see the whole organization and mechanism in order to be able to make perhaps some suggestions in this regard. From this, too, you will see that the plan seems very definite by now. Mr. Bartok is, of course, making this trip at his own initiative and expense, but I thought that it would perhaps be possible to arrange for him one or two lectures, thereby helping him to obtain a small fee. I am sure this would be most welcome. I am enclosing herewith again a list of lectures given by Mr. Bartok and I sincerely hope you will be able to consider this idea and to collect the necessary funds—we shall certainly not bargain over this particular part of the plan.

I would appreciate your answer as soon as possible and hope you will not mind nor misunderstand my suggesting this possibility to you.

With kindest personal regards and best wishes.

Very sincerely yours,
ANDREW SCHULHOF

LECTURES BY BELA BARTOK

Lectures on Piano Music:

1. *Contemporary music in elementary piano teaching.*

This lecture is accompanied by many examples on the piano, giving only easy pieces.

2. *Bela Bartok's piano compositions written with a pedagogical purpose.*

Lecture-recital with many examples on the piano, easy and more difficult pieces.

3. *Contemporary music in piano teaching.*

A cycle of three lectures, each about one hour, with many examples on the piano, easy and more difficult pieces.

Lecture on Hungarian Art Music:

4. *The relation between contemporary Hungarian art music and folk music.*

With many examples on the piano.

Lectures on Folk Music Research:

5. *Some problems of folk music research in East Europe.*

With examples played on gramophone records.

Some examples (scales and melodies only) are played on the piano. Slides are used in illustrating this lecture.

6. *The same lecture can be divided and extended to three lectures:*
   a. Hungarian folk music
   b. North-Slave *[sic]* and Roumanian folk music
   c. South-Slave *[sic]* (Serbo-Croatian and Bulgarian) folk music

Each lecture will have a duration of about one hour and is illustrated with gramophone records, slides and a few examples on the piano.

[Original in English]

251. C. P. WOOD — TO L. P. SIEG
SEATTLE

[*Seattle*] *October* 3, 1941

Dear President Sieg:
The attached letter just came from Mr. Bartok's agent and I submit it for your information (I have not yet replied).

If Bartok visits us on a weekend as he suggests any lecture would be impracticable, but if you are to be in your office I should like to bring him over. As soon as his appointment is made definite perhaps we can reopen the matter of an allotment for library material for graduate study in music to supplement our regular amount.

Cordially yours,
CARL PAIGE WOOD

*

L. P. SIEG — TO C. P. WOOD

Prof Wood
Glad to see him. Of course lectures are out if we are going to have him here for an extended period.

PRES

[Original in English]

252. C. P. WOOD — TO A. SCHULHOF
NEW YORK

[*Seattle*] *October* 6, 1941

Dear Mr. Schulhof:
President Sieg will be very glad to meet Mr. Bartok, and I hope we shall know at that time whether the appointment will be for next year or not.

I am afraid lectures are out of the question, since we are planning an extended engagement later. Even if this were not so, a week-end would never do for us.

Cordially yours,
CARL PAIGE WOOD

[Original in English]

253. TO C. P. WOOD—SEATTLE

[3]

3242, Cambridge Avenue
Riverdale, The Bronx, *N. Y.*
October 8. 1941

Dear Prof. Wood,
I am very happy that my suggestion has been accepted.
I have some concerts at the West coast: Palo Alto Nov. 26. and Portland Dec. 1. 2. As I have 3 free days between these dates, I should like very much to spend them in Seattle in order to see you and to talk over some questions (technicalities) connected with my eventual future job in Seattle. May I ask you if you are at that time in Seattle?

Yours, very sincerely
Béla Bartók

[Original in English]

254. C. P. WOOD—TO BÉLA BARTÓK
NEW YORK

[Seattle] October 15, 1941

Dear Mr. Bartok:
We are looking forward to seeing you next month, as Mr. Schulhof already advised me that you might be here. I am sure that I shall be here on the week-end between November 28 and December 1, and if President Sieg is in town you can confer with him. I hope that you will be able to tell us when you will be ready to come for the Walker-Ames appointment, as we cannot make it formal until we know the date.

Cordially yours,
Carl Paige Wood

[Original in Hungarian]

255. TO HIS SON BÉLA BARTÓK, JR.—BUDAPEST

[7]

3242, Cambridge Avenue
The Bronx, *N. Y.*
October 17th, 1941

My dear Son,
It is a long time since I last wrote to you, but I am still rather depressed and haven't felt like writing. My last 2 letters were written and mailed:

(1) a few days before Aug. 20th; this was the letter sent for your birthday;

(2) on Sept. 6th; in this letter I enclosed a statement from the Consulate certifying to my continued existence.

The last letter I received from you was dated August 22nd. I have also received your card from Transylvania.

Some person has seen Sumner Welles himself on Péter's behalf, and we've had a cable from Hajnal to say that a U.S. visa has already been issued for him. The question now is: how can he obtain the most essential transit visa? But you will no doubt know of these developments.

Owing to a variety of 'indescribable' circumstances, our return to Hungary has once more receded into the misty future. I cannot say what will happen. It's unlikely that my work at Columbia University can be extended. This is all the more annoying because it means that in July, 1942, I shall thus be compelled to leave this very interesting work unfinished. On the other hand, I am being offered some work for 42/43 at Seattle (University of Washington). That really is at the end of the world. It is a lovely place, of course—I won't say it isn't. But we are not too pleased to have to move on again like wandering gypsies.

Concerts are few; if we had to live on this, we should go hungry.

Otherwise we are managing somehow. The doctor (the one who examined my 'internal parts' in July) has given me X-ray treatment for my left shoulder.

Result: 00. But that doesn't matter, for at least I am able to play the piano—though I was able to do that before the X-ray invasion.

If Péter can manage to leave, you will handle the money alone, as you think fit. I wonder if that 'life' certificate I mentioned has reached you.

I shall try to write to you every month, although there isn't much to write about. Or rather, what there is to write about you can't. Please always tell everyone whom it concerns, whenever you receive a letter from me. It's impossible to write to everyone!

Much love to you both, from

YOUR DAD

[Original in English]

256. TO WILHELMINE CREEL—SEATTLE

[3]

3242, Cambridge Avenue
The Bronx, Riverdale
N. Y.
October 17, 1941

Dear Mrs. Creel,
I hope you are not angry with [me] for not having written you yet; but you know by experience how difficult I am in letter writing!

Now I have news for you: I am coming to Seattle for a few days. On Nov. 26. I have a lecture in Palo Alto, on Dec. 1. 2. in Portland, so I can spend the interim in Seattle where I want to talk over with Dr. Wood something (probably you know about it). For the rest of the time I am at your disposal if you want to have some lessons. I will arrive on Nov. 28. and leave Dec. 1. morning. This time I will be alone. Would you ask Mrs. Beck if I could stay in her house? And if not what hotel would you recommend? Perhaps one near the campus.

I prefer to *tell* you than to write about all our good- and mishaps (in fact a great deal of mis-, and tiny bits of good-). My intended letter was to be a very long and very un-American letter—complaints and complaints (here one *must* always feel fine and excellent even if dying). The only bright spot is my work at Columbia University: studying serbo-croatian *[sic]* folk-music material from really unique records, belonging to the Harvard University. But—hélas—this is only a temporary job and the work probably must remaine *[sic]* unfinished, so even there is mingled a bitter drop.

If I tell you that we have for this season one orchestra-engagement, three two-piano recitals, four minor engagements (piano solo or lecture) and that is all, then you easily see how precarious our situation is.

Our son Peter just got the American (visitor) visa, the difficulty is now to get for him the transit visa through the wild-beasts-land. But I don't know if it would not be more advisable for us to go back than for him to come over - - - that of course is only a vague idea.

We had the thrilling experience of the world-famous New-York-summer-time. I can bear it comparatively easily, but not my wife. So we went for several weeks to a quite *[sic]* place in North Vermont.

I hope you are well and had good time for practising and progress. This is all I wanted to tell you, for the moment.

Yours, very sincerely
BÉLA BARTÓK

Best regards from Ditta.

[Original in English]

257. TO C. P. WOOD—SEATTLE

[4] *Palo Alto, November* 25, 1941

Dear Prof. Wood,
I want only to tell you that I will arrive in Seattle on Nov. 28 at 5.30 p.m.

Perhaps next morning we could have that discussion, mostly about technicalities: I should like to know and to see what grammophones *[sic]* there are (copying machine?), what material (with Indian folkmusic) you have, if and how their texts are already transcribed etc.

Yours, very sincerely
BÉLA BARTÓK

P.S. I got an invitation from Mrs. Beck and will stay in her house.

[Original in English]

258. TO HENRY MISHKIN—AMHERST (MASS.)

3242 Cambridge Avenue
The Bronx, *N. Y.*
January 23. 1941
[*On the envelope:* 1942]

Dear Mr. Mishkin,
I am sending you the program for our 2-piano recital. I believe it is an evening concert. We will arrive on Febr. 23 early in the afternoon and should like to have a rehearsal of about 2 hours, in order to see and try the pianos.

Would you be so kind as to make reservation for us at a hotel. May we have two students for the evening to turn pages?

Yours, very sincerely
BÉLA BARTÓK

Christian Bach:	Sonata in G major
Domenico Zipoli:	Suite in four parts (trans. Heinrich Simon)
Friedemann Bach:	Sonata in F major
Bartók:	[Suite for Two Pianos, op. 4b (1941):]
	Serenata
	Allegro diabolico
	Scena della Puszta
	Per finire
	Six pieces from Mikrokosmos
Colin McPhee:	Balinese Ceremonial Music (trans.)
	[Pemoengkah–Gambangan–Taboeh teloe]
Liszt:	Concert pathétique

[Original in English]

259. TO C. P. WOOD—SEATTLE

[5]

3242, Cambridge Avenue
The Bronx, *N. Y.*
February 28.1942

Dear Professor Wood,
after long waiting for the decision of the respective committee, yesterday at last I got the news about it: the validity of my appointment has been extended for one more semester, i.e. until end of Dec. 1942.

So I can be at the disposal of the University of Washington either during the full academic year of 1943–4, or during the full calendar year of 1943 (2. semester of one academic year, and 1. semester of the other year), according to what you prefer.

I sent a letter of a similar content to Pres. Sieg, at the same time.

Yours, very sincerely
Béla Bartók

[Original in English]

260. TO WILHELMINE CREEL—SEATTLE

[4]

3242, Cambridge Avenue
Bronx, *N. Y.*
March, 2, 1942

Dear Mrs. Creel,
I got all your letters, telegrams etc. and we are very sorry indeed that we could not see you in Chicago, and especially for the reasons which prevented you to come there. You probably would have been

interested in our programs. We plaid *[sic]* rather well, and got very bad criticisms. In fact, 1 was good, 1 rather lukewarm, and [1 was] as bad as I never got in my life. Just as if we were the last of the last pianists. So you see your choice of piano-teacher was a very bad one!

I delayed my answer to your letters because I wanted to let you know my plans for the future. So I had to wait for the decision of Columbia University which I got a few days ago, and which says that the validity of my engagement has been extended until end of Dec. 1942. From that time on I can be at the disposal of Washington University whenever they want me to be there. Of course, I wrote a letter in this sense both to Pres. Sieg and to Prof. Wood.

[About ten lines missing.]

And now our personal affairs. First there is one good news: our son Péter arrived safely in—Lissabon *[sic]*, on Febr. 10. He got a special permit from the U.S. government, needed since the outbreak of war. So everything has been settled from U.S. point of vue *[sic]*. The Hungar. govern. too, apparently made no difficulties. But what happened in Lissabon! At the last moment, the British refused him the sailing permit! Now again, we are sending cables to London, to Lissabon, to Washington and are anxious to know what will happen.

I am still a 'visitor'; special preexamination is now needed to obtain an immigrant visa, and I don't know when it will be granted.

And now the bad knews *[sic]*. Our situation is getting daily worse and worse. All I can say is that never in my life since I earn my livelihood (that is from my 20th year) have I been in such a dreadful situation as I will be probably very soon. To say dreadful is probably exaggerated, but not too much. Mrs. Bartók bears this very valiantly: the worse the happenings, the more energetic, confident and optimistic she is. She tries to do some work, teaching for instance. But how to get pupils or a job! She asks you to give us some advice if you can. Could you send us the folder of that agency you were in negotiation with last year? And what is your opinion about this? I am rather pessimistic, I lost all confidence in people, in countries, in everything. Unfortunately, I know much better the circumstances, than Ditta does, so probably I am right in being pessimistic. Do you remember what I said just one year ago: I wonder if it is not too late (concerning war preparations). Now, I am afraid it *is* too late. And I whish *[sic]* only to be wrong in this my feeling.

Until know *[sic]* we had from Baldwin piano company two free pianos, a baby grand and an upright. Just today I got the news the upright will be taken from us. Of course we have no money to hire a second piano. So we will have no possibility to study two-piano works. And each month brings a similar blow. I am wondering and asking myself what next?

With these dissonant chords, I finish my letter, and am

Yours, very sincerely
BÉLA BARTÓK

Post scriptum.

For some reasons the mailing of this letter has been delayed. In the mean time *[sic]* I got news from Pres. Sieg that it has been decided that the decision should be postponed until 1943 spring—

[Original in English]

261. L. P. SIEG—TO BÉLA BARTÓK
NEW YORK

[*Seattle*] *March* 4, 1942

My dear Mr. Bartok:
This is to acknowledge your letter of February 28, in which you indicate that you might come to the University of Washington for the full academic year 1943–44, or, as an alternative, from January 1943 to December 1943.

At the time I discussed this matter with you last fall, we had not anticipated this serious war. As matters stand now, I feel that commitments of any sort for any great time in advance are extremely hazardous. We have no present way of knowing what our income will be on our invested funds.

It is my opinion that we ought to hold this matter in abeyance until sometime in the spring of the year 1943. By that time we should be able to know whether our finances will be sufficient to justify carrying through the proposed appointment.

I am sorry that I am not in a position to make engagements for the somewhat distant future, but that is simply one of the hazards of war.

Sincerely yours,
L. P. SIEG
President

[Original in English]

262. C. P. WOOD—TO BÉLA BARTÓK
NEW YORK

[*Seattle*] *March* 16, 1942

Dear Mr. Bartok:
I received your letter, and a copy of President Sieg's letter to you. I am sorry that the appointment is to be delayed again. So far as I know there is no specific reason to think that the funds will not be sufficient, but as the president says it is too far ahead to make firm commitments.

I shall try to bring the matter up again in the summer or fall, so that we can consider the earlier date for beginning, i.e. January 1943. Meanwhile please keep us informed of any change in your plans.

Cordially yours,
CARL PAIGE WOOD

[Original in English]

263. A. SCHULHOF—TO C. P. WOOD
SEATTLE

[*New York*] *April* 24, 1942

Dear Dr. Wood:
I was very glad to receive your letter of April 18th and I spoke immediately with Mr. Bartok. He would very much like to come to Seattle, but he is not sure at the moment whether he will be finished with his work here in New York until the coming fall. However, should he know early enough, he might be able to arrange something beginning with June 1942. Please let me know somewhat more in detail about your plans and in the meantime—perhaps in two or three weeks—I will be able to give you more definite news.

May I tell you rather confidentially that Mr. Bartok is receiving a fee of $1500 for each term at Columbia University ($3000 yearly) and that he receives naturally enough liberty to fulfill his various concert and lecture engagements, which are generally during a certain period of the year where they do not interfere too much with his work . . .[1]

With best regards.

Very sincerely yours,
ANDREW SCHULHOF

[1] In further passages, Schulhof discusses certain plans which in no way concern Bartók.

[Original in English]

264. TO C. P. WOOD—SEATTLE

[6]

3242 Cambridge Avenue
Bronx, *N. Y.*
July 7, 1942

Dear Prof. Wood,
thank you so much for your kind letter of March last in which you asked me to inform you of me *[sic]* plans. This is to tell you that I have a very important engagement with the N.Y.Philh. end of January and some other pending engagement in the second half of the season, all in the East. Therefore, it would be better to accept the idea of President Sieg and postpone the decision until next spring, as he wrote me in his letter.

Yours, very sincerely

BÉLA BARTÓK

[Original in English]

265. TO YEHUDI MENUHIN—ALMA (CALIF.)

[1]

3242 Cambridge Ave
Bronx, *N. Y.*
October 7. 1942

Dear Mr. Menuhin,
I am very glad to see from your letter that you are interested in my violin-concerto and are studying it.

You are quite right; a public performance with piano accompanyment *[sic]* would do no good, is—I would say—impossible. Now, of course, it is probably too late to find an orchestra for the work in this season, but I am sure you will find one for the next season.

I would be very glad to meet you when you will be in New York. Let me know the time of your visit in advance in order to make an appointment for our meeting.

Yours, sincerely
BÉLA BARTÓK

[Original in English]

266. TO WILHELMINE CREEL—SEATTLE

[5]

3242, Cambridge Ave
Bronx, *N. Y.*
December 31, 1942

Dear Mrs. Creel,
first of all we thank you very much for the two books. I already went through them, and liked them very much. The Cross Greek is really a touching book; I was especially interested in the chapter 'Our daily bread'! you know I always am very much interested in exotic authochtonous *[sic]* food. If I can't try them, I at least enjoy their description.

In the meantime some important events happened around us. As you perhaps know my son arrived (after leaving Budapest just before Xmas 1941) on Apr. 20.—I met him quite unexpectedly at our subway station 231st Street; it was like a scene in those old stories. The censor cut out the name of the boat from his Lissabon *[sic]* cable, so we did [not] know when to expect him. It is quite amazing how he could find his way through so many difficulties. But now, as he is 18, he probably must go to the army in a few months, in spite of his being here as a 'visitor'. This is not [a] too exhilarating view for us! Otherwise he is well, attends a 'night school' to study American history, economics and English. Another event is less joyful. It concerns my health which is impaired since the beginning of April: since that time I have every day temperature elevation (of about 100°) in the evening, quite regularly and relentlessly! The doctors cann't *[sic]* find out the cause, and as a consequence, cann't *[sic]* even try a treatment. Is not that rather strange? Fortunately, I can do my work; only it may happen for instance this: in Oct. I had a lecture in New York at the Musicological Society. It was aggravated by a dinner and discussions: when I came home, I had 102.

At Columbia, I am 'dismissed' from Jan. 1 on; they seem to have no more money for me. This is annoying because little more than half of the work (connected with the Parry collection) could be achieved during these 2 years; and I hate incompletness *[sic]*. If it ever can be continued, Heaven only knows. But from Febr. on, I am invited to Harvard University to give there a certain number of conferences and lectures during the 1st semester. This gives us a respite until next fall (no possibilities with concertizing or lecturing;

we have a 'unique' engagement in Jan. with the New York Philh. Society, but this is a 'family' business, the engagement was made through my friend Fritz Reiner who is guest conductor in some of those concerts).

So we are living from half-year to half-year. I still don't know what to decide about Seattle. What you write in your letter in this connection, is not very encouraging.

I was very busy during the whole year with my book. One, you know, is on Serbo-Croatian folkmusic, this I have finished in October; it ought to be published by the Columbia Press, as an Appendix to my work done there. The other is on my Rumanian folkmusic material: 2500 melodies published in two volumes, of course, with introductions and all. There is hope that it will be published.—All this was a rather tiresome work (and my struggling with the English language) but very interesting indeed.

Do you know that my article on Parry you corrected in Seattle appeared in the New York Times in June? I still don't know who sent it in; this is a rather mysterious business. But, at least, it was I who got the fee. So, with my books and articles I am gradually advancing to the position of an English writer (I don't mean it seriously, of course); I never had an idea that this will be the end of my career! Otherwise, my career as a composer is as much as finished: the quasi boycott of my works by the leading orchestras continues, no performances either of old work[s] or of new ones. It is a shame—not for me of course.

With this melancholy chord I close my letter, wishing you a very very happy happy *[sic]* new year.

Yours, very sincerely
BÉLA BARTÓK

My best regards to Mrs. Beck.

Your Japanese teaching is a 'defense work' isn't it? It must be awfully difficult.

(I am not moving to Boston, will go there each week for 1 or 2 days)

[Original in Hungarian]

267. DITTA PÁSZTORY—TO JÓZSEF SZIGETI

May 23, 1943

Dear Szigeti,

The card which arrived today gave me great, great joy; alas, I don't show it to Béla – – –

Koussevitzky visited B. in the sanatorium, and I know that B. was very pleased about it. (There was an interesting article by K. in last Sunday's Times.)

They agreed upon a purely orchestral work; it was Béla's idea to combine chorus and orchestra. I am so glad that plans, musical ambitions, compositions are stirring in Béla's mind—a new hope, discovered in this way quite by chance, as it were incidentally .

One thing is sure: Béla's 'under no circumstances will I ever write any new work ---' attitude has gone. It's more than three years now ---

And to whom do we owe most thanks for this?

You know, of course: to Szigeti.

The past week was very bad—rising temperature, 40° yesterday.

And the doctors are *not* certain what the primary disease may be.

Much love to Wanda,

Your ever grateful,
DITTA

[Original in English]

268. C. P. WOOD—TO BÉLA BARTÓK
NEW YORK

[*Seattle*] *June* 12, 1943

Dear Mr. Bartok:

It is almost a year since you wrote me that you would postpone the decision as to your engagement here.

Although the war is making many changes here I have no reason to think we cannot go through with our plans for an appointment on the Walker-Ames Foundation, since your work would not depend mainly on a large enrollment of students.

Please let me know very soon what your wishes are so that I can set the machinery in motion again.

Cordially yours,
CARL PAIGE WOOD

[Original in English]

269. TO C. P. WOOD—SEATTLE

[7]

32 Park Avenue
Saranac Lake, N. Y.
June 30, 1943.

Dear Prof. Wood,

thank you so much for your kind letter.

Perhaps you heard about the misfortune which befell me: since *[sic]* 1½ year I am ill! During the 1st 10 months I could still do my job, but since a worsening in March I am unfit for any continuous work outside of my house. The doctors cannot find out the cause of my illness; therefore, no cure and no treatment is possible, and the prospects of the future are rather gloomy. For the time being I can not even think of accepting a job anywhere!

Yours, very sincerely
BÉLA BARTÓK

[Original in English]

270. TO WILHELMINE CREEL—SEATTLE

[6]

32 Park Avenue
Saranac Lake, N. Y.
August 17, 1943

Dear Mrs. Creel,
I was very much surprised seeing the content *[sic]* of your letter, and at the same time deeply touched by your care. Only I have to tell you, you must not do this again; I know you are not a well to do person, and am very much worried by the thougt *[sic]* of your privations incurred by such acts. Under this condition I accept this time your offer, and if you allow me to give you a Ms. of one of my works as a souvenir. I succeeded to bring over many of them, but since they are now kept somewhere in New York, I can send it only after my return, which probably will be in Oct.

The situation concerning my disease is practically unchanged. Further examinations, made in this place, remained unsuccessful: the doctors cannot find out what the trouble is; as one of them put it 'it is a baffling case'. But this is getting to be a rather annoying subject, so I leave it.

What you are telling me about your language work is very interesting, at least to me. As you perhaps know it always was one of my hobbies to study languages. I read somewhere how terribly difficult the Japanese is. And what about the Korean? Is it related to the Chinese, or to the Japanese? I am sure I could not master any of these terrific language[s] (I had even my difficulties with the Turkish which is said to be one of the easiest languages, having no irregular verbs, nouns!) But I think it is too much for you these three languaged *[sic]*. I would have refused the Korean in your stead; you should be careful not only about other peoples' health, but about your own, too, and avoid to[o] much strain.

I kill the time by reading much (there is a 'Free library') and just finished Don Quixote in a 330 [-year-] old translation 'the which' did not give me particular difficulties.

We both send you our kindest regards.

Yours, very sincerely
BÉLA BARTÓK

[Original in English]

271. C. P. WOOD—TO BÉLA BARTÓK
NEW YORK

[*Seattle*] *October* 23, 1943

Dear Mr. Bartok:
I was fortunate in hearing your violin concerto last Sunday. It is a beautiful work and superlatively played.

I was happy to hear them say that your health is improved. If you feel able to reconsider the idea of coming out here please let me know at any time.

Cordially yours,
CARL PAIGE WOOD

[Original in English]

272. TO C. P. WOOD—SEATTLE

[8] Hotel Woodrow, 35 W. 64th
New York, N. Y.
November 27, 1943

Dear Prof. Wood:
many thanks for your kind letter of Oct. Yes, my health improved very much since end of August, I feel almost as well as before my illness. However, matters are not as simple as this: the doctors say I am now in a state of reconvalescence, and must be extremely careful during this winter in order to avoid a relapse which would be disastrous. Therefore, they want to send my *[sic]* somewhere to South-Caroline *[sic]* for the winter (with the aid of ASCAP). In spite of my not yet completely cured illness, I got an appointment at Columbia University for one semester. I can, of course, not work there now. So I will have to do this work (research work) when I come back from the South about end of April, in May and June, then, after the summer interruption continue it in Oct.–Dec. The earliest time I could come to Seattle would be therefore Jan. 1945. —In April 1944 I will again write to you and give you a picture of the situation as it will have developped *[sic]* until that time—as we all expect favorably.

The queer thing about all this is that the doctors still do not know exactly what the trouble was with my health!

Yours, very sincerely
BÉLA BARTÓK

P.S. In the meantime, Mr. Menuhin played my violin concerto in Minneapolis, and will play it in Apr. in Washington and in Baltimore. The performance in New York was really marvelous *[sic]:* all the 3 factors (soloist, conductor, orchestra) were the best a composer could wish for his work.

[Original in Hungarian]

273. TO JÓZSEF SZIGETI—PALOS VERDES ESTATES (CAL.)

[2]

Albemarle Inn,
Asheville, N.C.
January 30th, 1944.

My dear Joe,
excuse me for not writing all this long time. It can't be helped, I am an incorrigibly bad correspondent—apart from the fact that I am continuously overburdened with work—urgent work, as there is no knowing for how long it will be possible for me to carry on. But God knows (if He knows), I have often thought of you and I planned to write you a nice long letter from Saranac. But that is just the trouble: I didn't want to write a short one and to write a long one requires great determination. But enough of that - - -

I am really very sorry that it was not you who gave the première of the violin concerto. You may remember that 3 years ago, before the arrangement for piano came out, I had a copy sent to you—it was only a photostat. No one else had had a copy at that time. There might still be a possibility with Ormándy. He wrote to me about another matter and mentioned how sorry he was, etc., and how he would like to play it with you in Phil., because he had heard it on the radio and thinks that such a viol. concerto had not been written since Beeth., Mendels. and Brahms. Sic Ormándy!—The performance was really excellent. My greatest joy was that there was no trouble with regard to the instrumentation. Nothing had to be changed. For an orchestral 'accompaniment' to the violin is a very delicate matter.—The critics, of course, remained true to themselves, though they wrote a shade more kindly than usual.

I would not even mention them but for the fact that one of them made an asinine remark to the effect that he did not think this work *would squeeze out* the concertos of Beeth., Mendels. Brahms. How is it possible to write such stupidities? Who but a candidate for a lunatic asylum would want to 'squeeze out' these works. If he had written that he did not think my work could stand comparison with them, or something like that, that would have been all right. But enough of this, too.

My health suddenly improved at the end of Aug. At present I feel quite well, I have no temperature, my strength has returned, and I am able to take nice walks in the mountain forests—yes, I climb mountains (only very cautiously, of course). In March my weight was 87 lbs., now it is 105 lbs. I am getting stout. Too stout. As stout as anything. You will not recognize me.—Perhaps it is due to this improvement (or it may be the other way round) that I have been able to finish the work that Koussevitzky commissioned. The whole of September—pretty well day and night—I worked on it. It is supposed to be performed about the 17th or 18th of March; at that pair of concerts in which you are to be the soloist. I should be happy if you could at least manage to hear the rehearsal. I am very disappointed that I cannot be there. But it's like this: my doctors (I wish I might never see a doctor again) have exiled me from the inhuman northern winter to convalesce in this place until the end of April. Then, if no more unexpected troubles come along, they will give me my freedom.

Here I have started on an interesting (but, as always, lengthy) task which I've never attempted before. It is not exactly a musical job; I am organizing and clarifying the texts of Wallachian folk-songs, 2,000 of them. I think many interesting things will come to light, at least concerning the peasants. For example, it is much worse for a girl to be left in the lurch than it is for a boy. We knew this before, but now it can be proved with statistical data, in *svarc-aufvejsz* [*schwarz auf weiß*]. Then, the girls (or women) are far more violent and bad tempered* there are many more texts with curses in which the girls complain of the faithlessness of the boys than *vice versa*. These curse texts what's more are exceptionally distinctive. They are amazing, quite Shakespearian in their fantasy. Unfortunately I cannot quote the Wallachian because you would not understand it. But we Hungarians have plenty of them, e.g.:

May a row of thirteen apothecaries' shops
Empty themselves in you;

May nine cartloads of hay and straw
Rot in your bed.
May your towels pour out flames,
And the water you wash in turn to blood.

Or even

God punish you with money-bought bread,
Money-bought bread and a harlot to wed.

Money-bought bread—American townspeople could not understand that because we all pay money for bread, don't we? Yes, but not the peasant small-holder: he grows the wheat himself, he bakes the bread himself, but when the hail destroys his harvest, he has to buy the bread; yes, but where can he get the money from, eh?!

Similarly 'incomprehensible' is the Wallachian girl's curse 'May God punish you with nine wives' (when she has just hoped that you would 'Have a fit on your way to your wedding' and similar nice things). An American would say that this is not such a bad wish: *varietas delectat!* Yes, but there is no divorce among peasants. Only death can bring a 'change' of wife. And death is a very troublesome affair for them: it costs money and involves all kinds of other disturbance.

The 'indecent' texts, too, are quite extraordinary. Not disgusting urban army-filth but full of surprising ideas. Good humour and boisterous mockery.

This is how I am occupied now—while awaiting the end of my exile.

That Vecsey–Saint-Saëns affair happened as follows: We were in Portugal, in Oporto, at the time. Saint-Saëns was also there. Papa Vecsey was intent on bringing him and Frankie together. I don't know which concerto was to be 'performed', I can't remember even the key, nor anything else about it, except that the son played the (2nd) andante movement at an impossibly slow tempo—obviously following his father's advice. The composer arrived in the room of the hotel, and we started to play. When we reached the 2nd movement, Saint-Saëns interrupted with: 'It's impossible to play it like that,' and, going up to the piano, he corrected it to a proper andante tempo. That made this otherwise boring (at least for me) piece at least tolerable. Saint-Saëns then left, and old Vecsey burst out, 'Oh, he does not understand, he is not a violinist!'** Why are you interested, or what made you think of it?

Dorothy Parrish-Domonkos wrote enthusiastically about her summer visit to you. How did she come to play for you?

I should be very happy to hear from you about the Boston performance.

With best wishes and warm regards,

BÉLA

* I think we knew this, too, or didn't we?

** this happened in March, 1906

[Original in English]

274. TO YEHUDI MENUHIN—ALMA (CALIF.)

[2] *June* 30, 1944

Dear Friend,

many thanks for the minute work you have spent in fingering and bowing of the sonata, and for everything else you have done. As for the exclusivity, I think one year is a too short period, and I would offer you at least two years.—It is only from your letter I learned about that concert plan: Mr. Heinsheimer did [not] want to tell me as long as it is not fixed. Now, of course, we talked over the program; it will be a wonderful evening.

Here follow[s] my answer to your questions.

1st mov., bar 43. Of course the whole chords are meant to be pizz.

1st mov., bar 66. The sixth note is 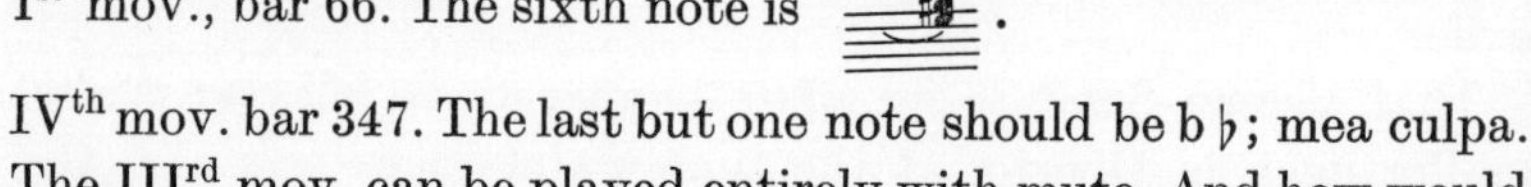 .

IVth mov. bar 347. The last but one note should be b ♭; mea culpa.

The IIIrd mov. can be played entirely with mute. And how would it be altogether without mute?

I am very glad to hear that the work is playable. But I am still concerned about certain positions. Are not the bars 99–100 in the 1st mov. too high? I mean whether they sound well in such a high pitch? If not then I could find another solution.

Would you mind a few changes (very few)? I made the following slight changes:

1st mov., bars 17, 18, 23; the pizz chord should be ;

bar 42; the last note changed into

bar 53; the 2nd chord should be (this was the original

form, then I thought it is unplayable. But now it appears not to be too difficult).

1st mov., bars 84–86. Would it not be better to have in the lowest part always [musical example] ? (This was the original form.) It may be up to you to decide this question.

2nd mov., bar 62. The 3rd quaver should be [musical example]

4th mov., bars 101–105 should be [musical example]

4th mov., bar 353: [musical example]

That is all. And I promise you to make no more changes, except for your suggestions.

Your account of the reaction of that Alaska crew to my sonata movement is quite amazing. I would never have expected this.

I had a good time in Asheville. However, my health is not as good as it should be, the doctors still tamper with me; they say something is wrong with my spleen, with my blood corpuscles, with this, with that – – – heaven knows what is wrong with me (surely not the doctors). Let us hope for the future.

July, August and Sept. I am spending at Saranac Lake, N. Y. (32 Park Avenue), and will then again return to New York.

Yours, very sincerely
BÉLA BARTÓK

[Original in Hungarian]

275. TO PÁL KECSKEMÉTI AND WIFE, *née* ERZSÉBET LÁNG—NEW YORK

[1] [*Saranac Lake*] *August* 22nd, 1944

Dear Erzsi and Pali,
I'm enclosing the cheque for Ditta's rent. I'm finding these housing difficulties rather upsetting: either I or Ditta—or even the two of us—continue to have no home. It's the eternal refrain once more: how I wish this exile would end at last!

This summer has been an extraordinarily hot one, it seems. Last year I almost froze here; this year, however, we have had day after day when the temperature has been above 90°. The peak was reached some 8 or 10 days ago, with 96°. Even the nights were so hot that one could not bear to have more than a sheet on the bed. But here this 96° (35° C in Hungarian) was quite agreeable. I would have been rather pleased about it if I hadn't known how unbearable it must have been in New York.

The Columbia Press have been disturbing me in my work. For a month, I have been chewing over colons and semi-colons, new paragraphs, and I have drafted hundreds of new counter-proposals. The battle will take place in October. In case you can't guess what it's all about, I'll whisper it: they have sent me the revised and typed copy of the preface to the Serbo-Croatian volume. All the trouble they must have taken and the number of corrections they have made is really astounding. Only they've often gone too far. The whole thing is very interesting and, above all, most instructive, but sometimes tiresome and annoying just because of this over-fussiness.

I would feel happy about what there is to feel happy about if I didn't always have the feeling that all this comes too late. Too late perhaps for me, and how much more so for those who are being killed off in the meantime.

Gloomily but with love, BÉLA

PS. Is there a gentleman called Plamenac (must be pronounced like the Hungarian c) in the Yugoslav section of the OWI?

[Original in Hungarian]

276. TO PÁL KECSKEMÉTI AND WIFE, *née* ERZSÉBET LÁNG—NEW YORK

[2] [*Saranac Lake*] *September* 1, 1944

Dear Erzsi and Pali,

Thanks for your letter and the one forwarded (it had a printed programme inside). One of my reasons for writing now is to ask you to do something: it is about the time when we should be receiving, from the Federal Tax people, that certain quarterly warning which you surely know—its envelope is brownish, its contents sweet. They usually send it addressed to 'Bela & Edith Bartok'. If one of these arrives, or has already arrived, please send it *to me*, here (not to Ditta's address). There's an important (tax register page-?) number in it. Though, I must say the tax people won't get much joy from me, for I've arrived at the point where they owe me instead of me owing them. I don't know if I told you the reason, viz. my

English taxes. I've been notified that 800 dollars have just been sent to me from London, but half of this has been deducted by *His Majesty's Tax Office*[1]. However, these 400 dollars can be put to the credit of my account here. The tax rate here is 25% only, my income here is not great, so it will turn out that Uncle Sam owes me 200. I'll hold out my palm, but obviously nothing will drop into it. Though, mind you, extraordinarily honest things do occur here. As you perhaps know, since last year, 25% of the State taxes are being remitted. Last year I deducted this all right; this year, however, I forgot to do so.—And, lo, what do I get but a letter from the State people, enclosing a cheque to repay the 25%, without my having asked for it! Could anything like that happen in Hungary? Obviously not, and not even if one did ask for it.

Then, I also wanted to write to you to say that I'm not always as blue as I was when I last wrote. Though there's always a good reason for worrying—almost without respite. In June I felt worried about Caen. Well, that's done for. Then, about Coutance, St. Malo, and later about Florence and Paris. And now about Hungary. There is some comfort, though, in that disconsolate state of affairs, if comfort it can be called. It is my firm conviction that whatever Hungary had done, she could not have changed her fate. The most she could have done would be to expose herself to great destruction (though that may still come!). Poland and the Baltic states are cases in point.

Sometimes my thoughts stray onto lighter subjects. For example: how many legs has a crab? The Wallachian folk-song says:

Opt	*picioare*	*racu*	*are.*
(< *octo*)	(= leg)	(< crab)	(*habet*)

Is this statement true or false?

A trick in the Wallachian (lyrical) texts seems to be traceable back to the times when the ancestors of the Wallachs were still in Italy, as I have realized. This technical trick manifests itself in a certain ornamental use of

the *frunză verde* or *Foaie verde* lines.
(< *fronda*) (< *folium*)

Nothing like this occurs in the village poetry of any other European people—except Italian. At home (in Budapest), I have a collection of folk texts from the Florence region; there are lines in it with

[1] In English.

exactly the same function, beginning with the words *Fronda verde* (or *verte?*)

I wonder whether there's a *fronda*-like word in Latin, meaning leaf of a tree.

I'll have to look it up in New York libraries, it seems, if I want to quote *fronda verde* sources. Maybe I'll find some.

The z<d change in *frunză—fronda* is completely regular: *zi<dies, zeu<deus, căzut <cadutus?, căzînd<cadentum.*

That 'preface' calls itself preface only out of sheer false modesty; actually, it's a full-scale treatise of 138 typed pages.

I am now ready with my anti-revision.

But the row won't take place before Oct. (talks with the *editor*)[1]. Meantime, I have been having a lot of trouble with the copyist (he was here quite by chance, on holiday) who calligraphed the musical part. He writes beautifully and is a good musician, but he's very stubborn on minor questions of detail. I've succeeded in getting over these troubles, too, without falling out with him.

I never go to the cinema. But now I've decided to go and see the newsreels on Paris as they get here.

Ditta played 2 weeks ago, then yesterday, and she's playing today, too (in a big sanatorium, for the sick). She enjoys it very much (I'm happy if I needn't play the piano).

All good wishes,

BÉLA

Just one more *quiz*:[1]
How would you translate this:

into old, classical English?

[Original in English]

277. C. P. WOOD—TO BÉLA BARTÓK
SARANAC LAKE

[*Seattle*] *September* 13, 1944

Dear Mr. Bartok:
In your last letter dated November 1943 you said you might be ready this fall to consider the idea of coming to the University of Washington in 1945.

[1] In English.

If nothing has occurred in the meantime to change your plans perhaps we ought to begin talking about it again. I shall be glad to learn how you feel about the proposal as it was originally outlined so long ago.

With best wishes and regards to Mrs. Bartok I remain

Cordially yours,
CARL PAIGE WOOD

[Original in Hungarian]

278. TO PÁL KECSKEMÉTI AND WIFE, *née* ERZSÉBET LÁNG—NEW YORK

[3] *Saranac Lake, September* 29th, 1944

Dear Erzsi and Pali,
I got Ditta's letter about this business of the apartment. Many thanks for your help! You see, I wasn't far off the mark when I mentioned homelessness.

But to return to the crab's eight legs—well, provided we're speaking about legs, then it has eight of them. But if about limbs, it has ten, the first pair having been grown into pincers. Thus, he, too, is right who asserts that the crab has ten legs.—As for the other question, the answer would be: '*Frailty, thy name is woman.*'[1] Frail or fickle—these are about the same.—All this is, however, only raillery and teasing. But what I'm going to say now is deadly serious:

'70% of my Wallachian singers were women, 30%, men. 90% of a certain sort of texts were supplied by women, 10%, by men (in the case of the other texts the proportion was: 76% women, 24% men; and 47% women, 53% men, respectively). What would the percentage be for the different types of texts if 50% of the singers had been women and 50% men?'

I wonder if you could work this out in your spare time (if you have any). I found it a very difficult problem; I tried to approach it by empirical methods before finding, at last, the mathematical formula. (I even thought of consulting Einstein who is, or rather was, on vacation here, on the shores of one of the lakes; once he even tumbled into the water because he miscalculated the effect of the force of the wind on the sails.)

It is best to portion out things in pairs, so I'm sending you herewith the first product of my career as an English poet. Can you find

[1] In English.

out what this is? If not, show it to Ditta; but if you can, still give it to her. (The insertions in red are corrections by someone else; all the rest is my own, original invention.)

Pali, have you a Thukidydes? *(Θουκυδίδης?)*
y?i? *ί?ν?*

For I would like to quote a sentence from it, from the part immediately preceding the funeral speech of Pericles. True, only in an English translation; although it would be nice to include the original as well, but I can't do that because it would look as though I understood Greek, which is not the case.—I've found a book here: an anthology of Greek literature. I thought it would be a good idea to read some of it. Well, in the explanatory text I came across, among others, the following gem:

'*But the ancient Greeks did their work under limitations* (poor things!). *They were pagans* (poor, unhappy people!). *They had not the light of the sun to see by* (poor, unhappy, wretched people!). *They groped for the truth, and they missed it*[1] – – – – (shall I continue?!)' Upon which I had a closer look at the title page and, lo, it turned out that the anthology was a school textbook by some rogue-pedagogue. The Americans of course, sanctified by God's Word, they are close to the Light, Truth and Beauty, not like those miserable Greeks.

These are the lighter aspects of life. As for the gloomier ones—the standstill in both East and West, the Arnhem adventure, Warsaw, Hungary—well, let's drop the subject!

To all this, of course, I only expect an oral answer.

I'll be writing to Ditta once more from here.

All good wishes.

BÉLA

[Original in Hungarian]

279. TO ERNŐ BALOGH—NEW YORK

[*Saranac Lake*] *October* 4, 1944

Dear Ernő,

Thank you for your letter of September 20. Tomorrow, I leave for New York; and I'll ring you up on, or some time after, Friday. The

[1] Text in italics in English.

latest trouble is—for there always has to be some trouble or other—that one cannot find an apartment in New York—in fact, no accommodation at all. Ditta is a permanent visitor at Woodrow, but every room is occupied for the time being. Ditta was turned out of that one-room flat she had last year, but fortunately she succeeded in getting a two-room one in the same house (309 West 57, apartment 503). The provisional solution is my going to live there. Even so, of course, it will be very tight for us in these two rooms: myself, with my bag and baggage, and she, with her piano. But at least the piano is on the spot in case I ever need to practise.

It is with a tense interest that I am looking forward to the negotiations with Elkán. I'll discuss the exact time with you, in N. Y.; actually, I could make it any time.

I have tried to practise here; and it seems as if I could still play the piano. I say this in connection with the proposed recordings. The Suite op. 14 (9½ minutes), the Sonatina (4 minutes), perhaps 2 or 3 Burlesques (2 minutes each), 1st Rumanian dance (4½ minutes), something from among the 15 Peasant Dances—these could be considered as pieces which neither Continental nor Columbia have recorded with me. Perhaps some others, too. For instance, I don't know whether those people have the Allegro Barbaro and Bear Dance.

As far as my health is concerned, from one point of view it might be called health. At least the local doctor here says that the lung trouble, erroneously diagnosed last year, and several times at that, as TB, has completely disappeared. Seen from another point of view, of course, all this is rather 'half-ness' than 'whole-ness.' Spleen, blood and goodness knows what else must be subjected to periodical checking up. But this, allegedly, is a phenomenon of old age (or senility?—I don't mind which). As for work, I've done some, only maybe not precisely what they are awaiting from me.

But I can't work two ways together, any more than a healthy-eyed man can squint in two directions.

To cut a long story short, I have been working exclusively on those Wallachian texts and have written my essay on them. I hope it is 'epoch-making' or at least 'fundamental'; the only pity is that there's no one likely to be interested or in a state of mind to appreciate it. But, for the time being, I don't mind even this. As I said earlier in New York, this study has been my way of working off my last (½-year) Columbia University commission. So it's not just wasted effort.

We're having a good summer here, sometimes it's been 96 degrees, not cold enough to make you shiver as it was last year. In addition, we enjoyed a bit of earthquake, and Ditta had her share of hurricanes into the bargain. So we have not suffered from any lack of entertainment.

Till we meet again *(so long! see you later!)*[1],

many greetings,
Yours,
BÉLA

[Original in French]

280. TO RADIO BRUSSELS
[PAUL COLLAER]

[2] *New York, October* 24th, 1944

I am so pleased to have had news of M. Paul Collaer and to learn that he has been able to resume his activities with Radio Brussels. For the last four years now I've been in the United States as a voluntary refugee. Many, many times, during these four long years, have I thought of all my Belgian friends and asked myself how they could endure all the ordeals of such a long, inhuman occupation. I am very glad to learn that the devastation was not as great as one had feared. I salute the valiant Belgian people in this hour of their liberation. And my special congratulations go to the Flemish department of the Belgian Radio for having again succeeded in enlisting the services of M. Paul Collaer who did so much for modern music before the war in Brussels.

As for what I have myself composed during this difficult period, I have little to tell. In the course of the first years, I threw myself heart and soul into the study, at Columbia University, of Serbo-Croatian folk music. The result of these studies is an essay about this music, which is going to be published by Columbia University Press. Another, and less agreeable, result of this seclusion and of the ceaseless and tiring work was that I fell ill from exhaustion. However, I somehow got over this ordeal, too, and finally I was able to resume my activities as a composer. Thus I was able to write, about a year ago, a Concerto for a large orchestra in five movements, for the Koussevitsky Foundation. This year I have composed a violin solo Sonata for Yehudi Menuhin, who will give the first performance of it at his Carnegie Hall recital in November. Menuhin, by the way,

[1] In English.

at his concerts in the United States and in England, has been playing my Concerto for the violin and my first violin and piano Sonata, these works being part of his repertoire.

BÉLA BARTÓK

[Original in English]

281. TO WILHELMINE CREEL—SEATTLE

[7]

New York, 19, N.Y.
309 West 57th St.
December 17, 1944.

Dear Mrs. Creel:
Is not this a most extraordinary stationary *[sic]* to write on? Yet, are we not supposed to regard as our patriotic duty to save paper in this acute paper shortage, are not we? Though, of course, there still appear the advertisements of Lucky Strikes, Chesterfields etc. urging people to buy them though they have no stocks to sell. But this is a different business: nothing is allowed to interfere with the high principles of advertising business, shortage of paper or no shortage; or else the world would crumble.—So, when I got this *[sic]* (one sided) copies made expressly for you, and saw these nice blank pages, I could not resist to fulfil my patriotic duty – – –.

To be so late in answering your letters is quite inexcusable. I will not even try to find and enumerate excuses, instead I will begin to give you a description of the most essential happenings of this year in my life.

You said in one of your letters that my recovering was a miracle. This is true only with some reservations: it was only a hemisemidemi-miracle. Of course, that lung-infection disappeared as mysteriously as it came—this you know from my last letter. There are, however, —and almost continuously—some minor troubles which probably never can be completely cured and make a regular job or concertizing etc. impossible for me. So for instance, last April my spleen became rebellious. My Asheville doctor mistook it for a pleuresy. He would have me *[sic]* quite gallantly treated me against it, but fortunately I had to come back to New York where the mistake was at once discovered, and my spleen punished by a rude X-ray treatment. Then it appeared there is disorder in my blood-picture, so they poisoned me with arsenic. Shall I continue? I think better not.

A few weeks ago I said: 'Tell me, doctor, exactly what my ailment is! Choose a nice Latin or Greek word and tell me.' After a moment's hesitation he emitted: 'Polycythemia' *[sic]*. There we are again! Only, 2 years ago this meant too many red corpuscules, and now it means too many white ones.

Surely, I do not feel as agile and lively as 4 years ago, and must take great care of myself especially in unfavorable weather and so on. But I can do work, mostly 'housework'; could, among others, teach. However, I have no pupils, only occasionally. So, for instance, last May Dorothy Parrish came to New York to have a few lessons. She was at that time pregnant, expected her child for December, wanted to come to New York for the winter. But I do not have news from her, except that somebody told me her husband is overseas. At X-mas time I will have here another former pupil of mine, Agnes Butcher from Canada.

I have another new work: a sonata for violin alone, written in Asheville for Menuhin. He played it in his New York recital on Nov. 26., it was a wonderful performance. It has 4 movements, and lasts ca. 20 minutes. I was afraid it is too long; imagine: listen[ing] to a single violin during 20 minutes. But it was quite all right, at least for me.—If he ever goes to Seattle for a recital try to induce the manager of the concert to ask for this piece. For orchestral works of mine can scarcely be performed there, anyway.

The first performance of my orchestra work, written in Sept. 1943 for the Koussevitzky Foundation took place on Dec. 1. 2. in Boston. We went there for the rehearsals and performances—after having obtained the grudgingly granted permission of my doctor for this trip. It was worth wile *[sic]*, the performance was excellent. Koussevitzky is very enthusiastic about the piece, and says it is 'the best orchestra piece of the last 25 years' (including the works of his idol Shostakovich!). At least this is his personal opinion – – –. He will play it in New York in Jan. Menuhin played my concerto this year in Washington, Baltimore, Pittsburg *[sic]*, and (in Sept.) in London (B.B.C.) twice! Next season he is going to play it in Philadelphia and probably in Boston.

I spent all my time—except those few weeks needed for the solo-violin sonata—to do some special scientific work. Perhaps you know that [I] gave the final shape to the musical part of the Rumanian Folk Music collection during my illness. These consist *[sic]* of two volumes: I: instrumental, II vocal melodies. Now, this year I worked on and almost finished the IIIrd volume, comprising all the texts. This was quite an unusual work for me. First, I had to devise a classifying system for these 1700 texts; then I studied and examined the classified material from the most various angles, and finally I made a lot of deductions on the basis of my studied *[sic]*. You see one of these deductions on p. L–LI; how do you like them? I had made the copy of these pages mainly to show you 3 text translations (marked with red). The first is a literal one in prose, the 2nd and 3rd I tried to translate in the original metre. In addition I am sending you another translation of – – – – now, I wonder, if you recognize it?

(interruption of a few days)

In the mean time your package with the two books arrived. And I did not even tell you anything about last year's books! Isak Dinesen's is a wonderful one. And it has a certain European flavour; I often wondered if it was originally written in English, or whether it is a translation. By the way: I never knew that Isak is a female name! Eliot seems to be a remarkable poet—though, of course, I am an incompetent judge of English poetry because of language difficulties. I know some of his earlier poems from an Anthology.

And now a short account of family-life. There is a housing-shortage in New York. So I stay with Ditta in a two room apartment which is, of course, too small for both of us. We very often hamper each other in our activities, but we must be glad to have got such an apartment, at least. My plan is to stay during the whole winter time in New York, and I hope the rude winter climate will not do any damage to my health.

Peter—after objection, and its revoking, joined last Febr. the Navy, had to attend there a 6 month's *[sic]* electric engineering course. Since Sept. he is stationed in Panama and seems to like the place.

We all are very much worried about the situation in Hungary and especially in Budapest, and are cursing the Germans; but this does not give any remedy.

Are you still teaching those oriental languages? Or are your activities only in music?

Best regards and wishes from us both for X-mas and New Year.

Yours, very sincerely
BÉLA BARTÓK

Some time ago Prof. Wood wrote me a letter. I will answer him soon: it is very improbable that I ever can go to Seattle!

[Original in English]

282. TO WILHELMINE CREEL—SEATTLE

[8]

309 W 57
New York
X-mas day 1944

Dear Mrs. Creel:
I hope you got my extremely long letter by this time. This 'unexpected' letter is to tell you that my 'Concerto for Orchestra' is going to be again performed in Boston on Dec. 29 and 30, and the latter will be broadcast by the 'Blue Network' at 8:30 p.m. Eastern Time (that is 5:30 in Seattle; or is it 4:30?). I don't know if you can listen to such broadcasts. The 1st item to be broadcast is the Moussorgsky 'Bald Mountain' piece, and after that comes my piece.

I forgot to tell you about my 'living' conditions in my last letter. This is now fairly well settled. This year I had an income of about $1400 from sale of my music and performance fees (in the U.S. and Britain) and in addition some other income. Now I made an agreement with Boosey & Hawkes according to which they will pay me an advance of $1400 yearly during the following three years, in addition to my regular income from sales and performances. So, for the next three years, a modest living is secured for us. (Doctors' expenses for me, if necessary, are still paid by the Ascap.) And after three years—heaven knows what will happen.

I received your 'Four B^s' program this morning. Was this a deliberate act of yours? This reminds me of a criticism appearing in Jan. 1944 in the San Francisco Chronicle and saying: 'the sonata (1st violin piano sonata, played there by Menuhin) emphasizes again what has often (?!?) been suggested in these columns—that Bartok is the fourth in the procession of the great B'^s of music.' This is, by the way, an amplification of the 'jeu de lettres' invented by Bülow—if I remember well— at the occasion of the 1st performance of Brahm's *[sic]* 1st symphony.

My piano pieces 'For Children' will come out in a few weeks in a revised (improved) edition, published by Boos. & Hawkes. I will make [them] send you a copy.

Happy New Year from both of us

BÉLA BARTÓK

[Original in English]

283. TO YEHUDI MENUHIN—NEW YORK

[3]

309 W 57
New York
April 5, 1945

Dear Friend:
my doctor is quite enthusiastic about California as a summer place for me, and so am I. Therefore, we are very happy to be able to accepte *[sic]* your kind invitation. We will go there for about 3 months and will leave New York about June 15. We will send you news about our arrival in San Francisco in time.

Don't hurry with and worry about the solo violin sonata; you will return it to me in Alma during our stay there.

Our best regards to you both!

Yours, very sincerely
Béla Bartók

[Original in English]

284. TO YEHUDI MENUHIN—ALMA (CALIF.)

[4]

309 W 57th
New York 19, N.Y.
June 6, 1945

Dear Friend:
I am so sorry to have to tell you that we cannot come to California! I do not feel quite well, and—for variety's sake—now Mrs. Bartók was ill for several weeks and does not yet feel quite well. We simply are scared to try such a long journey, connected, especially now, with all kind of annoyances. I scarcely can tell you how I regret this. I had so many musical plans connected with my stay there. All this now comes to nothing. And what makes things still worse is that you generally are too busy here in the East during the season to have a few quiet hours for discussing things. However, somewhere we must try to settle the final form of the solo sonata next winter; fortunately, it is not so urgent. I would be very pleased if you could write me about your stay in England, about your plans for the next season, when will you be in New York, and so on.

Yours, very sincerely
Béla Bartók

[Original in Hungarian]

285. TO JENŐ ZÁDOR—HOLLYWOOD

89 Riverside Drive
Saranac Lake, N. Y.
July 1st, 1945

Dear Mr. Zádor,
Thank you for your letter of June 19th. Just a year ago I was approached by someone else with the same request. On that occasion I said that, in principle, I was willing to do it, but asked for precise details from Mr. Schildkret. After that I heard nothing more until your letter arrived. And now I can again only give you the same reply: in principle I am willing to do it but would want to know some particulars. Namely: 1) What is required—an orchestral piece or a vocal one (chorus, or chorus with soloists, or doesn't it matter which?); or should it be orchestra with chorus? If it is a purely orchestral piece (further on in your letter you refer to it as a 'prelude'), how am I to show the biblical character of the work?

2) Is there any deadline?

3) a) I presume that what you have in mind would entail only the transfer of gramophone-recording rights. In that case, of course, the work could not be published (for, if it were, then, thanks to the wise *Zwangslizenz* system, other parties would be free to make recordings of it, too). b) For what period (five years, ten years, for ever) are the rights to be transferred?

4) It would be somewhat complicated to transfer to Mr. Sch. the copyright for publication also, as I have an exclusive contract with Boosey & Hawkes. But in respect of any work which I do not hand over to B. & H. for publication I am free to dispose of the gramophone-recording rights.

I would therefore be obliged if Mr. Schildkret would send me detailed information. (The above address is valid till mid-Sept.; after that date, my address will be: 309 West 57th New York.)

We have been receiving some extremely depressing news from Hungary: appalling devastations, terrible misery, chaos threatening (a great number of Hungarian newspapers from Budapest are finding their way—presumably through the Russian Embassy—to a Hungarian Communist newspaper here, which reproduces them in facsimile; also a few people have received news through private channels). As I see it, for the time being one cannot even think of returning to Hungary. Nor is there any means of doing so—neither transport nor (Russian) permit. But even if there were means, in my opinion it would be better to await developments. Heaven knows how many years it will be before Hungary can pull herself together in some measure (if at all). And yet I, too, would like to return, for good - - - - -

With kindest regards,

Yours sincerely,
BÉLA BARTÓK

[Original in Hungarian]

286. TO PÁL KECSKEMÉTI AND WIFE, *née* ERZSÉBET LÁNG—NEW YORK

[4]

Saranac Lake, N.Y.
89, Riverside Drive,
July 7, 1945

My dear Children,

At last we have safely—but not agreeably—arrived here. We were able to get into the train ½ an hour before departure, but even so we only got seats because of the astuteness of our porter. (True, the crowd thinned out after Albany.) It was very hot! Some cooling device did function, but feebly and ineffectively. Whenever the train stopped (and how often and how long it stopped), the device had a rest, too. Train-cooling is very nice indeed, but when it doesn't work properly, any European has a good mind to grab an axe and smash all the windows which, according to the American custom, should not, must not, and cannot be opened.

Once here, we realized that it was exactly as hot as in New York the day before. Still, it's quite different here. We live in a good-sized cottage (or hovel or hut) on a hill. The staircase is narrow like that of an attic, but there are lots of steps leading up. There's electricity for lighting and cooking, but to warm your bath-water you have to lay a fire in the stove. There's a tub in the bathroom but no wash-basin. There's an icebox, but it works with natural, god-created ice (delivered every other day). Generally speaking, goods are not delivered (they were last year), but the landlady often goes into 'town' in her car and takes Ditta with her.—Still, it's much better here than in that monstrous city. Within a few days Ditta livened up so much that it was a joy to look at her.

I should have liked to liven up, too, but so far it hasn't been possible. On July 2, I set out to emigrate and then to immigrate again. The first phase took place at dawn on July 3, the second, late at night the same day. From 9 in the morning until 6.30 in the evening (with only a break for lunch) I loafed, loitered and sat around in that Consulate, consumed with anger and anxiety. It almost seemed that I wouldn't get those precious documents that day (they covered a ton of paper with their futile scribbling in these times of paper shortage). In that case I might have had to wait until July 5, (National Holiday). What is more, the Consulate isn't open on July 2 either (Canadian Holiday!). It's a good thing I didn't start one day earlier. The surprises that can befall a man! But who would think of Canadian holidays when dealing with a U.S. Consulate.

All the same, it was better to emigrate and immigrate from and to this place than from N. Y., I think.

I hear there's a big heat-wave in N.Y. You poor things! If you are able to hold a pen in such heat, do write! And tell us where you're going to spend your holidays.

Pali, please do not forget to pay my rent at the beginning of Aug. Did you pay at the beginning of July to Johnson or whoever the person concerned may be?

In Montreal—a nice little city—I ate meat, regularly. Here they gave us all the 5 pounds of sugar at once for the ration card!

I have brought a French-language newspaper with me. I learned that 3 million French live there in a bunch.

Many greetings,
BÉLA (AND DITTA).

[Original in Hungarian]

287. TO PÁL KECSKEMÉTI AND WIFE, *née* ERZSÉBET LÁNG—NEW YORK

[5] *August* 11, 1945.

Dear Erzsi and Pali,
Péter will be home again any day now, please will you give him the enclosed letter?

Pali! You don't study our Szabadság[1] carefully enough. Otherwise you would have noticed that wonderful text and would have mused—as I am musing—over what a 'tall' drink could be like. I've seen tall houses, tall trees, tall mountains and even tall snow in my life; but a tall drink—that must be something marvellous. But what trifles all these problems are compared to that atomic

[1] Probably the Hungarian-language paper appearing in Cleveland.

what-not (it was back in 1940 that I first read about U.235, only a few grammes of it existed then at Columb. Univ.) – – –

Best wishes to you.

BÉLA

My dear, good and beloved friend Heinsheimer visited me here a few days ago. He couldn't bear this long separation. Really!

[Original in English]

288. TO DOROTHY PARRISH

[7] *August* 30, 1945

Dear Dorothy: many thanks for your letter. This morning we left (veteran Peter included) Saranac Lake for N.Y. If you want to call me on phone, do it after 5 P.M. (till 10). We left sooner [than] we wanted; Ditta does not feel quite well, and I too have abnormal temperature. Yes, Mrs. Creel is now in N.Y. only I don't have her address there. She expects me to be back in N.Y. about mid-September, and will call me up at that time. I began to write some works in Saranac, could unfortunately not finish them, and am wondering whether it will be possible to continue the work in N.Y.

Yours very sincerely
BARTÓK

[Original in Hungarian]

289. [WORLDS CONTENDING]

Three different worlds contended with each other
Three different worlds, three different countries.
The name of the one was the country of the sunrise,
The name of the second was the country of the sunset,
The name of the third was the country of the south.
Then up spake the country, the first kind of country,
The first kind of country, the country of the sunrise,
'Finer than both of you, better than both of you,
I am the loved one of the bright sun himself,
The bright sun himself visits me before you,
Visits me before you, so dearly he loves me.'
Then up spake the second, that fine and lovely country,

['*Worlds Contending*'. . .]

Fine and lovely country, country of the sunset.
'Finer than both of you, better than both of you,
I am the loved one of the bright sun himself,
The bright sun himself stays with me the longest,
Stays with me the longest, so dearly he loves me.'
Then up spake the third, that fine and lovely country,
'Finer than both of you, better than both of you,
I am the loved one of the bright sun himself,
The bright sun himself smiles on me more warmly,
Smiles on me more warmly, so dearly he loves me.'
Thus they contend, the fine and lovely countries,
The countries of the sunrise, the sunset and the south.
Their quarrel is heard by the Lord of all the countries,
The Lord of all the countries, the Lord Almighty God.
'Why do you contend, fine and lovely countries.
Bootless contestation { is of no avail / leads to nothing good.
(Leads to nothing good, and is of no advantage.)
Better that you show me, fine and lovely countries,
Fine and lovely countries, the thing you can create.
Who creates the loveliest, let her be the first,
Let her be the first and let her be my choice.'
Then the three countries consulted all together,
Consulted all together, ready for the contest
— — — — — — — — — — — —[1]

[1] Left unfinished by Bartók.

APPENDICES

THE PUBLICATION OF BARTÓK'S CORRESPONDENCE

The collection and publication of material and records relating to Béla Bartók was first begun in Hungary at the end of 1947, less than three years after the composer's death.

The first tangible results of the work appeared soon afterwards in the form of the first volume of his correspondence published in 1948 at the instigation of Zoltán Kodály. This collection contained more than a hundred letters, most of them found among the papers of Bartók's mother after her death. The most valuable letters in that collection are those shedding light on Bartók's youth, particularly his student years at the Budapest Academy of Music.

The second volume, containing another two hundred letters, followed in response to the world-wide welcome accorded the first, and was published in 1951. The research work, begun in the composer's native country, encouraged former pupils and admirers living abroad (including many who had emigrated from Hungary) to come forward and place the Bartók letters in their possession at the disposal of researchers in Hungary. The majority of these letters throw vivid light on the giddy round of his European recital tours. Others acquaint us with the humanism of Bartók's spirit, and they conclude with a moving picture of the bitter years of emigration. A number of letters had originally been written in foreign languages, but in this volume they were published in their Hungarian translation alone.

The third volume (1955) revealed another aspect of Bartók—the creative artist. This edition of three hundred letters was a joint enterprise undertaken by Hungarian, Rumanian and Slovak musicologists, and gives the reader a workshop view of Bartók the folklorist. These letters reflect difficulties encountered by the composer in the publication of his collections of folk music. As reading for pleasure they may not prove to be always very entertaining, but they are absolutely necessary for an understanding of Bartók's life and work, and this third volume, containing an impressive body of material, constituted a great step forward in Bartók research. In this volume letters in foreign languages were published in the original together with their Hungarian translations.

A total of more than six hundred of Bartók's letters, therefore, were published in these three volumes during the years 1948–1955.

A French translation of a volume of essays edited by Professor Bence Szabolcsi, published in 1956, contained a selection of forty letters taken from this material. Although only a handful, they were the first of Bartók's letters to be translated into one of the principal languages of the world. With the addition of one further letter, a German-language edition of the same volume came out in 1957.

The success these editions achieved abroad suggested the idea of translating a comprehensive selection from Bartók's letters previously published in Hungarian. As a result, a German edition appeared in 1960 with a selection of nearly two hundred letters. These letters, however, were not merely taken from the three volumes of correspondence already published in Hungarian; a third of them had not appeared in those volumes, and of this third some had never been published before in Hungarian or any other language, and the latest results of the continuing research on Bartók were thus incorporated.

The present (fifth) volume is the first ever published in English. While designed along the same lines as the German edition, it may nevertheless be considered a new publication in its content. Containing nearly three hundred letters, and consequently equal in size to the Hungarian–Rumanian–Slovak joint edition of 1955, it is one of the largest selections to appear in print. Sixty of these letters are here published for the first time, and as the preceding German edition also contained a good deal of original material, in all, more than a third of the letters in this book have in fact not yet appeared in an edition for the Hungarian-reading public.

At the request of Corvina Press, Mrs. Edith Pásztory-Bartók and Mr. Béla Bartók jr. have given their permission for the publication of this volume.

NOTES ON THE PRESENT EDITION

Approximately two out of every three letters were written in Hungarian, and they are here given in translation. More than a third of the correspondence was originally written in one of several foreign languages, most of them (seventy-one letters or a quarter of the present selection), in English.

Most of Bartók's letters were written in his own hand; there are a few typewritten, and a handful Mrs. Bartók wrote in his name. Where, in certain unavoidable cases, the text has been taken from copies of originals, it is invariably recorded in the Notes.

Bartók carefully dated most of his letters, adding his address after the name of the city. In the case of undated letters, references contained in the text have provided clues for approximate dating.

As a rule, the date heads the top right-hand corner of the letter. When it appears elsewhere—as at the bottom left of the page—it has been added to the top as well for easier reference. Where the date of the postmark differs from the date of the letter, the former is also given within square brackets. Bartók's slips in dating have been retained, but the correct date as reconstructed is also given.

The letters are arranged in chronological order. Bartók was eighteen when he wrote the first letter, and sixty-four when he wrote the last, shortly before his death.

There are some letters included which were not written by Bartók. They were all written to him or about him and are an important part of this collection.

As the arrangement of the letters is strictly chronological, the correspondence carried on with any particular person is inevitably interspersed among letters to other correspondents. Yet some sort of classification according to the recipients is essential for easier handling and study. Every letter, therefore, is headed by the name of the recipient and its number in the chronological series, but also carries a subsidiary number in a bracket to indicate its position in the series of letters to that particular person. Letter No. 37 in the collection, for instance, is subnumbered [21]—the twenty-first letter written to his mother—the next letter to his mother [22] is 101 in the chronological series.

The volume contains a series of notes on Bartók's principal correspondents and other points of interest occurring in the letters and, in certain cases, notes giving an account of the recovery of various letters; they also acknowledge the assistance of those who have kindly contributed letters in their possession.

A list of correspondents gives an exact survey of the addressees of Bartók's letters (260 Bartók letters addressed to 82 persons or institutions) and of other documents (29 letters of 10 persons). Nos. 17, 28, 156, 190, 210 and 289 are not letters but handwritten notes or drafts.

A brief survey of Bartók's compositions is also given.

The division of the book into five sections, representing important stages in the development of Bartók's art, has been adopted due to the success of this method in Hungary.

J. D.

LIST OF LETTERS

I

(1899–1905)

1	To István Thomán, Budapest [1]	Pozsony, September 8th, 1899
2	To his mother, Pozsony [1]	Budapest, January 21st, 1900
3	To his mother, Pozsony [2]	Budapest, November, 1902
4	To his mother, Pozsony [3]	Budapest, January 9th, 1903
5	To his mother, Pozsony [4]	Budapest, January 17th, 1903
6	To his mother, Pozsony [5]	Budapest, April 1st, 1903
7	To his mother, Pozsony [6]	Budapest, June 18th, 1903
8	To János Batka, Pozsony [1]	Passail, July 7th, 1903
9	To János Batka, Pozsony [2]	Passail, July 16th, 1903
10	To István Thomán, Budapest [2]	Passail, July, 1903
11	To his mother, Pozsony [7]	Gmunden, August 23rd, 1903
12	To his mother, Pozsony [8]	Gmunden, September 8th, 1903
13	To his mother, Pozsony [9]	Gmunden, September 23rd, 1903
14	To his mother, Pozsony [10]	Berlin, October 29th, 1903
15	To his mother, Pozsony [11]	Berlin, December 3rd, 1903
16	To István Thomán, Budapest [3]	Berlin, December 16th, 1903
17	Text draft of *Kossuth* symphony [12]	1903/4
18	To his mother, Pozsony [13]	Bowdon, February 12th, 1904
19	To Lajos Dietl, Vienna [1]	Berlin, March 17th, 1904
20	His mother to Mrs. Gyula Baranyai, Szeged	Pozsony, April 4th, 1904
21	To Kálmán Harsányi, Rákospalota [1a, 1b]	Regensburg, August 21st, 1904
22	To Kálmán Harsányi, Rákospalota [2]	Gerlicepuszta, September 18th, 1904
23	To István Thomán, Budapest [4]	Gerlicepuszta, September 18th, 1904
24	To Lajos Dietl, Vienna [2]	Pozsony, December, 1904
25	To his mother, Pozsony [14]	Paris, August, 1905
26	To Irmy Jurkovics, Nagyszentmiklós	Paris, August 15th, 1905
27	To his mother, Pozsony [15]	Paris, September 10th, 1905
28	*Curriculum vitae*	Sopron, December, 1905

II

(1906–1919)

29 To Lajos Poszvék, Sopron	Vienna, January 30th, 1906
30 To Péter König, Szeged	Pozsony, March 14th, 1906
31 To his mother, Pozsony [16]	Madrid, March 26th, 1906
32 To his mother, Pozsony [17]	Coimbra, April 11th, 1906
33 To his mother, Pozsony [18]	Venice, May 26th, 1906
34 To his mother, Vésztő [19]	Keresztúr, July 15th, 1906
35 To his mother, Pozsony [20]	Keresztúr, September 10th, 1906
36 To Lajos Dietl, Vienna [3]	Pozsony, November 3rd, 1906
37 To his mother, Rákospalota [21]	Bánffyhunyad, July 5th, 1907
38 To Etelka Freund, Annenheim [1]	Csík-Karczfalva, July 30th, 1907
39 To Stefi Geyer [1]	August 16th, 1907
40 To Etelka Freund, Annenheim [2]	August 17th, 1907
41 To Stefi Geyer, Budapest [2]	Vésztő, September 6th, 1907
42 To Stefi Geyer, Budapest [3]	September, 1907
43 To Gyula Sebestyén, Budapest	Rákospalota, October 9th, 1907
44 To Etelka Freund, Budapest [3]	Baden, June 28th, 1908
45 To Etelka Freund, Vitznau [4]	Zurich, July 20th, 1908
46 To Etelka Freund, Vitznau [5]	Argentières, July 27th, 1908
47 To István Thomán, Ungvár [5]	Geneva, July 31st, 1908
48 To Etelka Freund, Vitznau [6]	Geneva, July 31st, 1908
49 To Etelka Freund, Vitznau [7]	Albertville, Savoie, August 11th, 1908
50 To Etelka Freund, Vitznau [8]	Les Saintes-Maries, September 2nd, 1908
51 To Etelka Freund, Vitznau [9]	Chambéry, September, 1908
52 To Etelka Freund, Vitznau [10]	Chambéry, September, 1908
53 To Irma Freund, Budapest	Torockó, October 7th, 1908
54 To Etelka Freund, Budapest [11]	December 21st, 1908
55 To Etelka Freund, Budapest [12]	Vésztő, December 24th, 1908
56 To István Thomán, Budapest [6]	Berlin, January 3rd, 1909
57 To Etelka Freund, Budapest [13]	Budapest, January 28th, 1909

58 To Etelka Freund, Budapest [14] — Nagyvárad, July 17th, 1909
59 To István Thomán, Ungvár [7] — Beszterce-Marosludas, August 31st, 1909
60 To Etelka Freund, Budapest [15] — Mezőkoók, August 31st, 1909

61 To Etelka Freund, Budapest [16] — January 5th, 1910
62 To Rudolf Ganz — Budapest, 1910
63 To Sándor Kovács, Paris [1] — Budapest, February 18th, 1910
64 To Sándor Kovács, Paris [2] — Budapest, February 21st, 1910
65 To Sándor Kovács, Paris [3] — Budapest, March 5th, 1910
66 To Sándor Kovács, Paris [4] — Budapest, March, 1910
67 To Sándor Kovács, Paris [5] — Budapest, April, 1910
68 To Sándor Kovács, Paris [6] — Budapest, April, 1910
69 To Sándor Kovács, Paris [7] — Budapest, April 21st, 1910
70 To Dumitru G. Kiriac, Bucharest [1] — Budapest, April 29th, 1910
71 To Etelka Freund, Budapest [17] — Zurich, May 31st, 1910
72 To Frederick Delius, Paris [1] — Budapest, June 7th, 1910
73 To Frederick Delius, Dresden [2] — Budapest, 1910
74 To Frederick Delius, Dresden [3] — Budapest, 1910
75 To Etelka Freund, Budapest [18] — Topánfalva, January 4th, 1911
76 To Frederick Delius [4] — February 17th, 1911
77 To Turócszentmárton Printing Press — Budapest, February 25th, 1911
78 To János Buşiţia, Belényes [1] — March, 1911
79 To Frederick Delius, Paris [5] — Budapest, March 27th, 1911
80 To Frederick Delius, Grez-sur-Loing [6] — Rákoskeresztúr, July, 1911
81 To János Buşiţia, Belényes [2] — Budapest, December 18th, 1911
82 To János Buşiţia, Belényes [3] — Rákoskeresztúr, January, 1912
83 To Erich Moritz von Hornbostel, Berlin — May 22nd, 1912
84 To János Buşiţia, Belényes [4] — Svolvaer, July 12th, 1912
85 To Mrs. Kodály (Emma Gruber), Budapest — September 9th, 1912
86 To János Buşiţia, Belényes [5] — November–December, 1912
87 To Sámuel Bobál, Egyházmarót [1] — Rákoskeresztúr, December 16th, 1912

88	To Vilmos Géza Zágon, Paris [1]	Budapest, April, 1913
89	To Vilmos Géza Zágon, Paris [2]	Budapest, May 3rd, 1913
90	To Sámuel Bobál, Egyházmarót [2]	Spring, 1913
91	To Vilmos Géza Zágon, Paris [3]	Biskra, June 19th, 1913
92	To Kálmán D'Isoz, Budapest	Biskra, June 19th, 1913
93	To Vilmos Géza Zágon, Saint-Malo [4]	Vésztő, August 22nd, 1913
94	To Ion Bîrlea, Máramarossziget	October, 1913
95	To Sámuel Bobál, Egyházmarót [3]	Rákoskeresztúr, November 3rd, 1913
96	To Dumitru G. Kiriac, Bucharest [2]	Rákoskeresztúr, December 18th, 1913
97	To Imre Waldbauer, Paris	Budapest, June 15th, 1914
98	To Sámuel Bobál, Egyházmarót [4]	October 30th, 1914?
99	To János Buşiţia, Belényes [6]	Budapest, May 20th, 1915
100	To Budapest Philharmonic Society	Rákoskeresztúr, December 10th, 1915
101	To his mother, Pozsony [22]	Budapest, March 21st, 1917
102	To János Buşiţia, Belényes [7]	Budapest, May 6th, 1917
103	To János Buşiţia, Belényes [8]	Rákoskeresztúr, August, 1917
104	To János Buşiţia, Belényes [9]	Rákoskeresztúr, January 28th, 1918
105	To János Buşiţia, Belényes [10]	Rákoskeresztúr, September 14th, 1918
106	To János Buşiţia, Belényes [11]	January 31st, 1919
107	Zoltán Kodály to Hung. Min. of Culture	September, 1919
108	To his mother, Pozsony [23]	Rákoskeresztúr, October 23rd, 1919
109	To his mother, Pozsony [24]	November 28th, 1919

III

(1920–1926)

110	To Gyula Wlassics, Budapest [1]	Rákoskeresztúr, February 3rd, 1920
111	To Editor of *Szózat*, Budapest	Budapest, February 20th, 1920

112 To Géza Révész, Rostock [1] — Vésztő, August 22nd, 1920
113 To János Buşiţia, Belényes [12] — Budapest, May 8th, 1921
114 To Géza Révész, Amsterdam [2] — Budapest, March 3rd, 1922
115 To Géza Révész, Amsterdam [3] — Budapest, March 9th, 1922
116 To his mother, Pozsony [25] — Aberystwyth, March 16th, 1922
117 To his mother, Pozsony [26] — London, March 20th, 1922
118 To Géza Révész, Amsterdam [4] — London, March 22nd, 1922
119 To his mother, Budapest [27] — Paris, April 15th, 1922
120 To his mother [28] — Kassa, April 5th, 1923
121 To his mother [29] — Malvern Wells, May 4th, 1923
122 To Géza Révész, Amsterdam [5] — Budapest, May 27th, 1923
123 Gyula Wlassics to Béla Bartók [Draft] — Budapest, October 1st, 1923
124 Gyula Wlassics to Béla Bartók — Budapest, October 1st, 1923
125 To Edward Joseph Dent, London — Budapest, October 2nd, 1923
126 Gyula Wlassics to Béla Bartók — Budapest, May 27th, 1924
127 To Gyula Wlassics, Budapest [2] — Budapest, June 5th, 1924
128 To János Buşiţia, Belényes [13] — Budapest, May 15th, 1925
129 To Jenő Takács, Bremen [1] — Budapest, December 31st, 1925
130 To Constantin Brăiloiu, Bucharest [1] — Budapest, May 6th, 1926
131 To Constantin Brăiloiu, Bucharest [2] — Budapest, June 27th, 1926
132 To Antal Fleischer, Judendorf bei Graz [1] — Courmayeur, July 26th, 1926

IV

(1927–1940)

133 To Antal Fleischer, Barcelona [2] — Budapest, March 12th, 1927
134 To his mother [30] — Philadelphia, December 30th, 1927
135 To his mother [31] — Los Angeles, January 9th, 1928
136 To his mother [32] — Seattle, January 18th, 1928
137 To Péter Bartók, Budapest — St. Paul, January 24th, 1928

No.	Letter	Place and date
138	To Matica Slovenská, Turócszentmárton [1]	Budapest, May 16th, 1928
139	To Frigyes Reiner, Westport	Budapest, October 29th, 1928
140	To József Szigeti [1]	Budapest, October–November, 1928
141	To Oxford University Press, London [1]	Budapest, November 17th, 1928
142	To Ditta Pásztory (Mrs. Bartók), Budapest [1]	Moscow, January 2nd, 1929
143	To Ditta Pásztory (Mrs. Bartók), Budapest [2]	Kharkov, January 7th, 1929
144	To Ditta Pásztory (Mrs. Bartók), Budapest [3]	Rome, April 12th, 1929
145	To Michael D. Calvocoressi, London	Berlin, December 11th, 1929
146	To Ernő Südy, Békéscsaba [1]	Budapest, May 17th, 1930
147	To Octavian Beu, Bucharest [1]	Budapest, November 5th, 1930
148	Béla Balázs to Béla Bartók	Paris, November 15th, 1930
149	To Miklós Radnai	Budapest, November 21st, 1930
150	To his mother, Pozsony [33]	Freiburg, December 6th, 1930
151	Miklós Radnai to Béla Bartók	Budapest, December 10th, 1930
152	To Octavian Beu, Bucharest [2]	Berlin–Budapest, January 10th, 1931
153	To Oxford University Press, London [2]	Budapest, February 16th, 1931
154	To Constantin Brăiloiu, Bucharest [3]	Budapest, February 22nd, 1931
155	To László Pollatsek, Budapest	Budapest, February 23rd, 1931
156	To Société Internationale de la Musique Contemporaine	Budapest, May, 1931
157	To Oxford University Press, London [3]	Budapest, May 30th, 1931
158	To Oxford University Press, London [4]	Budapest, May 31st, 1931
159	To his mother, Budapest [34]	Geneva, July 9th, 1931
160	To his mother, Budapest [35]	Mondsee, July 13th, 1931
161	To Imre Weisshaus, Dessau	Mondsee, August 4th, 1931
162	To Max Rostal, Berlin	Budapest, November 6th, 1931
163	To János Bușiția, Belényes [14]	Budapest, December 20th, 1931
164	To Jenő Takács, Cairo [2]	Budapest, May 8th, 1932
165	To B.B.C. Music Department, London [1]	Budapest, September 6th, 1933

166 To B.B.C. Music Department, London [2] — Budapest, September 30th, 1933
167 To B.B.C. Music Department, London [3] — Budapest, October 7th, 1933
168 To Matica Slovenská, Turócszentmárton [2] — Budapest, October 8th, 1933
169 To B.B.C. Music Department, London [4] — Budapest, October 19th, 1933
170 To B.B.C. Music Department, London [5] — Budapest, October, 1933
171 To Ernő Südy, Békéscsaba [2] — Budapest, January 20th, 1934
172 To B.B.C. Music Department, London [6] — Budapest, May 9th, 1934
173 To Oxford Univ. Press, London [5] — Budapest, May 9th, 1934
174 To Oxford Univ. Press, London [6] — Solda, July 2nd, 1934
175 To Vinko Žganec, Zombor [1] — Budapest, October 27th, 1934
176 To Oxford Univ. Press, London [7] — Budapest, November 2nd, 1934
177 To Vinko Žganec, Zombor [2] — Budapest, November 7th, 1934
178 To Oxford Univ. Press, London [8] — Budapest, December 3rd, 1934
179 To Raïna Katzarova, Sofia — Budapest, February 27th, 1935
180 To Imre Deák, Pasadena — Budapest, March 5th, 1935
181 To Vinko Žganec, Zombor [3] — Budapest, July 3rd, 1935
182 To Oxford Univ. Press, London [9] — Budapest, July 4th, 1935
183 To B.B.C. Music Department, London [7] — Budapest, December 10th, 1935
184 To B.B.C. Music Department, London [8] — Budapest, December 14th, 1935
185 To László Rásonyi, Ankara [1] — Budapest, December 18th, 1935
186 To Vinko Žganec, Zombor [4] — Budapest, December 23rd, 1935
187 To Kisfaludy Society, Budapest — Budapest, December 29th, 1935
188 To B.B.C. Music Department, London [9] — Santpoort, January 13th, 1936
189 To B.B.C. Music Department, London [10] — Liverpool, January 16th, 1936
190 To Budapest newspapers, on Ferenc Liszt — February 3rd, 1936
191 To Jenő Takács, Cairo [3] — Budapest, February 16th, 1936
192 To László Rásonyi, Ankara [2] — Budapest, April 16th, 1936

193 To Brigitte Schiffer-Oelsner, Cairo — Budapest, July 14th, 1936
194 To László Rásonyi, Mátrafüred [3] — Budapest, August 21st, 1936
195 To Hugó Kelen, Budapest — Budapest, September 28th, 1936
196 To Sándor Albrecht, Pozsony [1] — Ankara, November 15th, 1936
197 To János Buşiţia, Belényes [15] — Ankara, November 18th, 1936
198 To Ahmed Adnan Saygĭn, Istanbul [1] — Budapest, January 2nd, 1937
199 To Ahmed Adnan Saygĭn, Istanbul [2] — Budapest, January 14th, 1937
200 To Mme Müller-Widmann, Basle [1] — Brussels, February 3rd, 1937
201 To Mme Müller-Widmann, Basle [2] — Budapest, May 24th, 1937
202 To Board of Governors, Sárospatak Sec. School — Budapest, May 26th, 1937
203 To Ahmed Adnan Saygĭn, Kadi-Köy [3] — Budapest, June 20th, 1937
204 To Géza Voinovich, Budapest — Budapest, September 14th, 1937
205 To Paul Collaer, Brussels [1] — Amsterdam, January 25th, 1938
206 To Sándor Albrecht, Pozsony [2] — January 31st, 1938
207 To Wilhelmine Creel, Tokyo [1] — Budapest, January 31st, 1938
208 To the Editor of *Az Est*, Budapest — Budapest, March 27th, 1938
209 To Mme Müller-Widmann, Basle [3] — Budapest, April 13th, 1938
210 To Ákos Weress — May, 1938
211 To Mme Müller-Widmann, Basle [4] — Budapest, May 29th, 1938
212 To Mme Müller-Widmann, Davos [5] — Budapest, October 9th, 1938
213 To Mme Zoltán Székely, Amsterdam — Budapest, October 24th, 1938
214 To Hans Priegnitz, Berlin — Budapest, January 12th, 1939
215 To Matica Slovenská, Turócszentmárton [3] — Budapest, January 28th, 1939
216 To Dorothy Parrish, Huntingdon [1] — Budapest, February 8th, 1939
217 To Denijs Dille, Antwerp — Budapest, May 19th, 1939
218 To Dezső Zádor, Ungvár [1] — Budapest, June 24th, 1939
219 To Béla Bartók, Jr., Orosháza [1] — Saanen, August 18th, 1939

220 To Dorothy Parrish, Huntingdon [2] — Budapest, January 17th, 1940
221 To Dezső Zádor, Ungvár [2] — Budapest, February 3rd, 1940
222 To Mme Müller-Widmann, Basle [6] — Naples, April 2nd, 1940
223 To Dorothy Parrish, Huntingdon [3] — New York, May 17th, 1940
224 To Gyula Kertész, Budapest — Budapest, July 14th, 1940
225 To Mme Müller-Widmann, Basle [7] — Geneva, October 14th, 1940

V

(1940–1945)

226 To Dorothy Parrish, Huntingdon [4] — New York, November 30th, 1940
227 To his sons Béla and Péter [2] — Long Island, December 24th, 1940
228 To Dorothy Parrish, Huntingdon [5] — Long Island, January 7th, 1941
229 To Dorothy Parrish, Huntingdon [6] — Long Island, January 15th, 1941
230 To Wilhelmine Creel, Seattle [2] — February 1st, 1941
231 To Béla Bartók, Jr., Budapest [3] — Jersey City, February 11th, 1941
232 To Béla Bartók, Jr., Budapest [4] — New York, April 2nd, 1941
233 To Douglas Moore, New York — New York, April 18th, 1941
234 To Béla Bartók, Jr., Budapest [5] — New York, May 7th, 1941

Figures in parentheses—from 1 to 30—indicate items from the collection of Bartók material in the University of Washington, Seattle (1941–44)

235 C. P. Wood to Béla Bartók — (1) Seattle, May 22nd, 1941
236 H. W. Heinsheimer to C. P. Wood — (2) New York, May 29th, 1941
237 To C. P. Wood, Seattle [1] — (3) New York, June 9th, 1941
238 C. P. Wood to Dr. Padelford — (4) Seattle, June 19th, 1941
239 To Béla Bartók, Jr., Budapest [6] — New York, June 20th, 1941
240 C. P. Wood to Béla Bartók — (5) Seattle, June 24th, 1941

241 C. P. Wood to Béla Bartók (6) Seattle, July 1st, 1941
242 A. Schulhof to C. P. Wood (7) New York, August 6th, 1941
243 L. P. Sieg to Béla Bartók (8) Seattle, August 20th, 1941
244 C. P. Wood to A. Schulhof (9) Seattle, August 21st, 1941
245 To C. P. Wood, Seattle [2] (10) Riverton, August 26th, 1941
246 To L. P. Sieg, Seattle (11) New York, September 8th, 1941
247 A. Schulhof to C. P. Wood (12) New York, September 20th, 1941
248 L. P. Sieg to Béla Bartók (13) Seattle, September 22nd, 1941
249 C. P. Wood to A. Schulhof (14) Seattle, September 25th, 1941
250 A. Schulhof to C. P. Wood (15) New York, October 1st, 1941
251 C. P. Wood to L. P. Sieg (16) Seattle, October 3rd, 1941
252 C. P. Wood to A. Schulhof (17) Seattle, October 6th, 1941
253 To. C. P. Wood, Seattle [3] (18) New York, October 8th, 1941
254 C. P. Wood to Béla Bartók (19) Seattle, October 15th, 1941
255 To Béla Bartók, Jr., Budapest [7] New York, October 17th, 1941
256 To Wilhelmine Creel, Seattle [3] New York, October 17th, 1941
257 To C. P. Wood, Seattle [4] (20) Palo Alto, November 25th, 1941
258 To H. Mishkin, Amherst New York, January 23rd, 1942
259 To C. P. Wood, Seattle [5] (21) New York, February 28th, 1942
260 To Wilhelmine Creel, Seattle [4] New York, March 2nd, 1942
261 L. P. Sieg to Béla Bartók (22) Seattle, March 4th, 1942
262 C. P. Wood to Béla Bartók (23) Seattle, March 16th, 1942
263 A. Schulhof to C. P. Wood (24) New York, April 24th, 1942
264 To C. P. Wood, Seattle [6] (25) New York, July 7th, 1942
265 To Yehudi Menuhin, Alma [1] New York, October 7th, 1942
266 To Wilhelmine Creel, Seattle [5] New York, December 31st, 1942
267 Ditta Pásztory (Mrs. B.) to József Szigeti New York, May 23rd, 1943
268 C. P. Wood to Béla Bartók (26) Seattle, June 12th, 1943
269 To C. P. Wood, Seattle [7] (27) Saranac Lake, June 30th, 1943
270 To Wilhelmine Creel, Seattle [6] Saranac Lake, August 17th, 1943
271 C. P. Wood to Béla Bartók (28) Seattle, October 23rd, 1943
272 To C. P. Wood, Seattle [8] (29) New York, November 27th, 1943

273 To József Szigeti, Palos Verdes [2] — Asheville, January 30th, 1944
274 To Yehudi Menuhin, Alma [2] — June 30th, 1944
275 To Pál Kecskeméti & Erzsébet Láng, N. Y. [1] — Saranac Lake, August 22nd, 1944
276 To Pál Kecskeméti & Erzsébet Láng, N. Y. [2] — Saranac Lake, September 1st, 1944
277 C. P. Wood to Béla Bartók (30) — Seattle, September 13th, 1944
278 To Pál Kecskeméti & Erzsébet Láng, N. Y. [3] — Saranac Lake, September 29th, 1944
279 To Ernő Balogh, New York — Saranac Lake, October 4th, 1944
280 To Radio Brussels [2] [Paul Collaer] — New York, October 24th, 1944
281 To Wilhelmine Creel, Seattle [7] — New York, December 17th, 1944
282 To Wilhelmine Creel, Seattle [8] — New York, Christmas, 1944
283 To Yehudi Menuhin, New York [3] — New York, April 5th, 1945
284 To Yehudi Menuhin, Alma [4] — New York, June 6th, 1945
285 To Jenő Zádor, Hollywood — Saranac Lake, July 1st, 1945
286 To Pál Kecskeméti & Erzsébet Láng, N. Y. [4] — Saranac Lake, July 7th, 1945
287 To Pál Kecskeméti & Erzsébet Láng, N. Y. [5] — Saranac Lake, August 11th, 1945
288 To Dorothy Parrish [7] — August 30th, 1945
289 'Worlds Contending. . .' — —

NOTES

Vol. I in Hungarian (1948)
Vol. II in Hungarian (1951)
Vol. III in partly bilingual edition (1955)
Vol. IV in German (1960)
More details about volumes I–IV are in the Bibliography

1 (September 8th, 1899)
Letters II/17. Ib.
(Reproduced in facsimile on pp. II–IV of Appendix.)

István Thomán (1862–1940). Professor of the piano, pianist; a pupil of Ferenc Erkel, Sándor Nikolits and Robert Volkmann and, later, of Ferenc Liszt (who honoured him with his friendship and took him as a companion on his travels). Bartók (like Ernő Dohnányi some years previously) studied under Th. at the Budapest Academy of Music from September, 1899, to June, 1903. In later years, Bartók would remember with gratitude his former professor at the Academy, whose vacant chair he occupied in 1907.

Pozsony. Bartók spent the most valuable years (1892–3 and 1894–9) of his youth in Pozsony, the musical centre of the northwestern part of old Hungary. As early as the Middle Ages, the town had been noted for its lively musical life, and it was here that the Hungarian Diet held its sessions between 1526 and 1848. While present-day Budapest (then Buda and the small satellite towns of Pest and Óbuda) was occupied by the Turks (1541–1686), Pozsony escaped occupation and the ravages of war, and its proximity to Vienna had a decisive influence on its cultural development. Since 1920, Pozsony (for many centuries referred to in German as Pressburg) has been part of Czechoslovakia and —as Bratislava—is now the cultural centre of Slovakia.

Gizella Révffy. A pupil of I. Thomán and a native of Pozsony, who died at an early age. She was a fourth-year student of the piano at the Academy in the school year 1899–1900.

During his illness, which lasted for several months, Bartók was not allowed to play the piano, nor was he able to attend school regularly. A school friend used to call on him and keep him abreast of the lessons set in school; in this way Bartók was able to pass the final examination in June, 1899. He then spent the summer with his mother at Eberhard, where he regained his health.

Shortly before being taken ill, in January, 1899, Bartók left Pozsony for Budapest, where he was given an audition by Professor Thomán. Bartók recalled the occasion as follows: '. . . I did well at my audition: the maestro recognized my talent, and I returned to Pozsony with the assurance that, after passing my last year at the secondary school, I should go up to the Academy of Music as Thomán's pupil...' 'Bartók Béla — Thomán Istvánról' (Béla Bartók on István Thomán), *Zenei Szemle* XI [1926–7] pp. 93–95.

Some of Bartók's letters to István Thomán first came to light in 1950. In Letters II and Letters III there have been published 17 and 27 letters to Thomán, respectively. Of these, seven letters are included in the present volume; they are: Nos. 1, 10, 16, 23, 47, 56 and 59.

These letters are addressed to: 'Budapest, Fürdő u. 6, III. em., Ngys. Thomán István Úrnak.'

The letters are published by permission of Miss Erzsébet Thomán, daughter of Professor Thomán.

2 (January 21st, 1900)
Letters I/15–17

Mrs. Béla Bartók, Sr. (*née* Paula Voit; b. January 16th, 1857, Turócszentmárton; d. December 19th, 1939, Budapest). Bartók's mother. Married Béla Bartók, Sr. (b. November 19th, 1855, Újvár), at that time principal of the agricultural school at Nagyszentmiklós, on April 5th, 1880. Widowed on August 4th, 1888, she thenceforth maintained herself and brought up her son, Béla, and her daughter, Elza, who became a primary-school teacher. She went to Pozsony, where young Béla started school, entering the second form of the secondary school during the school year 1892–3. In April 1894, she went to live in Pozsony; here her son continued to attend the secondary school, and here he passed his final examination. She was compelled by circumstance to stay in Pozsony even after her son had gone to Budapest—to which fact we owe the most valuable items of the family correspondence: Bartók's many letters written to his mother as a young man. Except for the years between 1907 and 1909—when she lived with her son in or near Budapest—Mrs. Bartók, Sr., remained a resident of Pozsony, where she stayed on even after the town had become part of Czechoslovakia following the First World War. Only in the 'thirties did she leave Czechoslovakia for Hungary (Budapest), so that she could live—and die—near to her son.

Lujcsi, Uncle Lujcsi. Brother of Bartók's mother, Lajos Voit, was a farm bailiff in Csorvás (Békés County, Orosháza district).

Ernő Dohnányi (b. July 27th, 1877, Pozsony; d. February 9th, 1960, New York). Celebrated Hungarian composer and piano virtuoso who as a pianist greatly influenced the young Bartók, although the latter soon found himself in opposition to Dohnányi's artistic and political views (see No. 13). Rooted as it was in traditional German romanticism (Brahms), Dohnányi's conservative music found more sympathy among the Hungarian ruling circles than did Bartók's and Kodály's new music based on ancient Magyar folk-song. For a quarter of a century (1919–44), Dohnányi was both president and conductor of the Hungarian Philharmonic Society, and a prominent figure in the musical world in Hungary.

Hubay–Popper String Quartet. For many years the Jenő Hubay and Dávid Popper Quartet educated the taste of Hungarian audiences by performing works by Hungarian and foreign composers. Works first played by this Quartet include all Brahms's chamber music (in the case of several of these pieces it was their first performance anywhere in the world). With the appearance (1909–10) of the Waldbauer–Kerpely String Quartet, the Hubay–Popper Quartet immediately became less important. The new Quartet presented to the public chamber music by Bartók and Kodály.

Jenő Hubay (1858–1937). Violinist, composer and professor of music; a pupil of Joachim. After successful performances abroad, he became professor in the Department of Violin at the Budapest Academy of Music. His most noted pupils—Joseph Szigeti, Stefi Geyer and Ferenc Vecsey—all became associated with Bartók and are referred to in Bartók's later letters, some of which were written to them.

Dávid Popper (1846–1913). One of the most famous cellists of his day; from 1886, professor at the Budapest Academy of Music.

Imre Waldbauer (1892–1952). First violin in the famous string quartet named after him. The first performance of chamber music by Bartók and Kodály is associated with his name.

Emil Sauer (1862–1942). Pianist, former pupil of Liszt. Frequently gave recitals in Hungary.

Eugène d'Albert (1864–1932). Pianist, former pupil of Liszt. Of some note as a composer.

Valkyrie. During his first year at the Academy, Bartók was an enthusiastic student of Wagner's later operas. In one letter (fragment, Letter II/22), he copied 26 bars of *The Ride of the Valkyrie* for his mother.

Miss Révffy. Gizella Révffy (see above), who, together with Ilona Durigo and Arnold Székely, received the 400-Kr. Liszt Scholarship. Bartók was granted a 300-Kr. bursary.

Elza. Bartók's sister—four years his junior—whom Bartók, because of her German-sounding name, addressed in his letters written in the autumn of 1903 by the Hungarian pet name 'Böske' (Bess).

The letters left behind by Bartók's mother came to light early in 1948. Of these letters 79 appeared in Letters I, and another 31 (including 6 that were corrected), in Letters II. These two volumes contain a very substantial number of the letters found among Mrs. Bartók Sr.'s papers. These letters were directly handed over to the collector by Elza Bartók (Mrs. Emil Oláh Tóth, d. September 11, 1955) and were then published without Béla Bartók, Jr. (the composer's son) having given his consent.

The letters contained in this volume (Nos. 2–7, 11–15, 17–18, 25, 27, 31–35, 37, 101, 108–109, 116–117, 119–121, 134–136, 150 and 159–160) are published with the consent of Mr. Béla Bartók, Jr.

The letters are addressed to: 'özv. Bartók Béláné Úrnőnek',
Pozsony, Kórház u. 3,
Vésztő (Békés megye),
Rákospalota, Mária u. 15,
Bratislava, Széplak u. 53,
Budapest, Krisztina körút 159.

3 (November, 1902)
Letters I/23–25 (incomplete)

Mrs. Gruber. This was the name by which Emma Schlesinger (later Sándor) was known (after her first husband, Henrik Gruber) until 1910 when she married Zoltán Kodály. She died as Mrs. Kodály on November 22nd, 1958. Emma Sándor was an accomplished composer and pianist: Ernő Dohnányi composed variations on one of her musical themes, and a number of her minor pieces and songs are incorporated in the works of Bartók and Kodály.

Mrs. Gárdony. Mrs. (Róza) Zsigmond Gárdony was the patroness of the young Bartók; it was she who paid for him to go to Meran, where he had treatment (November 15th, 1900, to April 1st, 1901) which completely restored him to health.

The Arányis: Titi and Adila. Of the three daughters (Hortense, Adila and Jelly) of police counsellor Taksony Arányi, Adila—and, more particularly, Jelly—grew up to be violinists with an international reputation. At the time of Bartók's visit, Hortense was a third-form student in the piano preparatory school, under Szendy, and Adila is known to have been Hubay's pupil; but Jelly was then only seven years old. In 1921 and again in 1922, Bartók dedicated to Jelly his two remarkable and experimental sonatas for violin and piano. Adila and Jelly were well-known personalities in musical circles in London. Adila (Mme Fachiri) died on December 15th, 1962, in Florence.

József Joachim (1831–1907). Hungarian-born violinist, composer and teacher of note.

László Toldy (1882–1929). Composer and writer on music. He wrote music for the theatre, orchestral and chamber music, and contributed articles on music to periodicals in Hungary and abroad.

4 (January 9th, 1903)
Letters I/25

At a private session (December 22nd, 1902) of the professors of the Academy of Music, Bartók performed a piano transcription of Strauss's *Ein Heldenleben*, to such effect that news of this feat reached Vienna, where shortly afterwards he was invited to play this contemporary 'modern' work to the conservative music-lovers of Austria (January 26th, 1903).

Professor Dohnányi. Frigyes Dohnányi, Ernő's father and Bartók's physics teacher in the 7th and 8th forms of the secondary school in Pozsony.

Viktor Herzfeld (1856–1919). Composer and second violin in the Hubay–Popper String Quartet. From 1888, Professor of Musical

Theory at the Academy of Music; in 1908, succeeded Koessler (see Note No. 5) in the chair of Musical Composition.

Ferdinand Löwe (1865–1925). Noted Viennese conductor; it was he who conducted on the memorable occasion when Bartók's 1st Suite for large orchestra was performed in Vienna on November 29th, 1905.

Aurél Kern (1871–1928). Composer and writer on music; music critic for several conservative dailies. Held a number of senior posts in Hungarian musical institutions.

Árpád Szendy (1863–1922). Pianist, composer and instructor. A former pupil of Liszt and Koessler, he was professor at the Academy of Music from 1890.

5 (January 17th, 1903)
Letters I/26–27

'*Symphony*'. This was the Symphony in E flat major, soon disowned, of which only the Scherzo came to be performed, on February 29th, 1904, and again on March 15th, 1905, in Budapest. On the second occasion it was played in place of Scherzo op. 2 (1904), written for piano and orchestra, which the Hungarian Philharmonic's musicians could not manage to play. (The 2nd and 3rd movements of the Symphony in E flat major were performed on September 28th, 1961, in Budapest, at a historic concert on the Hungarian Radio. The score was reconstructed for the occasion by Denijs Dille.)

Hans Koessler (1853–1926). After Robert Volkmann's death (1883), Professor of Composition at the Budapest Academy of Music. An exponent of the conservative, classicist tradition of the school of Brahms. He was the young Bartók's professor at the same time as István Thomán, from 1899 to 1903. He did not consider Bartók to be the best pupil in his composition class. He retired in 1908 but later resumed work as head of the Composition Department of the Academy of Music from 1920 to 1925.

Aunt Irma. Irma Voit, sister of Bartók's mother who lived with the Bartóks. Most of Bartók's letters to his mother written between 1919 and 1931 are addressed 'Dear Mama and Aunt Irma . . .'

6 (April 1st, 1903)
Letters I/30–32

On March 27th, 1903, in the concert room of the Royal Hotel in Budapest, Bartók performed his composition for piano, *Fantasy*, dedicated 'To Mrs. Emma Gruber' and dated February 8th, 1903.

'*Pens made in Vienna*'. An allusion to the *Kossuth* symphony on which Bartók was then working and, in particular, perhaps, to one passage in it which is a travesty of the Austrian Imperial Anthem.

Bartók's musical riddles referred to pseudo-folk-songs, then much in vogue.

Dr. Theodor Helm referred to the Vienna performance of *Heldenleben* in the 'Vienna Music Letters' column of *Pester Lloyd* (a German newspaper issued in Budapest) of February 24th, 1903.

In the same paper, on March 28th, 1903, he discussed the unsuccessful first performance of Richard Strauss's *Macbeth,* adding that it would be useful if Bartók were to prepare an illuminating piano transcription of this work, as he did with *Heldenleben.*

István Bárci. Correctly spelt, Bárczy. Then mayor of Budapest.

Pál Sándor. Expert in commercial matters, Hungarian M.P. from 1901. Brother of Mrs. Zoltán Kodály (Emma Sándor).

'*Ex-lex*'. The period following parliamentary refusal to pass the budget at the beginning of a new financial term. A period of '*ex-lex*' began on May 1st, 1903, and continued until March 30th, 1904.

7 (June 18th, 1903)
Letters II/44–46

Bernhard Stavenhagen (1862–1914) a pupil of Ferenc Liszt, German pianist, at the time Director of the Munich Academy of Music.

The reply from the Concertverein concerned the recital, planned for and actually held on December 14th, 1903—Bartók's first independent piano recital abroad.

The Lioness. This was the nickname given to Helen Trofimoff, to whom Bartók gave piano lessons. (The nickname is based on a pun of the Hungarian words for 'lion' or 'lioness'—*oroszlán*—and 'Russian girl'—*orosz lány.*)

Károly Gianicelli (1860–1939). Taught the double-bass at the Academy of Music and was associated with the reorganization of the Philharmonic Society (1887); a close friend of the Wagner family, he encouraged the study and performance of Wagner's works.

Hans Richter (1843–1916). Hungarian-born conductor of note, an admirer and zealous advocate of Wagner's works. From 1875 to 1877 he worked chiefly in Vienna, after 1877 in England. One memorable occasion of his later years as a conductor was a performance of Bartók's *Kossuth* symphony in Manchester on February 18th, 1904.

The Bayers. A pharmacist and his family at Nagyszentmiklós. The Bayer girls (Emília and Anna) were—like the Jurkovics sisters—inhabitants of Bartók's native town and admirers of the young Bartók. (As to Bartók's birthplace Nagyszentmiklós, see also Footnote of No. 26.)

'*4 Songs*'. The only MS. of the music of the *Four Songs* was lost in 1943. (This information was provided by Mrs. Emil Oláh Tóth, *née* Elza Bartók, 1948.) These were not identical with the four songs written in 1902, with words by Lajos Pósa.

8 (July 7th, 1903) A Slovak translation of the letter was published by Zoltán Hrabussay: 'Nevydané listy Bélu Bartóka v Archíve mesta Bratislavy', *Slovenská Hudba* (Bratislava), II/10 (October, 1958), pp. 446–448. The Hungarian original was published by Rezső Szalatnai: 'Két ismeretlen Bartók-levél' (Two Unknown Bartók Letters), *Muzsika* (Budapest), II/9, (September,

1959), pp. 28–29. Reprinted in *Documenta Bartókiana* Vol. III, edited by D. Dille, Budapest, 1968, Akadémiai Kiadó, pp. 268–269.

János Batka (Jr.) (1845–1917). Pozsony archivist and writer on music. Bartók '. . . during his later years at Pozsony, continued his musical education under the guidance of János Batka'. (Aladár Tóth: 'Bartók'. [Bence Szabolcsi and Aladár Tóth: *Zenei Lexikon,* 1930, Vol. I, p. 75.])

A photostat copy of the letter was received from Dr. Ladislav Burlas (Bratislava, 1958).

9 (July 16th, 1903)
(i.q. Note No. 8)

10 (July, 1903)
Letters III/338–342
(Photostat copy)

The photostat copy shows the letter-paper Bartók used in the year 1903, with the embossed crown and coat of arms of Hungary surmounted by the opening line of the Hungarian national anthem: 'Bless the Magyar, o Lord . . .' *(Isten, áldd meg a magyart . . .)*

'Sonata for left hand'. A movement from a projected sonata for piano which was published as No. 1 of *Four Piano Pieces,* with the title Study for the Left Hand, dedicated to István Thomán, dated January, 1903.

By permission of Mr. Tamás Gallia (grandson of the addressee). Collected by Ferenc Bónis.

11 (August 23rd, 1903)
Letters II/47–48

Ödön Mihalovich (1842–1929). Composer and teacher. From 1887 to 1919, Director of the Academy of Music.

Ritter Victor von Miller zu Aichstein (correctly *Aichholz).* An enthusiastic patron of Brahms's music. (Cf. passages in Max Kalbeck's *Johannes Brahms,* Vol. IV, p. 405 *et seq.*)

Margit Kunwald. E. Dohnányi's sister-in-law, mother of the Hungarian-born conductor Antal Doráti. (Dohnányi's first wife was Elza Kunwald.)

'Slow movement of the Sonata for violin'. As early as his last year as a student at the Academy, Bartók had been planning to write a sonata for violin and piano. The 3rd movement of the composition was actually performed at an Academy concert on June 8th, 1903, by Bartók and Sándor Kőszegi. After the first and last movements, Bartók eventually wrote the slow, middle movement. The complete work was performed at a Budapest concert on January 25th, 1904, by Bartók and Jenő Hubay.

Ludwig Bösendorfer (1835–1919). Piano manufacturer, a dynamic and enterprising figure in the musical life of Vienna.

Péter König. See Note No. 30.

12 (September 8th, 1903)
Letters I/42–45

Bartók's mother and aunt, like most of the educated people in

Pozsony, tended to speak German or at least to employ some German words and idioms.

This long letter contains the young Bartók's noblest expression of his credo—to which he remained loyal throughout his life.

The Biermanns. Friends of the Bartók family in Pozsony. According to his mother Bartók 'was already giving lessons at the age of 17, and he also accompanied a cellist, Mr. Biermann, and was payed for this'. (Letters II/209.)

Jenő Rákosi (1842–1929). Author, well-known Hungarian chauvinist journalist.

Row over 'Gotterhalte'. Resentment against the use of German as the language of command in the Austro-Hungarian army would often break out on festive occasions when there were sometimes mass demonstrations against the Austrian imperial anthem. There were frequent clashes between demonstrators and police.

István Tisza (1861–1918). A Hungarian politician and landowner. In 1903 the Emperor Francis Joseph appointed him to be Prime Minister of Hungary—for the first time.

László Lukács (1850–1932). A Hungarian politician, Minister of Finance in the first István Tisza cabinet.

Emsyke, Emsy Jurkovics. See Note No. 26.

Lajos Dietl. One of the partisans of the young Bartók, who was to play an important part as a member of the Rubinstein Competition in Paris. See Note No. 19.

13 (September 23rd, 1903)
Letters I/46–47 (A photostat is printed on pp. 190–193.)

On the letter-paper, this time without the usual embossed heading, Bartók drew Hungary's coat of arms (in the form used by Lajos Kossuth in the Hungarian War of Independence, without the crown) and inscribed the motto, *Le a Habsburgokkal!* ('Down with the Hapsburgs!')

Grosz. Probably a concert agent.

Rigele. The name of a prominent Pozsony family. Its most celebrated member was Alajos R., a sculptor. The letter refers to Ágost Rigele, a concert director.

'I shall be playing with the Grünfelds on Febr. 3rd'. On the day indicated, Bartók played in the programme of chamber music given by the Fitzner String Quartet in Vienna: he performed his Sonata for violin and piano, partnered by the Austrian violinist Rudolf Fitzner.

A few days afterwards, February 7th, 1904, Bartók took part in a performance of Dvořák's Piano Quartet (op. 87) in one of the Grünfeld–Bürger String Quartet's Sunday-afternoon concerts.

Vilmos Grünfeld (1855–1921). Violin teacher at the Academy of Music from 1898 to 1919. In 1894, together with Zsigmond Bürger (1856–1908), cello teacher at the National Music School, he had founded a string quartet.

'. . . a corrupt, predatory, murderous lot'. The background of Bartók's outburst is the so-called Chlopy General Order issued one

week previously (on September 16th), in which Francis Joseph, Emperor of Austria and King of Hungary, declared that he did not wish to introduce Hungarian as a language of command in the army, and in which he referred to the Hungarians as one of the 'ethnic groups' of Austria-Hungary.

14 (October 29th, 1903)
Letters II/51–52

Ferenc Vecsey (1893–1935). A celebrated Hungarian violinist of the time. He studied under Hubay, and later under Joachim in Berlin. He made his first public appearance at the age of 10. When he toured Spain and Portugal in the spring of 1906, he was partnered by Bartók. (See Nos. 31 and 32.) More information about Vecsey and his family is found in Nos. 34 and 273.

Leopold Godowsky (1870–1938). Polish pianist whom Bartók met in Budapest.

Fritz Kreisler (1875–1962). Austrian violinist.

Lajos Dietl. See Note No. 19.

'Sun., Oct. 2nd'. A slip of the pen: Bartók meant to write Nov. 2nd, since he was in Vienna from November 3rd to 5th. However, November 2nd was not Sunday but Monday. The two dates in the next passage (Feb. 3rd and Feb. 5th) are likewise erroneous, since he obviously meant November.

15 (December 3rd, 1903)
Letters I/47–49

16 (December 16th, 1903)
Letters II/53–54

The photostat of the programme of the Berlin piano recital, December 14th, 1903, is to be found in Letters I/194–195.

Ferruccio Benvenuto Busoni (1866–1924). Italian pianist and composer who was looked upon in his day as a new Franz Liszt. From 1894 on, he lived in Berlin, where he was active at the Academy of Music. 'Something really new at last...' was his comment on Bartók's *Fourteen Bagatelles.* (See Note No. 44.)

For a reprint of the review in German published in the *Vossische Zeitung* see *Zenetudományi Tanulmányok* (Musicological Studies), Vol. II, p. 409.

17 (1903/1904)
Letters II/54–55

Page 1 of the photostat of the draft programme published: *Egyetemi Nyomda Diáriuma,* March, 1948 (János Demény); all four pages of the photostat of the draft programme published: *Zenei Szemle,* August, 1948 (Bartók Number), pp. 426–9. (János Demény). A musical analysis of the composition was published in the January 11th, 1904 issue of *Zeneközlöny.* A reprint appears in *Zenetudományi Tanulmányok* (Musicological Studies) edited by Bence Szabolcsi and Dénes Bartha, Vol. II, pp. 422–429. (János Demény: 'Bartók Béla tanulóévei és romantikus korszaka' (Béla Bartók's Student Years and Romantic Period).

18 (February 12th, 1904)
Letters I/49–50

When recovered, the envelope of this letter was found to contain also a cutting from the *Manchester Courier* with a brief notice of Bartók's forthcoming visit, and a gilt-edged card, written to Bartók's mother from 'The Firs' (Cheshire) and dated '12-2-1904', on which Marie Richter informs Bartók's mother of her son's arrival.

19 (March 17th, 1904)
Letters I/51

Lajos Dietl. Pianist, professor at the Vienna Academy of Music and a supporter of the young Bartók. Also played an important part as one of the judges at the Rubinstein Competition in Paris (1905). (See Note No. 25.)

This letter is taken from the hand-written original, by courtesy of Mr. Jenő Kenessey, conductor of Budapest's State Opera (1948).

See also Notes Nos. 24 and 36.

20 (April 4th, 1904) Unpublished

Mrs. Gyula Baranyai (*née* Emília Quinz). Teacher in a girls' school in Szeged. From 1889 to 1892, the Bartóks lived at Nagyszőllős where Gyula Baranyai was the principal of the local school. It was here that young Béla's musical talent first became evident—when he played *The Danube River,* on May 1st, 1892. Bartók's mother kept up her friendly relations with the Baranyais long after they had left the district. At the time this letter was written, Gyula Baranyai was principal of a school in Szeged.

The letter came to light, through the agency of Mr. Sándor Veress, in 1948, by courtesy of the addressee.

21 (August 21st, 1904) The original text was published by Klára Gárdonyi (Mrs. Csapodi): 'Bartók Béla levelei Harsányi Kálmánhoz' (Béla Bartók's Letters to Kálmán Harsányi). *Irodalomtörténeti Közlemények,* Vol. IX (1956), No. 3, pp. 364–366.

Kálmán Harsányi (1876–1929). Poet. He met Bartók in the summer of 1904 at the Harsányis' summer residence at Gerlicepuszta, Gömör County, where B. had retired for several months to compose and prepare himself for the forthcoming concert season.

The *élan* of Bartók's message carried him on to a second postcard (the last, unfinished sentence of postcard No. 1 continues on No. 2). He posted them separately.

The originals of the letters and postcards are in the National Széchényi Library, Budapest, Archives of Manuscripts.

See also Note No. 22.

22 (September 18th, 1904)
See Note No. 21

'Oak Leaf'. The title of a long narrative poem by Kálmán Harsányi.

The work in question is probably by Henry Thode (1857–1920), a German art historian and poet. According to his family, Harsányi liked to browse in second-hand bookshops and would now and then send a volume to Bartók.

'Shadows of Rodostó'. A lyric poem by Harsányi about Hungarian exiles in Turkey after the defeat of Prince Rákóczi during the War of Independence (1703–1711).

'The Thirteen' (or 'The Thirteen of Arad'). A lyric poem about the thirteen martyred Hungarian leaders who were executed at Arad in 1849 after the defeat of the War of Independence. This is a kindred theme to that of Bartók's *Kossuth* symphony.

23 (September 18th, 1904)
Letters II/56

Bartók's new Scherzo was not performed on March 15th, 1905. Instead, his other Scherzo, written two years earlier, was played. See Note No. 5.

(The first performance of the new 'Scherzo' op. 2, [1904] was as late as September 28th, 1961, in Budapest, at the Hungarian Radio's historic concert of that date.)

Bartók's performance of Liszt's *Danse Macabre* (*Totentanz*) received a tremendous ovation. The next generation had an opportunity of admiring his interpretation when Bartók performed the work again in 1936.

24 (December, 1904)
Letters I/80–81 (erroneously dated). The approximate date of the letter was ascertained when later research elicited the source and date of the enclosed newspaper cutting. A photostat of the letter appears in *Alkotás,* Vol. I, Nos. 1–2 (January-February, 1947), p. 52.

The first performance of the quintet, scheduled for December 4th, 1904, did not take place. Instead, Bartók took part with the Grünfeld–Bürger String Quartet in a performance of Schubert's *Trout Quintet.* And yet, in a review in *Az Ujság* the following day there is a reference to the 'pronounced Hungarian quality' of the Bartók quintet! Bartók returns to this point in a later letter (No. 78).

'All the wonderful reviews' refer to the performance in Vienna of Bartók's quintet: it was given at a concert of chamber music on November 21st, 1904, by the Prill String Quartet Society, with Bartók participating.

25 (August, 1905)
Letters I/53–55

Having run out of letter-paper, Bartók wrote the last line of this letter on the back of a leaf from a pocket diary. The printed date on the leaf is August 8th. He probably wrote his letter during the evening of that day or on any day after that date (but certainly before August 15th which is the date of his next letter, written in Paris).

Rubinstein Competition. Anton Rubinstein (1829–1894), Russian composer and pianist, had entrusted a vast capital sum to the care of the Petrograd Conservatory which he had founded. The interest on this capital amounted to 10,000 francs every five years, and he directed that this sum should be equally divided between the young composer and the young pianist securing the highest marks in a Rubinstein Competition to be held once every five years. The opening competition in the series was held in 1890—when the founder was still alive—in Petrograd. The second (1895) was held in Berlin, the third, in Vienna (1900), and the fourth was the one referred to here and held in Paris. (The last Rubinstein Competition, so far as we know, was held in 1910, again in Petrograd.) In Paris the Piano Prize was awarded to the Leipzig-born pianist Wilhelm Backhaus (1884–1969), who was appointed Professor at the Royal College of Music in Manchester in that same year. The Composition Prize was not awarded.

Othmár Ságody (1881–1945). Writer on music and composer; the other Hungarian competitor in the contest, whom the judges unanimously disregarded.

Attilio Brugnoli (1880–1937). He was judged to be Bartók's equal as a composer and, like him, was honoured with a diploma. Later he taught in Parma and Florence, wrote some pieces for the piano and became a music critic.

Bartók's *Rhapsody* for piano and orchestra was performed by the Lamoureux Orchestra conducted by Camille Chevillard, with the composer as soloist.

The *Sonata for violin* was performed by Lev Zeitlin and the composer.

The president of the panel of judges was the Hungarian-born Leopold Auer (1845–1930), founder of the Petrograd Violin School.

Richard von Perger (1854–1911), referred to in Bartók's letter, was between 1899–1907 the Director of the Vienna Conservatory and headed the Gesellschaft der Musikfreunde. Conservative in taste, he composed music in the manner of Brahms.

Gustav Holländer. Violinist, composer and writer on music. Director of the Stern Conservatory in Berlin.

Two further accounts of the Rubinstein Competition are mentioned here since they contain information that usefully complements Bartók's own account: Caesar Hochstetter, of Leipzig, in *Signale für die Musikalische Welt*, 63/49, September 6th, 1905 ('Zum diesjährigen Wettstreit um den Rubinsteinpreis'), and Dr. Otto Neitzel, of Cologne, in *Die Musik*, IV/24, pp. 405–409 ('Der Rubinstein-Preis 1905').

26 (August 15th, 1905)
Letters I/56–61

Irmy Jurkovics (1882–1945). Daughter of Othmár Jurkovics, Judge of Nagyszentmiklós District Court. Together with her sister, Emsy, and the Bayer girls (see Note 7), she made an idol of Bartók at his first public recital at Nagyszentmiklós on April 13th, 1903. No. 3 (Fantasy II) of the *Four Piano Pieces* is dedicated To Misses Emsy and Irmy Jurkovics', Berlin, October 12th, 1903.

For a more detailed exposition of the philosophical subjects touched upon here, see Nos. 41 and 42.

Nagyszentmiklós (now Sînnicolaul Mare, Rumania). It was in this district in the southeastern part of pre-1914 Hungary that Bartók was born on March 25th, 1881, and here he lived for the first eight years of his life. Nagyszentmiklós was situated in the northern part of the former County of Torontál (of which, for a short time, it was the administrative centre); it comprised the most backward area of Hungary—and the one with the most troubled history. It was devastated in successive invasions during the Great Migration and again in later centuries. It has been part of Rumania since 1920 when it was renamed Sînnicolaul Mare.

After 1945, the original of the letter passed into Viktor Papp's hands; publishing rights were bought by the Hungarian Arts Council for Letter I.

27 (September 10th, 1905)
Letters I/67–69 (Unfinished?)

This letter to his mother fits in well with the philosophical comments contained in the preceding letter.

On the back of the letter-paper, upside down, we find the first lines of an unfinished letter to Richardis Richter, daughter of the conductor Hans Richter:

Paris, 18, Rue Clément-Marot
August 22nd, 1905.
Liebes Fräulein Richter!
Vielen für Ihre lieber...

It is just possible that a finished version of this letter—written in correct German—was, and still is, in existence; if so, it has yet to be traced. Bartók wrote to his mother on the spoilt letter-paper for the sake of economy.

28 (December, 1905)
Letters I/69

The short autobiographical note was written for Géza Mayer, a journalist, when Bartók gave a guest performance in Sopron (December 9th, 1905).

Keresztély Altdörfer (1825–1898). Organ player and composer. Was a visitor at Nagyszőllős.

First published: *Sopronvármegye,* May 7th, 1922. (Information received from Dr. Endre Csatkai, d. 1970.)

29 (January 30th, 1906) Original published by Gyula László: 'Bartók Béla soproni kapcsolatairól' (Béla Bartók's Connections with Sopron). *Soproni Szemle,* Vol. X (1956), No. 3, p. 280.

Dr. Lajos Poszvék. Physician; Vice-Chairman of the Sopron Literary and Artistic Society.

The proposed concert never took place, and Bartók's connections with Sopron were severed for the next twenty years.

30 (March 14th, 1906) Original published by Mrs. Pál Kollár: 'Újabb Bartók-levelek' (More Bartók Letters), *Új Zenei Szemle,* Vol. VI, Nos. 7–8 (July–August, 1955), pp. 6–7.

Péter König (1870–1940). Director of Szeged Municipal Music School. This letter requests subscriptions for *Hungarian Folk-Songs, for Voice and Piano* (Rózsavölgyi edition, 1906), in which the piano accompaniment for the first ten songs was written by Bartók, and for the remainder, by Kodály. See also No. 35.

31 (March 26th, 1906)
Letters I/73–74

Ferenc Vecsey. See Note No. 14.

32 (April 11th, 1906)
Letters I/75 part only, Letters II/59–60 in full

The *subscription list* was part of the preparations for the projected issue of a collection of folk-songs.

33 (May 26th, 1906)
Letters I/76

34 (July 15th, 1906)
Letters I/76–78 (without the concluding part of the letter)

This date must be either a slip of the pen or a printer's error. According to Béla Bartók, Jr., his father gives—in an unpublished letter of May 29th, 1906—the date of the fair at Gyula as July 20th. Accordingly, the letter ought to be dated July 25th.

The names mentioned in the letter are those of farm managers employed on the various Wenckheim manors. Further information on this subject is supplied by Béla Bartók, Jr., in his 'Bartók Béla Békés megyei kapcsolatai' (Béla Bartók's Connections with Békés County), *A Gyulai Erkel Ferenc Múzeum Kiadványai* (Publications of the Ferenc Erkel Museum at Gyula), No. 24 (1961), pp. 5–8.

Veritable Confidential Privy Councillor (the German *Geheimrat*)—a title conferred upon ministers and secretaries of state. Originally an office of much importance in the German states, it had now only titular significance.

The concluding part, published in this book for the first time, was addressed to Béla Oláh Tóth, the 18-month-old son of Bartók's sister.

35 (September 10th, 1906)
Letters I/78–79 (fragment)

Kodály says in the preface:
'The vast majority of Hungarian society is not yet sufficiently conscious of being Hungarian, is no longer sufficiently unsophisticated and yet still not educated enough, for these songs to go to its heart. These people still find it strange to hear Hungarian folk-songs in the concert hall! They are not ready to accept the idea that they rank with the masterpieces

of written music—and the folk-songs of other nations! But the time will come when this will be so . . .'

36 (November 3rd, 1906)
Letters I/79–80 and a photostat in *Alkotás*, Vol. I, Nos. 1–2 (Jan.–Feb., 1947), pp. 50–51.

Tulip League or Tulip Garden Association. A social movement launched in 1905 for the promotion of Hungarian industry; its emblem was a tulip.

Albert Count Apponyi (1846–1933). A Hungarian conservative statesman. (Also mentioned in Letter 103.)

37 (July 5th, 1907)
Letters I/82

At Körösfő Bartók had some carved furniture in Kalotaszeg style, made for him by a local carpenter (Kalotaszeg was a part of Transylvania with a tradition of Hungarian folklore).

'*Moroccan filth*'. This is no imaginary comparison. During his tour of Spain and Portugal, just one year before, Bartók had made a short trip across the Mediterranean to North Africa. For a photostat of his picture-postcard from Tangier, dated May 18th, 1906, see Letters III/361–362.

38 (July 30th, 1907)
Letters II/65

Etelka Freund. Pianist, former pupil of Busoni; studied composition under Bartók at the beginning of 1903 (Letters II/32). Her brother, Róbert Freund, a pupil of Liszt, later became professor at Zurich Conservatory. Later she married Móric Milch, a physicist and engineer.

In the Hungarian-inhabited hills of Csík, Transylvania, Bartók worked on the concluding part of the score of his 2nd Suite for orchestra, which he had left unfinished in 1905.

Bartók's letters to Etelka Freund have been secured with the help of Mr. Sándor Veress. Etelka Freund (Washington, D.C., U.S.A.) sent typewritten copies of these letters together with photostats of the most interesting of the postcards (those with musical notations and photographs.) Nearly all these letters—18—are included in this collection (see Nos. 40, 44–46, 48–52, 54–55, 57–58, 60–61, 71 and 75). Letter 53, written to Irma Freund, Etelka's sister, also belongs to this group of letters.

Their addresses:

'Annenheim am Ossiacher See, Kurhotel, Frl. Etelka Freund, Karintia.'
'Budapest, Mérleg u. 4., Freund Etelka úrhölgynek.'
'Vitznau (am Vierwaldstätter See), Park Hotel, Frl. Etelka Freund, Suisse.'
'Nagys. Milch Móricné úrnőnek, Budapest, Mérleg u. 4. Ungarn.'

39 (August 16th, 1907)
Letters II/65–70

Stefi Geyer (b. June 23rd, 1888, Budapest; d. December 12th, 1956,

Zurich). Eminent Hungarian violinist. From 1920 until her death, she lived in Switzerland, married to the composer and concert manager Walter Schulthess. Bartók's early two-movement violin Concerto (written between July 1st, 1907, and Febr. 5th, 1908) was written for her; it was first performed at the Bartók Festival at Basle on May 30th, 1958, by the Swiss violinist Hans-Heinz Schneeberger, with Paul Sacher conducting.

The original of this letter was made available for inspection and publication by courtesy of Mrs. Stefi Geyer. She also provided photostats of two other letters (Nos. 41 and 42) as a further contribution to Hungarian research on Bartók.

40 (August 17th, 1907)
Letters II/70

Thus the 2nd Suite for orchestra was originally conceived by Bartók with the title 'Serenade'. The 4th movement here referred to has as its first theme the first predominantly pentatonic melody in Bartók's music. This is undoubtedly a quotation of the pentatony of the 'lost Székely tunes.'

41 (September 6th, 1907)
Letters II/70–77

42 (September, 1907)
Letters II/78–81

The music quotation in this letter fixes the date when Bartók conceived the musical *leitmotif* which assumed a decisive form (D–F sharp–A–C sharp) in works written in 1908 (*Two Portraits for Orchestra*; Nos. 13 and 14 *of Fourteen Bagatelles*; *Dedication of Ten Easy Piano Pieces*). In this letter it appears in the form of C sharp–E–G sharp–B sharp. Above the four notes Bartók wrote: 'This is your "*Leitmotiv*".'

43 (October 9th, 1907)
Letters III/364

Gyula Sebestyén (1864–1946). A pioneer of Hungarian folklore; Chairman of the Hungarian Ethnographic Society and editor of the review *Ethnographia;* one of the first to follow the example of Béla Vikár in using the phonograph to collect folk-music. His book (*Regös énekek*—Minstrel Songs, 1902) followed Vikár as the second collection based on phonograph recordings.

The selected ballads referred to are the notations and texts of Bartók's first scholarly folk-song publication; the most beautiful items of his collection from Csík County were published as *Székely balladák* (Székely Ballads) in *Ethnographia*, Jan. and March, 1908.

This letter is published by courtesy of the Hungarian Musicians' Association.

44 (June 28th, 1908)
Letters II/83

The composition here referred to is *Fourteen Bagatelles*, op. 6 (May, 1908).

45 (July 20th, 1908)
Letters II/83

The composition in question is: *Ten Easy Pieces for Piano* (June, 1908).

46 (July 27th, 1908)
Letters II/83

47 (July 31st, 1908)
Letters II/84

48 (July 31st, 1908)
Letters II/84

49 (August 11th, 1908)
Letters II/84

50 (September 2nd, 1908)
Letters II/85

Reproduced in facsimile in Table VII of Appendix; *Sa Vie et Son Oeuvre*, p. 221; *Weg und Werk, Schriften und Briefe*, p. 231; and IV, supplement between pp. 64–65.

51 (September 5th, 1908)
Letters II/85

At the top of the first page Bartók printed the word *Sürgős* (Urgent) several times in one continuous line, beginning and breaking off in mid-word, imitating the roller-stamp, in this manner:
ős!!! Sürgős!!! Sürgős!!! Sür

52 (September 6th, 1908)
Letters II/85

The picture postcard shows women in folk-costume. On the skirt of one woman Bartók drew a big X and added the comment in the letter. (Written information from the addressee.)

53 (October 7th, 1908)
Letters II/86

Irma Freund. Etelka's sister, later Mrs. József Hercz.

By courtesy of Miss. I. Freund, Budapest.

Addressed to:
'Budapest, Mérleg u. 4.
Freund Irma Úrnőnek.'

54 (December 21st, 1908)
Letters II/86

István Kerner (1867–1929). Conductor, chief musical director of the Budapest Opera; Chairman of the Budapest Philharmonic Society from 1895 to 1919.

The first complete performance in Hungary of the 1st Suite for full orchestra was planned for the Philharmonic Society's 5th concert during the 1908/9 season. (The 1st, 2nd and 5th movements had already been performed at an Academy of Music concert on May 15th, 1907.) The first performance of the full work, scheduled for December 21st, 1908, was cancelled; it was replaced in the programme by the 1st and 2nd Suites of *L'Arlésienne* by Bizet. Nevertheless, the first performance of the full work in Hungary did take place during the 1908/9 season, but by the Academy Orchestra instead of the Philharmonic Society, and was conducted by Jenő Hubay (on March 1st, 1909). See also No. 187.

55 (December 24th, 1908)
Letters II/86

In Beethoven Hall, Berlin, Bartók, at Busoni's request, conducted the 2nd movement (Allegro vivace, G major) of his 2nd Suite for orchestra. This was the only occasion he ever took up the conductor's baton.

56 (January 3rd, 1909)
Letters II/87

Oscar Fried (1871–1942). Noted German conductor and composer.

57 (January 28th, 1909)
Letters II/87

The date, on which the 1st String Quartet (op. 7, 1908) was completed, is, therefore, January 27th, 1909.

58 (July 17th, 1909)
Letters II/88

59 (August 31st, 1909)
Letters II/88

When this postcard was written, Bartók had already started his tour to collect Rumanian folksongs—at Belényes, on July 18th, 1909, with the assistance of Ion Bușiția (see Note No. 78), a Rumanian school-master.

60 (August 31st, 1909)
Letters II/89 and facsimile plate VIII

61 (January 5th, 1910)
Letters II/91

Vincent d'Indy (1851–1931). French composer, one of the leading personalities in French music at the turn of the century; head of the celebrated Schola Cantorum.

Edouard Risler (1873–1929). French pianist.

Isidore Philipp (1863–1958). Hungarian-born music teacher who made a name for himself in musical circles in Paris. We are indebted to Mr. József Szigeti for the text of the letter in which Busoni recommends Bartók to him:

Cher Maître et ami,
Vous, qui êtes bon et intelligent et grand musicien aurez certainement plaisir à recevoir et connaître M. Béla Bartók, auteur hongrois de plusieurs compositions très intéressantes et originales, surtout pour piano.
Je me permets donc de vous l'envoyer et en vous remerciant de l'accueil que vous lui préparez je suis toujours votre très dévoué
Ferruccio Busoni
«partant pour l'Amérique»

62 (Early in 1910) Letter written in German. Translated into English: *Clavier* (Evanston, Illinois), Vol. I, No. 1 (March—April, 1962), pp. 10–11. The original text was published by János Demény in Bence Szabolcsi's *Béla Bartók*, Leipzig, 1968, Verlag Philipp Reclam jun., pp. 143–144. The original of the letter is in the possession of Dr. Hans Moldenhauer, University of Washington.

Rudolf Ganz (b. 1877). Swiss pianist; was one of the first recital artists to include Bartók's modern works in their programmes. Since the beginning of this century, he has lived in the United States (in Chicago, St. Louis and, finally, New York). He gave a recital in Budapest on March 11th, 1911.

Hugo Leichtentritt (1874–1951). German musicologist and critic. Writing of Bartók in Vol. 67 (1909), p. 14 of *Signale für die Musikalische Welt,* he declared that the Hungarian composer 'has no clear notion of the essential requirements necessary to give artistic significance to a composition'.

Maurice Ravel (1875–1937). Eminent French composer and pianist. (Another reference to him is made in Letter 96.)

A typewritten copy of the letter was made available by the composer Halsey Stevens, professor at the University of Southern California (Los Angeles, 1962).

63 (February 18th, 1910) Hungarian original still unpublished. A German translation has appeared in Letters IV/82. The programme of the first Paris recital is reproduced in facsimile in *Zenetudományi Tanulmányok* (Musicological Studies), edited by Bence Szabolcsi and Dénes Bartha, Vol. III, inset plate to pp. 360–361. (János Demény: *Bartók Béla művészi kibontakozásának évei. Találkozás a népzenével* [1906–1914] —The Years of Béla Bartók's Artistic Development. Encounter with Folk-Music [1906–1914].)

Sándor Kovács (1886–1918). The first piano teacher to apply the achievements of modern psychology to music teaching in Hungary. He was one of the first people to recognize the true significance of Bartók's art. His name is associated with the Festival Hongrois, Paris, March 12th, 1910, which for the first time called attention abroad to the modern movement in Hungarian music. He played an important part in the work of founding, in 1911, the New Hungarian Musical Society (UMZE—Új Magyar Zene-Egyesület).

Henry Expert (1863–1952). Librarian of the Conservatoire, an authority on old French music.

Kodály's birth date is in fact December 16th, 1882. His work in question is Sonate pour violoncelle et piano (2^{e} et 3^{e} parties).

A photostat of the letter has been obtained from the addressee's nephew, Dr. Pál K. Kovács, by Prof. Bence Szabolcsi. (1955)

See also Nos. 64–69.

Addressed to: 'M. Sándor Kovács, Paris, 99. Rue Notre-Dame des Champs.'

64 (February 21st, 1910)
(Cf. No. 63)

'*M. songs*'. Three songs by Ödön Mihalovich, sung by Mlle Trelli, accompanied on the piano by Sándor Kovács.

Árpád Szendy's 'bagpipe piece' ('Cornemuse' from *Sept poèmes hongrois*, op. 11) was not included in the programme.

65 (March 5th, 1910)
(Cf. Nos. 63 and 64)

Jules Ecorcheville (1872–1915). French writer on music, a pupil of C. Franck.

Pierre Aubry (b. 1874, d. Aug. 31st, 1910). French musicologist.

66 (March, 1910)
(Cf. Nos. 63–65)

Two concerts, held on March 17th and 19th, 1910, opened a new chapter in the history of modern Hungarian music. These concerts were given by a new string quartet (Waldbauer, Temesváry, A. Molnár, Kerpely), and the programme included chamber music by Kodály and Bartók, respectively. Bartók appeared at both concerts as pianist. In his letter Bartók refers to the Kodály programme of March 17th, 1910.

Concerning Imre Waldbauer, see also Note No. 2.

The Kodály programme included the *1st String Quartet* (op. 2, 1908–1909), *Piano Music* (op. 3, 1909) and the *Sonata for Violoncello and Piano* (op. 4, 1909–1910).

'*Villermose*' Emile Vuillermoz (1878–1960). French musicologist and aesthete.

Leó Weiner (1885–1960). Hungarian composer. His string trio had been played at the Paris concert. (At the time, Weiner used the Hungarian-sounding name of Vándor.)

Ervin Lendvai (1882–1949). Composer; a pupil of Koessler.

Géza Molnár (1870–1933). Hungarian musicologist and critic.

67 (April, 1910)
(Cf. Nos. 63–66)

Bartók's Rhapsody for piano and orchestra (op. 1) was performed at the 2nd orchestral concert (May 28th, 1910) of the 46th music festival of the Allgemeiner Deutscher Musikverein, at Zurich, conducted by Andreae Volkmar, with Bartók playing the solo part.

S.A.Újhely—Sátoraljaújhely, a Hungarian town near the Czechoslovak border.

Small piece in B flat minor. No. 1 ('Lento') of *Piano Music* (op. 3).

68 (April, 1910)
(Cf. Nos. 63–67)

'*Zágon songs*'. Music composed by Géza Vilmos Zágon (see Note No. 88).

Tivadar Szántó. See Note No. 163.

S.I.M.—Société Internationale de Musique. In November, 1911, the magazine published by the International Music Society brought out a number devoted to Hungary, to which Sándor Kovács contributed an article on modern Hungarian music (*La Jeune École Hongroise*, Vol. VII, No. 11, pp. 47–57).

'*Scarlatti publications*'. Sándor Kovács published pre-classical piano pieces (*Collections Sándor Kovács*): four volumes of music by

Scarlatti and two of music by 16th-century English composers.

69 (April 21st, 1910)
(Cf. Nos. 63–68)

70 (April 29th, 1910)
Letters III/26–27. Fragment, a typewritten copy of which has been obtained from George Breazul (Sinaia, Rumania, 1954). Original in French.

Dumitru G. Kiriac (b. March 6th, 1866; d. Jan. 8th, 1928). Rumanian composer and conductor of note, one of the pioneers of the modern Rumanian nationalist school.

For another letter written to Kiriac, see No. 96.

Cf. No. 77, similar in content but with reference to Slovakia.

71 (May 31st, 1910)
Letters II/91–92

'*Impression*'. Bartók is referring here to the Festival of the Allgemeiner Deutcher Musikverein.

Frederick Albert Theodore Delius (b. Jan. 29th, 1862, Bradford; d. June 10th, 1934, Grez-sur-Loing). Eminent English composer; from 1888 on lived in Paris.

72 (June 7th, 1910) Original in German. The original text was published by János Demény in Bence Szabolcsi's *Béla Bartók*, Verlag Philipp Reclam, jun., Leipzig, 1968, pp. 144–145.

Delius. See Note No. 71.

Bartók's journey to Norway took place in the summer of 1912 when he also crossed the polar circle to visit areas inhabited by the nomadic Lapps whose language is related to Hungarian. See Letters III/39–42 and No. 84.

Obtained in a typewritten copy from Mr. David Clegg, by kind permission of Mr. Alan Denson, Honorary Archivist of the Delius Trust.

See also Nos. 73, 74, 76, 79 and 80.

73 (1910) Unpublished. Original in German.

'*The business of the American copyright*'. Rózsavölgyi brought out an edition of Bartók's *Two Rumanian Dances*, stating on the title-page that they had been revised by Delius.

Delius's *Brigg Fair*, a work written for orchestra, was performed on February 15th, 1911, by the Orchestra of the Hungarian Philharmonic Society, conducted by István Kerner. In Bartók's words, this work is full of 'colours of marvellously fine texture, the magic atmosphere of folk-tales: that is the impression gained in listening to it by anyone with an ear for music'.

Percy Grainger (1882–1961). Australian-born English composer who was living in the United States since 1915. Bartók did not succeed in getting one of Grainger's works included in the programme of the Hungarian Philharmonic Society orchestra. But he kept in touch with Grainger and wrote an article in answer to

Grainger's study *Melody versus Rhythm*. See Letters III/396–400.

74 (Autumn/winter, 1910)
(Cf. No. 73)

75 (January 4th, 1911)
Letters II/92

76 (After February 17th, 1911)
(Cf. Nos. 73–74)

Delius's *Lebensmesse*, a grandiose work inspired by Nietzsche's *Zarathustra*, was performed in Vienna on February 17th, 1911. Bartók marked the occasion with an article, 'Delius's First Performance in Vienna' (*Zeneközlöny*, Budapest, Vol. XIV (1911), pp. 340–342).

77 (February 25th, 1911)
Letters III/229–230. First published translated into Slovakian (with part of the letter reproduced in facsimile): A. Baník: 'Belo Bartók a jeho záujem o slovenskú l'udovú pieseň. Venované 70. výročiu jeho narodenia.' *Hudba, Spev, Tanec* (Martin [Czechoslovakia]), Vol. II (March, 1951), No. 7, pp. 125–129; Hungarian original: János Demény: 'Bartók-dokumentumok Csehszlovákiából' (Bartók Documents from Czechoslovakia). *Új Zenei Szemle* (Budapest), IV/9 (September, 1953), pp. 7–9.

The letter is addressed to the Turócszentmárton Printing Company Limited (Turčiansky Svätý Martin, later Martin), publishers of *Slovenské spevy* (Slovakian Songs). This firm intended to publish these songs in three parts, from 1880 to 1907, but their publication was interrupted; the concluding section—Book 5—of the third part was not brought out until 1926.

This letter was referred to in 1912 by J. Skultéty, manager of Matica Slovenská and editor of *Slov. Pohl'ady*. (*Slovenská pieseň*, No. 2, p. 127.)

Twenty-one of the 43 pieces in Books III–IV of the series *For Children* (1908–1909) are versions of tunes taken by Bartók from the collection *Slovenské spevy*.

A typewritten copy of the letter has been supplied by Antal Ágoston Baník, Slovak musical folklorist and literary historian, librarian of Matica Slovenská.

78 (March, 1911) Hungarian original published by George Sbîrcea: 'Bartók Béla néhány ismeretlen levele' (Some Unknown Letters of Béla Bartók), *Korunk* (Kolozsvár–Cluj), Vol. XX (1961), No. 6, pp. 663–670.

Ion Bușiția (b. March 10th, 1875, Máramarossziget; d. Sept. 12th, 1953, Belényes). From 1897, teacher of drawing, geometry and music in the Rumanian Uniate Grammar School at Belényes. He was a man who found no professional outlet for his talents, a jack-of-all-trades who became at various times a sportsman, trainer of hunting-dogs, rambler, taxidermist and stage designer; he also played the violin well and founded a quartet. In the summer of 1909, he undertook to accompany Bartók on his tour of the villages of Bihar County and to give him all possible assistance in his work of collecting folk-songs. Later on, his association with Bartók deepened into a friendship too strong to be broken by the revised demarcation of the national frontier that separated them from one another, or poisoned by the atmosphere of national rivalry which was then encouraged.

With Bușiția's help Bartók collected the 371 Rumanian songs from Bihar County, which are contained in his first publication of Rumanian folk-songs.

The series of *Rumanian Dances* (of Hungary) composed by Bartók in 1915 were dedicated to Domnului Prof. Ion Bușiția. (It should be noted that from 1920 on Bartók used the Transylvanian Rumanian variant [Joan] of Bușiția's first name, whereas in the Hungarian addresses written prior to 1920, he would use the Hungarian [János].)

'Thank you for taking so much trouble!' Bartók is thanking Bușiția for his help in connection with the will of a deceased relative at Magyarcsék.

'The Monday concert'. A concert held on March 27th, 1911: At the 4th (Hungarian) concert of the Academy Orchestra during the 1910/11 season Bartók played Liszt's Piano Concerto in E flat major; in the same programme his 1st Suite for large orchestra was performed with Jenő Hubay conducting. (This was the second occasion on which the full Suite was performed in Hungary.) As an encore, Bartók played one of his *Rumanian Dances.*

'Quarantine'. Bușiția's children, Areta and Bubi, had been ill with scarlatina. Bartók's concern was for his son, Béla, who was six months old.

Ernő Keresztély and *Renée Engel.* Students taught by Bartók from 1907 to 1911 at the Academy of Music.

The incident referred to had in fact taken place seven, not five, years before. See No. 24.

The letters written to Bușiția came to light after his death, in 1955. These letters—there are 61—form the nucleus of the Rumanian section of Letters III. The letters to Bușiția have been published in Budapest by courtesy of the Rumanian authorities and by permission of the Folklore Institute of Bucharest (Viorel Cosma Collection). Bușiția himself, in a letter dated March 4th, 1952, expressed his desire to make these letters available to anyone engaged in Bartók research in Hungary.

Some of the most characteristic of the letters already published have been included in this volume, and to these have been added those letters which have been published since the appearance of Letters III (viz. in the German edition as well as in publications by Júlia Szegő, George Sbîrcea and Bence Szabolcsi).

They are addressed to:

'*Belényes.* Nagys. Bușiția János, főgymn. tanár Úrnak'

(from 1920 on)

'Domnului Prof. Joan Bușiția, *Beiuș*(Comitatul Bihor),*Rumänien.*'

79 (March 27th, 1911)
(Cf. Nos. 73–74 and 76)

'One-acter'. Bluebeard's Castle (op. 11).

A new work for orchestra (in 2 movements). *Two Pictures* (op. 10).

80 (July, 1911)
(Cf. Nos. 73–74, 76 and 79)

81 (December 18th, 1911)
(Cf. No. 78)

The first paragraph is probably a reference to the granting of some certificate for Bușiția's wife. The exact meaning is not known. However, Bușiția's wife was at that time contemplating a number of extravagant plans (taking up musical studies that would clearly be too much for her; visiting the French Riviera together with her children; and, meanwhile, seeing a well-known Budapest neurologist [Dr. Ernő Jendrássik, Letters III/36–37]); the certificate would probably concern one of these plans.

'Our New Year'. The Roman Catholic New Year as distinct from that of the Orthodox calendar.

82 (January, 1912) Letter written in Rumanian. Reproduced in facsimile in Júlia Szegő's book on *Bartók Béla, a népdalkutató* (Béla Bartók, the Folklorist). Bucharest, 1956, pp. 128/9, inset plate.

Enclosed with this letter, Bartók sent to Bușiția a copy of *Ady Endre legújabb versei: Az Illés szekerén* (Recent Poems by Endre Ady: On Elijah's Chariot), Singer és Wolfner, Budapest 1909, in which he indicated his favourite poems. (It is a small book, with only one poem printed—or beginning—on each page.) Bartók noted both the page number and the title of the first poem, and so it has been possible to identify the volume and the other poems for which he gave only the page number. (These poems are: *Magyar jakobinus dala, Magyar fa sorsa, Miért is tettem?, A téli Magyarország, A magyar vigasság, Nekünk Mohács kell, A grófi szérűn, Akit én csókolok, Májusi zápor után.*) Seven of the nine poems lament the backwardness and tragic fate of the Hungarian people; another is about motherhood; and the last is an ecstatic hymn to life, extolling peasant life.

Endre Ady (1877–1919). Poet and publicist; founder of modern Hungarian poetry. His appearance on the literary scene in 1905 coincided with the early folk-music collecting tours of Bartók and Kodály. Before long his revolutionary lyrics (symbolistic and immensely forceful) swept him to the centre of progressive intellectual life in Hungary. In 1916, Bartók set five of his songs to music (*Five Songs* for voice and piano, op. 16), none of which is among those listed here.

83 (May 22nd, 1912) Original in German. Reproduced in facsimile together with an English translation in the Berlin Phonogramme Archives by Kurt Reinhard. *The Folklore*

and Folk Music Archivist, Indiana University, Bloomington, Vol. V (Summer, 1962), No. 2, p. 3. The original text was published by János Demény in Bence Szabolcsi's *Béla Bartók*, Verlag Philipp Reclam, jun., Leipzig, 1968, pp. 145–146.

Erich Moritz von Hornbostel (1877–1935). German voice physiologist and ethnographer, was assistant lecturer under Professor Karl Stumpf at Berlin University; from 1906 was in charge of the Berlin Phonogramme Archives. He was one of the pioneers of comparative musicology and the collecting of tunes by phonograph recording. From 1922 on, co-operated with K. Stumpf in editing the series called *Sammelbände für vergleichende Musikwissenschaft*, of which the fourth volume (1923) consisted of the Rumanian folk-songs Bartók had collected in the Máramaros district.

Sándor Solymossy (1864–1945). Ethnologist. Secretary of the Hungarian Society of Ethnography from 1911 to 1914.

Willibald Seemayer (1868–1928). Ethnologist. Head of the Department of Ethnography at the Hungarian National Museum, Budapest, from 1902 to 1919.

Publication received from Mr. John S. Weissmann, London.

84 (July 12th, 1912)
(Cf. Nos. 78, 81 and 82)

On November 1st of the same year, Bartók returned D. C. Kiriac's Budapest visit in Bucharest. On that occasion he wrote to his mother: 'I have made a sally into the Balkan peninsula! Made friends with the Rumanians (since I can't make friends at home).' (Reproduced in facsimile in Letters I/196 with wrong date.)

85 (September 9th, 1912)
Letters I/84

Postcard written in pencil. First paragraph in French written in Greek characters; second paragraph continues in Hungarian but is still written in Greek characters; the remaining part is in Hungarian in Cyrillic characters.

By courtesy of Mrs. Zoltán Kodály (Emma Sándor), 1948.

Addressed to: 'Kodály Zoltánné úrnőnek, Budapest, Áldás u. 11.'

86 (November–December, 1912)
Hungarian original published by Prof. Bence Szabolcsi: 'Két Bartók-levél' (Two Letters of Bartók), *Magyar Zene*, Vol. I, Nos. 7–8 (August–October, 1961), pp. 147–152. Reproduced in facsimile in *Bartók Béla kézírása* (Béla Bartók's Handwriting), a collection of records containing 22 facsimile reproductions, edited by Prof. Bence Szabolcsi & Benjámin Rajeczky (1961).

About *Ion Bîrlea*, see Note No. 94.

Tiberiu Brediceanu (b. 1877). Rumanian composer.

For some time Bartók considered publishing the Rumanian folksongs he had collected in the Máramaros district in 1913 together with the material collected by Bîrlea and Brediceanu. (Letters III/59–65.)

On the last page of the letter there are 13 lines of a Rumanian folk ballad jotted down in pencil, in Bartók's hand:

Şi nimic nu mai vorbea
Şi el paşe îi d'id'ea
Pănă toate ea ardĕa.
Şi cenuşa să făcea
Şi în ciur el o punea
Şi afara mi—şi ieşea
Şi cu şiurnu şiuruia
Şi pre vânt o arunca
Şi din grai oşa grăia
Oi Ileana doamne mea
Ai fost şi nu vi mai fi
C'ai fost curvă tu săcească
Ca cin' să nu să mai nască.

For a photostat of the letter we are indebted to Dr. Alexander Buchner, of Prague (1961).

87 (December 16th, 1912) Hungarian original still unpublished. A Slovakian translation was published by Július Batel': 'Neznáme listy Bélu Bartóka', *Slovenská Hudba* (Bratislava), Vol. II, No. 1 (January, 1958), pp. 15–18. A German translation was published in Letters IV/92–93.

Fujara = (Standard Hungarian *furulya*). Very long shepherd's flute.

Bartók's four letters to the Rev. Sámuel Bobál, Slovak pastor of Egyházmarót village, have been translated into English from photostats of the originals. By courtesy of Dr. Ladislav Burlas (Bratislava, 1960).

88 (April, 1913) Hungarian original published by György Belia: 'Bartók Béla leveleiből' (A selection from Béla Bartók's Correspondence), *Csillag*, Vol. X, No. 7 (July, 1956), pp. 151–153.

Géza Vilmos Zágon (1890–1918). Composer and writer on music who helped to popularize modern music in Hungary before the First World War, especially the work of Debussy.

In June, 1913, Bartók was studying Arab folk-music in the Biskra district, and this letter describes the preparations for his journey. He gave accounts of his trip in 'A Biskra-vidéki arabok népzenéje' (Arab Folk-Music from the Biskra Region), *Szimfónia* (Budapest), Vol. I, Nos. 12–13 (September, 1917), pp. 308–323; and 'Die Volksmusik der Araber von Biscra und Umgebung', *Zeitschrift für Musikwissenschaft*, Vol. II, No. 9 (June, 1920), pp. 489–522.

Louis Laloy (1874–1944). French musicologist and critic.

Michael D. Calvocoressi. See Note No. 145.

Jean Marnold (1859–1935). French music critic, founder of *Mercure Musical*. Author of a book on Wagner and French translator of Nietzsche's *Die Geburt der Tragödie*.

Rózsavölgyi & Co. Music publishing firm and concert bureau. One of the publishers of Bartók's works from 1904 to 1915.

The English translation of Bartók's four letters to Géza Vilmos Zágon was prepared from the originals, kept in the Manuscript Archives of the National Széchényi Library, Budapest.

89 (May 3rd, 1913)
(Cf. No. 88)

Rozsnyai. Publishers of books and music; published some of Bartók's works from 1903 to 1910.

Addressed: 'À M. V. G. Zágon, 3, rue de l'Odéon, Paris.'

90 (After May 8th 1913)
(Cf. No. 87) Letters IV/98–99

91 (June 19th, 1913)
(Cf. Nos. 89 and 90)

92 (June 19th, 1913)
Letters III/369

Kálmán d'Isoz (1878–1956). Musicologist, secretary, then director, of the Music Department of the Hungarian National Museum. From 1934, Secretary of the Budapest Conservatory.

Published from the original. By courtesy of the Hungarian Musicians' Association.

Addressed to: 'd'Isoz Kálmán titkár úrnak, Budapest, Nemzeti Múzeum, Hongrie'

93 (August 22nd, 1913)
(Cf. Nos. 89–91)

Addressed: 'À M. G. W. Zágon, Saint-Malo, Hotel Central-Benoit, Frankreich'

94 (October, 1913)
Letters III/55–57

Ion Bîrlea (b. Jan. 11th, 1883, Berbeşti). Rumanian priest who accompanied Bartók on his folk-song collecting tour of Máramaros. By relieving Bartók of the administrative burden of collecting, he made it possible for the composer to collect in the space of two weeks the vast quantity of material—365 tunes—which makes up the Máramaros collection (March 15th to 27th, 1913).

Bârsănească. In Hungarian: *barcasági,* of the Barcaság, a region in the south-east Transylvania.

Fluer mare. (Rumanian) large flute.

Trişcă. (Rumanian) kind of bagpipe.

Tilincă cu dup and *tilincă fără dup.* (Rumanian) pipe with and without stop, respectively.

Bîrlea tells us that the majority of Bartók's letters to him were lost owing to the vicissitudes of the war. Even in the case of this letter the first leaf is missing.

This letter is published from a copy written by the addressee.

95 (November 3rd, 1913)
(Cf. Nos. 87 and 90)
Letters IV/101–102

96 (December 18th, 1913)
Letters III/67–68

Ilmari Krohn (1867–1960). Finnish folklorist and composer. In sketching out their plan for the collection of Hungarian folk-songs, in October, 1913, Bartók and Kodály opted for the system devised by the Finnish scholar. 'Ilmari Krohn has realized that the ending of each line of the melody is more important and more constant than the opening note . . . We, too, have adopted this system, with some modifications.' (Bartók and Kodály in 'Az új egyetemes népdalgyűjtemény tervezete' [Draft of the New Universal Collection of Folk-Songs], *Ethnographia*, 1913, Book V, p. 315.)

97 (June 15th, 1914) Hungarian original published by János Demény in 'Reflexiók egy francia vonatkozású Bartók-dokumentumhoz' (Reflections Concerning a Bartók Document Connected with France), *Élet és Irodalom,* Vol. IV, No. 39 (September 23rd, 1960), p. 5. Also reproduced in facsimile.

Imre Waldbauer. See Note No. 2.

Julien Tiersot (1857–1936). French musicologist and folklorist.

The letter is published from the original manuscript. By courtesy of the addressee's sister, Miss Ilona Waldbauer (Mrs. Frigyes Antal) (d. 1969.).

Addressed: 'À M. I. Waldbauer, 116 Rue d'Assas, Paris'

98 (October 30th, 1014)
(Cf. Nos. 87, 88 and 95)
Letters IV/104–105

99 (May 20th, 1915)
Letters III/92–93 (Cf. Nos. 78, 81, 82, 84 and 86)

'I have even found the time—and ability—to do some composing.' The *Sonatina, Rumanian Folk Dances* (from Hungary) and the *Rumanian Christmas Carols,* all written for the piano and all based on Rumanian folk-songs, were all composed in 1915.

100 (December 10th, 1915)
Letters III/373

At their guest concert on November 9th, 1915, in Vienna the Budapest Philharmonic Society had performed only three movements of Bartók's 1st Suite for large orchestra; they repeated this incomplete performance at their series of subscription concerts in Budapest on December 6th.

After this letter the Hungarian Philharmonic Orchestra did not again play a composition by Bartók until September 10th, 1918: they then played *Two Pictures* in Berlin, with the conductor István Kerner who had conducted the 1st Suite. (The performance was repeated in Budapest on October 7th, 1918.)

This letter is published from the original, now in the archives of the Hungarian State Opera, Budapest.

101 (March 21st, 1917)
Letters I/88–89

'I left at Emma's . . . I hope they have posted it.' Mr. and Mrs. Zoltán Kodály.

'The promised parcel . . .' 'a very special present'. Allusion to various foodstuffs amid wartime scarcity.

Egisto Tango (1876–1951). Italian conductor who worked with the Budapest Opera from 1912 to 1919. His name is associated with the first performances in Hungary of *The Wooden Prince* and *Bluebeard's Castle* (May 12th, 1917, and May 24th, 1918, respectively). During the 1919/20 season, he was at Kolozsvár, after which he would have liked to secure a contract once again in Budapest, but he was not admitted by the new, nationalist regime. In the mid-'twenties he organized an Italian opera company, went on a European tour and afterwards went to live in Vienna. From 1933 until his death, he lived in Copenhagen. Bartók dedicated *The Wooden Prince* to him: *Herrn Kapellmeister Egisto Tango in tiefer Dankbarkeit gewidmet,* printed on the title-page of the Universal Edition of 1921. Cf. the dedication to Reinitz in the 1920 Universal Edition of Ady songs: Note No. 122.

Violanta. Korngold's opera, produced by the Budapest Opera on February 27th, 1918.

'*Emil Ábrányi Jr.'s opera*'. *Don Quixote,* composed to the libretto by his father, E. Ábrányi, Sr. Produced on November 30th, 1917.

'*His Excellency*'. Miklós Count Bánffy, Director of Budapest Opera.

102 (May 6th, 1917)
Letters III/93–94 (Cf. Nos. 78, 81, 82, 84, 86 and 99)

Újtátrafüred (Slovakian: Novy Smokovec). A place in the Tatra mountains in Slovakia.

V.C.P.C. See Note No. 34

The Mareles. Isaia Marele, forest ranger, and family, hosts to Bartók at their home at Örvényes since 1914.

103 (August, 1917)
Letters III/102 and 104
First page reproduced in facsimile in Júlia Szegő's book *Bartók Béla, a népdalkutató* (Béla Bartók, Collector of Folk-Music), Bucharest, 1956, inset plate between pp. 128–129.

The three Hungarian books are the following:

(1) Béla Balázs: *Misztériumok* (Mystery Plays)—three one-act plays: *A kékszakállú herceg vára, A tündér, A szent szűz vére* (Bluebeard's Castle, The Fairy and The Blessed Virgin's Blood);

(2) Béla Balázs: *Játékok* (Plays): *A fából faragott királyfi* (The Wooden Prince), a ballet with illustrations by Miklós Count Bánffy; and *A halász és a hold ezüstje* (The Fisherman and the Silver Moon), a marionette show, with illustrations by Róbert Berény; and

(3) Zsigmond Móricz: *Az Isten háta mögött* (At the Back of Beyond), a novel.

ad (1): *Béla Balázs* (originally Herbert Bauer) (1884–1949). Librettist of two of Bartók's stage works. Poet of some note, novelist, dramatist and cinema aesthete; went into exile after 1919 because of his communist views and returned only in 1945. When *The Wooden Prince* and *Bluebeard's Castle* were revived and produced in Hungary in the mid-'thirties his name was suppressed. (See also Note No. 148.)

ad (2): *Róbert Berény* (1887–1953). Painter, a dynamic member of 'The Eight', a group of progressivist Hungarian painters in the late 1900s. Painted a portrait of Bartók (27″ × 18,4″) in the spring of 1913.

ad (3): *Zsigmond Móricz* (1879–1942). Hungarian writer of explosive energy. His depiction of the Hungarian rural scene made him one of the great critical realists in 20th-century Hungarian literature.

ad (1)–(3): Like the poet Endre Ady, all three men were intellectually akin to Bartók.

Albert Count Apponyi. (See Note No. 36.) He was re-appointed Minister of Education and Religious Affairs in July, 1917. A. wore a long beard.

Világ (Hung. for 'World'). Liberal daily newspaper started in 1910, to propagate progressive bourgeois ideas.

Nyugat (Hung. for 'West'). Literary magazine founded in 1908; it supported the modern trends in Hungarian arts and literature.

Ma (Hung. for 'Today'). Review founded in 1916 by Lajos Kassák, poet and painter; championed revolutionary trends in the arts.

Soldiers' Songs. A series of songs compiled and edited for the Musikhistorische Zentrale in Vienna.

104 (January 28th, 1918)
Letters III/106–107 (Cf. Nos. 78, 81, 82, 84, 86, 99, 102 and 103)

The programme of the Musikhistorische Zentrale's concert in Vienna on January 12th, 1918, included Bartók's *Slovak Folksongs* for a cappella male chorus and a number of ballads and soldiers' songs from his collection of Hungarian folk-tunes. Bartók co-operated in the organization of the concert and provided the piano accompaniment for Ferenc Székelyhidy's vocal items.

Published for the first time in the printed programme of the concert was a draft of the system of Hungarian folk-songs. (A = tunes of the Old Style; B = those of the New Style; C = miscellaneous tunes fitting into neither of the former classes. See Introduction to *A magyar népdal* [The Hungarian Folk-Song] by Béla Bartók, p. XIII, lines 3–8.)

Ferenc Székelyhidy (1885–1954). Celebrated Hungarian tenor, one of the ablest interpreters of Hungarian vocal music.

Rumanian Folk Dances. This composition of six short dances (piano pieces transcribed for orchestra) was presented by the Budapest Orchestra Society, conducted by Emil Lichtenberg, on February 11th (not 9th).

This letter is the translation of a copy of the original written in Mr. István Nagy's hand (Kolozsvár–Cluj, 1954).

105 (September 14th, 1918) Hungarian original published by George Sbîrcea in 'Bartók Béla néhány ismeretlen levele' (Some Unknown Letters of Béla Bartók), *Korunk* (Kolozsvár), Vol. XX (1961), No. 6, pp. 663–670; and by

Bence Szabolcsi in 'Két Bartók-levél' (Two Letters of Bartók), *Magyar Zene*, Vol. I, Nos. 7–8 (August–October, 1961), pp. 147–152.

The allusion is to the Felső-Szászberek country-residence of Baron Adolf Kohner, a great patron of arts.

Baron Kohner's three daughters (he had one son who was killed in the war): Ida, a painter; Lujza, a philologist; and Kató. Kató, Mrs. Antal Lukács, who was 12 years old at the time of Bartók's visit, lived in Montreal, Canada, until her death in April, 1964. The folk-song with piano accompaniment (see letter on p. 141) was written down and dedicated by Bartók to little Kató by way of compensation for the fact that, as a child, she had been sent to bed and so missed the folk-song singing during the evening. The dedication is missing from the MS., since the owner, fearing it might bring trouble, tore it off during the period of Nazi terrorism towards the end of the Second World War. (Written information from Mrs. Antal Lukács, dated September and October, 1961.)

Adolf Fényes (1867–1945). An outstanding name in modern Hungarian painting.

Sándor Bródy (1863–1924). Hungarian writer, author of the first naturalist Hungarian drama.

Menyhért Lengyel (b. 1880). Hungarian dramatist; has preferred exotic themes ever since his first play, *Typhoon,* met with world-wide success. Author of *The Miraculous Mandarin,* on which Bartók based his music.

Bujor. The name of Buşiţia's dog.

Headmaster Nutz. To help Bartók in his task of collecting Rumanian folk-music, Buşiţia wrote letters of introduction to a good many heads of schools in various districts. Bartók's inquiry concerns one of these.

106 (January 31st, 1919)
(Cf. Nos. 78, 81, 82, 84, 86, 99, 102–105)

Buşiţia's little son was carried off by the influenza epidemic raging throughout Europe.

'*. . . how things work out for you in the new world.*' At the end of the First World War, Transylvania was first occupied, and later, under the terms of the Trianon Peace Treaty, annexed, by Rumania. Belényes is situated in the territory thus annexed.

107 (Early September, 1919)
Letters I/92

For a year Bartók gave up his professorship at the Academy of Music and withdrew to hermit-like seclusion in his Rákoskeresztúr home. His petition to be granted leave (at first six months—later prolonged; see No. 109) was drafted by Zoltán Kodály as Assistant Director of the Academy.

Kodály's draft, written in his own hand, has been found in file No. 477/1919 in the archives of the Budapest Academy of Music.

108 (October 23rd, 1919)
Letters I/93–94

Zoltán. Zoltán Kodály, against whom disciplinary action was in fact subsequently taken.

'*A university professor who has "emigrated"* ...' Géza Révész. (See No. 112.)

Egisto Tango did in fact go to Rumania. He signed a contract with the Rumanian Opera of Kolozsvár, where he wanted to produce Bartók's opera, *Bluebeard's Castle.* He was frustrated in his attempt and not long afterwards dissolved his contract and left Rumania.

109 (November 28th, 1919)
Letters I/94–95 (incomplete)

110 (February 3rd, 1920) Hungarian original published, and reproduced in facsimile, by Iván Bognár along with an article entitled 'Kodállyal együtt ...' (Together with Kodály), *Irodalmi Újság,* Vol. VII, No. 12 (March 24th, 1956), p. 5

Baron Dr. Gyula Wlassics, Jr. In the first half of the 'twenties was appointed Director of Budapest Opera. Made a well-meaning but unsuccessful attempt to have Bartók's compositions for the theatre produced. (See Nos. 123, 124, 126 and 127.)

It should be noted that, almost simultaneously with, but independently of Bartók, Ernő Dohnányi also wrote in protest to Baron Wlassics.

111 (February 20th, 1920)
Letters III/377

Reporting the crisis about the directorship of the Opera on February 20th, 1920, the daily newspaper *Szózat* published the list of members of the newly formed 'Music Council' (President: Jenő Hubay; Vice President: Árpád Szendy; members: Béla Bartók, Béla Szabados, István Kerner and Ákos Buttykay; Secretary: Aurél Kern). Names omitted from the list were: Ernő Dohnányi, Zoltán Kodály and Egisto Tango. Bartók's letter of protest was printed on February 22nd.

Translated from the original. By courtesy of the Hungarian Musicians' Association.

112 (August 22nd, 1920) Hungarian original published by János Demény: 'Reflexiók egy kiadatlan Bartók-dokumentumhoz' (Thoughts on an Unpublished Bartók Document), *Élet és Irodalom,* Vol. V, No. 12 (March 24th, 1961), p. 3

Hornbostel. See Note No. 83.

Géza Révész (1878–1955). University professor, Hungarian pioneer of experimental psychology. During the Republic of Councils of 1919 he was given a post as head of a research institute, but after the successful counter-revolution, he was the subject of intrigue and was forced into exile. Later became Director of the Amsterdam Institute of Psychology and Pedagogy, and Bartók enjoyed his hospitality on his many tours of the Netherlands between 1923 and 1939. At the time Bartók wrote this letter, Prof. Révész was still trying to establish himself in Rostock.

Alfred Einstein (1880–1952). German musicologist, editor of the new edition of the Riemann Encyclopaedia; author of a number of well-known and learned essays on musicological subjects.

The polemics about Bartók's collection of Rumanian folk-songs appeared in the pages of *Nemzeti Újság, Új Nemzedék* and *Szózat* from May 19th until 28th.

'*...my Berlin trip*'. This took place at the end of February and early in March, 1920. It was Bartók's first post-war tour abroad.

'*Musical Quarterly of New York*'. The most influential music review issued in the United States.

Gyopár utca 2. This was the address of a villa owned by the banker József Lukács, father of Prof. György Lukács, the Marxist philosopher and literary critic. Here Bartók and his family enjoyed Lukács's hospitality for nearly two years.

Ani. Anne Gleimann, a pupil of Professor Révész (d. August, 1963, Budapest).

Translated from the Hungarian original. By courtesy of Mrs. Géza Révész (Magda Alexander), The Hague, 1960.

See also Nos. 114, 115, 118 and 122.

113 (May 8th, 1921) Hungarian original published by George Sbîrcea, in *Élet és Irodalom,* Vol. IV, No. 48 (November 25th, 1960), p. 5 ('Érdekes Bartók-levelet találtak Romániában'—Interesting Bartók Letter Found in Rumania).

'*London music periodical*' *The Sackbut;* the November 1920 issue carried an article on Bartók, written by Cecil Gray.

La Revue Musicale. In this review (March, 1921) there appeared an appraisal of Bartók's music by Zoltán Kodály. (Vol. II., pp. 205–217.)

'*The Anbruch of Vienna*'. *Musikblätter des Anbruch.* March 1st, 1921, printed a portrait of Bartók, his autobiographical notes and his music to a poem by Endre Ady, as well as contributions from Oscar Bie, Egon Wellesz, Felix Petyrek and Zoltán Kodály; also a German translation of Cecil Gray's study.

'*Italian music review*'. *Rivista Musicale Italiana.*

The 1920/21 season included two all-Bartók programmes:

(1) January 7th, 1921 (*1st String Quartet;* piano pieces, played by Ernő Dohnányi; *Piano Quintet,* with Bartók's participation).

(2) February 27th, 1921 (songs; soloist: Izabella Nagy; piano works, played by Bartók).

The latter all-Bartók concert was held in the morning.

The contract signed with Budapest Opera related to *The Miraculous Mandarin.*

114 (March 3rd, 1922)
(Cf. No. 112) Unpublished

Bartók's concert tour of Transylvania took place between February 19th and 26th, 1922, and comprised six recitals.

'The Frankfurt première' (of *Bluebeard's Castle* and *The Wooden Prince*) took place on May 13th (and not on April 30th).

115 (March 9th, 1922)
(Cf. Nos. 112 and 114) Unpublished

Egon Kornstein (b. 1891). Violinist; for many years played the viola in the Waldbauer–Kerpely String Quartet. Lives in the United States. Has changed his name to Kenton.

Addressed to: 'Géza Révész, Keizergracht 283, Amsterdam.'

116 (March 16th, 1922)
Letters I/103–104

Following his début in London on March 14th, 1922, Bartók gave the second recital of his tour of Britain, in Aberystwyth, on March 16th. He played some of his piano works and also played in a performance of Beethoven's Trio in E flat major (op. 70).

117 (March 20th, 1922)
Letters I/104

'A rich woman, a singer'. On March 19th, 1922, Bartók gave another recital in London, in the home of Miss Dorothy Moulton.

At his first London concert (on March 14th), he partnered Miss Jelly Arányi in his 1st Sonata for violin and piano.

118 (March 22nd, 1922)
(Cf. Nos. 112, 114 and 115)
Unpublished

Bartók's first tour of the Netherlands did not take place until the end of April, 1923. He then gave recitals in Amsterdam, Rotterdam and Utrecht.

119 (April 15th, 1922)
Letters I/104–105

Bartók's Paris concert took place at Le Vieux Colombier Theatre. He played his own and Kodály's works, accompanied Slivinsky in folk-song arrangements and played his Sonata for violin and piano with Miss Jelly Arányi.

Henri Prunières (1886–1942). French musicologist and writer on music.

'... as well as a few young (notorious) Frenchmen'. These are probably some of 'Le Groupe des Six': Honegger, Milhaud, Poulenc, etc.

Eugen Szenkár (b. 1891). Hungarian-born composer and conductor; worked with the Frankfurt Opera from 1920 until 1923; produced *Bluebeard's Castle* and *The Wooden Prince* on May 13th, 1922.

120 (April 5th, 1923)
Letters I/106–107

Kassa. The town—now Košice (Slovakia)—has belonged to Czechoslovakia since 1920.

Bartók's next concert at Kassa took place on April 20th, 1926.

However, he did give performances on the scheduled day in other towns of Slovakia; viz. on

February 5th, 1924, at Komárom (Slov. Komárno),

February 9th, 1924, at Losonc (Lučenec),

March 29th, 1924, at Rimaszombat (Rimavská Sobota).

Superscription—in an unknown hand—on the letter says: 'Recalling your first work—*The Danube River*—which you performed at the age of 10 in the banquet room of Nagyszőllős County Hall, a humble admirer at Nagyszőllős sends his respectful greetings and begs an autograph.'

121 (May 4th, 1923)
Letters I/107

Further recitals were given: on May 7th, London; May 9th, Huddersfield; and May 11th, London.

122 (May 27th, 1923)
(Cf. Nos. 112, 114, 115 and 118) Unpublished

Bartók dedicated his *Ady Songs* to Béla Reinitz—hence the '*quite a row*'.

Béla Reinitz (1878–1943). Composer, the first to set to music some of Endre Ady's poems. As a critic he was one of the first to recognize the significance of Bartók's and Kodály's art. Held a leading post (head of the Directory of Music) under the Republic of Councils of 1919; following the downfall of the Republic he was imprisoned and subjected to much vilification in the press ('a musical *condottiere* with a deranged mind, an indisciplined megalomaniac', etc.). These were the circumstances in which Bartók dedicated his *Ady Songs* to Reinitz 'with true friendship and affection'. Later Reinitz went into exile in Vienna but returned to Hungary at the end of the 'twenties.

123 (October 1st, 1923) Hungarian original published by János Demény, in *Kortárs*, Vol. IV, No. 9 (September, 1960), pp. 319–328 ('Kiadatlan Bartók-dokumentumok'–Some Unpublished Bartók Documents).

This is a draft—never actually sent off—of No. 124.

Translated from photostats of originals in the National Széchényi Library, Budapest (Fol. Hung. 2697). Through the agency of Mrs. Pál Haás (Miss Zsuzsa Kner).

See also Nos. 124, 126, 127, 148, 149 and 151.

124 (October 1st, 1923)
(Cf. No. 123)

The final, fair copy—which was actually sent—of No. 123.

125 (October 2nd, 1923) Published in *Documenta Bartókiana* Vol. II, edited by D. Dille, Budapest, 1965, Akadémiai Kiadó, p. 164 (facs.).

Edward J. Dent (1876–1957). British musicologist of note; Chairman of the International Society for Contemporary Music from 1922 to 1938.

Published from a copy of the

original made by Mr. D. Clegg, Lichfield, Staffordshire, England (1962).

126 (May 27th, 1924)
(Cf. Nos. 123 and 124)

127 (June 5th, 1924)
(Cf. Nos. 123, 124 and 126)

Although Bartók did not eventually manage to honour the deadlines indicated in this letter, the musical score of *The Miraculous Mandarin* may be assumed to have been completed in the autumn—or, at the latest, by the end—of 1924. As there are three different conclusions to this work (arrangement for piano for two hands, arrangement for piano for four hands, and a score), the history of the concluding part of this work cannot be regarded as having been cleared up in every detail. Aurél Nirschy's article ('Varianten zu Bartóks Pantomime: Der wunderbare Mandarin', *Studia Musicologica,* Vol. II [1962], Nos. 1–4, pp. 189–223) supplies many valuable additional facts about the history of the conception of *The Miraculous Mandarin.*

128 (May 15th, 1925)
Letters III/149–150 (Cf. Nos. 78, 81, 82, 84, 86, 99, 102–106 and 113)

Bartók's collection of *Rumanian Christmas Carols* was published by Universal Edition at Bartók's expense. (*Melodien der rumänischen Colinde,* Vienna, 1935.)

For letters written to *Oxford University Press,* see Nos. 141, 153, 157, 158, 173, 174, 176, 178 and 182. Some letters written by Bartók to Brăiloiu (see Nos. 130, 131 and 154) are relevant to these.

Bartók was awarded the Order *Bene Merenti* Class I on October 28th, 1924.

Bartók played in Prague on January 10th, 1925, and at Brno on March 2nd, 1925.

The tour of Italy, from March 10th to 14th, 1925, comprised piano recitals in Milan, Rome, Naples and Palermo.

129 (December 31st, 1925)
Letters I/111

Jenő Takács (b. September 25th, 1902, Cinfalva). Hungarian composer and pianist. Between the two world wars, professor at Cairo Conservatory, then, at the University of the Philippines, Manila; went to Switzerland after the Second World War. Now lives in the United States. See also Nos. 164 and 191.

Information received from Dr. Endre Csatkai, of Sopron, Hungary, 1948.

Addressed to: 'Herrn Jenő Takács, p. A. Kapellmeister Fall, Bremen, Rembertistrasse 91.'

130 (May 6th, 1926) Unpublished

Constantin Brăiloiu (1893–1958). Rumanian folklorist of note who published Rumanian versions of several of Bartók's essays on folk-music. (*Scrieri mărunte despre muzica populara românească* [Short Essays on Rumanian Folk-Music] Bucharest, 1937.)

Octavian Goga (1881–1938). Rumanian poet and statesman. Responsible for the Rumanian versions of many poems by Sándor Petőfi and of Imre Madách's verse drama *The Tragedy of Man*. His correspondence with Endre Ady is of historical significance.

Bartók's 14 letters to Brăiloiu are kept in the archives of the Rumanian Musicians' Association. Only two of them (Nos. 130 and 154) have been made public so far (at the 2nd Conference on Musicology held in the autumn of 1961, in Budapest), through the agency of Mr. Zeno Vancea.

131 (June 27th, 1926)
Letters III/167–176

Cluj. Klausenburg in the original; the Hungarian name was Kolozsvár.

Brăiloiu had asked Bartók for the revised versions of several of the tunes collected in Bihar County. Bartók wrote them down at the end of his letter.

'No. [—].' Bartók omitted the number, but, in the published volume, this *colinda* appears as No. 18. Thus, the completed text should read 'No. 18.'

132 (July 26th, 1926) Hungarian original published by Cs. P. (Péter Csobádi) in *Irodalmi Újság*, Vol. VI, No. 46 (November 12th, 1955), p. 1 (' "Lehetőleg egyszerű szobát . . ."—Új Bartók-levelek' 'A simple room if possible . . . —New Letters by Bartók).'

Antal Fleischer (1891–1945). Hungarian conductor; presented Bartók's early works in many European cities.

The concert in Barcelona was held on March 24th, 1927, after all: the local Philharmonic Orchestra, acting on Casals's advice, engaged the conductor of the Budapest Opera for two nights. The programme of the first concert included the works of certain Hungarian composers, among them Bartók's early Rhapsody (op. 1), with the composer as soloist.

Published from the original. By courtesy of Mrs. Antal Fleischer.

133 (March 12th, 1927)
(Cf. No. 132)

Addressed to: 'M. Anton Fleischer, Hotel Victoria, Barcelona, Espagne.'

134 (December 30th, 1927)
Letters I/115

During his long tour of the U.S., Bartók appeared with the Philadelphia Symphony Orchestra in that city on December 30th–31st, playing his early Rhapsody, with Frigyes Reiner conducting (see No. 139). On January 1st, 1928, in the same city, he played his 2nd Sonata for violin and piano together with Miss Jelly Arányi.

'*. . . from D.*' i.e. Ditta, Bartók's second wife. (See Note 142.)

135 (January 9th, 1928)
Letters I/115

At Los Angeles, on January 11th, 1928, Bartók gave a lecture on

Hungarian music and played his own and Kodály's works.

136 (January 18th, 1928)
Letters I/116–117 and the complementary part of the letter, with the Portland programme ib., pp. 197–198.

Bartók appeared in Seattle on January 15th, 1928.

'Emil'. Probably Emil Oláh Tóth, Elza Bartók's husband.

'Sánta Mónika', 'Sánta Katalina', 'Sánta Barbara.'—Untranslatable play on words. *Sánta* is Hungarian for 'lame,' 'limping'.

137 (January 24th, 1928) Unpublished. Displayed—by permission of Mrs. Ditta Bartók—at the Béla Bartók Memorial Exhibition, held in September, 1950, under the aegis of the Hungarian Musicians' Association. (See Dr. Ervin Major's Catalogue of the Exhibition, Item 61.)

Péter Bartók (b. July 31st, 1924), Bartók's second son, child of his second marriage, was three and a half years old at the time. (Concerning his mother, see Note No. 142.)

Date of Bartók's appearance at St. Paul: January 25th, 1928.

Addressed to: 'Bartók Péter úrfinak, Budapest, Szilágyi tér 4. *Hungary.*'

138 (May 16th, 1928)
Letters III/244–246

Matica Slovenská. The name of a Slovak cultural and scientific institute founded in 1861, during the period of Austrian 'absolutism', i.e. repression, political and otherwise, following Hungary's defeat in the War of Independence of 1848–9. In 1875—eight years after Austria and Hungary composed their differences in the 'Compromise' of 1867—the M. S. was dissolved and its property confiscated. The dissolution of the M. S. deprived the Slovaks of all opportunities of satisfying their cultural needs in their native tongue; hence they were driven to seek to establish cultural contacts with the Czechs.

In the Czechoslovak Republic, constituted after the First World War, the Matica Slovenská was reopened. Today it serves as Slovakia's National Library.

During the 'twenties, Bartók was busy preparing for the press his collection of Slovak folk tunes.

In the autumn of 1920, he consigned the first few pages of his collection to Miloš Ruppeldt, a representative of the Matica Slovenská. In 1921 a contract was concluded between Bartók and the M. S., under which Bartók undertook to consign to the M. S. the complete collection by September 30th, 1922; and the Matica, to publish the collection within four years at the latest. By October, 1922, Bartók had completed the first part of the collection; on July 15th, 1923, Viliam Figuš-Bystrý, who had been appointed editor of the collection, reported that 1,792 tunes—two-thirds of the collection—and the preface were ready to go to press.

In this letter, Bartók informs the Matica that he has completed the work. A receipt made out by the Czechoslovak Consulate in Budapest on June 22nd, 1928, shows that Bartók had on that date handed in the closing pages of his collection. Bartók's delay, it seems, was due to the failure of the Matica to go ahead with the printing or to Bartók's failure to receive the proofs of the first two-thirds of the collection which he had handed in some years previously.

For an account of subsequent developments, see also Nos. 168 and 215.

Published from a photostat by courtesy of Dr. Ladislav Burlas.

139 (October 29th, 1928)
Letters II/108–109

Frigyes (*Fritz*) *Reiner* (b. Dec. 19th, 1888, Budapest; d. Nov. 15th, 1963, New York). Noted Hungarian conductor, headed the Cincinnati Symphony Orchestra from 1922. His name is associated with first performances in the U.S.A. of several Bartók works. During Bartók's first tour of the U.S.A., he conducted the Cincinnati Symphony Orchestra's performance (in New York, February 13th, 1928; and in Cincinnati, February 24th–25th, 1928) of Bartók's 1st Piano Concerto.

The First Prize at the Philadelphia Music Fund Society's contest (600 entries) was divided between Bartók (for his 3rd String Quartet) and the Italian composer Alfredo Casella (1883–1947).

The 1st Piano Concerto was presented in Budapest on March 18th–19th, 1928, with Ernő Dohnányi conducting. It was conducted by Hermann Abendroth in Cologne at the end of the same month and by Erich Kleiber in Berlin at the end of April, with the composer playing the solo part on both occasions.

Erich Kleiber (1890–1956). German conductor.

Pierre Monteux (1875–1964). French conductor; successfully championed the works of contemporary composers. Second conductor of the Concertgebouw Orchestra of Amsterdam from 1925.

Willem Mengelberg (1871–1951). Dutch conductor, responsible for the Concertgebouw's rise to world fame.

The new, 4th, String Quartet was written between July and September, 1928.

Bartók's letter is published from a typewritten copy received from Dr. Ottó Gombosi, by kind permission of the addressee (1949).

140 (October–November, 1928)
Letters III/388–389

József Szigeti (b. Sept. 2nd, 1892, Budapest). Celebrated Hungarian violinist, Hubay's pupil. Bartók dedicated to him his 1st Rhapsody, 1928 (referred to in this letter), and to him and Benny Goodman, the *Contrasts* (written in 1938) for violin, clarinet and piano. Szigeti transcribed some of the 85 pieces in *For Children* for the violin and piano, and performed them all over the world.

'*... some information about Russia.*' Szigeti had been to the Soviet Union on several occasions. Bartók now asks him for information before himself setting out for that country.

The English translation of this letter was made from a photostat of the original, by courtesy of the addressee. See also No. 273.

141 (November 17th, 1928) Unpublished

The Oxford University Press was headed by Hubert J. Foss, and the letters are addressed either to him or to the firm.

Ion Bîanu (1856–1935). Member, and Chief Librarian, of the Rumanian Academy; Professor of Rumanian Literature at the University of Bucharest. (In Letters III, twelve letters written by Bartók to Bîanu are printed: 6 in French, 5 in German and 1 in Rumanian. In these letters Bartók discusses the work involved in the projected edition of the tunes collected in Bihar County and the preparatory work for a Rumanian edition (which never materialized) of the Máramaros collection.)

A typewritten copy of the letter was provided by Mr. David Clegg, of Lichfield, U.K., and we are indebted to Prof. Gerald Abraham, of Liverpool, for a photostat.

See also Nos. 153, 157, 158, 173, 174, 176, 178 and 182.

142 (January 2nd, 1929) Hungarian original still unpublished. A German translation appeared in Letters IV/136.

Mrs. Béla Bartók (*née Ditta Pásztory*) (b. 1903, Rimaszombat). Bartók's second wife and former pupil whom he married on August 28, 1923. During the schoolyear 1922–23, Ditta Pásztory was a second-year student in the Piano Department of the Academy.

By courtesy of the Hungarian Musicians' Association, by kind permission of Mrs. Béla Bartók.

Addressed to:
'Bartók Béláné Úrnőnek, III. Kavics u. 10. Budapest, Ungarn/Hongrie.'

143 (January 7th, 1929) (Cf. No. 142) In German: Letters IV/136–138

Bartók's Kharkov recital was given on January 6th, 1929; it was followed by one in Odessa on January 9th, two appearances (January 16th and 20th) in Leningrad, and his final recital in Moscow on January 24th.

Ithma. The name of a Viennese concert agency with whom Bartók had a general contract. (Letters III/246.)

Addressed to:
'Bartók Béláné Úrnőnek,
III. Kavics u. 10.,
Budapest, Hongrie, Ungarn,
Венгрия.'

144 (April 12th, 1929) Unpublished. Displayed at the Hungarian Musicians' Association's Béla Bartók Memorial Exhibition in September, 1950, by permission of Mrs. Béla Bartók (Ditta Pásztory). (See

Dr. Ervin Major's Catalogue of the Exhibition, item 62.)

Nikolai Vassilievich Gogol (1809–1852). Russian writer.

At the Bartók–Szigeti concert in Rome on April 12th, 1929, one of the items of the programme jointly performed by the two artists was Bartók's 2nd Sonata for violin and piano.

Addressed to:
'Bartók Béláné Úrnőnek,
III. Kavics u. 10.
Budapest, Ungheria.'

145 (December 11th, 1929) Unpublished

Michael D. Calvocoressi (b. Oct. 2nd, 1877, Marseilles; d. Feb. 1st, 1944, London). Greek-born music critic; lived in Paris for many years, then, after the First World War, he lived and worked chiefly in London. The modern musical movement in Hungary was for the first time brought to the attention of the musical world in Britain in an article contributed by him to *The Musical Times* in the spring of 1913. In a series of lectures, delivered in Paris in February, 1914, he discussed modern trends in music, including the new music in Hungary, of which he said Bartók was the central figure. He was a gifted translator and was responsible for the English-language versions of the words of a number of Bartók's and Kodály's works.

Bartók's book on Hungarian folk-music (*A magyar népdal*, Rózsavölgyi és Társa, Budapest, 1924), in which 320 tunes are printed, was translated and brought out in German and English editions: *Das ungarische Volkslied*. Walter de Gruyter, Berlin, 1925; *Hungarian Folk Music*. Oxford University Press, London, 1931. Here Bartók is discussing the English-language edition.

Typewritten copies of the original were provided by Prof. G. Abraham, of Liverpool, and Mr. D. Clegg, of Lichfield.

146 (May 17th, 1930) Hungarian original unpublished. In German: Letters IV/138

Ernő Südy. A pharmacist in Békéscsaba, executive officer for arts in the Aurora Circle formed in 1913; Bartók stayed with him in Békéscsaba on five occasions between 1922 and 1936.

Robert Schmitz. Pianist. See Letter I/174 (picture taken on March 6th, 1928, on board the liner *George Washington*, shows him with Bartók and Pablo Casals).

Published from a copy written in the addressee's hand.

See also No. 171.

Addressed to:
'Ngs. Dr. Südy Ernő úrnak,
az "Aurora" kör elnöke [Chairman of the Aurora Circle], Békéscsaba.'

147 (November 5th, 1930) Letters III/184–185

Octavian Beu (b. July 9th, 1903, Orlați; d. Jan. 3rd, 1964, Sibiu). Rumanian folklorist who wrote to Bartók in connection with a radio talk about the composer.

Z. Székely.—See Note No. 213. See also No. 152.

148 (November 15th, 1930)
(Cf. Nos. 123, 124, 126 and 127)

By sending this letter, Béla Balázs removed the obstacle which had prevented a Budapest revival of Bartók's two stage works. See Note No. 103, *ad* (1).

Even so, it was not until a few years later that these two works reached the stage again: *The Wooden Prince* on January 30th, 1935, and *Bluebeard's Castle* on October 29th, 1936.

The royalties due to Balázs were paid by Bartók: they met abroad for this purpose. (Information received from Mr. Béla Bartók, Jr.)

149 (November 21st, 1930)
(Cf. Nos. 123, 124, 126, 127 and 148)

Miklós Radnai (1892–1935). Composer; professor at the Royal Hungarian Academy of Music from 1919; Director of Budapest Opera from 1925.

150 (December 6th, 1930)
Letters I/120

The London success that was 'overdue by about 24 years' must be a reference to Bartók's performance of his early Rhapsody for piano and orchestra, on Nov. 26th, 1930. This work at the Rubinstein contest in Paris had failed to bring him success, and as a solo piano piece had also been unfavourably noticed in the press after its first performance in Hungary on November 4th, 1906, in Pozsony.

151 (December 10th, 1930)
(Cf. Nos. 123, 124, 126, 127, 148 and 149)

152 (January 10th, 1931)
Letters III/189–195

Bartók writes this long letter to correct various statements made by Octavian Beu in his radio talk, the text of which had been submitted to him beforehand.

'*. . . when I was attacked . . . as a musical Scotus Viator*'. Allusion to the British journalist R. W. Seton-Watson who fell into disfavour with Hungarian chauvinists.

Emil Haraszti (1885–1958). Composer and music critic, the director of the Nemzeti Zenede (the National Conservatorium of Music) between 1918 and 1927. He spoke depreciatingly about Hungarian folk-music that was discovered thanks to Bartók's and Kodály's initiative and research, and Bartók disliked him because of this.

Bartók wrote a postcard on March 29th, 1931, supplementing what he said in this long letter:

'I am sending you the 2nd piece ('Village Dance') of the *Deux Images* as a supplement to my last letter. The themes owe something to Rum[anian] influence.'

153 (February 16th, 1931)
(Cf. No. 141)

As no headway had been made, either in Rumania or in England, with the proposed editions of his collection of *colinda*, Bartók was evidently contemplating an edition at his own expense (which was eventually brought out in 1935.) It would seem that this is why he asks for the manuscript to be returned to him.

In arriving at this decision he may have been stimulated by the publication in Rumania in 1929 of a collection of *colinda* (by Sabin V. Drăgoi) which must have directed Bartók's attention to his own, unpublished, collection. (See No. 163.)

154 (February 22nd, 1931) (Cf. No. 130)

To commemorate his 50th birthday, Bartók's Rumanian admirers proposed to put up a commemorative plaque on the wall of his native home at Nagyszentmiklós. This project came to nothing, like the Budapest Opera's plan to produce *The Miraculous Mandarin.*

Bartók's request to have a Hungarian inscription engraved on the tablet *next to* the Rumanian one was misreported in some Hungarian newspapers which stated that he insisted on the inscription being written in Hungarian *instead of* in Rumanian.

155 (February 23rd, 1931) Reproduced in facsimile headlined 'Egy újabban előkerült Bartók levelezőlap' (A Recently Discovered Bartók Postcard) in *Új Zenei Szemle,* Vol. IV, Nos. 7–8 (July–August, 1953), p. 55. (Edited by István Szelényi.)

László Pollatsek (Pataki). Hungarian writer on music, living in Tel-Aviv, Israel.

In its 1912 edition (by Rózsavölgyi), *4 Nénies* is mistakenly marked op. 8b. The same opus number was given to the piano piece *2 Elegies.*

Esquisses is marked only op. 9. Therefore, the opus number of *4 Nénies* correctly is op. 9a, that of *Esquisses,* op. 9b.

156 (May, 1931) Reproduced in facsimile, with the heading 'Írásaiból–szavaiból' (Some Sayings and Writings of Bartók) in *Új Zenei Szemle,* Vol. VI, No. 9 (September, 1955), p. 6. (Edited by István Szelényi.)

For having publicly refused, in 1931, to conduct *Giovinezza,* the Fascist anthem, Toscanini was banished from Italy.

The *UMZE*—Új Magyar Zene-Egyesület (New Hungarian Music Association) registered support for Toscanini in a letter to the executive committee of its parent organization, the International Society of Contemporary Music (Société Internationale de la Musique Contemporaine). The draft was written in Bartók's hand and has been made public by courtesy of Mr. Zoltán Kodály.

157 (May 30th, 1931) (Cf. Nos. 141 and 153)

158 (May 31st, 1931)
(Cf. Nos. 141, 153 and 157)

159 (July 9th, 1931)
Letters I/121

Bartók, as a member of the Comité International de Coopération Intellectuelle, had been invited to attend the first session of the League of Nations in July 1931; there, on July 7th, he read his proposal concerning gramophone recordings.

He was leaving Geneva for Mondsee, where he had been invited to teach at the annual music course of the Austro-American Conservatory of Music and Art of the Stage.

The letter written to Cairo presumably related to the congress on Arab folk-music, which was to be held in that city in March, 1932, and to which Bartók had been invited to attend as the representative of Hungary. Efforts to trace the letter have so far been unsuccessful. Mustafa Rida Bey, to whom it was addressed, died in the early 1950s.

Bartók first met *Thomas Mann* (1875–1955) in Budapest, at Gyopár utca 2 (see Note No. 112); he also met the great humanist author in later years (they met for the last time at Lajos Hatvany's home in Budapest on June 8th, 1936).

160 (July 13th, 1931)
Letters I/122–126

Karel Čapek (1890–1938). Czech humanist writer.

Gilbert Murray (1866–1957). British classical scholar. Chairman of the League of Nations 1923–1938, joint-president from 1938 onwards.

Gheorghe Oprescu (b. 1881). Professor at Bucharest University. Corresponding Member of the Rumanian Academy. Director of Toma Stelian Museum.

Paul Valéry (1871–1945). French lyric poet, philosopher and essayist.

Ugo Ojetti. Permanent correspondent for cultural affairs at the League of Nations.

Henri Focillon (1881–1943). French art historian.

Nini Roll-Anker (1873–1942). Norwegian authoress. Used the *nom de plume* Kåre P. in the 1930s.

'*Generalsekretär*'. Fritz E. Krombholz, of Vienna.

Mrs. P. = Katherine Buford Peeples. Founder of the Austro-American Conservatory, Professor of Music; University of Redlands, Calif.

Mrs. C. = Mrs. Artie Mason Carter.

Paul Weingarten (b. 1886, Brno; d. 1948, Vienna). Professor at the National Academy of Music in Vienna.

161 (August 4th, 1931) Hungarian original unpublished. In German: Letters IV/145–146

Imre Weisshaus (b. 1905). Composer and pianist. Bartók's pupil at the Academy of Music 1921–1925. (His name is also written 'Weiszhausz' in the Academy registers.) Has lived in Paris for several decades; has assumed the name Pál Arma and is known as a composer and the author of illustrated articles on musical subjects.

'. . . *the Róths*'. The Róth Quartet (Ferenc Róth, Jenő Antal, Ferenc Molnár and Albert van Doorn).

'*And as for my Sonata, I have already played it there.*' On October 12th, 1927. Another recital, at Dessau, so far as we know, was never given.

Wilhelm Kienzl (1857–1941). Austrian composer, author of the opera *Evangelimann*. Honorary President of the Austro-American International Conservatory.

Rosina Lhévinne (b. 1880, Kiev). Russian-born pianist, wife of Josef Lhévinne. Taught at the Juilliard Graduate School, New York.

Bartók's remark at the end of his letter alludes to the addressee's addiction—having been influenced by the *Art Nouveau* movement—to the use of lower-case letters, even in writing the initials of his name.

Published from a typewritten copy received from the addressee, who has, however, omitted the form of address.

162 (November 6th, 1931) Letters II/111–113 (only in Hungarian). In German: Letters IV/146–148

Max Rostal (b. 1905). Violinist. Lived in London for many years. Included in his programme was Bartók's Violin Concerto (1937–8). Has lived in Switzerland since 1958. Head of the Violin Department at the Berne Conservatory. When this letter was written, he was living in Berlin, where his string quartet included some of Bartók's works in its programmes. It was while rehearsing the quartets that he had doubts as to the correctness of the metronome signs, and he asked Bartók to check the markings for the 1st and 4th String Quartets. Bartók examined the passages that had been indicated and, in his letter, made a large number of important corrections of nuance.

Mr. Endre Gertler, the eminent Hungarian violinist living in Brussels, has compared the points in this letter relating to the 1st String Quartet with the score in his possession, on which notes have been made in Bartók's own hand. As a result, he has added the following two corrections:

1st movement 10: [*long* pause]
3rd movement 32: L'istesso tempo

The letter is from a typewritten copy received from the addressee and checked by the late Mátyás Seiber (1950)

163 (December 20th, 1931) Hungarian original unpublished. In German: Letters IV/149–150

Tivadar Szántó (1877–1934). Pianist and composer. Knight of the Legion of Honour following the First World War.

'*Drăgoi's colinda collection*'. Sabin V. Drăgoi's book (*303 colinde cu text şi melodie*) is undated. The preface was dated January, 1925. According to information kindly supplied by the author, it was in 1929 that his book appeared.

Published from a handwritten copy obtained from Mr. István Nagy (Kolozsvár–Cluj, 1954).

164 (May 8th, 1932) Letters I/127–128. Published from the text as printed in an article in *Sorsunk* (Pécs, Hungary), November, 1946. The author of the article—Prof. Jenő Takács, composer and pianist—had the letter reproduced in facsimile and published at a later date, *Feuilles Musicales*, Vol. III, Nos. 9–10 (September–October, 1950), p. 122.

Jenő Takács was at that time professor at the Cairo Conservatory and attended the congress as adviser to the Egyptian Radio on Arab music.

Polnauer. The name of the Hungarian Consul General in Alexandria at the time and whose support Professor Takács sought to obtain for Bartók.

'*. . . your new country*'. Manila, the Philippines, where the addressee lived for nearly three years.

See also Nos. 129 and 191.

165 (September 6th, 1933) Unpublished. Original written in English.

Most of the letters are addressed to the Music Department, British Broadcasting Corporation, No. 166 to Mr. Tillett, and Nos. 188 and 189 to Mr. Clark.

Bartók appeared at the Berkeley Hall, Glasgow, on November 2nd, 1933.

At his London concert (at Queen's Hall) on November 8th, 1933, he played his 2nd Piano Concerto, with Sir Adrian Boult conducting.

A typewritten copy of the letter has been received from Mr. D. Clegg, Lichfield.

See also Nos. 166, 167, 169, 170, 172, 183, 184, 188 and 189.

166 (September 30th, 1933)
(Cf. No. 165)

167 (October 7th, 1933)
(Cf. Nos. 165 and 166)

168 (October 8th, 1933)
Unpublished

After Bartók had submitted to the Matica Slovenská (see Note No. 138) the concluding part of his collection of Slovak folk tunes (in 1928), three editors in succession worked on the volume:

(1) *Miloš Ruppeldt*. He asked Bartók to omit a certain type of folk tune from the collection. Bartók flatly rejected this request, considering that to do so would be quite unscientific.

(2) *Ján Valašťan-Dolinský*. He was not satisfied with the words of the tunes as noted down by Bartók; he therefore wrote to the teachers and notaries of the villages, where Bartók had done his collecting, and had them revise the words of the folk-songs.

(3) *Ivan Ballo*. He began to restore the revised words from literary Slovakian to the original dialects.

In the course of this prolonged work, some tension began to arise between Ballo and the Matica, and between the Matica and Bartók. Several times Bartók wanted to cancel his contract but again and again was persuaded to grant an extension of time.

The Matica had to bring an action against Ballo to get the manuscript back from him—which it did not manage to do until the beginning of 1935.

A photostat of the letter has been received from Mr. Antal Ágoston Baník, of Martin, Czechoslovakia.

See also No. 215.

169 (October 19th, 1933)
(Cf. Nos. 165–167)

170 (End October, 1933)
(Cf. Nos. 165–167 and 169)

171 (January 20th, 1934)
(Cf. No. 146) Hungarian original unpublished. In German: Letters IV/151–152

Bartók's concert was given at the Aurora Circle's Bartók Festival on February 15th, 1934. In Békéscsaba the population is mainly Slovakian; at Bartók's wish, the Slovak songs were given Slovak titles in the printed programme to emphasize that this was a concert for a national minority. The Slovak songs were sung by Szidi Elek, accompanied on the piano by Bartók. For Bartók's views on national minorities see also Letter No. 104.

172 (May 9th, 1934)
(Cf. Nos. 165–167, 169 and 170)

The B.B.C.'s Bartók programme—on May 25th, 1934—included *Cantata Profana* (The Nine Enchanted Stags), for double mixed chorus, tenor and baritone soloists, and orchestra, with Trevor Jones (tenor), Frank Phillips (baritone), the Wireless Chorus (leader: Leslie Woodgate) and the B.B.C. Orchestra (leader: Laurence Turner), conducted by Aylmer Buesst. The first part of the programme included *Two Pictures* and the 2nd Piano Concerto.

173 (May 9th, 1934)
(Cf. Nos 141, 153, 157 and 158)

174 (July 2nd, 1934)
(Cf. Nos. 141, 153, 157, 158 and 173)

175 (October 27th, 1934) Hungarian original published by János Demény in *Új Zenei Szemle*, Vol. VII, No. 9 (September, 1956), pp. 11–14 ('Bartók-dokumentumok Jugoszláviából'—Bartók Documents from Yugoslavia).

Vinko Žganec (b. Jan. 22nd, 1890, Vratišinec). Croatian folklorist to whom Bartók wrote while working on his book *Népzenénk és a szomszéd népek népzenéje* (The Folk Music of Hungary and of the Neighbouring Peoples). Bartók found much to help him in Žganec's work *Hrvatske pučke popijevke iz Međumurja* (Croatian Folk-songs from the Muraköz), Vol. I: Secular Tunes; published by the Zagreb Academy of Sciences, Zagreb, 1924: this was his chief source for the closing chapter of his own book ('Serbo-Croatian Folk Music and the Folk Music of Hungary').

'I hope the bitter irony in the last paragraph on p. 33 of my booklet will not be misunderstood.'

'The four main Hungarian folk-songs publications contain between them about 230 ancient pentatonic tunes; whereas this Muraköz [collection contains] 190. We may say confidently that anyone wishing to gain a thorough knowledge of the old-style Hungarian folk-song should study this Croatian-language edition of Muraköz [tunes]. We certainly ought to be grateful to the Zagreb Academy of Sciences for bringing out—even though with Croatian words—so many Hungarian tunes! If things go on as they are now—if a universal edition of Hungarian folk-songs is delayed much longer—then we shall soon reach the stage when far more Hungarian songs are available with words in Croatian or Slovakian, Ruthenian or Rumanian, than with the original Hungarian words; [and] other nations will get to know the music of the Hungarian village in *that* form—with *foreign-language* words, presented as the folk music of all sorts of non-Hungarian-speaking peoples. Then however much we protest that these songs have been *borrowed* from the Hungarian body of folk music, people will not believe us, all the less so because we shall not even be able to produce what would be the most convincing evidence—the universal edition of the 10,000 Hungarian folk-songs so far collected.'

A foot-note added later to the above passage reads:

'Meantime—after my manuscript had gone to press—the Hungarian Academy of Sciences decided to grant, for this half-year and, as far as possible, for the next few years, certain sums for the universal edition of Hungarian folk-songs. If other official bodies were to make the effort to do likewise, we might hope to see the [proposed] edition materialize within the next few years.'

Bartók was not to see his hope come true during his lifetime. The first volume of the projected edition was issued by the Hungarian Academy of Sciences in 1951. Six volumes of the series had been brought out by 1966.

Franjo Xaver Kuhač (1834–1911). Croatian folklorist. Graduated from a teachers' training college and studied music in Budapest. Studied under Liszt in Weimar. Lived in Zagreb from 1871. His principal work: *Južno-slovjenske narodne popievke* (South-Slavonic Folk-songs, with piano accompaniment), Vols. I–IV, 1879–1881.

Ludvik Kuba (1863–1956). Czech painter and collector of folk-songs. Principal work: *Slovanstvo ve svych zpěvech* (Slavs Singing), a collection of Czech, Moravian, Slovak, Polish, Ukrainian, Byelorussian and other songs arranged in ten volumes which appeared from 1884 to 1895. In addition three volumes of Southern Slav and Bulgarian folk-songs appeared between 1927 and 1929.

The English translation of the letter has been made from a handwritten copy sent by the addressee.

See also Nos. 177, 181 and 186.

176 (November 2nd, 1934)
(Cf. Nos. 141, 153, 157, 158, 173 and 174)

177 (November 7th, 1934)
(Cf. No. 175)

178 (November 3rd, 1934)
(Cf. Nos. 141, 153, 157, 158, 173, 174 and 176)

179 (February 27th, 1935)
Letters III/402

Raïna Katzarova-Kukudova. Bulgarian student of folk-music.

Géza Fehér (1890–1955). Hungarian Byzantine scholar. For several years studied pre-historic Hungarian relics in Bulgaria.

Published from a photostat of the original manuscript obtained from Bulgarian authorities by the Hungarian Institute for Cultural Relations (1954).

Addressed to:
'Mme Raïna Katzarova, Sofia. Musée d'Ethnographie, Bulgarie'

180 (March 5th, 1935)
Letters II/114–115

Imre Deák (b. Feb. 2nd, 1892, Szombathely; d. Nov. 17th, 1945, Pasadena, Calif.). Pianist and musicologist. A pupil of Thomán and Bartók. Lived abroad from 1921.

In September, 1934, Bartók, at the request of the Hungarian Academy of Sciences, was relieved of his teaching duties, and it became his official task to devote three afternoons a week to the preparatory arrangement of the collection of Hungarian folk tunes and the revision of phonogrammes.

Bartók, so as to recover at least part of the cost—met by him—of the publication of his volume of *colindas,* collected subscriptions for the book. (See also Note No. 153.)

A typewritten copy of the letter was sent (1949) by Professor Stephen Deák, brother of addressee, University of Southern California. Checked from a photostat (1969).

Addressed to:
'Mr. Imre Deák, 1800 San Pasquale Street, Pasadena, California, U.S.A'

181 (July 3rd, 1935)
(Cf. Nos. 175 and 177)

'Melodije iz Južne Srbije.' Srpske narodne melodije (Južna Srbije). Songs from Macedonia. A collection by Vlad R. Georgevitch, published by Ernest Closson, 1928.

'Od Timok do Vita'. Narodni pesni ot Timok do Vita, a work by Vassil Stoin, containing 4,076 Bulgarian tunes. Sofia, 1928.

Vassil Stoin. Bulgarian student of folk music. Head of the Folk Music Department of the Sofia Museum of Ethnography from 1924. His '2nd big volume'—containing 2,718 tunes from the northern region of Bulgaria—was published in 1931.

Dr. István Ecsedi (1885–1936).

Folklorist. Director of the Déri Museum at Debrecen.

'I didn't even know you had written an opera.' This was a misunderstanding on Bartók's part. Replying to Bartók, Žganec, in his letter of July 25th, 1935, wrote:

'It was on my collection of Muraköz folk-songs that our composer Krsto Odak based his opera *Dorica pleše,* produced during the past season at the Zagreb, Belgrade and Ljubljana Operas. That is the opera your friend has been telling you about. It was written by my friend Odak, not by myself, though he worked from notes made by me.' (Information kindly supplied by Mr. V. Žganec.)

182 (July 4th, 1935)
(Cf. Nos. 141, 153, 157, 158, 173, 174, 176 and 178)

183 (December 10th, 1935)
(Cf. Nos. 165–167, 169, 170 and 172)

The year 1936 opened for Bartók with a tour of England and Holland: on January 7th, he played at a 'Prom' (Promenade Concert) at the Queen's Hall with the B.B.C. Symphony Orchestra; the first part of the concert, conducted by Sir Henry Wood, with Bartók's 2nd Piano Concerto as its centre piece, was broadcast.

184 (December 14th, 19365)
(Cf. Nos. 165–167, 1, 1790, 172 and 183)

After his appearances in Holland, Bartók returned to Britain, where he gave a guest performance at Liverpool on January 16th, and on January 17th and 18th played for the B.B.C. Midland Region at Birmingham. (There he played his 2nd Piano Concerto with Leslie Howard conducting.)

185 (December 18th, 1935)
Letters III/406–408

László Rásonyi (b. Jan. 22nd, 1899, Liptószentmiklós). Hungarian–Turkish language scholar. Lecturer on Turkish–Hungarian linguistic and historical relationships in the Department of Hungarian Studies, Ankara University, from 1935 to 1942. It was his idea that Bartók should be invited to Turkey to organize the collecting of Turkish folk-songs or, at least, to undertake one collecting tour in that country.

Paul Hindemith (1895–1963). German composer. Emigrated from Nazi Germany. From 1935 to 1937, lived and worked chiefly in Turkey, in 1938–39 in Switzerland. In 1939 went to the United States and was appointed professor at Yale, then at Harvard University; in 1953 returned to Switzerland, where he lived until his death, in 1963.

Mátyás Seiber (1905–1960). Hungarian-born composer and cellist. Studied at the Budapest Academy of Music under Schiffer ('cello) and Kodály (musical composition). Lived in England and died in a road accident on a trip to South Africa. Regarded as one of the distinguished names in modern British music.

Iván Engel (b. 1899). Pianist and

music teacher. A former pupil of Professor Thomán, he studied musical composition under Kodály and Leó Weiner. Frequently played Bartók in his recital programmes. Lives in Switzerland.

Lajos Kentner (b. 1905). Pianist. Studied at the Budapest Academy of Music under Arnold Székely, Herzfeld, Kodály, Weiner and Koessler. Bartók entrusted him with the first performance of his 2nd Piano Concerto in Budapest in 1933. Lives in England.

Sándor Veress (b. 1907, Kolozsvár). Hungarian composer of note, pianist, folklorist and teacher. A former pupil of Kodály. Has lived in Switzerland since 1949; was head of the Dept. of Composition at Berne Conservatory. Professor at the University of Berne since March, 1968 (*Vollamtlicher Extraordinarius für Musikwissenschaft*).

Mahmud Raghib Gazimihâl (b. 1900, Istanbul). Turkish music research scholar. Lecturer on musical theory and musical history at Ankara State Conservatory. Worked in Istanbul in the 1920s and 1930s. Turkish contributor to *Zenei Lexikon* (Encyclopaedia of Music) edited by Bence Szabolcsi and Aladár Tóth (Budapest 1930–31, 1935).

Published from the original by courtesy of the addressee.

See also Nos. 192 and 194.

Addressed to:
'M. le Prof. Dr. László Rásonyi
Ankara Demirtepe, Akbay-sok. 10.
Törökország (Turquie)'

186 (December 23rd, 1935)
(Cf. Nos. 175, 177 and 181)

187 (December 29th, 1935)
Letters III/409–410

Kisfaludy Society. The most important literary society in Hungary before the Second World War. Conservative in character; in 1936 celebrated the 100th anniversary of its foundation.

Every six years the Society awarded prizes from its own funds for works chosen from the six departments of creative activity (literature, painting, dramatic art, sculpture, architecture and music). These were called Greguss Prizes, after Ágost Greguss, literary aesthete, founder of this prize fund.

The Music prize in 1917 was awarded to Jenő Hubay (for his *Symphony*); in 1923, to Árpád Szendy (*Helicon Suite*); and in 1929, to Ernő Dohnányi (*Ruralia Hungarica*).

Viktor Papp, music critic, in his 1935 annual report to the Greguss Committee, recommended Bartók's 1st Suite for large orchestra for the prize.

As Bence Szabolcsi tells us, Papp was acting in good faith in making his infelicitous recommendation: he was anxious to find some means of securing the prize for Bartók; he knew that the society was too conservative to accept a new work and considered it more prudent to suggest the 1st Suite.

The letter appeared in print for the first time in the January 3rd, 1936 issue of *Népszava*, the Social Democrats' daily newspaper. The music editor was Sándor Jemnitz, and so no doubt he was responsible for its publication.

188 (January 13th, 1936)
(Cf. Nos. 165–167, 169, 170, 172, 183 and 184)

The letter is addressed to *Edward Clark*, conductor (May 10th, 1888, Newcastle-upon-Tyne—May 5th, 1962), whose name is associated with the first performance in Britain of Bartók's 1st Piano Concerto (October 10th, 1927).

189 (January 16th, 1936)
(Cf. Nos. 165–167, 169, 170, 172, 183, 184 and 188)

190 (February 3rd, 1936)
Letters III/410–411

On February 3rd, 1936, Bartók gave an inaugural lecture at the Hungarian Academy of Sciences. The subject of his lecture was Franz Liszt. He was asked by the Secretariat of the Academy to write a *résumé* of his lecture for the daily press, which, however, was not printed by any of the Budapest dailies.

Bartók's manuscript has been obtained for publication from the Hungarian Academy of Sciences. Information furnished by Dr. Pál Gergely.

191 (February 16th, 1936) Published in *Documenta Bartókiana*, Vol. III, ed. by D. Dille, Budapest, 1968, Akadémiai Kiadó, p. 285. (Cf. Nos. 129 and 164.)

Bartók is referring to: *Pet hrvatske pjesme* (*Five Slavian Melodies*) for voice and piano, op. 36 (1934–5, Siegendorf, Paris).

For the tunes mentioned in the letter (see pp. 248–9). By courtesy of Professor Jenő Takács, of Cincinnati, 1961.

Addressed to:

'Jenő Takács, 22, rue Aboul Sebaa, le Caire, Egypt.'

192 (April 16th, 1936)
Letters III/411–412

'*Halk Evi*' or 'Halkevi' = People's House or House of Culture. As the addressee kindly informs us, there were at the time some 350 such houses throughout Turkey, the largest and most important being the one in Ankara.

The programme, so far as the addressee remembers, included Kodály's *Dances of Marosszék* and one of Liszt's Rhapsodies.

193 (July 14th, 1936) German original in Letters IV/168

Brigitte Schiffer-Oelsner. Composer and folklorist. Studied musical composition under Heinz Tiessen at the Berlin Conservatory 1930–35; pupil of Curt Sachs and E. M. von Hornbostel at Berlin University up to 1933. Her collection of Arab tunes was completed in 1933. Her Ph.D. thesis (*Die Oase Siwa und ihre Musik*, Berlin, 1935) she sent to Bartók.

The Hungarian pianist Lajos Hernádi, a former pupil of Bartók, obtained a photostat of the letter from the addressee during his concert tour of Egypt (1958).

194 (August 21st, 1936)
Letters III/413

The addressee was spending his summer vacation at Mátrafüred, Hungary.

The collection in question would seem to be the collection of Turkish folk tunes by the Hungarian Turkish scholar Ignác Kúnos (1860–1945).

195 (September 28th, 1936)
Letters III/413–414

Hugó Kelen (1888–1956). Composer, chorus leader. He tried to persuade Bartók to alter a couple of bars of the tenor part in *Cantata Profana,* which seemed impossible to sing; the singer E. Rösler had refused to sing the part, thereby jeopardizing the first performance of the work in Hungary.

Kelen, who was Rösler's singing-teacher, agreed to mediate and wrote to Bartók, asking him to change the bars, but Bartók refused. Later, however, after listening to Rösler's lengthy plea, the composer yielded and (in the singer's words) 'allowed himself to be talked into the alteration'. He produced from his pocket an altered version of the two bars which he had after all already prepared. It was with this alteration that the *Cantata Profana* was eventually performed for the first time in Hungary on November 9th, 1936.

Endre Rösler (1904–1963), tenor of the Hungarian State Opera, had preserved Bartók's variant of those two bars and made it available for publication as a supplement to the letter.

The letter has been published from the original handwritten copy, by courtesy of Mr. Hugó Kelen (1952).

Addressed to:
'Ngys. Kelen Hugó tanár úrnak, Budapest, II. Margit u. 9. sz.'

196 (November 15th, 1936)
Letters III/314

Sándor Albrecht (b. August 12nd, 1885, Arad; d. July 30th, 1958, Bratislava). Composer, organist and conductor. Studied at the Budapest Academy of Music as a pupil of Thomán, Koessler and Bartók. From 1908 onwards organist, then conductor, at Pozsony Cathedral. Under Bartók he studied the last year of the piano course in the schoolyear 1907–8; but his friendship with Bartók dates back to Bartók's early years in Pozsony, and they continued to correspond until the late 'thirties.

The majority of Bartók's letters to S. Albrecht were destroyed during the Second World War; the 22 surviving letters are the longest and most important items of the Slovakian material of Letters III.

Published from a photostat obtained with the help of Dr. Ladislav Burlas.

See also No. 206.

Addressed to:
'Ngys. Albrecht Sándor
Igazgató úrnak, Bratislava,
Schiffgasse 12., Tchécoslovaquie.'

197 (November 18th, 1936)
Letters III/209 (Cf. Nos 78, 81, 82, 84, 86, 99, 102–106,

113, 128 and 163). Reproduced in facsimile in *Bartók Béla, a népdalkutató* (Béla Bartók, the Folklorist) by Júlia Szegő, Bucharest, 1956, inset plate to pp. 288–289.

Bartók's last known lines written to Buşiţia. Only a fragment of the picture postcard has survived. The entire address is missing, as well as a few sentences from the text.

198 (January 2nd, 1937) French original unpublished. German translation in Letters IV/170–171

Ahmed Adnan Saygin (b. 1907, Ismir). Until 1941–42 he wrote his name Saygĭn, later Saygun. Turkish composer and folklorist. Professor of composition at the Ankara State Conservatory. One of the party which accompanied Bartók on his collecting tour in Turkey. His reminiscences ('Bartók in Turkey') appeared in *The Musical Quarterly*, Vol. XXXVII, No. 1 (January, 1951), p. 5 ff.

On January 11th, 1937, Bartók gave a talk on Radio Budapest about his folk-song collecting tour in Turkey. His talk was illustrated with songs sung by the distinguished singer the late Mihály Székely, with Tibor Polgár at the piano; Miklós B. Fehér played the violin.

In his letter Bartók refers to the Adana earthquake.

The book which Bartók was 'eagerly awaiting' was probably an offprint of the French version (*Études sur l'Europe Centre-Orientale*, No. 5, Budapest, 1937) of *Népzenénk és a szomszéd népek népzenéje* (The Folk Music of Hungary and of the Neighbouring Peoples). (*Archivum Europae Centro-Orientalis*, Budapest, 1936, pp. 197–232 and I–XXXII.)

Published from the original by courtesy of the addressee.

See also Nos. 199 and 203.

Addressed to:
'Bay Ahmed Adnan Saygĭn, Conservatoire de Musique, Istanbul, Turquie.'

199 (January 14th, 1937) (Cf. No. 198) German translation in Letters IV/172

In the second half of January, 1937, Bartók went on a concert tour of Switzerland, Holland, France, Belgium and England that lasted nearly a month.

200 (February 3rd, 1937) Hungarian translation: Letters II/121–122. German original in Letters IV/172–173

Frau Professor Dr. Oscar Müller-Widmann, who died in 1965, was a Basle admirer with whom Bartók often stayed during his European tours in the second half of the 1930s. For an account of how Frau Müller-Widmann met Bartók, see Willi Reich: *Béla Bartók — Eigene Schriften und Erinnerungen der Freunde* (Benno Schwabe & Co. Verlag, Basel/Stuttgart, 1958), pp. 137–138.

Dates of the performances mentioned in the letter (all in 1937):

January 28th—Radio Hilversum

January 29th—Lecture in Amsterdam

January 30th—Radio Paris

February 3rd—2nd Piano Concerto, Bruxelles

. . . Performances in London

February 11th—Radio Hilversum

Zoltán Székely (b. Dec. 8th, 1903, Kocs). Hungarian violinist and composer. Studied at the Budapest Academy of Music, under Hubay and Kodály. From 1922 lived in Holland; from 1948, in the U.S.A. Founder and leader of the Hungarian String Quartet. Prepared a transcription for violin and piano of Bartók's *Rumanian Folk Dances*, composed for the piano. Bartók's 2nd Rhapsody, written in 1928 (and revised in 1944), for violin and piano, and for violin and orchestra, as well as his Violin Concerto (1937–8), were dedicated to him.

Wladimir Vogel (b. 1896, Moscow). Swiss composer. Pupil of Busoni. A friend of the Müllers.

Conrad Beck (b. 1901). Distinguished Swiss composer. An enthusiastic mountaineer.

Typewritten copies of Bartók's 29 letters to Mrs. Müller-Widmann have been obtained, with the addressee's consent, and with the intention of assisting Bartók research in Hungary, from Dr. Ottó Gombosi (Basle, 1949). 23 of these letters were translated into Hungarian and printed in Letters II. Six letters appear, in their original German version, in Letters IV.

See also Nos. 201, 209, 211, 212, 220 and 222.

201 (May 24th, 1937)
Letters II/122–124
and IV/173–175 (Cf. No. 200)

Bartók co-operated in the inaugural concert, on May 7th, 1937, of the 'Singing Youth' movement, by playing 11 of the easier, and 5 of the more difficult pieces from the *Mikrokosmos* cycle. Bartók's appearance on that occasion was a notable event, for it was the first time for nearly eight years that he had played his own works at a concert in Budapest.

Of Bartók's 27 new choral pieces, 19 were sung on this occasion by five different school choirs. (One of these was from a school in the suburbs—the Liget Utca Boys' School Choir, conducted by László Preisinger [Perényi]; their programme included Nos. 3, 4, 13 and 6 of the 27 children's choruses.)

202 (May 26th, 1937) Unpublished. Original in Hungarian

English translation from the original, kept in the archives of Sárospatak College. By courtesy of Dr. Kálmán Újszászy.

Typewritten letter bearing Bartók's signature.

203 (June 20th, 1937)
(Cf. Nos. 198 and 199) German translation in Letters IV/175–178

István Count Zichy (1879–1951). Painter. Student of Hungarian pre-history. From 1934 until 1944 he was the director of the Museum of History, Budapest.

Addressed to: '*M. le Prof. Achmed Adnan Saygĭn, 127 Mühürdar caddesi, Kadĭköy, Istanbul, Turquie.*' (The envelope bears an Austrian postage stamp; readable part of rubber-stamp torn off. Place where the letter was registered is stated on the registration receipt: Heiligenblut.)

204 (September 14th, 1937) Hungarian original published in 'Bartók Béla levele a magyar népzenegyűjtemény kiadási munkálatairól' (Letter from Béla Bartók Concerning the Publication of the Hungarian Folk-Music Collection), *Új Zenei Szemle*, Vol. VI, No. 11 (November, 1955), pp. 7–8, edited by István Szelényi).

Géza Voinovich (1877–1952). Aesthete and literary historian. Author of dramas on themes derived from Hungarian history.

In September, 1937, the Hungarian Academy of Sciences decided to seek financial support from the Ministry of Religious Affairs and Education for a projected edition of the folk-music material collected by Bartók and Kodály, whose preparatory work had been going on for years. (Cf. Notes No. 175 and 180.) It was about this project that Voinovich had asked to be informed. Although, in his reply, the Minister of Education admitted the importance of the project, he ruled that the matter be shelved, 'since, in the appropriations of the 1938–9 budget, no fund has been provided for subsidizing the efforts of the Academy of Sciences to preserve our folk-songs.'

The volumes *A Magyar Népzene Tára* (*Corpus Musicae Popularis Hungaricae*) have only been published since 1951, and six volumes have appeared to date (I: *Children's Games;* II: *Great Days;* IIIA–IIIB: *Wedding Songs;* IV: *Pairing Songs;* V: *Dirges*). The publication was in the hands of Zoltán Kodály until his death on March 6th, 1967. He was relying on preparatory work done jointly by Bartók and himself.

205 (January 25th, 1938) Unpublished

Paul Collaer (b. 1891, Boom). Belgian conductor. Writer on music, ethno-musicologist, one of the most widely known authorities on modern music.

On January 30th, 1938, a programme of Bartók's works was broadcast by Radio Bruxelles, Station No. 2, with Bartók himself playing *Suite* op. 14, *Night Music, Preludio all'Ungherese;* he also accompanied Mlle Martin-Metten who sang eight songs from *20 Hungarian Folk-Songs* (1929). The programme also included his 2nd Sonata for violin and piano.

Published from a photostat, by courtesy of the Hungarian Musicians' Association.

See also No. 280.

Addressed to: 'M. Collaer, 67 Av. E. Béco, Ixelles, Bruxelles, Belgium.'

206 (January 31st, 1938)
Letters III/317 (Cf. No. 196)

'Sl. Mat.' Concerning the Matica Slovenská, see Notes No. 138 and 168.

'Tromba', *'corno'*. References to certain sums of money, royalties, etc., which Bartók had put aside in Pozsony in case he had to repurchase the manuscript of his collection of Slovak folk-songs.

Bartók's Sonata for two pianos and percussion was performed by himself and Mrs. Bartók at Basle, on the occasion of the 10th anniversary of the Basle branch of the International Society for Contemporary Music. Then followed his tour of Holland and Britain. His performance on Radio Luxembourg took place on January 29th, 1938: he played with the Radio Orchestra in a performance of his 2nd Piano Concerto. The appearance in Brussels, of which he writes in the preceding letter (No. 205), took place towards the end of his tour.

207 (January 31st, 1938) English original unpublished. Hungarian translation: Letters II/127–128; German translation in Letters IV/180–181

Wilhelmine Creel (Mrs. Harold E. Driver). U.S. pianist and Oriental philologist, one of the most notable of Bartók's pupils. Studied under Bartók in Budapest, March, 1936, to June, 1937. She had studied earlier in Chicago where she had taken a degree of 'Master of Music' at the American Conservatory of Music (her piano teacher had been Mrs. Louise Robyn, and she had studied musical composition under Adolf Weiding). Went to live in Peking in 1932 to study Chinese language and philosophy. From China she had come directly to Hungary to study the piano under Bartók.

From August, 1937, to June, 1940—at the time, that is, when this letter was written—she was living in Tokyo and was one of the first pianists to present many of Bartók's piano pieces in Japan.

Miss Creel is an untiring propagator of Bartók's works in the United States, and one of his compositions is usually included in her frequent piano recitals. From 1940 to 1950, she taught at Washington University, Seattle. Since then she has been living in Bloomington and teaches at Indiana University.

Published from a photostat of the English original. By courtesy of Mrs. Harold E. Driver. (1949)

See also Nos. 230, 256, 260, 266, 270, 281 and 282, and the full Washington University correspondence of 30 letters (Nos. 235–238, 240–254, 257, 259, 261–264, 268–269, 271–272 and 277).

208 (March 27th, 1938) Reproduced in facsimile in Károly Kristóf's *Beszélgetések Bartók Bélával* (Talks with Béla Bartók), Budapest, 1957, inset plate to pp. 144–145.

In the October 10th, 1937, number of the daily paper *Pesti Napló*, Bartók had explained why he refused to permit the Hungarian Radio to transmit his public performances to Germany and Italy. The reason, he wrote, 'is quite simple; namely,

I have never given broadcast performances for the radio networks of either Italy or the Third *Reich;* what is more, I have never even been asked by those two broadcasting corporations to perform directly for them. Under the circumstances, I thought it would be unfair to myself to allow the Hungarian Radio to offer these two broadcasting corporations my recital performances on Radio Budapest as a sort of gift . . .'

In March, 1938, certain newspapers returned to the theme and even added that Bartók had written to the German authorities on the subject.

This new development induced Bartók to make a statement for the daily *Az Est.*

Typewritten letter bearing Bartók's signature.

209 (April 13th, 1938)
(Cf. Nos. 200 and 201) Letters II/130–133 and IV/182–184

U.E. = Universal Edition, Viennese publishers of Bartók's music from the summer of 1918 onwards.

A.K.M. = Gesellschaft der *A*utoren, *K*omponisten and *M*usikverleger. See No. 129.

Stagma. Name of the copyright office of Nazi Germany.

Paul Sacher (b. 1906). Director of the Basle Chamber Orchestra, noted interpreter of modern orchestral compositions. We are indebted to him for three of Bartók's major works which he commissioned: Music for Strings, Percussion and Celesta (1936); Sonata for two pianos and percussion (1937) and Divertimento for string orchestra (1939). For more details see Willi Schuh: 'Bartóks Basler Auftragswerke', *Musik der Zeit* (1954), No. 9, pp. 45–48, with passages from Bartók's letters to Paul Sacher.

210 (May, 1938) Reproduced in facsimile in István Lakatos: 'Ismeretlen Bartók-kézjegy' (An Unknown Note of Bartók), *Utunk* (Kolozsvár), Vol. XI. No. 40 (October 5th, 1956)

Ákos Weress. Engineer. A music-lover who collected in his keepsake album the three most important wishes of musicians, writers and other artists. Bartók recorded his own three wishes on page 314 of Weress's album.

211 (May 29th, 1938)
(Cf. Nos. 200, 201 and 209) Letters II/134–135 and IV/185–186

On May 21st, 1938, Bartók began to send his most important music MSS. to Mrs. Müller-Widmann, so that they would be in a safer place, as he feared possible unrest and upheaval in Hungary. In each of his letters he would state which of his MSS. he had posted.

The second part of the letter discusses political oppression in Rumania: at the time, Rumanian chauvinists, with the Iron Guard movement at their head, were pursuing a policy of national hatred directed against the Hungarian minority.

212 (October 9th, 1938)
(Cf. Nos. 200, 201, 209 and 211) Letters II/138–140 and IV/186–188

'*Ch.*' = Chamberlain.
'*H.*' = Hitler.
'*I have finished the violin Concerto*'. Bartók later recorded the date of completion at the end of the score as December 31st, 1938.

'*Two pieces for Szigeti*'. *Contrasts* for clarinet, violin and piano. According to the date on the score, it was completed on September 24th, 1938. In reality, probably only the two dances (*Recruiting Dance, Fast Dance*) were completed. For it was in this two-movement form that the work was performed in New York on January 9th, 1939 (by József Szigeti, Benny Goodman and Endre Petri). The title of the middle movement is *Relaxation*.

213 (October 24th, 1938)
Letters III/433

In this letter, written to Zoltán Székely's wife (see Note No. 200), Bartók congratulated them on the birth of a son.

A typewritten copy of the letter has been obtained from Professor H. Stevens, Los Angeles (1952).

214 (January 12th, 1939)
Letters III/438

Hans Priegnitz (b. Oct. 20th, 1913, Berlin). German pianist. As a demonstration against the Hitlerite régime, P. decided to play some contemporary work on the German *Reich* Radio. This project was sympathetically received by the conductor Karl List. Priegnitz understood that Bartók had written a 3rd Piano Concerto, and so he wrote asking for the MS. (Bartók did write a 3rd Piano Concerto—in 1945! Priegnitz's information was based on an inaccurate statement in a German musical review.)

'*. . . such "degenerate" music . . .*' This refers to a Nazi exhibition under the same title where, Bartók learnt with indignation, his works were not displayed—evidently out of political tact towards the pro-Nazi Hungarian government.

Typewritten letter bearing Bartók's signature.

Published from a photostat made by the addressee. By courtesy of Professor Bence Szabolcsi.

215 (January 28th, 1939) Unpublished. Original in Hungarian and English as well.
(Cf. Nos. 138 and 168)

Early in 1935, the Matica Slovenská, by taking legal proceedings, managed to regain possession of the MS. of Bartók's collection of Slovak folk music from Ivan Ballo. Even so, the task of preparing it for the press went on as slowly as before and eventually came to a halt, with only the first 75 pages corrected. On August 20th, 1937, Bartók wrote to Albrecht: '. . . Those damned people still are doing nothing at all. In fact they are displaying the most outrageous indifference, so that now I'll have to assert my rights and get the manuscript back, even if I have to sue them ...' (Letters III/315) The mounting tension accompanying the deteriorating political situation was not favourable to the projected edition. International relations went rapidly from bad to worse. From one of Bartók's letters of a later date (No. 206), we learn that the Czechoslovak authorities did not permit him to give the recital scheduled to take place at Bratislava. The constant menace of the Third *Reich* strengthened national feeling in the little states of Central and Eastern Europe, and in the resulting atmosphere of mistrust, scientific cooperation became an impossibility. Such were the circumstances culminating in Bartók's embittered letter which, regrettably, brought his connection with the Matica Slovenská to an end.

Musicologists in present-day Slovakia are making amends for the sins committed there in the past in the name of nationalism and are now publishing Bartók's collection of Slovakian folk-songs from the MS. which has remained there. The first volume—containing 788 tunes—of a projected three-volume edition has already appeared. (Béla Bartók: *Slovenské l'udové piesne,* Vol. I. Vydavatel'stvo Slovenskej Akadémie Vied, Bratislava, 1959. Preface by Oskár Elschek.)

This letter is typewritten, in Hungarian followed by an English version. Both versions were signed by Bartók. It should be noted that Bartók's correspondence of a legal nature at that time was typed by Dr. István Török.

216 (February 8th, 1939) English original unpublished. German translation in Letters IV/190–191

Dorothy Parrish. American pianist. She studied at the Academy of Music (Budapest) from 1933 to 1935 as a government exchange student, under the auspices of the International Institute of Education. From 1935 to 1937 she took private piano lessons from Bartók. Back in the United States, she married Dr. Anthony Domonkos, a Hungarian physician—hence the address Mrs. Dorothy Parrish Domonkos, on Bartók's later letters to her. She lives in New York and performs Bartók at her recitals.

'*Sonata for two pianos and percussion*' was first performed in Europe as follows:

(1938)	
January 16th	Basle
June 11th	Luxembourg
June 20th	London
October 31st	Budapest
November 15th	Amsterdam
November 20th	Brussels
(1939)	
February 17th	Zurich
February 27th, March 6th	Paris
April 8th	Venice

Typewritten letter bearing Bartók's signature. Published from a photostat of the English original.

See also Nos. 220, 223, 226, 228, 229 and 288.

217 (May 19th, 1939) French original unpublished. Hungarian translation: Letter II/144

Denijs Dille (b. Feb. 21st, 1904, Aarschot). Belgian musicologist and Bartók scholar. Author of two books on Bartók, written in Flemish (Brussels, 1939 and 1947, respectively). In his second book there is a document in facsimile relating to this letter: the first four bars of the 1st movement of *Contrasts*, written out in Bartók's hand, with a dedication to Dille: *À M. Denijs Dille avec toutes mes sympathies. Béla Bartók, Budapest, le 19 Mai 1939.* Until the summer of 1961, D. D. was Professor of French Language and Literature in Antwerp. Chief Assistant in charge of the Bartók Archives in Budapest since its foundation in September, 1961.

Published from a photostat of the handwritten original, by courtesy of the addressee (Antwerp, 1949).

Addressed to: 'M. Denijs Dille, Minderbroederstraat 2/2, Antwerpen, Belgium'

218 (June 24th, 1939) Hungarian original published by László Sándor: 'Két ismeretlen ukrán vonatkozású Bartók levél' (Two Unknown Letters of Bartók Referring to the Ukraine), *Irodalmi Újság*, Vol. VII, No. 33 (August 18th, 1956), p. 5.

Dezső Zádor (b. Oct. 20th, 1912, Ushgorod [Ungvár]). Composer, folk-song collector and pianist from Carpatho-Ukraine. 1943: Professor at Cluj Conservatory; 1945–1949: Principal of Ushgorod Music School; since 1952: Arts Director of the Carpatho-Ukrainian Regional Philharmonic Society and the local Folk-song Choir. In the weeks following the Vienna Arbitration of 1938, D. Z. sent his collection of Ukrainian folk-songs to Budapest.

Molnár. Dr. Imre Molnár (b. 1888). Writer on music, singer and singing teacher. Professor at the Budapest Conservatory from 1928 onwards. D. Zádor's collection first came into his possession through Endre Zádor, one of his pupils and younger brother of the addressee. As he could not make use of the material at the Conservatory, he handed it over to Bartók as a contribution to his material on East European folklore.

The letter was dictated by Bartók to his wife and the final copy signed by him.

Published from the original, by courtesy of László Sándor (Ushgorod [Ungvár], 1956).

See also No. 221.

Addressed to: 'Nagyságos Zádor Dezső úrnak, Ungvár, Drugeth tér 13.'

219 (August 18th, 1939) Letters I/132–133

Béla Bartók, Jr. (b. Aug. 22nd, 1910). Bartók's first-born son. Engineer, technological adviser to the Hungarian State Railways (Budapest).

'Szőllős' = Szőllőspuszta, a farmstead near Orosháza.

The date written beside the last bar of the score of *Divertimento* is the same as that given in the letter: Saanen, August 2nd–17th, 1939.

The 6th String Quartet had indeed been completed (Saanen–Budapest, August–November, 1939), but it was dedicated to the Kolisch Quartet.

At *Scheveningen,* near The Hague, on June 30th, 1939, Bartók played the 2nd Piano Concerto, with The Hague Orchestra conducted by Carl Schuricht.

Published from the handwritten original, by courtesy of the addressee.

See also Nos. 227, 231, 232, 234, 239 and 255.

Addressed to: 'Ifj. Bartók Béla mérnök úrnak, Orosháza, Szőllőspuszta, László major.'

220 (January 17th, 1940)
(Cf. No. 216) Letters IV/195–196

On April 15th and 16th, 1940, at Huntingdon, Pa., in response to an invitation from Huntingdon Juniata College, Bartók gave a recital and lecture.

Andrew Schulhof. Representative of Bartók and of Boosey & Hawkes (the new publishers of Bartók's works). His name appears—both as addressee and as writer—in the Washington University's batch of 30 letters.

221 (February 3rd, 1940)
(Cf. No. 218) (Also reproduced in facsimile)

László Sándor writes: 'Those few lines in which he replies to Zádor's complaint about Ukrainian orthography are most typical of Bartók's political views. As is well known, following the Vienna Arbitration, the Hungarian government tried by every means to separate the Carpatho-Ukrainians from the eastern Ukrainians – even by means of their orthography. It introduced the so-called Harajda Hungarian. Russian orthography which was totally different from the one accepted and current in Soviet Ukraine.' (Ushgorod [Ungvár], 1956.)

222 (April 2nd, 1940)
(Cf. Nos. 200, 201, 209, 211 and 212) Letters II/149–150 and IV/197–198

Bartók's mother had died on December 19th, 1939.

On April 13th, 1940, in Washington, Bartók and József Szigeti played Bartók's 1st Rhapsody and 2nd Sonata at one concert of the Elizabeth Sprague-Coolidge Festival. He took part in several other concerts, the last one on May 1st, 1940, in New York, at the Bartók Concert sponsored by Columbia University.

223 (May 17th, 1940)
(Cf. Nos. 216 and 220) Letters IV/198–199

224 (July 14th, 1940)
Letters I/134. Part of the letter reproduced in facsimile: *Magyar Kórus,* Vol. XV, No. 2 (December, 1945), p. 1141

Gyula Kertész (1900–1967). Church choir conductor. Composer and collector of folk-songs. A pioneer of the choral movement in Hungary. Co-editor (with Lajos Bárdos) of *Magyar Kórus* (from 1931 onwards) and (with György Kerényi) of *Énekszó* (from 1933 onwards). Responsible for the publication of Bartók's choral works (*Székely Songs* for male chorus [1932]; *27 Choruses* for 2 and 3-part children's or women's chorus [1935]; *From Olden Times* for 3-part male chorus [1935]).

Published from the handwritten original, by courtesy of the addressee.

225 (October 14th, 1940)
(Cf. Nos. 200, 201, 209, 211, 212 and 222) Hungarian translation: Letters II/153–154; German original: *Béla Bartók. Eigene Schriften und Erinnerungen der Freunde*, by Willi Reich, Basle, 1958, pp. 65–66.

226 (November 30th, 1940)
(Cf. Nos. 216, 220 and 223) Letters IV/200

On January 25th–26th, 1940, in Pittsburgh, Bartók played his 2nd piano Concerto, with Fritz Reiner conducting.

In a letter dated October 27th, 1940, written from the Bermudas, Bartók tells his son, Béla Bartók, Jr., how his luggage came to be left behind:

'. . . We arrived at the Spanish frontier on the 16th in the morning. It was here that the trouble started. It turned out that that was as far as the motor-coach went. The customs officers intended to show no mercy. We were pressed for time because our train was leaving; I had forgotten my Spanish. They came up with the suggestion that I should register our luggage sealed, then it would pass the customs without being opened . . . It turned out 3 days later, at Badajoz, that they had sent the luggage by 'express goods' service . . . and we learned that there was no chance of express goods reaching the place for another 5 days! I found a customs officer who could speak French: I had to ask this man to take charge of our luggage. He would send it on to Lisbon, and from there it would go to New York on the next ship to sail. And so, well, we just continued our journey *without any luggage! ...*' (Letters I/135)

Bartók's luggage finally reached him on February 11th, 1941. (See No. 231.)

Mr. Barone = probably Prof. Gyula Baron, one of the executors of Bartók's will.

227 (December 24th, 1940)
Letters I/137–140

'a kind of Dean' = President Nicholas Murray Butler.

'a son of the Hungarian Plains' = Béla Bartók.

'a son of France' = Dr. Paul Hazard.

'an English scholar' = Sir Cecil Thomas Carr.

'a professor of the United States' = Dr. Karl T. Compton.

Oszkár Jászi (1875–1957). Sociologist, author. Pioneer of sociological writing in Hungary, and intellectual forerunner and chief theoretician of the bourgeois-democratic revolution of 1918. Following the débâcle of the revolutions, J. went into exile and lived in Austria until 1926 when he emigrated to the U.S.A.

228 (January 7th, 1941)
(Cf. Nos. 216, 220, 223 and 226) Letters IV/201–202

229 (January 15th, 1941)
(Cf. Nos. 216, 220, 223, 226 and 228) Letters IV/202

230 (February 1st, 1941)
(Cf. No. 207) Letters II/155–156

Edmond Meany. Hotel near Washington University, Seattle.

Mrs. Turner. Cornelia Turner, the Seattle representative of New York concert agencies.

Dr. Ottó Gombosi (1902–1955). Hungarian musicologist. After graduating from the Budapest Academy of Music, he went on to study at the University of Berlin, where he took a degree in Music in 1925. A contributor to numerous music reviews both in Hungary and abroad. Author of *Jacob Obrecht* (Leipzig, 1925); published the works of the 16th-century minstrels Bálint Bakfark and Thomas Stoltzer. Lived in the U.S.A. from 1940 onwards.

231 (February 11th–12th, 1941)
Letters I/140–142

Columbia University extended Bartók's commission to cover the whole of the following academic year (1941/42), and again for another half-year (the first half of the academic year 1942/43).

232 (April 2nd, 1941)
Letters I/142–143

'*a Harvard professor*' = Milman Parry (d. 1935). Professor of Classical Philology at Harvard University. In 1933 and 1934, accompanied by a student named Albert Lord, he went to Yugoslavia to study folk poetry in that country. They were excellently equipped and had been coached for the work by Dr. György Herzog, Columbia University's expert on folk music. Their collecting tour yielded more than 2,200 double-sided discs on which they had recorded songs sung by 90 singers. On a further 350 double-sided discs they had made another 300 recordings of various types of song—some in Turkish and Albanian—and a number of folk tunes performed on instruments. The collection also included two epic poems which rival the Odyssey for sheer length (13,000 odd and 12,000 lines, respectively). Most of the songs and tunes they collected—Serbo-Croatian epics—are survivals of popular customs several thousand years old and may possibly be traced back to Antiquity, to the age of the Homeric epics.

Funds from the Ditson Foundation enabled Bartók to take an appointment as Visiting Associate in Music at Columbia University, where he then studied this collection for two years (1941 and 1942). Contributions from a number of admirers made it possible for him to stay there for another half-year, preparing the material for publication.

The collection was published only after Bartók's death. (*Serbo-Croatian Folk-Songs*, Columbia University Press, New York, 1951.)

233 (April 18th, 1941) English original unpublished. Hungarian translation in Letters II/157–158.

Douglas Stuart Moore (b. Aug. 10th, 1893, Cutchogue, N.Y.). Composer and writer on music. Executive Officer of the Columbia University Music Department.

'*... the long Turkish occupation ...*' In 1389, following the Battle of Kossovo Plain, Serbia was reduced to the status of a feudal province of the Ottoman empire. It regained its independence only in the 19th century. The Turkish garrisons were withdrawn from the country in 1867. The Bulgarians, too, were subjected to more than four and a half centuries of Turkish occupation. — The Turkish occupation of Hungary is counted from 1526 (when the national army of Hungary was annihilated in a battle near Mohács) to 1686, the year Budavár, the capital of the country, was recaptured from the Turks.

Published from a typewritten copy, by courtesy of the addressee (1950).

234 (May 7th, 1941)
Letters I/143–144

Bartók was 60 years old on March 25th, 1941.

235 (May 22nd, 1941)
Letters III/454 English original (1)

Carl Paige Wood (b. Dec. 20th, 1885; d. Jan. 16th, 1947). Professor at the Washington University, Seattle. Taught organ, theory and composition. Executive Officer of the Music Department.

C. P. Wood wanted to persuade Bartók to accept a post on the staff of the University. Visiting scholars of note were usually given appointments for three, six or nine months at the University. Bartók was invited for a complete year, but since he was already working at Columbia University and sometime later was in any case too unwell to undertake long journeys, the offer was repeated for three consecutive years. In happier circumstances C. P. Wood had fully intended that Bartók's one-year assignment would be followed by the offer of a permanent appointment to a professorship.

(Information received from Mrs. Harold E. Driver.)

The Washington University material is listed (1–30) in Note No. 207.

236 (May 29th, 1941)
Letters III/456 English original (2)

Hans Walter Heinsheimer (b. Sept. 25th, 1900, Karlsruhe). Music aesthete. Representative of the firm Boosey & Hawkes (deputy for Andrew Schulhof). In his book *Fanfare for 2 Pigeons* (New York, 1952), he pays tribute to Bartók in a chapter ('Cortège', pp. 104–123).

237 (June 9th, 1941) Hungarian translation: Letters II/159. English original: Letters III/458 (3) [Copy]

238 (June 19th, 1941) Letters III/460 English original (4)

Dr. Padelford. Chairman of the Graduate Council in charge of the Walker-Ames Appointments, who had the final voice in the awarding of grants.

239 (June 20th, 1941) Letters I/145–147

240 (June 24th, 1941) Letters III/460 English original (5)

241 (July Ist, 1941) Letters III/462 English original (6)

Lee Paul Sieg. President of Washington University 1934–1946.

242 (August 6th, 1941) Letters III/462 English original (7)

243 (August 20th, 1941) Letters III/464 English original (8)

244 (August 21st, 1941) Letters III/464 English original (9)

245 (August 26th, 1941) Hungarian translation: Letters II/162–163 English original: Letters III/466, 468 (10)

246 (September 8th, 1941) Hungarian translation: Letters II/163–164 English original: Letters III/468 (11) [Copy]

247 (September 20th, 1941) Letters III/470 English original (12)

248 (September 22nd, 1941) Letters III/470 English original (13)

249 (September 25th, 1941) Letters III/472 English original (14)

250 (October 1st, 1941) Letters III/472, 474 English original (15)

251 (October 3rd, 1941) Letters III/476 English original (16) *ad* 251 (16): memorandum, L. P. Sieg to C. P. Wood.

252 (October 6th, 1941) Letters III/476 English original (17)

253 (October 8th, 1941) Hungarian translation: Letters II/164–165 English original: Letters III/478 (18)

254 (October 15th, 1941) Letters III/478 English original (19)

255 (October 17th, 1941) Letters I/149–150

'*. . . and we've had a cable from Hajnal . . .*' Dr. Tibor Hajnal, Chief Physician of 'Tábor' Deaconess Sanatorium, Budapest, specialist on diseases of the lung and other internal diseases, was the guardian of Bartók's second son, Péter.

256 (October 17th, 1941) (Cf. Nos. 207 and 230) Letters II/165–166

Mrs. Beck. Broussais Beck (Eleanor Nordhoff Beck) was harpist in the Seattle Symphony Orchestra and a patroness of the arts. She entertained Bartók on several occasions.

257 (November 25th, 1941) Hungarian translation: Letters II/167 English original: Letters III/480 (20) (reproduced in facsimile).

During his stay in Seattle, probably on November 29th, Bartók had a long discussion with Professor Melville Jacobs of the Department of Anthropology in the Institute, who had collected the bulk of the Indian folk-music material in 1936–9.

258 (January 23rd, 1942) Unpublished

Mr. Henry Mishkin. Professor at Amherst University.

A typewritten copy of the letter has been obtained from Mr. János Neubauer, Amherst, Mass., 1958.

259 (February 28th, 1942) Hungarian translation: Letters II/168 English original: Letters III/482 (21)

260 (March 2nd, 1942) (Cf. Nos. 207, 230 and 256) Letters II/169–170

261 (March 4th, 1942) Letters III/482 English original (22)

262 (March 16th, 1942) Letters III/484 English original (23)

263 (April 24th, 1942) Letters III/484 English original (24)

264 (July 7th, 1942) Hungarian translation: Letters II/171 English original: Letters III/486 (25) (reproduced in facsimile).

265 (October 7th, 1942) English original unpublished. Hungarian translation: Letters II/173

Yehudi Menuhin (b. Apr. 22nd, 1916, New York). World-famous violinist. Former pupil of Adolf Busch (Basle) and George Enescu (Paris); devoted interpreter of Bartók's works of violin. By commissioning Bartók to write for him a sonata for violin solo, he was able to assist the composer materially. Later he invited him to his home in California where, so he hoped, Bartók would be able to create more works—but the visit never materialized because of the grave nature of Bartók's illness.

Cf. Yehudi Menuhin: 'Bartók as I Knew Him'. *The Long Player*, Vol. II, No. 10 (October, 1953), pp. 28–29.

Published after a typewritten copy received from the addressee.

See also Nos. 274, 283 and 284.

266 (December 31st, 1942) (Cf. Nos. 207, 230, 256 and 260) Letters II/173–175

'Cross Creek'. Title of a novel by Marjorie Kinnan Rawling.

Bartók's vast collection of Rumanian folk music: *Román népzene* (Rumanian Folk Music), Vols. I–III, ed. by Benjamin Suchoff, published in 1967, The Hague, Martinus Nijhoff. (Vols. I–II contain 2,555 tunes; Vol. III contains words of 1,752 tunes.)

Bartók's article ('Parry Collection of Yugoslav Folk Music') appeared in *The New York Times*, June 28th, 1942.

'... *defense work* ...' The addressee taught Japanese to soldiers at the university.

267 (May 23rd, 1943) Letters III/489 (incomplete)

Dr. Serge Koussevitzky (1874–1951). Conductor. Commissioned Bartók, then gravely ill and deeply depressed, to write a piece of orchestral music in memory of his wife, the late Natalie Koussevitzky. After years of dormancy, Bartók's creative ambition was aroused, and he composed the first of his three major works written in America—the Concerto for orchestra (written between August 15th and October 8th, 1943).

Published from a typewritten copy of the original letter.

Submitted by Ida Kenton (d. 1955), by courtesy of Mr. József Szigeti (1951).

268 (June 12th, 1943) Letters III/488 English original (26)

269 (June 30th, 1943) Hungarian translation: Letters II/178 English original: Letters III/490 (27) in facsimile. It is reproduced in facsimile in *Bartók Béla kézírása* (Béla Bartók's Handwriting), a collection of records containing 22 facsimile reproductions, edited by Bence Szabolcsi & Benjámin Rajeczky. Editio Musica, Budapest, 1961.

270 (August 17th, 1943) (Cf. Nos. 207, 230, 256, 260 and 266) Letters II/178–179 English original reproduced in facsimile in *The New Hungarian Quarterly* (Budapest), Vol. II, No. 1, inset to pp. 24–25.

Enclosed with this letter, Mrs. Harold E. Driver sent one instalment of the tuition fee which Bartók had refused to accept at the time when (1941) he was giving lessons to her. She proposed to go on sending these instalments each month.

'... *a 330[-year-]old translation* ...' The translation of *Don Quixote* which Bartók read could not have been so old, as only the first part of Cervantes's famous novel had been written by 1613: either it was a translation of only part of the book (possibly Part I), or it is a slip of the pen.

271 (October 23rd, 1943)
Letters III/492 English original (28)

Bartók's (2nd) Violin Concerto was played in New York on October 13th, 15th and 17th, 1943, by Tossy Spivakovsky, with Arthur Rodzinski conducting. Of these performances the one on the 17th fell on Sunday, therefore C. P. Wood must have heard that one.

272 (November 27th, 1943) Hungarian translation: Letters II/179–180 English original: Letters III/492, 494 (29)

273 (January 30th, 1944)
Letters II/183–185

Camille Saint-Saëns (1835–1921). French composer. Bartók met him on his tour of the Iberian peninsula. See Nos. 31 and 32.

274 (June 30th, 1944)
(Cf. No. 265) Hungarian translation: Letters II/185–187

The work referred to in this letter (one of the three major works composed in America) is the Sonata for solo violin completed in Asheville on March 14th, 1944.

The '*Alaska crew*' had been composed of members of the U.S. Air Force.

In a letter dated August 17th, 1949, Mr. Yehudi Menuhin kindly informs us that the concert took place at the local U.S. Air Force theatre at Kodiak, the Aleutians, before an audience of about 400, who responded to Bartók's sonata movement with unexpected enthusiasm and, after the concert, inquired about gramophone records of the work.

Published from a photostat of the letter, by courtesy of the addressee.

275 (August 22nd, 1944)
Letters II/188

Pál Kecskeméti (b. Oct. 31, 1901, Makó). Philosopher and sociologist. His wife (*née* Erzsébet Láng), a former pupil of Bartók (1908 to 1911), became an eminent cembalo player. Both Mr. and Mrs. Kecskeméti became closely associated with Bartók in 1943. For a long time they lived in the same apartment building and saw a great deal of one another.

Bartók's housing difficulties concerned a lease signed by Mrs. Bartók, which the landlord refused to recognize as valid. As the former tenant's lease had not yet expired, there was a fear that he might return to New York and claim the apartment. That was what actually happened. In the meantime, however, the Bartóks had succeeded in finding another apartment (of two rooms) in the same building.

'*... what there is to feel happy about ...*' Allied successes in France.

Dragan Plamenac (b. 1895). Yugoslav musicologist. Worked

for the Office of War Information Department. He was put in touch with Bartók by Pál Kecskeméti.

Published from a photostat of the letter, by courtesy of Mrs. P. Kecskeméti (d. 1959), 1948.

See also Nos. 276, 278, 286 and 287.

276 (September 1st, 1944) Letters II/189–190 (incomplete)

The solutions of *'how many legs has a crab?'* and of the musical *'quiz'* can be read in Letter No. 278.

See also No. 279.

277 (September 13th, 1944) Letters III/494 English original (30)

278 (September 29th, 1944) Letters II/190–192

'Frailty, thy name is woman!' Shakespeare: *Hamlet,* Act I, scene 2.

The music quoted in letter 276 is the famous *canzone* from Verdi's *Rigoletto.*

'The first product of my career as an English poet . . .' This is the English version of the words of *Cantata Profana.* There are only very few corrections, 'the insertions in red', in Bartók's translation.

279 (October 4th, 1944) Hungarian original (with first passage reproduced in facsimile) printed in *Új Zenei Szemle,* Vol. VI, No. 1 (January, 1955), pp. 42–43, edited by István Szelényi.

Ernő Balogh (b. 1897, Budapest). Hungarian-born pianist living in the U.S.A. Bartók's pupil at the Budapest Academy of Music from 1909 to 1913. Emigrated from Hungary after the First World War.

280 (October 24th, 1944) (Cf. No. 205)

Statement sent to liberated Radio Brussels.

281 (December 17th, 1944) (Cf. Nos. 207, 230, 256, 260, 266 and 270) Letters II/192–195

Bartók is writing on the back of pages from the English-language MS. of his collections of Rumanian folk-songs.

' . . . hemisemidemi-miracle . . .' Pun made by Bartók, meaning 'more or less a miracle'. Unhappily, even this did not prove to be true.

' . . . another translation . . .' The English-language version of the words of *Cantata Profana,* sent by Bartók to the Kecskemétis as well. See No. 278.

The two books, according to information kindly submitted by the addressee, were: *Winter Tales* by Isak Dinesen; *Four Quartets,* by T. S. Eliot.

282 (Christmas, 1944) (Cf. Nos. 207, 230, 256, 260, 266, 270 and 281) Letters II/195–196

ASCAP = *A*merican *S*ociety of *C*omposers, *A*uthors and *P*ublishers. The Society helped Bartók in various ways (by providing medical treatment, paying for holidays, etc.).

On Decembrr 7th, 1944, Mrs. Harold E. Driver gave a concert of the 'four B's' (i.e. her programme included works by *B*ach, *B*eethoven, *B*rahms and *B*artók).

Hans Guido Bülow (1830–1894). Pianist and conductor. An outstanding intellectual in the musical life at the period.

In January, 1945, Bartók revised his 85-piece piano series *For Children* (1908–9), rewriting several pieces and omitting a few. The revised series consists of 79 pieces.

283 (April 5th, 1945)
(Cf. Nos. 265 and 274) Hungarian translation: Letters II/196–197

Enclosed with this letter (pasted on to the letter-paper) was a cutting from an unidentified Hungarian-language U.S. newspaper with the following comment (written in Bartók's own hand): 'This will perhaps interest you.' The news item was as follows:

'Mr. Gábor Rejtő, the distinguished Hungarian cellist, will shortly terminate his concerts with the Gordon Quartet this year as he will be spending the summer months on Mr. Yehudi Menuhin's ranch in California. Mr. Rejtő also enjoyed the world-famous violinist's hospitality last year, and Mr. Menuhin has now repeated the invitation. As before, they will be playing a good deal of chamber-music at Menuhin's lovely home in California.'

From a typewritten copy obtained from the addressee. A photostat was made available later (also of Letter 284).

Addressed to: 'Mr. Yehudi Menuhin, 10 East 77 St., New York, N. Y.'

284 (June 6th, 1945)
(Cf. Nos. 265, 274 and 283) Hungarian translation: Letters II/197

Addressed to: 'Mr. Yehudi Menuhin, Box 32, Alma, Santa Clara County, California.'

285 (July 1st, 1945)
Letters I/150–151

Jenő Zádor (b. Nov. 5th, 1894, Bátaszék). Hungarian composer living in Hollywood. He made an attempt to help Bartók financially by giving him a commission. This was done through the conductor Schildkret who was planning to bring out a gramophone album entitled *Genesis,* the movements of which he commissioned celebrated composers to write (Stravinsky, Milhaud, Schoenberg and others). It was hoped that Bartók would write the opening number, but he turned the offer down and sent back the 250 dollars advance.

Published from a photostat by courtesy of the addressee.

Addressed to: 'Dr. Eugene Zador, 1433 N. Sycamore Ave, Hollywood 28, Cal.'

286 (July 7th 1945)
Letters II/197–198

This letter was written during Bartók's last stay at Saranac Lake where he composed his third (and last completed) major work written in America, the 3rd Piano Concerto.

'On July 2, I set out to emigrate ...' Originally Bartók had entered the U.S. on a visitor's visa. However, he decided that it would be better for him to get an immigrant's visa. In these circumstances he was required by law to leave the territory of the U.S. so that he would be able to receive the new visa abroad. For this purpose Bartók went to Montreal, Canada, a place relatively not far from Saranac Lake.

287 (August 11th, 1945)
Letters II/202

'Péter will be home again ...' Péter was expected to arrive home from military service in Panama.

Here Bartók is poking fun at the corrupted Hungarian spoken by Hungarians living in the U.S.A. (e.g. *magas ital* is a literal translation of 'tall drink').

'... tall snow ...' A playful reference to the authoress Ila Unger who wrote under the *nom de plume* of *Alba Nevis* (Latin for 'white snow'). She was very tall.

288 (August 30th, 1945)
(Cf. Nos. 216, 220, 223, 226, 228 and 229) Unpublished

289 (Date unknown) Hungarian original was published (along with facsimile reproduction) by Mária Keresztury, below the headline 'Egy Bartók-vers' (A Poem by Bartók), for the first time in *Magyar Nyelv,* Vol. LII, No. 1 (March, 1956); for the second time in *Új Zenei Szemle,* Vol. VII, No. 6 (June, 1956), pp. 16–19.

This fragment of a poem, in tone and style reminiscent of a Hungarian ballad, seems to indicate that Bartók had in mind a composition akin to *Cantata Profana.* Bartók was intending to enlarge the *Cantata Profana* (which is based on a Rumanian ballad) into a work in three movements by adding one composition based on a Hungarian, and one based on a Slovak ballad. This suggestion is made in a letter written in the early 1930s to Sándor Albrecht:

'As for the oratorio—in fact, it is no oratorio but a cantata, for double chorus, orchestra, and baritone and tenor solo (I wrote it back in 1930!); *c.* 18 minutes. The choral and solo parts are very difficult but not the orchestral parts. However, it is not going to be published (or performed) for the time being because I am planning to add to it 3 more pieces of similar length in such a way that, while they will be linked together by some connecting idea, it would be possible to perform each of the three separately. It will be 1 year or 2 at least before I can see whether there is any likelihood of my achieving this.' (Letters III/279)

The expression '3 more pieces of similar length' is a slip of the pen instead of saying '2 more pieces of similar length'—a lapse corrected in the concluding part of the sentence.

LIST OF CORRESPONDENTS

The numbers in brackets refer to the total number of letters written to the addressee.

Those in the second column refer to the numbering of the present volume.

No.	Correspondent	Letters	Numbers
1	Albrecht, Sándor	[2]	196, 206
2	'Az Est' (Editor)	[1]	208
3	Balogh, Ernő	[1]	279
4	Bartók, Béla, Jr.	[7]	219, 227, 231, 232, 234, 239, 255
5	Bartók, Béla, Mrs., mother (Paula Voit)	[35]	2–7, 11–15, 17, 18, 25, 27, 31–35, 37, 101, 108, 109, 116, 117, 119–121, 134–136, 150, 159, 160
6	Bartók, Béla, Mrs., wife (Ditta Pásztory)	[3]	142–144
7	Bartók, Péter	[1]	137
8	Batka, János	[2]	8, 9
9	'BBC' (London)	[10]	165–167, 169, 170, 172, 183, 184, 188, 189
10	Beu, Octavian	[2]	147, 152
11	Bîrlea, Ion	[1]	94
12	Bobál, Sámuel	[4]	87, 90, 95, 98
13	Brăiloiu, Constantin	[3]	130, 131, 154
14	Bușiția, János	[15]	78, 81, 82, 84, 86, 99, 102–106, 113, 128, 163, 197
15	Calvocoressi, Michael	[1]	145
–	Clark, Edward	[–]	(188) (189) See 'BBC' (London)
16	Collaer, Paul [Radio Brussels]	[2]	205, 280
17	Creel, Wilhelmine	[8]	207, 230, 256, 260, 266, 270, 281, 282
18	'Curriculum vitae' (Sopron)	[1]	28
19	Deák, Imre	[1]	180
20	Delius, Frederick	[6]	72–74, 76, 79, 80
21	Dent, Edward	[1]	125

22 Dietl, Lajos	[3]	19, 24, 36
23 Dille, Denijs	[1]	217
24 Fleischer, Antal	[2]	132, 133
— Foss, Hubert	[–]	(141) (157) (158) (174) (176) (182) See 'Oxford Univ. Press'
25 Freund, Etelka	[18]	38, 40, 44–46, 48–52, 54, 55, 57, 58, 60, 61, 71, 75
26 Freund, Irma	[1]	53
27 Ganz, Rudolf	[1]	62
28 Geyer, Stefi	[3]	39, 41, 42
29 Harsányi, Kálmán	[2]	21, 22
30 Hornbostel, Erich	[1]	83
31 d'Isoz, Kálmán	[1]	92
32 Jurkovics, Irmy	[1]	26
33 Katzarova, Raïna	[1]	179
34 Kecskeméti, Pál	[5]	275, 276, 278, 286, 287
35 Kelen, Hugó	[1]	195
36 Kertész, Gyula	[1]	224
37 Kiriac, Dumitru	[2]	70, 96
38 'Kisfaludy' (Soc.)	[1]	187
39 Kodály, Zoltán, Mrs., (Emma Gruber)	[1]	85
40 Kovács, Sándor	[7]	63–69
41 König, Péter	[1]	30
42 'Matica Slovenská'	[3]	138, 168, 215
43 Menuhin, Yehudi	[4]	265, 274, 283, 284
44 Mishkin, Henry	[1]	258
45 Moore, Douglas	[1]	233
46 Müller-Widmann, Mrs.,	[7]	200, 201, 209, 211, 212, 222, 225
47 'Newspapers' (Budapest)	[1]	190
48 'Oxford Univ. Press'	[9]	141, 153, 157, 158, 173, 174, 176, 178, 182
49 Parrish, Dorothy	[7]	216, 220, 223, 226, 228, 229, 288
50 'Philharm.' (Budapest)	[1]	100
51 Pollatsek, László	[1]	155
52 Poszvék, Lajos	[1]	29
53 Priegnitz, Hans	[1]	214
54 Radnai, Miklós	[1]	149
55 Rásonyi, László	[3]	185, 192, 194
56 Reiner, Frigyes	[1]	139
57 Révész, Géza	[5]	112, (114, 115,) 118, (122)
58 Rostal, Max	[1]	162
59 'Sárospatak' (Board of Gov.)	[1]	202

60 Saygïn, Adnan	[3]	198, 199, 203
61 Schiffer-Oelsner, Brigitta	[1]	193
62 Sebestyén, Gyula	[1]	43
63 Sieg, L.P.	[1]	246
64 'SIMC'	[1]	156
65 Südy, Ernő	[2]	146, 171
66 Székely, Zoltán, Mrs.,	[1]	213
67 Szigeti József	[2]	140, 273
68 'Szózat' (Editor)	[1]	111
69 Takács, Jenő	[3]	129, 164, 191
70 Thomán, István	[7]	1, 10, 16, 23, 47, 56, 59
— Tillett (Mr.)	[—]	(166) See 'BBC' (London)
71 'Turócszentmárton' (Press)	[1]	77
72 Voinovich, Géza	[1]	204
73 Waldbauer, Imre	[1]	97
74 Weisshaus, Imre	[1]	161
75 Weress, Ákos	[1]	210
76 Wlassics, Gyula	[2]	110, 127
77 Wood, C. P.	[8]	237, 245, 253, 257, 259, 264, 269, 272
78 'Worlds Contending' (Poem)	[1]	289
79 Zágon, Géza Vilmos	[4]	88, 89, 91, 93
80 Zádor, Dezső	[2]	218, 221
81 Zádor, Jenő	[1]	285
82 Žganec, Vinko	[4]	175, 177, 181, 186

Letters written by others

Balázs, Béla	[1]	148*[1]
Bartók, Béla, Mrs., wife (Ditta Pásztory)	[1]	267
Bartók, Béla, Mrs., mother (Paula Voit)	[1]	20
Heinsheimer, H.W.	[1]	236*
Kodály, Zoltán	[1]	107
Radnai, Miklós	[1]	151*
Schulhof, Andrew	[4]	242, 247, 250, 263
Sieg, L. P.	[3]	243*, 248*, 261*
Wlassics, Gyula	[3]	123*, 124*, 126*
Wood, C. P.	[13]	235*, 238, 240*, 241*, 244, 249, 251, 252, 254*, 262*, 268*, 271*, 277*

[1] (*To Béla Bartók)

Letters written in Bartók's name;
their place to be found in List of Letters

Bartók, Béla, Mrs., wife (Martha Ziegler)	[–]	(114, 115, 122) See Révész, Géza

A BRIEF SURVEY OF BÉLA BARTÓK'S COMPOSITIONS

A detailed catalogue of the works of Béla Bartók, prepared by András Szőllősy, has been published by the Corvina Press.[1]

The present survey of Bartók's works should be regarded only as an outline needed for this collection of letters; it is mainly based on the text of a newer list of works prepared by Professor Halsey Stevens.[2]

[1] *Bartók: Sa Vie et Son Oeuvre.* Publié sous la direction de Bence Szabolcsi, Éditions Corvina, Budapest, 1956. Deuxième édition remaniée: Éditions Corvina—Boosey and Hawkes, Budapest—Paris. Printed in Hungary 1968. *Bartók: Weg und Werk, Schriften und Briefe.* Zusammengestellt von Bence Szabolcsi. Corvina, Budapest, 1957.

[2] *The Life and Music of Béla Bartók,* by Halsey Stevens. Oxford University Press, London, Oxford, New York, 1953. Revised edition 1964.

BARTÓK'S COMPOSITIONS

1902: *Four Songs* ('Négy dal'), for voice and piano, with texts by Lajos Pósa.
Symphony.
Scherzo for orchestra.

1903: *Sonata for violin and piano.*
Kossuth (symphonic poem in ten tableaux).
Marcia funebre from the 'Kossuth' for piano.
Four Piano Pieces ('Négy zongoradarab').

1904: *Piano Quintet.*
Rhapsody, op. 1 for piano; also for piano and orchestra, and for two pianos.
Scherzo (op. 2) for piano and orchestra.

1905: *Suite No. 1,* op. 3 for large orchestra.

1906: *Twenty Hungarian Folk-Songs* ('Magyar népdalok'), for voice and piano. (1–10: Bartók; 11–20: Kodály) (Revised version 1938.)

1905/7: *Suite No. 2,* op. 4, for small orchestra. (Revised versions 1920 and 1943.) Transcribed as *Suite for Two Pianos,* 1941.

1907: *Three Folk-Songs from Csík County* ('Három csíkmegyei népdal').

1907/8: *Violin Concerto* (No. 1). (First movement incorporated into the *Two Portraits,* op. 5.) *Two Portraits* ('Két portré'), op. 5, for orchestra.

1908: *Fourteen Bagatelles* ('Tizennégy bagatell'), op. 6, for piano.
Ten Easy Piano Pieces ('Tíz könnyű zongoradarab').
String Quartet No. 1, op. 7.

1908/9: *Two Elegies* ('Két elégia'), op. 8b, for piano.
For Children ('A gyermekeknek'), for piano. Original version, 85 pieces in four volumes; revised version (January, 1945), 79 pieces in two volumes, Vol. I based upon Hungarian folk tunes, Vol. II, on Slovakian folk tunes.

1908/10: *Seven Sketches* ('Vázlatok'), op. 9, for piano.

1909/10: *Two Rumanian Dances* ('Két román tánc'), op. 8a, for piano.

1910: *Four Dirges* ('Négy siratóének'), op. 9a for piano.
Two Pictures ('Két kép'), op. 10, for orchestra.

1908/11: *Three Burlesques* ('Három burleszk'), op. 8c, for piano.

1911: *Bluebeard's Castle* ('A kékszakállú herceg vára'), op. 11. Opera in one act, libretto by Béla Balázs.

1911: *Allegro barbaro,* for piano.

1912/21: *Four Orchestral Pieces* ('Négy zenekari darab'), op. 12.

1912: *Four Old Hungarian Folk-Songs* ('Négy régi magyar népdal'), for 4-part male chorus, a cappella.

1913: *First Term at the Piano* ('Kezdők zongoramuzsikája'), for piano. (Eighteen elementary pieces for the piano method of Sándor Reschofsky.)

1915: *Sonatina,* for piano, based on Rumanian folk tunes. Transcribed for orchestra as *Dances of Transylvania* ('Erdélyi táncok'), 1931; also for violin and piano by Endre Gertler, 1931.
Rumanian Folk Dances from Hungary ('Magyarországi román népi táncok'), for piano. Transcribed for small orchestra, 1917, as *Rumanian Folk Dances* ('Román népi táncok'); also for violin and piano by Zoltán Székely.
Rumanian Christmas Songs (Colindas) ('Román karácsonyi dallamok'), for piano. (Two series of ten each.)
Two Rumanian Folk-Songs ('Két román népdal'), for 4-part women's chorus.
Nine Rumanian Folk-Songs ('Kilenc román népdal'), for voice and piano.

1914/16: *The Wooden Prince* ('A fából faragott királyfi'), op. 13, ballet in one act, libretto by Béla Balázs.

1916: *Suite,* op. 14, for piano.

1915/16: *Five Songs* ('Öt dal'), op. 15, for voice and piano. (Author of some texts not stated [1–3], others attributed to Béla Balázs [4–5].)

1916: *Five Songs* ('Öt dal'), op. 16, for voice and piano. Poems by Endre Ady.

1907/17: *Eight Hungarian Folk-Songs* ('Nyolc magyar népdal'), for voice and piano.

1914/17: *Fifteen Hungarian Peasant Songs* ('Tizenöt magyar parasztdal'), for piano. Nos. 6–12, 14, 15 transcribed for orchestra as *Hungarian Peasant Songs,* 1933.
Three Hungarian Folk-Tunes, for piano. Published in the collection *Homage to Paderewski,* 1942.

1915/17: *String Quartet No 2,* op. 17.

1917: *Five Slovak Folk-Songs* ('Tót népdalok'), for 4-part male chorus.
Four Slovak Folk-Songs ('Négy tót népdal'), for 4-part mixed chorus and piano.

1918: *Three Studies* ('Három tanulmány'), op. 18, for piano.

1918/19: *The Miraculous Mandarin* ('A csodálatos mandarin'), op. 19, pantomime in one act. Libretto by Menyhért Lengyel.

1920: *Improvisations on Hungarian Peasant Songs* ('Rögtönzések magyar parasztdalokra'), op. 20, for piano.

1921: *Sonata No. 1,* for violin and piano.

1922: *Sonata No. 2,* for violin and piano.

1923: *Dance Suite* ('Táncszvit'), for orchestra.

1924: *Five Village Scenes* ('Falun, népdalok'), for voice and piano.
Village Scenes ('Falun'), for four or eight women's voices and chamber orchestra.

1926: *Sonata,* for piano.
Out of Doors ('Szabadban'), for piano.
Nine Little Piano Pieces ('Kilenc kis zongoradarab'), for piano.
Concerto No. 1, for piano and orchestra.

1916/27: *Three Rondos on Folk Tunes,* for piano.

1927: *String Quartet No. 3.*

1928: *Rhapsody No. 1,* for violin and piano. Also versions for 'cello and piano; violin and orchestra.
Rhapsody No. 2, for violin and piano. Also for violin and orchestra (revised 1944).
String Quartet No. 4.

1929: *Twenty Hungarian Folk-Songs* ('Húsz magyar népdal'), for voice and piano. Five of the songs transcribed in 1933: *Hungarian Folk-Songs* ('Magyar népdalok'), for voice and orchestra.

1930: *Four Hungarian Folk-Songs* ('Magyar népdalok'), for mixed chorus, a cappella.
Cantata Profana: The Nine Enchanted Stags ('A kilenc csodaszarvas'), for double mixed chorus, tenor and baritone soloists and orchestra.

1930/31: *Concerto No. 2, for piano and orchestra.*

1931: *Forty-Four Duos,* for two violins. Six of the duos transcribed in 1936: *Petite Suite,* for piano.
Hungarian Sketches ('Magyar képek'), for orchestra. Transcriptions of some piano pieces of the *Ten Easy Pieces, Four Dirges, Three Burlesques, For Children.*

1932: *Székely Songs* ('Székely dalok'), for male chorus, a cappella.

1934: *String Quartet No. 5.*

1935: *Twenty-Seven Choruses* ('27 két- és háromszólamú kórus'), for 2- and 3-part children's or women's chorus.
From Olden Times ('Elmúlt időkből'), after old Hungarian folk- and art-song texts, for 3-part male chorus, a cappella.

1936: *Music for Strings, Percussion and Celesta* ('Zene húros- és ütőhangszerekre, celestával').

1937: *Sonata for Two Pianos and Percussion* ('Szonáta két zongorára és ütőhangszerre'). Transcribed as *Concerto for Two Pianos, Percussion and Orchestra*, 1943.

1938: *Contrasts*, for violin, clarinet and piano.

1937/38: *Concerto for Violin and Orchestra* (No. 2).

1926/39: *Mikrokosmos*, 153 progressive pieces for piano. Seven of the piano pieces transcribed for two pianos.

1939: *Divertimento for String Orchestra.*
String Quartet No. 6.

1943: *Concerto for Orchestra.*

1944: *Sonata for Solo Violin.*

1945: *Concerto for Piano and Orchestra No. 3.* The last 17 bars were orchestrated by Tibor Serly.
Concerto for Viola and Orchestra. Unfinished; reconstructed and orchestrated by Tibor Serly.

LIST OF PLACES

Names of places mentioned in the letters in Hungarian, now no longer part of Hungary

Bánffyhunyad	Huedin
Belényes	Beiuş
Beszterce	Bistriţa
Biharfüred	Stina de Vale
Brátka (Barátka)	Bratca
Csík-Karczfalva	Cîrţa
Csík Szentdomokos	Sîndominic
Csucsa	Ciucea
Drágcséke	Drăgeşti
Dragomér[falva]	Dragomireşti
Egeg	Hokovce
Egyházmarót	Kostolné Moravce
Élesd	Aleşd
Esküllő	Aştileu
Felsőlefánt (Felsőelefánt)	Horné Lefantovce
Fillér	Filiar
Gerlice	Grlica
Glód	Glod
Gyalány	Delani
[Gyergyó]kilyénfalva	Chileni
Gyergyószentmiklós	Gheorgheni
[Gyergyó]tekerőpatak	Valea Strîmbă
Hédel	Hiadel' [Hjadel?]
Ipolyság	Šahy
Kassa	Košice
Kis-Báród	Borozel
Kolozsvár	Cluj
Kopárhegy	Krokava
Körösfő	Crişeni
Lissó	Lišov
Magyarcséke	Ceica
Máramarossziget	Sighet

Marosludas	Ludoşul de Mureş
Marosvásárhely	Tîrgu-Mureş
Mezőkók	(Cooc) Coc
Mezőtelegd	Tileagd
Nagy-Báród	Borodul-Mare
Nagyszentmiklós	Sînnicolaul-Mare
Nagyszőllős	Vinogradov
Nagyvárad	Oradea
Pozsony (Preßburg)	Bratislava
Ratkó	Ratková
Ratkósebes	Ratkovské Bystré
Szalatnya	Hontianska Slatina
Szászfalva	Măgeşti
Temesvár	Timişoara
Topánfalva	Cîmpeni
Torockó	Trăscău
Tőkésújfalu	Klátova Nová Ves
Tőtös	Groşi
Turócszentmárton	[Turčiansky Svätý] Martin
Újtátrafüred	Nový Smokovec
Ungvár	Užhorod, Ushgorod
Vársonkolyos	Şuncuiuş
Zágráb	Zagreb

BIBLIOGRAPHY

Letters I *Bartók Béla—Levelek, fényképek, kéziratok, kották* (Béla Bartók. Letters, Photographs, Manuscripts and Musical Scores). Collected and arranged for the press by János Demény. Preface by János Demény. Budapest, 1948, Magyar Művészeti Tanács, 212 pp.
Photostatic copies on pp. 157–208.
Hungarian versions only.
110 items.

Letters II *Bartók Béla levelei—Az utolsó két év gyűjtése* (Letters of Béla Bartók. Material Collected During the Last Two Years). Collected and arranged for the press by János Demény. Preface by András Mihály. Budapest, 1951, Művelt Nép, 236 pp., I–XVI photographic plates.
Letters written from Hungary, Switzerland and the United States.
Hungarian versions only.
196 items.

Letters III *Bartók Béla levelei* (Letters of Béla Bartók). Edited by János Demény.
Part I: 'Romániai levelek' (Rumanian Correspondence). Collected by Viorel Cosma. (Preface by Ferenc Bónis, unsigned.)
Part II: 'Csehszlovákiai levelek' (Czechoslovak Correspondence). Collected by Ladislav Burlas. (Preface by Ladislav Burlas, unsigned.)
Part III: 'Magyarországi levelek' (Hungarian Correspondence). Collected by János Demény. (Preface by János Demény, unsigned.)
Budapest, 1955, Editio Musica, 504 pp., and Supplement.
Letters in Hungarian, Rumanian and Slovak, together with Hungarian translations of letters written in the other two languages. Editor's preface by János Demény.
318 items (92 in Hungarian, 124 in Rumanian, 72 in Slovak, and another 30 in the Supplement).

Letters IV *Béla Bartóks ausgewählte Briefe*. Collected and edited by János Demény. German translation by Mirza Schüching. (Preface by József Ujfalussy, unsigned.) Budapest, 1960, Corvina Press, 292 pp.
A selection from Letters I—III and from recent Hungarian collection.
195 items.

Letters V See Preface of this volume.

Letters VI *Béla Bartók. Lettere scelte*. Edited by János Demény, translated by Paolo Ruziscka. Preface by János Demény. Milan, 1969'

il Saggiatore di Alberto Mondadori Editore, 510 pp.
A selection from Letters I–V and from recent Hungarian collection. 270 items.

Bartók. Sa Vie et Son Oeuvre. Edited by Bence Szabolcsi. Preface by Zoltán Kodály. Budapest, 1956, Corvina Press, 351 pp.
40 letters on pp. 199–294.

Bartók. Sa Vie et Son Oeuvre. Second, revised edition. Edited by Bence Szabolcsi. Preface by Zoltán Kodály. Budapest—Paris, 1968, Corvina Press—Boosey & Hawkes, 332 pp.
40 letters on pp. 195–276.

Bartók. Weg und Werk—Schriften und Briefe. Edited by Bence Szabolcsi. Preface by Zoltán Kodály. Letters and photographs selected by János Demény. Budapest, 1957, Corvina Press, 371 pp.
41 letters on pp. 207–312.
Second, revised edition in preparation.

Béla Bartók. Edited by Bence Szabolcsi. (Letters selected by János Demény.) Leipzig, 1968, Verlag Philipp Reclam jun., 207 pp.
14 letters and Notes on pp. 127–159, 194–198.

GENERAL INDEX

([C] see also List of Correspondents, p. 441. Numerals in italics indicate references in Notes)

Aberystwyth 157
Ábrányi, Emil 133, *397*
Adana 253, 254, *422*
advertising, wartime expenditure on 341
Ady, Endre 113, *392*
Albany (N. Y.) 347
Albertville 90
Albrecht, Sándor [C] *421*
Alexandria 221
Algiers 121, 123
Allegro molto (Kodály) 186
Alma (California) 345
Also sprach Zarathustra (Nietzsche, Strauss) 48
Altdörfer, Keresztély 54, 381
Amherst (Massachusetts) 318
Amsterdam 156, 157, 159, 190, 255, 263, 266, 276
Ankara 241, 250, 252, 253
Anschluss (1938) 267–8, 272, 276
Apponyi, Count Albert 68, 135, *383*, *398*
Arad 206
Arany, János 113
Arányi, Adila & Titi 18, 20, 21, *372*
Arányi, Jelly 156, 157, 159, 160, *372*, *405*
Argentières 89–90
Arles 91
Arnhem 338
Asheville 329, 333, 341, 342
astronomy 77, 79, 82
Athens 22, 242
atom bomb 348–9
Aubry, Pierre 99, *388*
Auer, Leopold 45, 46, *380*
autobiographical matter 54, 340–1
Avignon 91

Bach, J. C. 319
Bach, J. S. 17, 25, 50, 150, 181, 222, 223, 280, 284
Bach, W. F. 319
Backhaus, Wilhelm 45, 48, *380*
Baden 89, 269
Balánbánya 70
Balázs, Béla 136, 198, 199, *397–8*
—, letter of 198
Ballo, Ivan 224, 275, *414–5*
Balogh, Ernő [C] *438*
Baltimore 300, 329, 342
Banat County 129, 233
Bánffy, Count Miklós 133, *397*
Bánffyhunyad 69
Baranyai, Mrs. Gyula [C] *378*
Barber of Seville (Rossini) 193
Barcelona 62, 64, 176, 177, 183
Bárci [Bárczy], István 22, *374*
Bartók, Mrs. Béla (B's mother) [C] 15, 25, 27, 54, 192, 267, 272, 281, 353, *370*, *430*
—, letter of 39
Bartók, Mrs. Béla (B's 1st wife) (see under Ziegler, Martha)
Bartók, Mrs. Béla (B's 2nd wife) (see under Pásztory, Ditta)
Bartók, Béla (B's son) [C] 134, 139, 140, 146, 163, 291, *429*
Bartók, Elza ('Böske', B's sister) 17, 22–5 *passim*, 29–31 *passim*, 34, 39–41 *passim*, 47, 53, 291, 293, 299, *370*, *371*
Bartók, Péter (B's son) [C] 193, 258, 291, 297, 303, 305, 307, 316, 317, 320, 324, 343, 348, 349, *406*, *438*
Basle 182, 255, 258, 264, 265, 273, 276
Batka, János [C] 33, *375*
Bayer (family) 24, *374*
Bayreuth 41–2, 43
BBC (London) [C] *414*
Bechert, Paul 226
Beck, Mrs. Broussais 317, 318, 325, *435*
Beck, Conrad 256, *423*
Beethoven, L. v. 17, 46, 48, 50, 149, 158, 181, 222, 280, 285fn, 329, 330
Békés County 30, 40, 69, 176
Békéscsaba 196
Belényes 58, 95, 112, 117, 125, 139
Belgrade 233
Benedek 65

Berény, Róbert 136, 139, *397*, *398*
Berlin 14, 18, 23, 32–5 *passim*, 38, 40, 48, 93–4, 97, 114, 152, 190, 194, 197, 199, 211, 216, 217
Berne 278
Beszterce-Marosludas 95, 200
Beu, Octavian [C] *409*
Bianu, Ion 191, *408*
Biermann (family) 29, 30, *376*
Bihar County 65, 102, 117, 128, 129, 135, 154, 155, 171fn, 201, 202, 230, 233, *391*, *405*, *408*
Biharfüred 154
Bîrlea, Ion [C] 118, *395*
Birmingham 240, 245
Biskra 57, 119, 121–3, 251
Bobál, Sámuel [C] *394*
Bolzano 228
Boosey & Hawkes 344, 346
Bösendorfer, Ludwig 28, 39, *375*
Boston 325, 332, 342, 344
Bowdon 37–8
Boxtel 38
Brahms, J. 28, 110, 161, 201, 204, 329, 330, 344
Brăiloiu, Constantin [C] 209–11 *passim*, 229, *404*
Bratislava 182 (see also Pozsony)
Bratka 113
Brediceanu, Tiberiu 118, *393*
Breitkopf & Härtel 89, 90, 197
Bremen 168
Brigg Fair (Delius) 105, 111, *387*
Brno 168, 195
Broadwoods 38
Bródy, Sándor 141, *399*
Bronx (N. Y.) 301, 305, 310, 315–21, 323–5
Brugnoli, Attilio 45, 46, *380*
Brussels 255, 263, 266, 276, 340
Bucharest 102, 103, 115, 167–71 *passim*, 191, 206, 209, 240, 250
Budapest (see List of Letters, p. 357, for Bartók's letters from Budapest; also frequent references pp. 15–64, 91–285. Thereafter, as follows) 289, 291, 297, 301, 305, 335, 343, 346, 353
—, Academy of Music 13, 52, 54, 114, 143–5, *370*, *372*
Bülow, Hans von 344, *439*
Bürger, Zsigmond (see under Grünfeld–Bürger Quartet)
Bușiția, Ion [C] 58, 138, *390–1*, *392*
Busoni, Ferruccio 35, 89, 93, 96, *377*, *386*
Butcher, Agnes 342
Byng, Mrs. Lucy 234, 236
Cairo 211, 221, 250
Calvocoressi, M. D. [C] 120, 130, 197, 209, 228, *409*
Čapek, Karel 212, 214, *412*
Carinthia 15
Carter, Mrs. Artie Mason 216, 217
Chamberlain, Neville 271, 272
Chambéry 91–2
Chamonix 90
Chevillard, Camille 46, 47
Chicago 192, 319
Chopin, F. 17, 22, 29, 35, 280
Chován, Kálmán 204
Cincinnati 190
Clark, Edward [C] (see under BBC)
Cleveland 291, 293
Cluj 170, 206, *405* (see also Kolozsvár)
Cociuba 113
Coeuroy, André 197
Coimbra 62–4
colinda, and B's work on this form 129, 138, 142, 167–77 *passim*, 182, 197, 201–10 *passim*, 228, 229, 234–40 *passim*, 259, *404*, *405*, *411*, *413*
Collaer, Paul [C] 340, *424*
Cologne 38
Columbia University 289, 293, 298–306 *passim*, 309–12 *passim*, 316–25 *passim*, 328, 334, 339, 340, 349, *432*
composer, Bartók as: performances 39–40, 54, 199, 342
—: publications 27, 38, 42–3, 90, 94
—: recognition (or otherwise) 22, 96–7, 123–4, 135, 146, 153–4, 158–60, 163, 181, 245, 302, 325, 329–30, 344
—: thoughts on composition 87, 105, 198, 200–3 *passim*, 218, 329, 332–3, 346
—: work on compositions 132, 278, 284
Condat, Mme 47, 51
copying scores, instructions for 34
Courmayeur 176
Creel, Wilhelmine [C] 349, *425*
Csábrágsomos 122
Csángó 270
Csetátja 107
Csík 57, 92, 134
Csík-Karczfalva 69
Csongrád 68
Csucsa 113
Czerny, C. 124

d'Albert, Eugène 16–17, *371*
Dances of Galánta (Kodály) 242, 245
Davos 134, 271
Deák, Imre [C] *417*
Debussy, C. 58, 201, 280
Delius, Frederick [C] 10, 104, *389*
Dent, Edward [C] *403*
Denver 186, 298
Dessau 193, 216, 217
Destrée, Jules 212–15 *passim*
Detroit 300
dietetic matters 19, 34, 62–3, 183, 185, 187, 222, 292, 324
Dietl, Lajos [C] 31, 33, 45–7 *passim*, 53, *376*, *378*
Dille, Denijs [C] *429*
d'Indy, Vincent 96, *386*
Dinesen, Isak 343
d'Isoz, Kálmán [C] *395*
Doboz 65
doctorate (Columbia University) 293, 298
Dohnányi, Ernő 16–22 *passim*, 27–32 *passim*, 38, 48, 97, 144, 145, 238, *370–1*, 400
Dohnányi, Frigyes 20, 27, 28, *372*
Don Quixote (Cervantes) 328, *436*
Dostoevski, F. 136
Drágcséke 112
Drăgoi, Sabin V. 221, *413*
Dragomérfalva 125
Drážovce 108
Dresden 106
Dumbravița de Codru 253
Dvořák, A. 28, *376*
Eberhard *369*
Ecorcheville, Jules 98–101 *passim*, *388*
Ecsedi, István 239, *417–18*
educational matters 76–7, 258, 324, *370*
Egeg-Szalatnya 118
Egyházmarót 118, 122
Einstein, Albert 300, 337
Einstein, Alfred 152, *401*
Eisner, Mór 45
Elberfeld, Mr. 111
Élesd 113
Eliot, T. S. 343
Elkán 339
emigration (of B. and of his son Péter) 267, 276, 279, 283–5 *passim*, 291, 294, 298, 305, 316–17, 320, 324, 347–8
Engel, Iván 242, *418*
Engel, Renée 110, *391*
Eötvös, József 204
Epitaphe (Kodály) 186
Erkel, László 54
Esküllő 113
Expert, Henry 97–9 *passim*, *387*

Fehér, Géza 237, 238, *417*
Fekete-Érpuszta 65
Felsőelefánt 109
Fényes, Adolf 140, *399*
Fenyves, Jenő [?] 159
Filimon, Nicolae 126
Fillér 109
financial matters: difficulties 17–18, 150, 153–4, 242, 266, 320–1, 327
—: expenses (food) 27, 28, 34, 38, 91
—: expenses (lodging) 16, 47, 62, 301, 305, 333
—: expenses (travel) 37–8, 192, 221
—: expenses (various, musical) 103, 126, 142, 146, 163, 254
—: personal income 34–5, 157, 160, 162, 165–6, 188, 189, 216, 269, 272–3, 298, 304, 307–10 *passim*, 322, 334–5, 344
Fionnay 257
Five Slavian Melodies op. 36 (Takács) 248–9, *420*
Flament, Edouard 45
Flaubert, G. 136
Fleischer, Antal [C] 245, *405*
Focillon, Henri 213, *412*
Fogaras 134
folk-music, Arab 57, 120–3, 130, 251, 256, 300
—: Bulgarian 233, 237, 244, 306
—: Hungarian 50, 57, 60, 82, 97, 102, 128, 182, 194–5, 200, 229, 239, 243, 247, 250, 260, 262, *409*
—: Indian (North American) 302, 304, 306, 318, *435*
—, Rumanian 57, 102, 103, 106, 112, 115–18, 125–6, 128, 129, 167, 171–7 *passim*, 182, 191, 196, 197, 199, 203, 208–11 *passim*, 233, 238, 289, 325, 342, 343, *436*
—, Ruthenian 277, 281
—, Serbo-Croatian 229–33, 244, 289, 299–301, 306, 310, 317, 324, 325, 340, *416*, *432–3*
—, Slovakian 57, 102, 108–9, 119, 121–2, 127–8, 129, 131, 149, 182, 188–9, 202, 224–5, 229, 264, 275, *390*
—, Székely (Hungarian) 74, 88, 116
—, Turkish 181, 243, 254, 255, 259–61, 289
—, Wallachian (and texts) 94–5, 330–1, 335–7, 339

—, compositions based on (consult Index of Bartók's Works)
folk-music collecting and research 57–8, 64–5, 68, 70–4, 94–5, 102, 107, 113–19 *passim*, 126, 131, 140, 153–4, 221, 238, 243, 250, 260, 270, 273
—: classification 128–9, 146, 342
—: notation 88, 103, 108–9, 231, 244, 259–60
—: publications and writings by Bartók 100, 144, 152–4 *passim*, 197, 229, 242, 259, 313–4, 325, 334, 336, 340
folk-music used in original compositions 198, 201–3, 220, 248–9
Forest Hills 290, 291–6, 300, 301
Foss, Hubert [C] 170, 228, 236
Franck, Mr. 65
Frankfurt 155, 156, 158, 161
Freiburg 199
Frescobaldi, G. 222
Freund, Etelka [C] 58, 97, *383*
Freund, Irma [C] *385*
Fried, Oskar 94, *386*
Fuller, Richard 309, 311

Galgóczy, Mr. 65
Gárdony, Mrs. Zsigmond 18, 21, *372*
Ganz, Rudolf [C] *387*
Geneva 89, 90, 211–15, 216, 284
Gerlice 42–3, 68, 109
Gertler, Endre *413*
Geyer, Stefi [C] 58, 269, 282, *383–4*
Gianicelli, Károly 24, 32, 42, *374*
Glasgow 222
Gleimann, Anne 152, *401*
Glód 125, 126
Gmunden 18, 27–32
Godowsky, Leopold 33, 35, *377*
Goga, Octavian 169, *405*
Gogol, N. 194, *409*
Gombosi, Ottó 297, *432*
Gömör County 40, 43, 68, 109, 119
Goodman, Benny 182, 272, 277, *407*
Götterdämmerung (Wagner) 24
Gounod, C. 49
Grainger, Percy 105, *389*
Gray, Cecil 197, *401*
Graz 24
Greguss Medal 245
Grez-sur-Loing 111
Grosz, Mr. 32
Gruber, Mrs. (see under Sándor, Emma)
Grünfeld, Vilmos (see under Grünfeld–Bürger Quartet)
Grünfeld–Bürger Quartet 32, 44, *376*
Gutmann, Mr. 39
Gyergyó 134
Gyergyó-Kilényfalva 70
Gyergyószentmiklós 70, 74
Gyula 64, 65, *382*

Hague, The 266
Hajnal, Tibor 316, *435*
Halle 197
Handel, G. F. 161
Haraszti, Emil 197, 202, 203, *410*
Harsányi, Kálmán [C] *378–9*
Hartmann, Mr. 33
Harvard 279, 299, 301, 317, 324
Háry János (Kodály) 242
Hauptmann, Mr. 102
Haydn, J. 46
Heiligenblut 259
Heinsheimer, Hans Walter 304, 332, 349, *433–4*
—, letter of 303
Heldenleben (Strauss) 19, 21, 22, 28, *372–4 passim*
Helm, Theodor 22, *373*
Herzfeld, Viktor 20, *372–3*
Hilversum 255
Hindemith, Paul 241, 251, *418*
Hitler, Adolf 271–2
Holländer, Gustav 46, *380*
Hont County 140
Hornbostel, Erich Moritz von [C] 152, 251, *393*
Hubay, Jenő 16, 20, 100 123, 124, 145–6, 152, 245, *371*
Huber, Mr. 269
Hunedioara 201
Huntingdon (Pennsylvania) 279, 280, 290, 291, 295, 296
Hunyad County 69, 117, 152
ill health 13, 15, 135, 142, 143, 253, 257, 282, 284, 289, 309, 316, 324, 326–8 *passim*, 330, 333, 339–42 *passim*, 345, 349, *369*, *435*, *436*
Ipolyság 119
Ischl 28
ISCM [C] 165, 208
Istanbul 243, 250, 253, 259

Janosko, Mr. 292–4 *passim*
Jászi, Oszkár 293, *432*
Jersey City 297
Joachim, József 19, 28, *371*, *372*
Jód 125
journalists, unreliability of 44, 110
Judendorf 177
Juon, Paul 35
Jurkovics, Emsy 31, 52, *380–1*

Jurkovics, Irmy [C] 14, 31, *380–1*

Kansas City 187, 298
Kassa 161, *402*
Katzarova, Raïna [C] *417*
Kecskemét 249
Kecskeméti, Pál & Erzsébet [C] 289, *437*
Kehlendorfer, Mr. 39
Kelen, Hugó [C] *421*
Kentner, Lajos 242, *419*
Keresztély, Ernő 110, *391*
Kern, Aurél 20–2 *passim*, *373*
Kerner, István 93, 133, *385*
Kertész, Gyula [C] *431*
Kharkov 192–3
Kienzl, Wilhelm 217, *413*
Kiev 192, 193
Kiriac, D. G. [C] 114, *389*, *393*
Kis Báród 113
Kisfaludy Society [C] 245, *419*
Kleiber, Erich 190, *407*
Kodály, Zoltán 106–7, 115, 144, 146, 151, 152, 197, 267, 268, 297, 299, 353, *372*, *401*
—, as collector of folk-music 57, 67, 109, 128, 188, 237, 239, 260, 262, *382*, *424*
—, as composer 97, 99–101, 104, 195, 204, 222, 242, 250, *388*
—, letter of 143
Kodály, Mrs. Zoltán (see under Sándor, Emma)
Koessler, Hans 20, 21, 23, 27, 28, 54, *373*
Kohner (family) 140, *399*
Kolisch Quartet 296
Kolozsvár 32, 215, 291 (see also Cluj)
König, Péter [C] 28, 68, *382*
Kornstein, Egon 157, 159, *402*
Körösfő 69
Kossar, Mrs. A. 240
Kossuth, Lajos 36
Koussevitzky, Serge 289, 326, 330, 340, 342, *436*
Kovács, Sándor [C] *387*, *388*
Kreisler, Fritz 33, 110, *377*
Krohn, Ilmari 128, *395–6*
Krokava 109
Kuba, Ludvik 233, 244, *416*
Kuhač, Franjo Xaver 233, 239, *416*
Kúnos, Ignác 252, *421*
Kunwald, Margit 28, *375*
Laloy, Louis 120, *394*
League of Nations 212–5, 221
lecturer, Bartók as 186, 241–2, 250, 255, 300, 306, 308, 311, 313–14, *420*
Leichtentritt, Hugo 96, *385*
Leipzig 92, 102
Lendvai, Ervin 100, *386*
Lengyel, Menyhért 141, *399*
Leningrad 192, 193
Les Saintes Maries 91
letter-writing 9–10, 256, 271, 316, 317, 329
Lhévinne, Rosina 217, *413*
linguistic matters: difficulties 63–4, 114, 136, 138, 158, 187, 237, 244, 252, 265, 277, 325
—: in folk-music collecting and translations 89, 91–2, 102, 116, 125, 127, 169, 195, 200, 209, 224, 234–6
—: interest in 38, 49, 65–6, 69, 266, 292, 327, 335–8 *passim*, 348
Lipótmező 23
Lipótváros 238
Lisbon 60–3 *passim*, 290, 294, 295, 320, 324
Lissó 118, 127, 130
Liszt, F. 13, 14, 17, 23, 25, 26, 50, 110, 197, 200, 204, 246–7, 250, 280, 319, *420*
Liszt Scholarship 22–3, *371*
Liverpool 246
Lobkovitz, Mr. 157, 158
London 37, 38, 153, 155–8 *passim*, 167, 169–71 *passim*, 191, 197–9 *passim*, 210, 223, 226–8 *passim*, 241, 246, 251, 266, 269, 276, 320, 335, 342
Los Angeles 184, 185, 194
Löwe, Ferdinand 20, *373*
Lucerne 89
Lukács, József 401
Lukács, László 31, *376*
Luxembourg 263, 266, 269, 276
Lyon 91

Madrid 60–2, 63
Magyarcséke 112
Malvern Wells 162
Manchester 14, 26, 33, 35, 37, 38 54, *374*
Mandl, Mr. 47, 53
Mann, Thomas 211, 214, *412*
Máramaros County 118, 129, 201, *393*, *394*, *408*
Marele (family) 135, 142, *397*
Marnold, Jean 120, *394*
Marosvásárhely 134
Marót 127–8, 130
Mass of Life (Delius) 107, 110, *390*
mathematical problem 337

Matica Slovenská [C] *406–7*, *414–15*, *427–8*
Maupassant, G. 49, 192
McPhee, Colin 319
Mendelssohn, F. 329, 330
Mengelberg, Willem 190, *407*
Menuhin, Yehudi [C] 289, 329, 340, 342, 344, *435*, *439*
Meran 13, *372*
Mertens, Mr. 276
Mezőkoók 95
Mezőség 95
Mezőtelegd 113
Michigan 305
Mihalovich, Ödön 28, 42, 52, 98–100 *passim*, 102, 124, *375*, *387*
Milan 64
Milford, Humphrey 209, 228
Milhaud, Darius 195, 196
Miller, Victor von 28, *375*
Minneapolis 329
Mishkin, Henry [C] *435*
Molnár, Géza 100, *388*
Molnár, Imre 277, *429*
Mondsee 211–17
Monteux, Pierre 190, *407*
Montreal 348
Moore, Douglas [C] *433*
Móricz, Zsigmond 136, *397*, *398*
Moscow 192, 194
Moussorgsky, M. 344
Mozart, W. A. 46, 181, 276, 280, 284
Müller-Widmann, Mme [C] 181, *422*
Munich 22, 42, 96, 197
Muraköz 229–33
Murillo, B. E. 48
Murray, Gilbert 212, 215, *412*

Nagy Báród 113
Nagyszentmiklós 13, 22, 50, 52, 54, 199, 200, 206, *381*
Nagyszőllős 54, 200
Nagyvárad 94, 131, 220
Naples 281
New York 152, 183, 192, 195, 197, 280, 282 (see also List of Letters, p. 357. Many references pp. 289–349.)
Nietzsche, F. 50
Nyitra County 108, 109

Odessa 192, 193
Ojetti, Ugo 213, *412*
Oporto 62–4 *passim*, 331
Oprescu, Gheorghe 213, 215, 221, *412*
Oradea 206
Ormándy, Jenő 329
Orosháza 171
Örvényes 154
Oxford University Press [C] 167, 170, 197, 210, *404*

Padelford, Dr. 307, *434*
Palermo 168
Palestrina, G. P. 26
Palo Alto 315, 317, 318
Panama 343
Paris 44–53 *passim*, 96, 100, 111–12, 120–1, 124, 130, 153, 155–60 *passim*, 183, 220, 255, 257, 275, 276 (see also Rubinstein Competition)
—, impressions of 48–50
Parrish, Dorothy [C] 283, 297, 331, 342, *428*
Parry, Milman 299, 300, 310, 324, 325, *432*
Parsifal (Wagner) 41–2
Passacaglia (Dohnányi) 23, 33, 43
Passail 22, 24–8 *passim*
Pásztory, Ditta (B's second wife) [C] 149, 183, 184, 211, 216, 260, 264–6, 276, 283–4, 289, 302–3, 317, 320, 333–4, 336–40 *passim*, 343, 345, 347, 349, *408*
—, letter of 325
Pável, Constantin 118
Peeples, Katherine Buford 216, 217, *412*
Péntek, György Gyugyi 69
performing standards 45, 93–4, 111, 124, 133, 190, 255–6, 264, 329
Perger, Richard von 46, 53, *380*
Pericles 338
Petőfi, Sándor 113
Petrova 125
Petrovosel 115
Philadelphia 183, 189, 329, 342
Philipp, Isidore 96, *386*
philosophical and religious matters 51, 53–4, 75–87, 265
pianist, Bartók as 13, 14, 19, 22, 31–5, 39, 40, 44, 54, 59, 61–2, 63, 150, 153, 155–7, 159, 161, 162, 177, 181, 192, 193, 217, 222, 249, 252, 263–4, 266, 290, 295, 306, 316, 317, 320, 323, 339
Piano pieces (Kodály) 99–101 *passim*, 222
Pittsburgh 290, 295, 342
Plamenac, Dragan 334, *437–8*
Plicka, Karel 202
Poieni 126
Poldini, Ede 204
political matters: effects on the arts and folk-music collecting 139, 182, 208, 220–1

—: Fascism and Nazism 257, 265–74 *passim*, 276, 278–9, 340
—: language, minorities and other concerns 29–31, 35–7, 50, 137, 201, 230, 281, 335, *375–6*, *377*, *415* (see also World Wars)
Pollák, Mr. 32
Pollatsek, László [C] *411*
Polnauer, Josef 221, *414*
Popper, David *371*
Portland 184, 186, 315, 317
Pozsony 13, 14, 15, 16, 24, 33, 35, 39, 40, 43–4, 54, 60, 67, 68–9, 115, 145, 154, 157, 158, 161, *369*, *370*
Poszvék, Lajos [C] *381*
Pulenc, Francis 196
Prague 122, 168, 191, 211, 213, 224, 225, 239, 240
Priegnitz, Hans [C] *427*
Princeton 300
Provo (Utah State) 298
Prunières, Henri 160, *402*
Psalmus Hungaricus (Kodály) 149, 195

Radnai, Miklós [C] *410*
—, letter of 199
Radulescu-Niger, Mr. 136
Raghib, Mahmud 243, *419*
Rákosi, Jenő 29, 42, *376*
Rákoshegy 126
Rákoskeresztúr 64, 111–4 *passim*, 120, 127–41 *passim*
Rákospalota 75, 88
Raphael 48
Rásonyi, László [C] *418*
Ratkó-Bisztró 43, 109
Ravel, Maurice 97, 128, 160, 195, *387*
Regensburg 41
Reger, Max 85
Reiner, Fritz [C] 325, *405*, *407*
Reinitz, Béla 397, *403*
Révész, Géza [C] 144, *400–1*
Révffy, Gizella 15, 17, *369*, *371*
Reynold, Gonzague de 213
Richter, Hans 24–6 *passim*, 35, 37, 42, 43, *374*
Rida Bey, Mustafa 211
riddles (musical) 20, 333–5, *373*, *438*
Rigele, Mr. 32, 33
Risler, Edouard 96, 99, 101, *386*
Rodope 239
Roll-Anker, Nini 215, *412*
Rome 194
Rösler, Endre 421
Rostal, Max [C] *413*
Róth Quartet 216, *413*
Rózsavölgyi & Co. 94, 99–101 *passim*, 121, 162, 228, 239, 260, 261, 283, 299, *389*, *395*
Rozsnyai 121, 204, *395*
Rubinstein Competition 14, 44–8 *passim*, 52, *378*, *379–80*
Ruppeldt, Miloš *414*

Saanen 278, 281
Sacher, Paul 269, 278, 279, *426*
Ságody, Othmár 46, *380*
St. Louis 298
St. Paul 187, *406*
Saint-Saëns, Camille 331, *437*
Salzburg 70
Sándor, Emma [C—as Kodály, Mrs. Zoltán] 18, 20, 23, 24, 35, 43, 53, 130, 133, *372*
Sándor, Pál 22, *374*
San Francisco 185, 298, 344, 345
Santpoort 246
Sarajevo 233
Saranac Lake (N. Y.) 326–9 *passim*, 333–40 *passim*, 346–9 *passim*
Sarkad 65
Sárospatak 258
Sátoraljaújhely 100, *388*
Sauer, Emil 16–7, 21, *371*
Savoie 91–2
Saygin, Adnan [C] *422*
Scarlatti, D. 101
Scheveningen 279, *430*
Schiffer-Oelsner, Brigitta [C] *420*
Schildkret, Nat 346
Schoenberg, Arnold 9, 58
Schmidt, Tibolt 168
Schmitz, Robert 195–6, *409*
Schubert, F. 17, 44, 50, 110, 201, 280, *379*
Schulhof, Andrew 280, 303, 309, 315, *430*
—, letters of 308, 311, 312, 322
Schulthess, Walter 226, 269, 284
Schumann, R. 17, 19, 280
Seattle 184–5, 296–8 *passim*, 302–4 *passim*, 307–18 *passim*, 321–2, 325–6, 328, 336, 342–4 *passim*
Sebestyén, Gyula [C] *384*
Seiber, Mátyás 242, *418*
Seemayer, Willibald 114, *393*
Shakespeare, W. 330
Shostakovich, Dmitri 342
Sieg, Lee Paul [C] 307, 309, 312–15 *passim*, 319–23 *passim*, *434*
—, letters of 308, 312, 321
Simon, Heinrich 319
Slavici, Ion 136
Sofia 238
Solymossy, Sándor 114, *393*
Sopron 54, 59, *381*

Sonata for 'cello and piano (Kodály) 97, 99
Stagma 269, 272, *426*
Stâna 168
Stavenhagen, Bernhard 24, *374*
Steiermark 95
Stencel (family) 34
Stein, Vassil 239, *417*
Strasbourg 32, 99
Strauss, Richard 13, 19, 21, 22, 31, 38, *374*
Stravinsky, Igor 58, 160
String Quartet (Kodály) 99, 101, 104
Südy, Ernő [C] *409*
Svolvaer 114
Symphony (Dohnányi) 20
Szabolcsi, Bence 353
Szántó, Tivadar 101, 220, *388*, *413*
Szászfalva 113
Szatmár County 136, 141, 197
Szeged 40, 60, 68
Székely, Arnold 17, *371*
Székely, Zoltán 182, 194, 196, 203, 220, 255, 274, 278, *423*
Székely, Mrs. Zoltán [C]
Székelyhidy, Ferenc 137, *398*
Szendy, Árpád 20, 98, 100, *373*
Szenkár, Jenő 161, *402*
Szentdomokos 74
Szigeti, József [C] 182, 194, 196, 220, 272, 279, 282, 289, 325–6, 371, *407*
Szőllőspuszta 278, *429*
Szymanowski, Karel 160

Takács, Jenő [C] *404*, *414*
Tamașiu, Mr. 206
Tango, Egisto 133, 135, 137, 144–5, *396–7*, *400*
Tannhäuser (Wagner) 17
Tausig, Carl 17
teacher, Bartók as: academic 52, 105, 143–4, 152, 215–17, 238, 241, 302
—: private 18, 23, 27, 47, 279–80, 283, 290, 295–7, 342, *376* (see also under lecturer, Bartók as)
Tekerőpatak 74
Thallóczy Lajos 33
Thode, Henry 42, *378*
Thomán, István [C] 13, 17, 20, 22, 23, 32, 43, 52–4, *passim*, 238, *369*, *370*
Thomas, Ambroise 49
Thucydides 338
Tiersot, Julien 130, *396*
Timisoara (also Temesvár) 206, 226, 249
Tisza, István 31, *376*
Tőkésújfalu 109
Toldy, László 19, *372*
Topánfalva 107
Torockó 92
Torontál County 115–18
Toscanini, Arturo 207–8, 212, 411
Totentanz (Liszt) 43, 250, *379*
Tóth, Emil Oláh 185
Tötös 113
transcription (for piano solo) 19, 21, 22, 26, *372*, *373–4*
Trautmannsdorf 27
travel, by rail 37–8, 61, 183–4, 242
—, by taxi 37, 183, 192, 221
Tristan und Isolde (Wagner) 41, 48
Trofimoff, Helen 24, 27, *374*
Turner, Cornelia 297, *432*
Turócszentmárton Press [C] 122

Újtátrafüred 134, *397*
Universal Editions 138, 189, 196, 198, 267, 268, 276, *404*, *426*
Utrecht 241

Vacarescu, Mme 221
Vágássy, Mr. 65
Valašťan-Dolinský, Ján *414*
Valence 91
Valéry, Paul 213, 214, *412*
Valkyrie (Wagner) 17, *371*
Várșonkolyos 113
Vaskóh 117
Vecsey, Ferenc 32, 60–2 *passim*, 331, *371*, *377*
Vecsey, Lajos 60, 63, 66, 331
Venice 64, 229
Veress, Sándor 242, *419*
Vermont 309, 317
Vésztő 66, 75–83, 93, 123, 152
Vidovszky (family) 65
Vienna 13, 14, 19–24 *passim*, 33, 37, 38, 43, 47, 48, 53, 54, 59, 67, 68, 89, 91, 107, 110, 111, 122, 132, 137–8, 144, 145, 154, 182, 216, 239, 249, 268, 272, *372*, *373*
Violanta (Korngold) 133, *397*
Visó 125
Vogel, Wladimir 256, *423*
Voinovich, Géza [C] *424*
Voit, Irma (B's aunt) 15, 22, *370*
Voit, Lajos ('Lujcsi', B's uncle) 15, 22, *370*
Volkmann, Robert 26–7, *373*
Vuillermoz, Emile 100, *388*
Wagner, R. 17, 19, 25, 38, 50, 247, *371*
Waldbauer, Imre [C] 161, *371*
Waldbauer Quartet 99, *371*

Warsaw 192, 338
Washington 320, 329, 342
Washington University 282, 302, 304, 305, 307, 308, 310, 312, 316, 319–21 *passim*, 336
Weimar 197
Weinberg, Jacob 45
Weiner, Leó 100, 101, *388*
Weingarten, Paul 216, 217, *412*
Weingartner, Felix 48
Weisshaus, Imre [C] *412–13*
Welles, Sumner 316
Weress, Ákos [C] *426*
Willner, Arthur 196
Wilson, Duncan 223, 226, 246
Wilson, Mrs. Woodrow 214–15
Wlassics, Gyula [C] *400*
—, letters of 163, 164, 166
Wood, Carl Paige [C] 308, 311, 312, 317, 320, 343, *433*
—, letters of 302, 304, 307, 309, 312, 314, 315, 322, 326, 328, 336
Wood, Henry 241
World War I 57, 130–2, 134–6, 149
World War II 182, 279, 301, 3 21 337–8, 343

Zádor, Dezső [C] *429*
Zádor, Jenő [C] *439*
Zágon, Géza Vilmos [C] 101, *388*, *394*
Zagreb 168, 230, 233
Zeitlin, Lev 45, 46, *380*
Žganec, Vinko [C] *415*
Zichy, István 260, *423*
Ziegler, Martha (B's first wife) 104, 134, 140, 149,
—, letters in B's name 155, 156, 162–3
Zipoli, Domenico 222, 319
Zólyom County 131
Zurich 89, 99, 101, 103, 104, 107, 165, 170, 225, 226, 228, 276

INDEX OF BARTÓK'S COMPOSITIONS REFERRED TO IN THE VOLUME

(Numerals in italics indicate references in Commentaries)

Allegro barbaro (1911) *149*, 159, 186, 339
Allegro diabolico (1941 – Suite for two pianos op. 4b, 2nd movement) 319
Bagatelles op 6. see *Fourteen Bagatelles*
Bear Dance (1908 – *Ten Easy Piano Pieces* No. 10) 159, 161, 186, 187, 215, 339
Bluebeard's Castle op. 11 (1911) *58*, 111, 124, 136, 139, 161, 164, 165, 198 *397*, *400*, *402*, *410*
Burlesques op. 8c see *Three Burlesques*
Cantata Profana (1930) *181*, *182*, 197, 203, 228, 252, *415*, *421*, *438*, *440*
Concerto for Orchestra (1943) *289*, 326, 330, 340, 341, 344, *436*
Concerto No. 1 for piano and orchestra (1926) *149*, 190, 197, 274, *407*, *420*
Concerto No. 2 for piano and orchestra (1930/1) *181*, 223, 256, 274, *414*, *415*, *418*, *430*, *431*
Concerto No. 3 for piano and orchestra (1945) *289*, *440*
Concerto for violin and orchestra (1907/8) *384*
Concerto for violin and orchestra (1937/8) *182*, 265, 272, 323, 328, 329, 341, *413*, *423*, *427*, *437*
Contrasts (1938) *182*, 272, 277, *407*, *427*, *429*

Dance Suite (1923) *149*, 202, 203
Dirges op. 9a see *Four Dirges*
Divertimento (1939) *182*, 278, 281 *430*

Eight Hungarian Folk-Songs (1907/17) 155, 159, 160
Elegies op. 8b (1908/9) *411*
Evening in the Country (1908 – *Ten Easy Piano Pieces* No. 5) 159, 186
Evening with the Székelys (1908 – *Ten Easy Piano Pieces* No. 5) 207, 215

Fantasia No. 1 (1903 – *Four Piano Pieces* No. 2) *13*, 35, 42, 43, *373*
Fifteen Hungarian Peasant Songs (1914/17) 227, 250, 339
Five Hungarian Folk-Songs (1929/33 – Transcription of *Twenty Hungarian Folk-Songs*) 269, *449*
Five Slovak Folk-Songs (1917) 137–8, 237, *398*
Five Songs op. 16 (1916) 162, 163, *392*, *397*, *403*
Five Village Scenes for voice and piano (1924) *149*, 196, 227, 256
For Children (1908/9) 97, 122, *182*, 227, 344, *390*, *407*, *439*
Forty-Four Duos for 2 violins (1931) *182*, 220, 270
Four Dirges op. 9a (1910) *57*, 186, 207, *411*
Four Hungarian Folk-Songs (1930) 197, 270
Four Old Hungarian Folk-Songs (1912) 197
Four Piano Pieces (1903) *13*, 38, *375*, *380*
Four Pieces for Orchestra op. 12 *58*
Four Songs (lost) 24, *374*
Four Songs (1902) 38
Fourteen Bagatelles op. 6 (1908) *57*, 89, 98, (*377*, *384*)

Hungarian Sketches (1931) 250

Improvisations on Hungarian Peasant Songs op. 20 (1920) *149*, 156, 160, 168, 217

Kossuth (1903) *13*, 23, 26–8, *passim*, 33, 35–7, 39, 40, 50, 54, *373*

Mikrokosmos (1926/39) *149*, *182*, 257, 280, 284, 319, *423*

Music for Strings, Percussion and Celesta (1936) *182*

Nine Little Piano Pieces (1926) *149*, *150*, 197, 217

Out of Doors (1926) *149*, 197, 217

Per finire (1941 – Suite for two pianos op. 4b, 4th movement) 319
Petite Suite (1936) 270
Piano Quintet (1904) *14*, 45, 46, 112, *379*
Rhapsody for Piano op. 1 (1904) *410*
Rhapsody for piano and orchestra op. 1 (1904) 45, 94, 99, 101, 250, *380*, *388*, *405*, *407*, *410*
Rhapsody No. 1 for violin and piano (1928) *181*, 191, 197, 202, 203, 207, *430*
Rhapsody No. 2 for violin and piano (1928) *181*, 197, 202, 203, 207, 256, 270, *423*
Rumanian Christmas Songs (1915) 186, 203, *396*
Rumanian Folk Dances (1915) 137–9 *passim*, 142, 161, 196, 203, *391*, *396*, *398*, *423*

Scena della Puszta (1941 – Suite for two pianos op. 4b, 3rd movement) 319

Scherzo for orchestra (1902) 23, 33, 38, *373*, *379*
Scherzo for piano and orchestra op. 2 (1904) *14*, 42, 43, *373*, *379*
Serenata (1941 – Suite for two pianos op. 4b, 1st movement) 319
Sketches op. 9 (1908/10) *57*, 203, 207, *411*
Slovakian Boys' Dance (1908 – *Ten Easy Piano Pieces* No. 3) 207
Sonata for piano (1926) *149*, 186, 197, 217, 222, 227
Sonata for 2 pianos and percussion (1937) *9*, *182*, 264, 265, 269, 276, *428*
Sonata for solo violin (1944) *289*, 332–3, 340, 342, 345, *435*, *437*
Sonata for violin and piano (1903) *13*, 28, 40, 45, 46, *375*, *380*
Sonata No. 1 for violin and piano (1921) *149*, 156, 159–61 *passim*, 168, 341, 344, *402*
Sonata No. 2 for violin and piano (1922) *149*, 168, 194, 263, *405*, *409*, *424*, *430*
Sonatina for piano (1915) 203, 220, 339, *396*
String Quartet No. 1, op. 7 (1908) *58*, 94, 101, 193, 218–19, *386*, *401*, *413*
String Quartet No. 2, op. 17 (1915/17) *58*
String Quartet No. 3 (1927) *182*, 197, *407*
String Quartet No. 4 (1928) *182*, 190, 197, 219, *497*, *413*
String Quartet No. 5 (1934) *182*
String Quartet No. 6 (1939) *182*, 278, 281, 296, *430*
Studies op. 18 see *Three Studies*
Study for the Left Hand (1903 – *Four Piano Pieces* No. 4) *13*, 23, 27, 33, 35, 43, *375*
Suite No. 1 for orchestra op. 3 (1905) *14*, 54, 93, 132, *181*, 247, *373*, *381*, *391*, *396*, *419*
Suite No. 2 for orchestra op. 4 (1905/7) *10*, *57*, *58*, 70, 75, 93, 94, 96, 104, 105, 111, *383*, *384*, *386*
Suite for piano op. 14 (1916) *58*, 160, 186, 339, *424*
Symphony (1902) *13*, 20–1, 25
Székely Songs (1932) 227
Székely Songs see *Eight Hungarian Folk-Songs*

Ten Easy Piano Pieces (1908) 89, *384*
The Miraculous Mandarin op. 19 (1918/19) *58*, 141, 154, 163–7, *passim*, *181*, 256, *399*, *401*, *404*, *411*
The Wooden Prince op. 13 (1914/16) *58*, 124, 134, 136, 155, 161, 164, 165, 198, *397*, *402*, *410*
Three Burlesques op. 8c (1908/11) *57*, 159, 186, 339
Three Rondos on Folk Tunes (1916/27) 197, 227
Three Studies op. 18 (1918) *58*, 168, 225
Twenty Hungarian Folk-Songs (1929) *181*, 197, 227, 263, 270, *424*
Twenty Hungarian Folk-Songs (with Kodály 1906) 97, 237
Twenty-Seven Choruses (1935) *182*, 257, 269, 283, 305
Two Pictures op. 10 (1908) *58*, 111, *396*, *410*, *415*
Two Portraits op. 5 *58*, *384*
Two Rumanian Dances op. 8a (1909/10) 160, 203, 339, *389*

Village Scenes for four or eight women's voices and chamber orchestra (1924) 196, 256 see also *Five Village Scenes*